Related titles of interest

COREA, *Need for Change: Towards the New International Economic Order*

JENNINGS and WEISS, *The Challenge of Development in the Eighties: Our Response*

LASZLO, *Systems Science and World Order: Selected Studies*

MENON, *Bridges Across the South: Technical Cooperation Among Developing Countries*

SAUVANT, *Changing Priorities on the International Agenda*

SCHOORL et al, *Between Basti Dwellers and Bureaucrats*

STREETEN and JOLLY, *Recent Issues in World Development*

UNESCO, *Scientific Forecasting and Human Needs*

Related journals*

HABITAT INTERNATIONAL The Journal for the Study of Human Settlements. Established at the UN Conference, Vancouver 1976

WORLD DEVELOPMENT The Monthly Multi-Disciplinary Journal Devoted to the Study and Promotion of World Development

ECONOMIC BULLETIN FOR EUROPE The Journal of the United Nations Economic Commission for Europe

* Free specimen copies available upon request

UNCTAD

AND

THE SOUTH–NORTH DIALOGUE

The First Twenty Years

Essays in memory of
W. R. MALINOWSKI

Edited by
MICHAEL ZAMMIT CUTAJAR

PERGAMON PRESS

OXFORD · NEW YORK · TORONTO · SYDNEY · PARIS · FRANKFURT

U.K.	Pergamon Press Ltd., Headington Hill Hall, Oxford OX3 0BW, England
U.S.A.	Pergamon Press Inc., Maxwell House, Fairview Park, Elmsford, New York 10523, U.S.A.
CANADA	Pergamon Press Canada Ltd., Suite 104, 150 Consumers Road, Willowdale, Ontario M2J 1P9, Canada
AUSTRALIA	Pergamon Press (Aust.) Pty. Ltd., P.O. Box 544, Potts Point, N.S.W. 2011, Australia
FRANCE	Pergamon Press SARL, 24 rue des Ecoles, 75240 Paris, Cedex 05, France
FEDERAL REPUBLIC OF GERMANY	Pergamon Press GmbH, Hammerweg 6, D-6242 Kronberg-Taunus, Federal Republic of Germany

First edition 1985

Library of Congress Cataloging in Publication Data
Main entry under title:

UNCTAD and the south–north dialogue.

1. United Nations Conference on Trade and Development—Addresses, essays, lectures.
2. International economic relations—Addresses, essays, lectures. 3. Malinowski, W.R. (Wladek R.)—Addresses, essays, lectures. I. Zammit Cutajar, Michael. II. Malinowski, W.R. (Wladek R.) III. United Nations Conference on Trade and Development.
IV. Title: U.N.C.T.A.D. and the south–north dialogue.
HF1411.U52   1984   341.7'54   84-6484

British Library Cataloguing in Publication Data

UNCTAD and the South–North dialogue.
1. United Nations. *Conference on Trade and Development* 2. Developing countries—Foreign economic relations 3. International economic relations I. Zammit Cutajar, M. II. Malinowski, W.R.
337'.09172'2   HF1410
ISBN 0-08-028144-3

Printed in Great Britain by A. Wheaton & Co. Ltd., Exeter

TO
WLADEK
AND
HALINA

EDITOR'S NOTE

This book is a collective tribute to the memory of W. R. (Wladek) Malinowski—a friend, a colleague, a guide, an exemplary international civil servant. It is a token of admiration and of support for the brave efforts which he made, until the very end of his life, to promote the ideals and objectives of the United Nations as an instrument of world peace and economic and social justice.

The book focuses on the evolution, achievements and perspectives of UNCTAD—the United Nations Conference on Trade and Development —one of the main organs through which the United Nations pursues its economic and social aims and of which Malinowski was a 'founding father'. UNCTAD was a child of the era of decolonization—the first institutional response in the economic sphere to the entry of the Third World on the international scene. The story of UNCTAD is an important and unfinished chapter in the record of that historical process whereby the forces of the Third World are being mobilized to restructure the international economic system to respond to their needs and their aspirations. Indeed, the story of UNCTAD contains the essence of the 'South–North Dialogue'—so called here since the initiative for structural change through negotiation has always started from the South, whereas the North has sought to preserve existing structures and has not been collectively disposed to contemplate more than a 'trickle down' of benefits and concessions, as conveyed by the more familiar term 'North–South'.

While this volume has been many years in gestation, it is perhaps fitting that it should come to light in 1984, the year of the twentieth anniversary of UNCTAD. This will be an occasion when all those who share the ideals which inspired the birth of this institution will want to reflect upon its achievements and on the obstacles on which it has stumbled, and draw from this reflection lessons for future struggles.

This book may also be considered timely in that its appearance happens to coincide with a new wave of political and ideological criticism of UNCTAD—generated within the United States Administration—aimed at curbing UNCTAD's mandate and its decision-taking process. The contents of the book may serve to enlighten the debate to which the criticism should give rise.

The contributions to this volume point to the successes of UNCTAD in generating new ideas on international policies for trade, finance and money, in promoting a climate of intellectual and political opinion more favourable to change in existing policies, in stimulating other institutions to be more responsive to the needs of the Third World, and in itself providing the framework for the negotiation of new policy measures. Negotiations in UNCTAD have resulted in the adoption of measures ranging from legal instruments (such as international commodity agreements, the Code of Conduct for Liner Conferences and, when it enters into force, the agreement on the Common Fund for commodities), through non-binding norms or codes of behaviour (such as aid targets or the principles and rules on restrictive business practices agreed upon in 1980), to unilateral concessions (such as the Generalized System of Preferences and the measures of relief for the official debt of the low-income developing countries adopted in 1978). The contributions also reflect the growing importance of economic co-operation among developing countries (ECDC), as well as the change brought about by UNCTAD in the modalities of negotiation between the Third World and the industrialized countries, notably through the consolidation of the 'Group of 77' as a Third World caucus. Moreover, one article analyzes the marked influence of UNCTAD on the emerging discipline of international development law.

At the same time, the various assessments of UNCTAD's work show up the main stumbling blocks which have impeded the restructuring of the international framework sought by the Third World through UNCTAD. In general, the main obstacle is seen to be the resistance to change by powerful corporate and governmental interests in industrialized countries. As is the case at present, this resistance is often stiffened by intellectual or ideological opposition to the measures proposed and it has been reinforced in recent years by unfavourable economic trends. Moreover, the dramatic rise in unemployment in these countries has pushed their organized labour into a protectionist stance. In face of such opposition, it is essential for the Third World to be at its most persuasive in presenting its negotiating positions. Yet the credibility of its collective proposals is often weakened by the appearance of divergent perceptions of short-term national interest with respect to specific measures proposed. The Third World needs to reconcile such divergences before sound negotiating positions can be presented. Furthermore, the present institutional compartmentalization in the economic field, notably among the IMF, GATT and UNCTAD, prevents issues of global economic management from being tackled seriously and comprehensively, permits governments to evade inconvenient problems by shifting them from one forum to another, and allows inconsistencies to occur in the positions taken by the same countries or groups in different forums.

The articles gathered in this volume also offer pointers to the directions in which UNCTAD's work may evolve in the coming years. One lesson which a reader may draw from them is that UNCTAD should devote more attention to research and deliberation on the long-term issues of reform in the international trading, financial and monetary systems and of mechanisms for global economic management. However inaccessible agreement on these issues may seem, they deserve to be kept alive. UNCTAD is the only specialized institution which can bring a truly universal viewpoint to bear on them, in the interest of the entire international community. To fulfil this mission, UNCTAD would have to regenerate its conceptual base, adapting it to the changing realities of the world economy. The present lull in negotiations on development issues provides an opportunity for UNCTAD to reinforce its work in this direction.

Another permissible conclusion from the evidence in this book is that the developing countries must intensify their efforts to realize their potential for mutually-beneficial economic exchanges and joint enterprises. Initially motivated by the desire to reduce the Third World's dependence on the industrialized countries, South–South co-operation is further justified by the rather gloomy prospects for economic growth in those countries and consequently for North–South development co-operation. UNCTAD and other institutions of the United Nations system have been helping developing countries to translate the aims of ECDC into concrete programmes and projects. This assistance needs to be increased, without thereby discouraging the Third World from building its own autonomous mechanisms and institutions for co-operation.

Finally, since the negotiation of changes in the international economic framework will remain in the forefront of UNCTAD's concerns, one may envisage UNCTAD playing a more active role in exploring selected areas in which South–North negotiations might have most chance of success. This exploration would include the identification of interests in both industrialized and developing countries which may be most responsive to specific cases for negotiated change. Of course, it would be for the parties to each negotiation to marshal their full bargaining leverage (and here again the strengthening of South–South co-operation is clearly relevant); it would also be for them to deal with the difficulties which they might encounter in their own camps. However, a specialized institution like UNCTAD may properly devote its energies, in the general interest, to presenting a well-articulated case for change and to mobilizing support for it.

All the contributors to this book have been associated with UNCTAD at various stages of its work, mostly as members of its secretariat. The three Secretaries-General of UNCTAD to date are among them, as are people whose first steps in the secretariat were steered personally by Malinowski as their supervisor. Brief biographical notes on the contributors are to be found at the end of the book.

We have not aimed to put together an exhaustive description and assessment of UNCTAD's work. Nor is this a primer on UNCTAD; the contributions assume a certain basic familiarity with the institution and the substantive issues which it addresses. Each contributor has been free to define his subject and to express his own views on it. It should not be assumed that each participant in this collective enterprise shares the views here expressed by the others nor—let it be said on behalf of all those contributors who are or were members of the United Nations Secretariat—do their views necessarily represent the official positions of the United Nations or its Secretariat, of which the UNCTAD secretariat forms part.

Yet, with all these disclaimers, we trust that the contents of the volume cover many important points of interest to present and future students of UNCTAD, of international economic relations and of international development diplomacy—and do so in an authoritative manner.

Many people other than the authors have helped to bring this book into being. To these un-named ones go our collective thanks. A special word of appreciation is due, moreover, to Carmel Greevy who worked with me on the preparation of all the edited texts.

The royalties from this book will be donated to support an activity connected with Wladek Malinowski's work and interests.

Geneva, June 1984   Michael Zammit Cutajar

CONTENTS

W. R. Malinowski (1909–1975)

WLADYSLAW R. MALINOWSKI
(1909–1975)

A biographical note and appreciation
by Zenon Carnapas

Wladyslaw Roman Malinowski was born in Lwow, Poland, on 18 September 1909. After completing studies in economics with distinction at the Jagellonian University, Krakow, he started upon a successful career as an economist and statistician in his country. The outbreak of war drove 'Wladek' and his wife Halina, whom he had married in 1935, into work for the Polish Labour Resistance Movement, first underground in Poland and later in Sweden, the USA and Britain.

After the war, Malinowski joined the United Nations Secretariat, where he distinguished himself over the years by his intellectual and political independence, his commitment to the ideals of the Organization, his advocacy of the cause of the emerging Third World and his part in setting up mechanisms to promote that cause. He was instrumental in the establishment of the United Nations regional economic commissions and encouraged the coalition of developing country interests that took shape as the 'Group of 77'. He shares with Raúl Prebisch the credit for the institution of UNCTAD as a permanent feature of the United Nations.

Malinowski was a trusted adviser to the first three Secretaries-General of UNCTAD and a dynamic director of its pioneering Division for Invisibles. In the latter function, he guided the developing countries toward the realization of their economic rights in shipping, insurance and technology. The adoption in April 1974 of the United Nations Code of Conduct for Liner Conferences, coinciding with his formal retirement from the United Nations Secretariat, was the crowning achievement of his contribution to UNCTAD. He continued to serve UNCTAD in an advisory capacity until his death in Geneva on 24 May 1975.

Son of a pioneer democratic socialist, Aleksander Malinowski, one of the founders of the Polish Socialist Party (PPS)—and, incidentally, named after his father's underground pseudonyms, 'Wladek' (diminutive for Wladyslaw) and 'Roman'—Malinowski grew up in a politically active and aware environment, undergoing the great historical influences of the time: the dissolution of European empires, from which Poland emerged once more as a State, the revolution in neighbouring Russia and the widespread suffering in Europe in the aftermath of the 1914–18 war. From his adolescence on, Malinowski was active in political life: first as a member of a clandestine socialist school organization and later, while a student in Krakow, as a member of the Independent Socialist Students' Association (ZNMS), which was at that time on the left-wing of the Polish Socialist Party. From these early days, too, he started to enquire into the problems of Latin America and of regions under colonial rule, problems little thought of in a Europe preoccupied with its internal threats. During these university years, Malinowski met Professor Oskar Lange, who was to exercise a profound influence on his thinking. Together, they edited an annotated bibliography on the theory of socialism, including forms and problems of the labour movement (Association of Workers' Colleges, Krakow, 1930).

Malinowski distinguished himself as a student of economics at the Jagellonian University. In 1931, he won the Solvay Prize, a competition among young Polish economists, with a study on currency stabilization in Poland after the first World War (published by the Economic Society, Krakow, 1932). In 1933, he obtained his doctorate in economics (actually an LL.D., since economics was taught in the law faculty) with a thesis on the quantity theory of money (Economic Society, Krakow, 1934). A year before that, he had started work at the Polish Bureau of Statistics, taking charge of the branch dealing with monetary and trade statistics. In 1934, he joined the editorial board of the Polish Statistical Year Book, of which he later became Chief Editor. During his years at the Bureau of Statistics, Malinowski travelled on official visits to the League of Nations and to the national statistical offices of Austria, Belgium, France and Germany. In 1938, he was given time off for post-graduate work and, as a Fellow of the National Cultural Foundation of Poland, spent a year studying at the London School of Economics and Political Science (LSE). In 1939, Malinowski was appointed Professor of Economics of the Polish Free University, at its Lodz campus.

This promising career in the service of his country was interrupted by the German invasion of Poland in 1939. True to his family history and to his personal principles, Malinowski chose the path of active opposition to the occupier and worked in the ranks of the underground Polish Labour Movement, the main workers' resistance movement. In 1940, together with his ever-supportive wife and companion, he undertook a perilous voyage as a courier to Sweden, where they remained for a while before travelling in 1941 to the United States, through the USSR and Japan. During the remainder of the war years Malinowski worked, mainly through writing and giving lectures, to mobilize support in the USA and Britain for the Polish Labour Movement in its underground resistance struggle. He was one of the editors of *For your Freedom and Ours,* an anthology of Polish progressive and democratic thought through the centuries, published in the USA with an introduction by Malcolm W. Davis (Frederick Ungar, 1943) and in the UK with an introduction by Bertrand Russell (George Allen and Unwin, 1944). This work was also published in Polish.

In the later war years, Malinowski became Assistant Financial Counsellor at the Polish Embassy to the USA and, in this capacity, obtained his first exposure to the process of international institution-building. It was the period when the post-war institutions of the United Nations system were being designed, and Malinowski served as adviser to the Polish delegation to several international conferences, including the International Labour Organization Conference in Philadelphia and the International Monetary and Financial Conference at Bretton Woods, both in 1944.

Much more could be said about this first half of Malinowski's life. This volume is however inspired by and focuses on his contributions as an international civil servant to the work of the United Nations. His first association with the world body came through an assignment with UNRRA in the immediate post-war period. This was followed, in April 1946, by his entry into the United Nations Secretariat as a regular staff member. The transition from national service to international service was a logical one for Malinowski, inspired by the same commitment and ideals, responding to his early interest in the world at large, and motivated by the crying need to rebuild a world which had been shattered by war. He was to serve the United Nations until his dying day, a thirty-year span during which, while loyally maintaining his Polish citizenship, he established an exemplary reputation for integrity and independence.

If Malinowski deserves a special place in the history of the United Nations, it is not simply because of his long, active and varied career. He belonged among those few officials of the Secretariat who left a marked and unmistakably personal influence on events at the United Nations, with a far-reaching impact on international economic relations. He did not serve the Organization merely as a detached intellectual, content with and stopping at the diagnosis of a problem. Nor did he behave as a bureaucrat, intimidated by the political and other undercurrents that flow in the United Nations as in any other organization. He fought with courage and tenacity, aloof from considerations of personal promotion and benefit, to bring about effective solutions to the economic and social problems of the Third World that were and are addressed by the international community in the United Nations. In this fight, his political acumen, vision, dedication and energy made him a formidable protagonist.

Malinowski was primarily a political activist. His career in the United Nations was a series of battles, often fought in opposition to powerful political forces. He was, indeed, a representative of a novel breed of international civil servant, determined to be objective but not neutral in the face of inequity, oppression and discrimination in whatever form. Promulgating this credo, he dismayed many of his contemporary colleagues and some traditional diplomats, encumbered as they were with the notion that international civil servants should serve only passively.

In his first years at the United Nations, Malinowski helped to deal with the relief, rehabilitation and economic reconstruction of countries devastated by war, notably in Europe and East Asia. Those were the pressing problems facing the Organization at that time. Its response to them led to the establishment in 1947 of the United Nations Economic Commissions for Europe (ECE) and for Asia and the Far East (ECAFE, later ESCAP). Malinowski was involved in these processes, developing his own ideas on the potential role of the regional commissions. He saw them as essential elements in the development of their respective regions and advocated the strengthening of their functions and of their autonomy in social as well as economic matters. His duties in the Secretariat led him into the position of 'anchor man' for the commissions at Headquarters, a position formalized in 1952 with his assignment to head the newly-created Regional Commissions Section of the Department of Economic and Social Affairs. He worked hard for the establishment of the Economic Commissions for Latin America (ECLA, 1948) and for Africa (ECA, 1958), the latter at a time when the decolonization of Africa was only beginning and there were only a handful of independent African developing countries pressing for the Commission to be set up.[1] Malinowski's contacts with and visits to developing countries in the performance of these duties deepened his awareness of the problems of development and established his reputation as a trustworthy ally of the Third World in its struggle for political and economic emancipation.

The vision which Malinowski had of the role of the regional economic commissions is apparent from some of his ideas and actions from their early days. He saw the ECE as a means for the United Nations to play a role in European affairs. Writing in January 1948 to his old friend and fellow militant Gunnar Myrdal, the first Executive Secretary of the ECE, Malinowski suggested that in a period of deep political division in Europe, the ECE could become a bridge between East and West, so long as it resisted pressures which would have it degenerate into an appendix of the Marshall Plan. Similarly, he was conscious of the need for ECLA to develop independently of influences from outside the region, and played a little-known but important part in holding off plans for a merger between ECLA and the Organization of American States.

Later, fighting for the establishment of the Economic Commission for Africa, Malinowski faced the opposition of those, who setting themselves against inevitable historical evolution, were apprehensive that the presence of a regional commission in Africa would act as an additional spur to the process of decolonization. Malinowski realized that the process was irreversible; he recognized the duty of the international community, participating in the United Nations, to encourage decolonization, and to contribute to a common effort to support the building and development of the African States. He believed that Africa, more than any other continent, was being neglected and left helpless by its colonial rulers. In this connection, in November 1956, he wrote to a friend:

> It seems obvious that colonization is rapidly declining in Africa. In the same way as it was timely to establish ECAFE in Asia at the time of rapid colonial decline there, it would seem timely [to establish a regional commission] in Africa. The obvious policy, in my view, in periods of disintegration of the old system, when new independent states and nationalism are mushrooming and growing, is for the UN to step in. And in this respect, our experience with the regional commissions in under-developed areas is most encouraging ... Enlightened people ... should understand that such moves ... are making a transition possible to another system in which the colonial powers would be less hated than otherwise ... The establishment of a regional commission may and should increase drives for independence and against colonialism....

Malinowski's work with the regional commissions brought him into close contact in 1949 with Raúl Prebisch, then Executive Secretary of ECLA. Prebisch, with his innovative theories on trade and economic development, his political vision and his reforming zeal, was later to become the most articulate spokesman of the Third World in international development diplomacy and, through the establishment of UNCTAD, the initiator of a far-reaching process of institutional reform within the United Nations, to make it more responsive to the needs of developing countries. He had a most profound influence on Malinowski, just as Malinowski made a considerable impact on Prebisch. A bond of mutual respect and close friendship grew between them.

Impressed by the acknowledged success of ECLA and of Prebisch, particularly in the area of economic co-operation and integration, and frustrated by the climate of opinion prevailing at United Nations Headquarters toward the regional commissions, Malinowski became convinced of the need to strengthen the position of the commissions through a process of decentralization, particularly in the area of operational activities. Malinowski belonged to those who believed that the commissions, in close touch with national experts and continuously exposed to the economic and social difficulties of the countries of their regions, were better equipped than

Headquarters to understand many of the problems in those regions and contribute to their solution. Despite the force of this argument, however, there were still major interests in favour of retaining the management and control of operational activities at Headquarters, while confining the commissions to purely deliberative functions. The debate on this issue, both among governments and within the Secretariat, was protracted. It culminated in the adoption by the United Nations General Assembly in 1961 of two resolutions[2] which decided the issue in favour of decentralization. The first resolution recommended the establishment of regional development and planning institutes closely linked to the respective regional commissions, while the second aimed, through a variety of measures, at enhancing the role of the commissions and strengthening their capacity and functions.[3]

By that time, Malinowski had been appointed Secretary of the UN Economic and Social Council (ECOSOC) and of the Second Committee (Economic and Financial) of the General Assembly. While he retained overall responsibility for relations with the regional commissions, his new duties enabled him to devote his energies to wider issues of international economic relations. The Assembly and ECOSOC were the two fora in which the developing countries could voice their aspirations for economic and social justice, though their negotiating position was then a weak one. These institutions, by their nature, could produce only guidelines for action rather than negotiated agreements. Moreover, the developing countries were in a minority in ECOSOC at that time. The decisive institutions in international economic relations were those established at Bretton Woods (IMF and IBRD) and the GATT, the only element salvaged from the aborted Havana Charter for an International Trade Organization. In these institutions, the developing countries were and still are at a disadvantage before the economic weight of the industrialized countries and are handicapped by the mechanisms by which decisions are reached.

From this frustration flowed a number of policy objectives for the developing countries: their equitable representation in ECOSOC (which they have since approached though not attained through its successive enlargements), an effective say in the decision-taking processes of the Bretton Woods institutions (which still eludes them), and the creation of new United Nations institutions in the economic field which respond to their concerns, give them a full part in decision-taking and can lead to the negotiation of concrete agreements. Their search for such an institution in the field of trade and related aspects of development led, in due course, to the establishment of UNCTAD. Meanwhile, the developing countries continued to exert pressure in available fora, succeeding in pushing through the International Development Strategy for the 1960s, which were designated by the General Assembly as the first United Nations Development

Decade, and participating, as producers, in the negotiation of individual commodity agreements under United Nations auspices.

At the helm of the secretariat of ECOSOC and of the General Assembly's Second Committee, a man of Malinowski's dedication to the cause of development had ample opportunities to play a critical role in promoting the cause of the developing countries. Malinowski rose to the occasion. His solid grasp of substantive problems, his judgement and his flair for political activity in which he always engaged with inexhaustible energy and obvious zest made him an outstanding Secretary of ECOSOC and gave a new character to that post. He stood ready to help all delegations with substantive information, data, and advice. He considered it his special duty to provide such assistance to delegations from developing countries, who often worked without the support services provided to representatives of developed countries by their capitals or by their regional organizations. Above all, he made it one of his missions to assist developing countries to coalesce into a single, united group, so as to strengthen their negotiating position. He can be seen, in retrospect, as a seminal figure in the formation of the 'Group of 77', whose activities now permeate the entire United Nations development system and are a stimulus for greater Third World collective self-reliance.

In the drive for a new international trade institution, Malinowski and Raúl Prebisch formed a redoubtable team. The political energy of the one complemented the analytical power of the other, and together they left their mark on the history of economic development. Their work was instrumental in shaping and promoting the decisions taken in 1962 by ECOSOC and the General Assembly, which led to the convening of the first United Nations Conference on Trade and Development in Geneva in 1964 and, subsequently, to the establishment of UNCTAD as an organ of the General Assembly for deliberation and negotiation in the field of trade and development.[4]

In the preparation of the 1964 Conference and at the Conference itself, Malinowski served as Executive Assistant to the Secretary-General of the Conference (Prebisch), while retaining his responsibility for the ECOSOC secretariat. At the Conference, Malinowski had a special assignment to support work on the institutional follow-up of the Conference and, through his role in the negotiations on that issue, was instrumental in defining the nature and *modus operandi* of UNCTAD. He was among those who resisted the attempts by developed countries to ensure they held a privileged position in decision-taking, through weighted voting or the introduction of the consensus 'principle', a principle tantamount to a power of veto by any dissenting country and likely to lead either to paralysis in decision-taking or to complete satisfaction of the positions of the dissenting party as a condition for its joining the consensus. Although the various negotiating groups of UNCTAD have always striven for agreements in which all countries could join, some votes have been taken and UNCTAD has been criticized on this account as being 'confrontational'. It should be left to historians to assess whether decisions taken by weighted voting or by consensus are more conducive to the most favourable long-term evolution of the development process than decisions taken by voting, reflecting the views of the majority of the negotiating parties at the time they were taken, and often accepted by some if not all of the dissenters subsequently.

Malinowski's role as one of the main architects of UNCTAD has been widely recognized and was even the subject of a special tribute by the President of the first Conference, Abdel-Moneim El-Kaissouni (then Vice-President of the United Arab Republic), in his final speech to the Conference.[5]

Prebisch invited Malinowski to join him in the fledgling secretariat of UNCTAD, which began to be formed in 1965, once the General Assembly had established the new institution. Political pressures prevented Prebisch from appointing Malinowski as Deputy Secretary-General of UNCTAD, as he had wished, or even as Director of Co-ordination (the proposed third-ranking post). Neither post was, in fact, filled during Prebisch's term of office and the latter was never established subsequently. Instead, Malinowski accepted the post of Director of the Division for Invisibles. It says much for his character and his pioneering spirit that, in face of what to a lesser man might have been grave disappointments, he gave up the prestigious post of Secretary of ECOSOC in order to take on a job which presented a challenge that was both institutional and personal. It was a challenge to UNCTAD in that, for the first time, an international organization was to deal with the economic aspects of maritime transport and of insurance, despite fierce opposition from vested interests in countries that were the traditional suppliers of services in these areas. Indeed, such opposition had foiled early attempts to set up a specialized agency for maritime transport in the United Nations system and had permitted only the establishment, in 1948, of the Intergovernmental Maritime Consultative Organization (IMCO, now IMO) to deal with the technical and legal, but not economic, aspects of shipping. It was a personal challenge in that it projected Malinowski into a field of professional activity to which he had no previous exposure, whether in his national career or as an international civil servant. He surmounted the challenge with distinction, serving UNCTAD through his divisional work and as a trusted adviser to its three Secretaries-General over a span of ten years, in fact until the end of his life.

The Division for Invisibles was responsible for work in a variety of fields and within those fields for a variety of aspects. It encompassed shipping, insurance and initially tourism, though this activity was discontinued after a while. A later addition was the important area of transfer of technology. In shipping, the Division dealt with problems of development of national merchant fleets, freight rates, shipping services, market structures, practices in liner shipping 'conferences' and their effects on shipping, protection of shippers' interests, economic co-operation in shipping, multi-modal transport, ports, and international shipping legislation. In the field of insurance, the problems addressed mainly concerned the development of national insurance industries in developing countries, while in that of transfer of technology, the work of UNCTAD dealt mainly with the terms, conditions and practices related to the supply of technology to the developing countries and the promotion of indigenous technological capacities in those countries.[6]

In all areas of the Division's work, Malinowski attached the highest importance to the training of competent national personnel for the administrations and enterprises of developing countries. He considered training to be an essential complement of research and negotiation, and initiated a number of training schemes in his Division's programme.

Malinowski saw the areas of economic activity covered by the work programme of his Division as essential links in the process of development. He set out to make that programme a means to increase the participation of developing countries in these areas, so that they might achieve higher levels of employment and income, provide ancillary support to other economic activities, principally trade, and reduce the economic and consequently political dependence of the Third World on the industrialized countries. An equally fundamental part of his approach was his unflinching conviction that the United Nations, and UNCTAD in particular, had a responsibility, indeed a moral obligation derived from their legislative mandates and perhaps foremost from the spirit and ideals of the United Nations Charter, to promote more equitable international economic relations by formulating and helping to implement policies which would achieve those objectives.[7] In rigorously pursuing the tasks entrusted to him, Malinowski remained true to his own commitment to social justice and to the principles of equity and fair distribution of income on the national and the international levels.

He quickly succeeded in building around himself a team of competent professionals, many of them young, all of whom he inspired with his own example of industry and devotion. Only those who did not know Malinowski would have been surprised to see that he established one of the most effective divisions of the UNCTAD secretariat which won respect within and outside the United Nations even in the first years of its existence, for an output that constitutes an impressive pioneering contribution to development economics in shipping and insurance.

One of the early findings of the work of the Invisibles Division in the area of shipping was that the cartel-like system of liner shipping conferences, dominated by corporations in the traditional maritime nations of Western Europe, were damaging many of the interests of developing countries. The liner conferences operated, with the indulgence of their home governments, in a *laissez faire* environment, subjected to no discipline of regulations other than self-imposed forms of control, calculated to serve their own interests. They jealously protected their privileges by effectively preventing shipping companies in developing countries from joining these conferences, or from acquiring a share in the carriage of cargoes commensurate with the trade generated by the developing countries concerned.

Malinowski concentrated a great deal of his efforts on bringing to fruition, in a major breakthrough in international economic relations, the desire of the developing countries, and of some of their enlightened partners in the North, to formulate an international and binding agreement to regulate liner conferences and safeguard the interests of developing countries. It was a lengthy, painstaking task, which he pursued with the full support of the then Secretary-General of UNCTAD, Manuel Pérez Guerrero. After many years of analysis, debate and negotiation, a United Nations Conference of Plenipotentiaries, working under the auspices of UNCTAD, adopted the United Nations Convention on a Code of Conduct for Liner Conferences on 6 April 1974. Malinowski served as Director-in-charge of that Conference. It is not an exaggeration to say that without his perseverance the Convention, which represents a pioneering achievement in its area, might never have seen the light of day. (It entered into force in October 1983.)[8]

The contribution of the Invisibles Division in the area of insurance was also substantial and equally alarming to established interests. It must perhaps be seen as a reflection of the importance of that work and as a personal tribute, even if a rueful one, that the London weekly publication *The Economist* once referred to the "formidable Mr. W.R. Malinowski...a skilful and provocative Pole...who has now established himself as the demon-king in the folklore of British insurance".[9]

Finally, in transfer of technology, the Division under Malinowski's guidance sowed the seeds for an International Code of Conduct on the Transfer of Technology, negotiations on which are now in their final stages, again under the auspices of UNCTAD.

No achievement would induce Malinowski to leave the battlefield. After the adoption of the Liner Code and his retirement from the United Nations Secretariat, he accepted the invitation of the newly-installed Secretary-General of UNCTAD, Gamani Corea, to serve as his Special Adviser at a time when, following the sixth Special Session of the General Assembly and the adoption of its resolutions on a New International Economic Order, international economic relations were entering a new critical phase. However, he did not live long enough to see UNCTAD, an institution so dear to his heart, contribute to the ambitious enterprise launched by the sixth Special Session, which was inspired in large measure by UNCTAD's own work. His death in May 1975 put a premature end to Malinowski's fight for his beliefs and for the cause of the Third World.

Those who met Malinowski cherish a vivid memory of the man. Those who were privileged to work with him remember him with admiration, while even those who worked to opposite ends could not but respect him as a staunch adversary. His younger colleagues, whom he guided conscientiously, diligently and with affection both as professionals and as people, remember him with profound gratitude. He was a man ahead of his time, a man working for a future in which injustice and oppression would have no place.

Note:

The main professional positions held by W.R. Malinowski, in chronological order, were: 1932–39, Chief, Department of Foreign Trade and Money Market Statistics, Bureau of Statistics of the Republic of Poland, Warsaw; 1934–39, Member, Editorial Board, later Chief Editor, *Concise Statistical Year Book of Poland*; 1943–45, Assistant Financial Counsellor, Polish Embassy, Washington D.C.; 1945–46, Economic Affairs Officer, United Nations Relief and Rehabilitation Administration (UNRRA), Washington D.C.; 1946–1952, Economic Affairs Officer, United Nations Secretariat, New York (Economic and Employment Committee, Temporary Sub-Commission on Economic Reconstruction of Devastated Areas, Regional Economic Commissions Section); 1952–59, Chief, Regional Economic Commissions Section, UN Department of Economic and Social Affairs; 1959–1965, Secretary, UN Economic and Social Council (ECOSOC) and Secretary, Second (Economic and Financial) Committee of the UN General Assembly; 1963–64, Executive Assistant to the Secretary-General of the UN Conference on Trade and Development; 1965–1974, Director, Division for Invisibles, UNCTAD, Geneva; 1973–74, Director-in-Charge, UN Conference on a Code of Conduct for Liner Conferences; 1974–75, Special Adviser to the Secretary-General of UNCTAD.

---

1. When the ECA was established it had as members only seven independent developing countries (Ghana, Liberia, Libya, Morocco, Sudan, Tunisia and the United Arab Republic), together with South Africa and six European countries with colonial ties to Africa.

2. General Assembly resolutions 1708 (XVI) *Planning for economic development*, and 1709 (XVI) *Decentralization of economic and social activities of the United Nations and strengthening of the regional economic commissions.*

3. A review of the history of the debate and an analysis of the institutional background was given by Malinowski himself in his article on *Centralization and Decentralization in the United Nations Economic and Social Activities,* reprinted from *International Organization,* Vol. XVI, No. 3, 1962.

4. See *The Origins of UNCTAD,* by Sidney Dell, in this volume.

5. See *Proceedings of the United Nations Conference on Trade and Development*, Vol. II, *Policy Statements*, pp. 544–546, United Nations publication, sales No. 64.II.B.12.

6. On transfer of technology, see the contribution to this volume by Surendra J. Patel.

7. See, in this context, the following texts by W.R. Malinowski: *Toward a change in the international distribution of activities in shipping*, in *Shipping and Developing Countries, International Conciliation*, No. 582, pp. 66 (Carnegie Endowment for International Peace, March 1971); Introductory address at the symposium on *Studies in Maritime Transport* organized by the Gdansk Maritime Institute and UNCTAD's Division for Invisibles, entitled *Changing Political Climate in which UNCTAD Committee on Shipping has worked since its foundation*, p. 31 of the proceedings (Gdansk-Szczecin, October 26, 1971); *Shipping and the Third World*, an interview in *Inter-economics*, No. 1, p. 6 (Verlag Weltarchiv GMBH, Hamburg, 1971); *European Insurance and the Third World* in *Journal of World Trade Law*, Vol. 5, No. 5 (September-October, 1971), p. 545.

8. See the case study on the Liner Code by M. J. Shah, in this volume.

9. See *The Economist*, 24 June 1972, Survey on Insurance, p. 33.

PART ONE

Emergence and Evolution

TWO DECADES AFTER*

by Raúl Prebisch

Wladyslaw Malinowski was the great driving force behind the establishment of UNCTAD. I fully endorse what Sidney Dell says in this connection in his noteworthy contribution to this volume. Malinowski was an exceptional man, with a powerful intellect, strong convictions and a buoyant fighting spirit. His life in the United Nations was enthusiastically devoted to the cause of the developing countries with a fervour which naturally aroused great resistance in the major industrialized countries, stronger perhaps than that which I myself aroused. However, we could always count on the support of Secretary-General U Thant and of the developing countries. I was unsuccessful in my efforts to have Malinowski designated as my second-in-command in UNCTAD, a post which was eventually left vacant in my time, but he was my adviser and close associate, as well as a dear friend.

As I write these pages, I have a picture in my mind's eye of Wladek Malinowski and myself discussing the first two decades of UNCTAD while taking a stroll, as in times gone by, in the grounds of the Palais des Nations. Indeed, over 20 years have passed since the Preparatory Committee of the first United Nations Conference on Trade and Development embarked on the discussion of a vast international programme of action, from which UNCTAD emerged as an institution. We, who with great conviction and enthusiasm took part in its creation and its early evolution, believed that throwing light on the problems of development and international economic co-operation would gradually lead to reciprocal measures of benefit to the industrialized centres and to the vast periphery of the world economy. However, very little has been achieved despite the many lengthy meetings of the member governments of this international organization; and the present outlook is far from encouraging.

On careful reflection, it appears that the industrial centres are generally not interested in the development of the periphery except in so far as that suits their own development, or more precisely the interests of those of their enterprises which are linked in one way or another with the peripheral countries. Although those enterprises may be guided by long-term con-

---

* Translated from the original Spanish text

3

siderations in their own business affairs, they do not and cannot have a real grasp of the major objectives of development. Such a grasp may be expected of the governments of the industrialized countries; however, their commitment to development objectives has not been much in evidence, except in occasional statements on international co-operation which have very rarely been translated into positive measures.

I believe that this attitude on the part of the industrialized nations, stems from the dynamics of their own development. Contrary to what was maintained by conventional theories, there has not been a trend towards the world-wide spread of capitalism and the international distribution of the fruits of its rising productivity, itself the result of constant technological innovation. In the historical development of capitalism, those fruits have remained in the industrialized nations and have not led to a steady decline in prices. As a result, demand has grown in the industrial centres, constantly spurring on innovation, above all in industry. Rising productivity has made it possible to make new investments, leading in turn to further increases in productivity.

The periphery of the world economy has remained on the sidelines of this process, except in its role as supplier of primary commodities. The penetration of capital and technology from the industrialized centres has been confined to this and related activities. The bulk of the Third World's labour force has continued to earn a precarious living in pre-capitalist activities with very low productivity. In fact, rather than spreading smoothly and spontaneously to the periphery as it developed in the centres, industrialization sprang up in developing countries largely in reaction to the major crises of the advanced nations (notably two World Wars and the intervening Great Depression).

In order to industrialize, the peripheral countries resorted to protectionism, usually to an excessive degree, and to a variety of incentives; and this strategy continued even after the consequences of the crises had been overcome. Industrialization consequently developed in flagrant violation of conventional theory, which advocated a special form of international division of labour enshrining the concentration of technological progress and its benefits in the advanced countries.

The General Agreement on Tariffs and Trade was entirely based on that theory which, whatever its original scientific purity, was fundamentally geared to the development of the centres and relegated the periphery to a wholly secondary role. This is why the peripheral countries did not find an effective response to their developmental demands in the GATT principles: hence their struggle for a new trade and development organization which would accommodate their interests and aspirations.

What has happened in the two decades since UNCTAD set to work? My aim is not to restate what is already familar but rather to seek to understand its significance. This is of great importance for defining the orientation of current development policy.

Developing countries have learned to export manufactures. This opens up new horizons for the concept of comparative advantage in the trade of industrial goods. How can comparative advantage exist for such goods before industrialization has taken place? Now, the peripheral countries which have carried their industrialization furthest have a clear comparative advantage for a range of products whose technology they have fully assimilated. They should therefore be able to export those goods freely to the industrialized centres, where they can purchase goods which are more advanced technologically, until with the passage of time they can also participate as producers in the great trade currents that have developed for such goods.

In other words, as they develop industrially, the peripheral countries could be incorporated into the framework of the GATT principles. However, they are running into considerable difficulties in this process. Despite the persistent efforts of UNCTAD, it has not been possible to remove the tariff restrictions hindering imports of processed commodities, for which tariff rates escalate with the degree of processing. This contrasts with the great liberalization of trade in the technically more advanced goods of paramount interest to the centres. This liberalization, achieved through the Kennedy and Tokyo Rounds, has not reached such processed articles and barely affects the periphery's other exports of manufactures.

It is true that the Generalized System of Preferences has been established as a result of negotiations in UNCTAD. However, its clearly restrictive nature considerably limits its practical value. Furthermore, there is no binding agreement on the way it operates and it therefore remains open to serious damage caused by backsliding on the part of countries granting preferences. What is more, when some exports of manufactures from the periphery become sufficiently competitive internationally to penetrate the centres successfully, with clear comparative advantage, the centres resist this penetration by whatever means are available, even by flouting the basic principles of the GATT. A typical case is that of the Multi-Fibre Arrangement, which imposes quotas and growth limits on developing countries' exports and none on those of the industrialized nations: a combination of restriction and discrimination. This and other such arrangements are termed 'voluntary', since the developing countries have no other choice than to submit to them, after a fruitless struggle.

As a result of such arrangements, which it must be said affect not only the periphery but also trade among the industrialized countries, tariffs have been declining in importance, while various forms of non-tariff restrictions have emerged which sometimes wipe out the tariff cuts granted in trade negotiating rounds and increase the impact of tariffs which have not been cut. The UNCTAD secretariat, in its recent statements and documents on trade policy, has been drawing attention to the growth of what has come to be called 'managed trade'.[1] There is something else that is equally serious, however: the recent attempt to reopen the issue of reciprocity in trade relations between industrialized and developing countries. It had come to be understood that to apply a strict concept of reciprocity to the periphery, by demanding that it should grant the industrial nations tariff cuts similar to those it requested of them, would be a blow to its economic development. Now this understanding is being questioned.

In this connection, it is worth restating the nature of the problem. There is a tendency towards external disequilibrium in the development of the periphery, primarily because of the differences in the income-elasticity of demand. As a rule, the elasticity of demand in the centres for goods which they need to import from the periphery is smaller than the elasticity of demand in the periphery for imports from the centres. It is essential to counter this tendency by developing industrial production in the Third World, in the first place for domestic consumption and thereafter for export to the centres. However, in view of the great differences in productivity, owing to the historical lag in the periphery's development, the latter must resort to protection, and must also obtain tariff cuts from the centres. Now, if to grant such cuts the centres demand cuts from the periphery, the latter will be unable to counter the tendency towards disequilibrium, which seriously impairs its rate of development.

Furthermore, the call for reciprocity in tariff cuts fails to recognize a built-in reciprocity in North-South trade relations, inasmuch as the more the periphery can export, the more it will import from the centres. Protection by developing countries does not really diminish the amounts of such imports but rather changes their composition, which is a very important factor in the development strategies of these countries.

I have long argued that while the tariffs applied by the centres accentuate the tendency towards external disequilibrium of the developing countries, the tariffs set by the periphery, as long as they are not unreasonable, are essential in order gradually to correct that tendency. (I must emphasize the qualification to this statement, since developing countries have frequently resorted to excessive and abusive protection. It is in their own interests to be moderate in this respect, regardless of international negotiations.)

To return to the matter of the proliferation of non-tariff restrictions: I am inclined to think they are not merely a product of circumstances but rather a deep-seated problem unquestionably aggravated by the consequences of the international recession. This contention rests on a number of points.

First of all, let us return to the question of the centres retaining the fruits of their technical progress. For better or for worse, advanced capitalism has always functioned in this way. The industrial nations have retained those fruits, and their labour force has won an increasingly large share of them by exercising trade-union power and political leverage. In any event, those fruits have not spread to the periphery through lower prices, as had been assumed in conventional theory on the international expansion of capitalism.

Now, the growing competitiveness of peripheral manufactures is increasingly threatening this power of retention in the industries exposed to competition from such manufactures. For as a peripheral country assimilates production technology from the centres, while having a lower level of direct and indirect remuneration than the latter, it becomes more and more competitive. Hitherto this has occurred on a relatively small scale, but even so the centres are not only reluctant to make tariff cuts such as those that emerged from the two negotiating rounds, but also resort to the non-tariff restrictions mentioned above. The sheer scale this competitive process could reach may easily be imagined, through greater growth in the countries originally initiating it and through the inclusion of other developing countries in the process. How then would the centres react?

Would industrialized nations have any option but protectionism, which is condemned by the principles of the GATT? Would they follow the same advice in their own case as they have given to others in order to avoid protectionism? This advice is very simple: bring about external equilibrium by devaluation.

In assesssing the validity of this advice, a clear distinction must be drawn between the devaluation which inevitably accompanies inflation and the devaluation which is used as a substitute for protection and subsidies. I have always maintained, and still do, that in the latter case devaluation has harmful effects on the relative prices of goods which were already competitive, and that is why I have opposed the use of this instrument by the periphery.

What would happen if devaluation were used by the centres as a means to face up to increasingly stiff competition from the periphery, without visibly violating the principles of GATT by imposing non-tariff restrictions which are not provided for by those principles? It is not difficult to imagine the results, at least in theory. Devaluation would lower the wages of the labour force, so that the effects of competition on the industries concerned would be lessened as the prices of imports rose, while exports would be encouraged by lower prices. Devaluation would help to shift labour from threatened industries to export production, in other words, from less to more productive activities, with the ensuing growth of the total product of the economy. This at least is what conventional theory would predict.

However, this advantage could be largely offset or even cancelled out by the worsening of the relative prices of exports as a result of the devaluation.

This is not to mention the fact that the labour force would bring its political and trade-union power to bear to make up for the effect of the higher domestic prices resulting from devaluation, so that successive devaluations would become necessary.

We shall however leave these effects, very important though they may be, to one side so that we can get to the heart of the problem.

Will the centres permit a reversal of the historical tendency for the retention of the fruits of their technical progress? Their unwillingness to lower tariffs hindering peripheral imports and their use of non-tariff restrictions are evidence of their inclination to avoid or restrain competition rather than resort to a readjustment of incomes, which is inconceivable given the power of the labour force.

This all goes to show once again that the strong do not violate the principles they themselves have formulated: they simply either create new principles or continue to proclaim and formally respect the old ones while perverting them in practice! In any event, the periphery is faced with a new problem whose dimensions may become much larger. UNCTAD is playing a very important role in drawing attention to these problems and to the pressing need to arrive at reasonable solutions.

I do not believe that it will be possible to find solutions which will open wide the gates to imports from the periphery. Nor do I believe that the latter will be able to step up its exports of manufactures to the extent necessary to satisfy its huge needs of imports from the centres, above all of capital goods and intermediate goods and, in some cases, of grain, imports of which have been growing rapidly in a considerable number of developing countries. I do not wish to be dogmatic, however. This is a problem which must be analysed thoroughly, and at once.

In any event, the periphery will have to practise import substitution in so far as it is unable to develop its exports to the centres in order to pay for imports from them. This substitution, however, should not be carried out by each country in isolation. A vigorous policy of highly dynamic co-operation in industrial goods is necessary among developing countries: co-operation in production and reciprocity in trade. There have been experiments that are instructive as regards both what should be done and what should be avoided. UNCTAD and the regional economic commissions have a very important analytical and promotional role to play here.

It has to be admitted that import substitution has become discredited, in consequence of excessive protection, because it has been attempted in an unbalanced way, without a comparable effort to encourage exports of manufactures, and also because a number of countries allowed themselves to be dazzled during the long years of prosperity of the centres which ended in the first half of the 1970s. At the time it was believed that the centres would remain indefinitely open to exports from the periphery. Those hopes have been dissipated by the moderate growth prospects of the centres, even after the current recession has been overcome.

Furthermore, during those years of prosperity, extraordinary growth rates were achieved in a large number of developing countries. Unfortunately, the nations in question did not take advantage of the growth of total income to raise the rate of accumulation of reproductive capital, which increases both incomes and productivity. A privileged consumer society consequently developed in the upper and high-middle social strata. This process squandered a considerable potential for capital accumulation, which is necessary for the productive employment of the great mass of the population remaining on the margin of development at the bottom of the social structure.

Major changes in peripheral development are called for, as well as an enlightened policy of international co-operation: converging measures by the centres and by the peripheral countries. To speak of international cooperation today may seem to be no more than a way to open the door to new illusions and fresh frustrations. The centres, overburdened by their own problems, have become more reluctant than ever to co-operate in peripheral development. They are going through a crisis which, in my opinion, is basically structural, and they will not be able to overcome it entirely without very great changes on their own part. The direction of those changes is not yet clearly visible. However, crises have a habit of imposing changes and calling forth new ideas, as well as new men to put them into practice. We in the periphery must prepare ourselves for changes in the centres. We should not, however, wait passively, as we have much to do on our own. For we are still submerged in the past, victims of obsolete ideologies. New ideas are called for from us too, and we must begin to develop them in order to pave the way for the introduction of a global plan to reshape the present world order.

---

[1] I refer in particular to statements made by Reinaldo Figueredo, Director of the Manufactures Division of the UNCTAD secretariat, to Sessional Committee I of the Trade and Development Board at its meetings on 1 October 1981, 9 March 1982 and 8 September 1982.

THE ORIGINS OF UNCTAD

by Sidney Dell

1. Conceptual origins

From the very beginning the governments that established UNCTAD accepted a commitment "to lay the foundations of a better world economic order".[1] They recognized that "international trade is an important instrument for economic development".[2] In view of the importance attached to these basic ideas by those who were most active in creating the new institution, it is natural to begin by examining their origins and the character of the new departure that they represented.

The conventional wisdom about international trade, then as now, was grounded in neo-classical political economy, which asserted that spontaneous forces were always tending towards a benevolent equilibrium, and that any departures from this equilibrium would inevitably set in motion a self-correcting process of adjustment. Moreover, full employment, economic growth and the optimum utilization of resources were assured.

The first major challenge to neo-classical political economy was that of the Keynesian school in the 1930s, which showed that cyclical fluctuations in the level of output and employment were inherent in the system. Since spontaneous forces could not be relied on to eliminate the ups and downs of the trade cycle, it was incumbent on governments to provide the economic management needed to maintain full employment at all times. At the San Francisco and Bretton Woods conferences, governments expressed their determination to avoid a return to the conditions that had brought about the Great Depression of the 1930s. Accordingly, the charters of the United Nations and of the International Monetary Fund embodied a commitment to the objective of full employment.

There was no corresponding enlightenment or freshness of outlook with respect to world trade. In this area the old neo-classical precepts continued to prevail. Whatever happened in world trade had to happen by virtue of an international division of labour that was as inescapable as it was just.

The prevailing view in the first postwar decade was that if governments would only renounce the manipulation of exchange rates and dismantle the restrictions on trade and payments left over from the depression and the war, market incentives would be set free and would operate in such a way as to ensure the specialization of all countries along the lines best calculated to promote their development, based on the principle of comparative advantage. Indeed, the spontaneous forces in the system could be relied upon, in the long run, to bring about not only universal development but the progressive equalization of incomes worldwide, so that inequities in the intercountry distribution of income would disappear of their own accord. Thus while the attainment of full employment called for government intervention in the economy where needed, in international trade and payments diametrically opposed objectives were adopted.

To this vision of the world economy there emerged, soon after the end of World War II, a centre of strong opposition. This centre of opposition was located not in an academic institution, as the Keynesian school had been, but in the United Nations Economic Commission for Latin America, headed by Raúl Prebisch, who was later to become the first Secretary-General of UNCTAD. Prebisch confronted the conventional wisdom head on. So far from there being any spontaneous tendency towards a worldwide levelling of incomes, he showed that the forces tending towards the continuous polarization of economies, both internally and externally, were far stronger than those tending towards equilibrium. He demonstrated that if these cumulative forces of the world economy were not countered by deliberate action at the national and international level, the economic distance between rich and poor would grow ever wider.

The power of initiative and change rested with the industrial countries at the centre of the world economy, while the less developed countries at the periphery merely responded passively to the stimuli generated at the centre. The hegemony of the centre was, moreover, manifested both in the composition of its trade with the periphery and in the terms on which that trade took place.

The composition of trade was a survival of the old colonial order under which the metropolitan powers exported manufactures to their dependencies in exchange for imports of foodstuffs and raw materials. This pattern of specialization was promoted and preserved by the tariff structure of the industrial centres: while primary products were generally admitted duty free or at a low rate of duty, tariffs on manufactured imports were deliberately set to increase progressively with their degree of manufacture. This relic of mercantilism had survived into modern times.

Structural rigidity in the composition of trade between the centre and the periphery had major implications for the growth and the terms of trade. In the first place world demand for primary commodities tended to increase much more slowly than for manufactures. This was due partly to the fact that advances in real income were generally associated with relatively slower increases in the demand for foodstuffs and other staple consumer goods and with a shift in demand towards industrial goods and services. Moreover, technical progress was constantly tending to reduce the raw material content of final output both by making it possible to economize on the use of raw materials as well as by increasing the degree of fabrication of finished products. The development of synthetic products in the industrial countries further reduced the requirements of these countries for imports of natural materials from developing countries. Finally, the industrialization of agriculture in the developed countries made it possible for them to do without a number of the agricultural products previously imported from developing countries.

(a) Terms of trade

Coupled with the above trends was a tendency for the terms of trade of developing countries to deteriorate over time owing to declines in the prices of the primary commodities exported by them in relation to the prices of the manufactures that they imported from the industrial countries. Of the entire body of thinking developed by Prebisch and the ECLA school, this particular proposition was probably the most controversial, and became the subject of an extensive literature.

This is not the place for an in-depth review of the debate on the unequal terms of exchange, as it has been called. In part, the critics misunderstood what Prebisch was saying. As he pointed out in his report to UNCTAD I,[3] the terms of trade thesis "should not be regarded as an immutable law". Indeed, Prebisch pointed to the circumstances in which the inherent tendency towards deterioration might be offset or even reversed.

Consequently, much of the controversy about the historical trends was beside the point. Since Prebisch was not arguing that relative declines in the prices of primary products would take place under any and all conditions, but only that there was a *tendency* for this to occur in the absence of countervailing forces, it was not necessary for him to show that historical trends had invariably been in that direction.

It is true that in the course of his original exposition of the thesis in 1950, he cited data that indicated a long-run improvement in United Kingdom terms of trade from 1876–80 to 1946–47. Since United Kingdom imports consisted predominantly of primary commodities while its exports were mainly manufactures, he drew the conclusion that developing country exporters of primary commodities had suffered a symmetrical deterioration in their terms of trade. This reasoning has been criticized in the literature on various technical grounds, some valid, some invalid. It should, however, be borne in mind that the statistical evidence available to Prebisch in 1950 was extremely limited, and any alternative series that he might have used at that time would have been at least equally open to criticism.

More important, however, is the fact that empirical results for *any* period, however well based in statistical terms, could yield only suggestive and not conclusive evidence. The perceived trend in the statistics for any particular period should, properly speaking, be the starting point for further analysis of *all* the various factors involved, including both the inherent factors emphasized by Prebisch and the countervailing factors, if any.

It is therefore the analytical case that must be decisive, and here there can be little doubt that the general proposition advanced by Prebisch has been vindicated. As recently demonstrated by Professor Spraos,[4] rigorous analysis of the Prebisch thesis, reinterpreted as relating to the double factorial terms of trade, shows that "the exchange of primary exports against manufactured imports has been conducive to making growth incrementally inequalising for developing market economies." This conclusion emerges quite simply from the fact of the low income- and price-elasticity of demand for the primary commodities principally exported by developing countries. It is reinforced by the fact that while technical progress in the manufacturing industries of developed countries usually generates higher real wages and profits for the producers, corresponding advances in the technology of primary production tend to be passed on to consumers in the form of (relatively) lower prices.

(b) Adverse trends in world trade

At the level of international economic diplomacy, the most important factor in the convening of UNCTAD I was the progressively deteriorating situation of developing countries in world trade in the course of the 1950s and early 1960s. The contribution of the 'ECLA doctrine', as it came to be called, was that it was able to show that the adverse trends were not casual or accidental, but were deeply ingrained in the world trading system itself. While world trade as a whole more than doubled from 1950 to the early 1960s, exports from developing countries rose by only half. As a result, the share of developing countries in world trade declined steadily from nearly a third in 1950 to only slightly more than a fifth immediately before the Conference. The developing countries lost ground even in world trade in primary products, in which they were believed to have a comparative advantage. Thus the share of developing countries in world exports of primary commodities other than petroleum declined from 41% in 1950 to less than 30% in the early 1960s.

Some of the inherent factors tending towards this outcome have already been mentioned, notably the lower income-elasticity of world demand for primary products exported by developing countries than for manufactures, exported mainly by developed countries, and differences in market structure as between the two product groups. But there were additional factors tending in the same direction. Prominent among these were the restrictions on imports of primary commodities imposed by industrial countries, particularly in connection with agricultural support programmes. At the same time, the developing countries made little headway in manufactures: in fact their share in world exports of these goods was also declining. The main factor in this decline was the recovery in the export capacity for manufactures that had taken place in Western Europe and Japan, which was only to be expected. The developing countries were, however, concerned about various obstacles to their export trade in manufactures. In addition to maintaining the old colonial tariff structure, as noted earlier, the developed countries were beginning to take even more stringent measures against manufactured imports from developing countries, particularly cotton textiles.

In 1962, the developing countries found themselves compelled to enter into an international arrangement for the restriction of cotton textile exports to the industrial countries under the threat that, in the absence of such an arrangement, the industrial countries would impose even more severe import controls. This new development was clearly an ominous one, giving rise to the fear among developing countries that any success they might achieve in diversifying their exports into the field of manufactures would quickly meet with strong and discriminatory resistance from the industrial countries.

These various obstacles to the growth of exports of developing countries were compounded by a deterioration in their terms of trade: between 1950 and 1961, for example, the terms of trade of developing countries deteriorated by some 17%. Even without accepting the theory of unequal exchange, it was clear that the persistence of this trend would cause mounting difficulties for the developing countries.

(c) The 'trade gap'

It was not surprising in these circumstances that the export earnings of the developing countries should have increased much less rapidly than their import requirements. The issue of the 'trade gap' of developing countries, and the consequent foreign exchange constraints on their development was forcefully highlighted by UNCTAD I and placed firmly in the centre of international economic discussion.

In launching the first United Nations Development Decade in 1961 with the strong support of President Kennedy and other leaders of industrial countries, the General Assembly of the United Nations adopted the target of a minimum annual rate of growth of 5% in the real income of less developed countries by 1970. This was certainly not an inordinately ambitious target, and was not, in fact, much higher than the average rate of 4.4% per annum recorded in the 1950s. In view of rapid rates of population increase, the target rate of 5% per annum corresponded to an annual rate of expansion of little more than 2.5% in the average per capita income of the developing countries. For the poorer countries that accounted for about half of the population of the less developed areas, such a rate of growth implied that the period required to reach contemporary Western European living standards would be of the order of two hundred years.

The report of the Secretary-General of the Conference to UNCTAD I drew attention to the foreign trade implications of this minimal 5% growth target. On the basis of past experience, an overall growth rate of 5% per annum would necessitate a rate of increase of import volume of not less than 6% per annum. One of the main reasons for this was that any acceleration in the rate of growth would necessitate additional investment, and the import content of such investment was normally much higher than that of income as a whole because developing countries had relatively little capacity for production of machinery and equipment.

On the other hand, the volume of exports of developing countries had been increasing at a rate of only 4% per annum during the 1950s, and if petroleum-exporting countries were excluded the rate was even lower. At the same time, the effect of the deterioration in terms of trade was that the purchasing power of exports over imports rose more slowly still, by under 2% per annum.

This then, was the basis for the 'trade gap' of developing countries. Even at existing rates of growth there was a widening gap in their balance of payments. At higher rates of growth consistent with the quite modest objectives of the Development Decade, the gap would be magnified accordingly. It was estimated that if current trends in world trade continued, the trade gap of developing countries would be likely to reach an order of magnitude of about $20 billion by 1970, a daunting figure at the dollar prices prevailing in the early 1960s.

Projections of this type have since become commonplace, and are now carried out regularly not only by research departments of the United Nations but also by those of other international agencies such as the IMF, the World Bank and the OECD. At the time of UNCTAD I, however, the idea of a quantifiable foreign exchange constraint on growth created fierce controversy. A powerful intellectual barrage was mounted against the idea of a trade gap on the basis of a variety of arguments ranging from fundamental criticism of the concept itself to scepticism about the statistical techniques employed.

There was, of course, room for honest differences of opinion as to the precise magnitude of the trade gap. Being a residual, the gap between projected exports and imports was necessarily sensitive to the underlying assumptions made about the functional relationships between trade and growth in both developed and developing countries. But it could hardly be doubted that there *was* a gap, and that it was tending to increase. This was obvious from the fact that the volume of exports of developing countries was tending to rise more slowly than the volume of imports. This factor alone indicated a growing trade gap even if there was no further deterioration in terms of trade.

What was important was not the precise magnitude of the trade gap that had been projected, but the basic tendency that it indicated. It pointed clearly to the character of the measures that would be needed if the General Assembly's target rate of growth were to be realized. Either the gap would have to be bridged by a suitable expansion of trade or aid, or the developing countries would have to effect a fundamental re-orientation of their foreign trade pattern and possibly of their domestic economic policies as well. The only other possibility was a reduction in overall growth rates by the developing countries to the point at which their imports would rise no faster than the current slow rate of expansion of their exports, and this would mean the collapse of any hope of attaining the General Assembly's objectives.

Part of the opposition to the 'trade gap' analysis was based on concern in the developed countries that it was intended to use it to establish a case for $20 billion of additional aid annually. It is quite clear, however, that this was *not* Prebisch's intention. His main objective was to obtain acceptance of the proposition that the trade and aid objectives of the international community must be consistent with its growth objectives. Such consistency could, however, be achieved in various ways. Addressing the Federal German Society for Foreign Policy in Bonn in June 1965, for example, Prebisch said: "Allow us to export that much more and we will be a ready market for an additional 20 billion dollars' worth of your industrial products per year.". A few days earlier he had told the Canadian Manufacturers' Association in Toronto that "the fundamental long-term solution [to the problem of the trade gap] lies in trade—by increasing the possibilities of the developing countries to export more, so that they can import more". Aid, he said, could only be a temporary measure, though it might have to continue for some time for countries at a very low level of development.

II. Convergent measures to close the trade gap

How could such a transformation of the trade prospects of developing countries be accomplished? The answer lay in a programme of what Prebisch called "convergent measures"—mutually-supporting measures by both developing and developed countries. Great efforts by the developing countries themselves were indispensable—"the policy of international co-operation is only complementary, it cannot be a substitute for internal development policy".[5] In particular, effective steps would have to be taken to deal with the three main obstacles to the growth of productivity and per capita income in developing countries: land tenure, limited social mobility and ignorance in the masses, and the concentration of income in the hands of relatively small population groups.[6]

Prebisch was also very much aware of the cul-de-sac that Latin American countries had got themselves into by pursuing policies of what he called "inward-looking industrial growth, regardless of the outer world". He considered that "the countries now embarking upon industrialization should be warned against the grave mistakes we have made in Latin America because we were unable, within the framework of world production and trade, to start exporting manufactured goods at the very outset of our industrialization process."[7]

But if developing countries were to be encouraged to adopt more outward-looking policies, the international community must be ready to accept the implications for world trade and make room for the additional exports involved. "It is no good", said Prebisch, "to preach the need for [developing countries] to develop by their own efforts and at the same time to limit their possibilities of giving practical expression to that effort in the international field through the expansion of their exports. They must not be forced into a kind of closed development"[8].

(a) Commodity stabilization

Since the unregulated operation of market forces had been tending to bring about perverse transfers of real income from the poor countries to the rich, there was a strong case for corrective international action to counterbalance this process. Such action could take the form of internationally agreed measures to stabilize trade in basic commodities at a reasonable price level, and to promote the diversification of exports from developing countries so as to include a progressively growing proportion of manufactured products.

The industrial countries were aware, from their own experience, of the serious problems of domestic income distribution resulting from the chronic weakness of agricultural prices, and the consequent persistent tendency for the internal terms of trade to move against agricultural producers. It was for this reason that they had taken a variety of steps to support domestic agricultural prices or incomes through deliberate government regulation of commodity markets or provision of income supplements to farmers. They were nevertheless opposed to international intervention in commodity markets. While their opposition could be understood in terms of their short-term interests, it was less clear that it was rational in a longer run perspective, since rising real income in the developing countries was clearly in harmony with the interests of the developed countries from many points of view, including the larger markets for their exports that a prosperous Third World would imply. In fact, however, the policies of the industrial countries on agricultural production and trade had a doubly adverse effect on the developing countries. While their *laissez-faire* policies at the international level prevented the adoption of agreements to stabilize international commodity prices, their close regulation of internal agricultural markets created a stimulus to domestic producers and an additional obstacle to exporters in developing countries.

It was therefore not sufficient to expand the number and increase the effectiveness of international commodity agreements. It was also important to improve the access of primary commodities produced in developing countries to the markets of the industrial countries. Barriers to imports of such products should be progressively reduced and ultimately eliminated.

(b) Export diversification

But the real solution to the problem of insufficient growth of exports from developing countries lay in diversification of exports, particularly into the field of manufactures. Here there was a need for preferential treatment for the manufactured exports of developing countries in the markets of developed countries. The case for such preferences was that they could help in overcoming the initial difficulties and high costs of breaking into highly competitive markets in which established large scale industries in the developed countries had an overwhelming advantage. In other words, the case for preferences was a logical extension of the generally accepted argument for the protection of infant industries through import tariffs. In fact if infant industries needed protection in the domestic markets of developing countries because of their initially high costs of production, they obviously needed even more protection in foreign markets, whether developed or developing, in the form of preferential treatment.

Industrial growth in the developing countries could also be accelerated through concerted action within regional groupings of these countries, thereby increasing the scope for efficient import substitution by bringing into play the benefits of specialization, competition and economies of scale.

These were among the main features of a new world trade policy that would make a significant positive contribution to world development instead of creating obstacles to that development, as had too often been the case in the past.

(c) The role of trade in development

One of the major achievements of UNCTAD I was its acceptance, in principle, of the importance of trade as an engine of development. The very first paragraph of the Final Act of the Conference states that "In an age when scientific progress has put unprecedented abundance within man's reach, it is essential that the flows of world trade should help to eliminate the wide economic disparities among nations". That declaration reflected a new concept of international trade. As noted earlier, world trade had hitherto been viewed as the spontaneous and benevolent result of the operation of market forces. International action should therefore be limited to the creation of the freest possible environment for trade and payments, so that the beneficial effects of market forces could be maximized.

Now, however, it was gradually coming to be understood that international trade could and should be shaped to the goals of international policy. The Conference thereby marked a turning point in attitudes to the role and possibilities of international trade in promoting development in all countries, and especially in developing countries. The extent of the change should not, of course, be exaggerated. Whatever the texts agreed to at UNCTAD I may have contained, it certainly cannot be said that they embodied international agreement on the specific steps needed to promote development through trade. Indeed even today, a generation later, the battle for better access for the exports of developing countries to the markets of industrial countries remains to be won, and in some respects the protectionism of the industrial countries is even stronger in the 1980s than it was in the 1960s.

III. The concerns of the socialist countries of Eastern Europe

The socialist countries of Eastern Europe had long had their own reasons for urging the convening of a world economic conference devoted particularly to international trade problems. At the United Nations General Assembly in 1956, the delegation of the USSR proposed that such a conference be convened in the following year to consider "a further expansion of world trade and the establishment of a world trade organization within the framework of the United Nations."[9] A draft resolution calling upon the Economic and Social Council to consider the idea of a world economic conference was narrowly rejected by the Assembly's Economic and Financial Committee.[10] At frequent intervals thereafter the socialist countries continued to press their case, and when the developing countries began their own campaign for a conference on trade and development in the early 1960s, the two groups joined forces in furtherance of this objective.

(a) East-West trade

The principal motivation of the socialist countries in this regard derived from the fact that, as they saw it, they were subject to trade discrimination by the OECD countries as well as by many developing countries. It was true that most of the developed market economies had granted most-favoured-nation tariff treatment to the socialist countries. But the latter were concerned about cases of continuing tariff discrimination, and particularly about the EEC and EFTA programmes of mutual tariff reduction under their respective customs union and free trade area arrangements, which the socialist countries regarded as tantamount to raising barriers to traditional East-West trade.

They were even more disturbed by the widely prevalent practice in OECD countries whereby imports from socialist countries were subject to quantitative restrictions, and certain exports were subject to 'strategic' export controls. The socialist countries were also confronted with varying degrees of restriction on transferability of the currencies earned from exports to certain of the developed market economies. In the light of these considerations, the primary goals of the socialist countries were the mutual application by all countries of most-favoured-nation treatment in relation to both tariff and non-tariff restrictions, and a more flexible payments system. These objectives could not, they felt, be attained by means of negotiations within the General Agreement on Tariffs and Trade (GATT) to which they had not (except for Czechoslovakia) subscribed. As they saw it, GATT rules had been drawn up one-sidedly, reflecting the needs of market economies. State trading was treated in GATT only from the limited standpoint of the special conditions obtaining in a few relatively unimportant sectors of the market economies themselves. There had been no attempt in GATT to establish a mutually satisfactory regime for East-West trade.

The OECD countries, on the other hand, were concerned about the difficulties of giving any real meaning to the concept of non-discrimination in the context of a centrally planned economy. For example, they considered it virtually impossible for any external authority to ascertain either the criteria determining governmental trading plans and policies in the socialist countries or the methods whereby such criteria were translated into choices between competing sources of supply made by the agencies responsible for import decisions. On the other hand they insisted on the legitimacy of the EEC and EFTA arrangements in so far as they observed the principles for such arrangements laid down in GATT.

The socialist countries made common cause with the developing countries in seeking a world trade conference in the hope and expectation that the East-West trade issues in which they were interested would find a place on the agenda of the conference as well as in the work programme of any institution that the conference might establish. Prebisch's report to UNCTAD I did in fact contain a short section on East-West trade. While the report did not propose any specific solution of the controversy between the socialist countries and the developed market economies, it did support efforts to resolve that controversy. It pointed out, moreover, that "World trade is an intimately interrelated network, and the repercussions of obstacles in any one part are felt inevitably in all the others."[11]

(b) East-South issues

The developing countries had no objection to the discussion of East-West issues in UNCTAD and supported the socialist countries on the principle that East-West trade should be normalized. The OECD countries, however, did not regard UNCTAD as an appropriate forum for discussion of East-West issues, which it preferred to take up in the UN Economic Commission for Europe. The developing countries, for their part, saw no reason to press the OECD countries on this matter. On the contrary, they feared that prolonged and acrimonious debates on this subject might divert attention from the questions of trade and development that they considered of highest priority. Moreover, the exports of socialist countries to the OECD countries consisted largely of primary commodities and were therefore, to a considerable extent, in competition with the exports of developing countries. The developing countries were therefore concerned that any expansion of East-West trade should not be at the expense of developing country exports.[12]

Furthermore, developing countries expected the socialist countries to undertake specific trade and aid commitments within the framework of their planning processes. They should, for example, accelerate the growth of their imports from developing countries, reduce the differential between the import and domestic sales prices of commodities purchased from these countries, grant concessions equivalent to the preferential arrangements expected of the market economies, and refrain from re-exporting commodities imported from developing countries except with the permission of the latter. These and other requests addressed to the socialist countries placed them, in effect, in a position similar to that of the developed market economies vis-a-vis the Third World, and their role in UNCTAD gradually evolved accordingly.

IV. The need for a new institution

Was a new institution really necessary for the purposes that the developing countries had in mind? A basic factor in the circumstances leading to the establishment of UNCTAD was the lack of any international framework for dealing with problems of trade and development. There were, indeed, institutions that could have been adapted for this purpose, but there was little comprehension within these institutions of the need for such adaptation.

(a) The shortcomings of GATT

One such agency was GATT. In 1947, at a a conference in Havana, fifty-four countries drew up and signed a Charter for an International Trade

Organization (ITO). Just as the IMF had been set up to create an internationally agreed and supervised world monetary system, so the ITO was intended to establish an internationally acceptable regime for world trade, including special provision for trade in primary commodities.

Article 8 of the ITO Charter gave some recognition, in general terms, to the special importance of the development of underdeveloped countries, but as in the case of the Bretton Woods Conference of 1944, representation of the point of view of such countries was singularly weak at the Havana Conference. A number of these countries pressed for recognition of the special relationship between economic development and world trade, but without success. The Charter emerged as a document designed mainly to promote the interests of the developed countries by establishing an Organization committed to promote non-discrimination in international trade and a general lowering of trade barriers. Not only did these twin objectives fail to take developing country interests into account: they were in many ways, in conflict with those interests, in that they denied the special protection that infant industries and infant economies needed.

The Havana Charter failed to secure ratification in the United States because of concern in that country regarding the possible efforts of an ITO to limit the freedom of action of individual countries with respect to trade policy. What remained was the General Agreement on Tariffs and Trade drawn up at about the same time. This was an inter-governmental agreement on the two main objectives of the Charter, but did not involve the creation of an Organization in the full sense of that term, and omitted the one feature of interest to developing countries: the ITO provisions regarding international commodity agreements.

The unconditional application of the most-favoured-nation principle appeared justified only as between countries of similar economic structure and levels of development, and therefore possessing equivalent bargaining power. Since the markets of developed countries were much more important to the developing countries than those of the developing countries were to the developed countries, bargaining power in GATT negotiations was inevitably weighted heavily on one side. Consequently, the principle whereby there was no obligation to negotiate on any particular product was used by developed countries to exclude from negotiations a wide range of goods of vital interest to developing countries. Moreover, the fact that developing countries were rarely principal suppliers of the products on which they were seeking concessions meant that they were relegated to an essentially passive role in negotiations, receiving only the indirect effects of concessions negotiated between the industrial countries. Nor were they able to obtain significant concessions with respect to non-tariff barriers on products of major interest to them, and this often negated any tariff concessions that might otherwise have been applicable.

The lack of a solid institutional basis for GATT was also a serious disadvantage for developing countries, particularly in relation to their efforts to secure recognition for new principles of international trade that would take their special circumstances and weak bargaining power into account. A fully fledged international trade organization, involving treaty obligations on the part of its members, would have meant the incorporation of Charter provisions into the national legislation of every member country. An agreement such as GATT presupposed, on the contrary, that national legislation took priority over GATT commitments, so that members were able to continue to apply previously introduced commercial policy measures even if they were inconsistent with the letter and spirit of GATT. Moreover, there were no sanctions for failure to comply with the provisions of GATT other than the authorization to injured members to retaliate—a useless safeguard for low-income countries.

The inadequacy of the legal basis for GATT also had the effect of putting a premium on flexibility in the interpretation of GATT provisions as a means of finding pragmatic solutions to the problems of the major trading countries. This led to a tendency to place the exceptions to GATT above the rules, and to legitimize the granting of permanent waivers despite the clear incompatibility of such waivers with the spirit of GATT. Thus, the cotton textile arrangement was a basic deviation from the principles of GATT whereby developing country exporters agreed to forego the protection against quantitative trade restrictions, expecially applied in a discriminatory manner, that was theoretically afforded by the General Agreement. This severely damaging concession was made by the developing countries under the threat of still more restrictive measures by the importing countries. It is difficult to see how the developing countries could have fared any worse in this particular instance if there had been no GATT at all.

The shortcomings of GATT were primarily the result of the framework within which it had been conceived and created, and of the fact that its objectives were mainly those of the developed country governments that dominated it. The GATT secretariat served these objectives with a high degree of dedication, professional skill and technical efficiency, but they had, prior to UNCTAD I, little interest in or understanding of the trade problems faced by the developing countries. Nor were they receptive to suggestions that were made to them well before UNCTAD I that if GATT remained unresponsive to the trade needs of developing countries, alternative machinery would have to be created for that purpose. Once UNCTAD was set up, the atmosphere in GATT changed, and efforts were made to correct the imbalance in its affairs, though even then with only limited practical effect. It was in this way that GATT missed the opportunity presented to it to head off the creation of a rival institution.

(b) The inertia of ECOSOC

A similar lack of understanding and vision prevented the Economic and Social Council (ECOSOC) from occupying the territory that was ultimately assigned to UNCTAD. The Charter of the United Nations had established the Council as a principal organ of the world body which, together with the General Assembly, was from the outset seized with development problems. At any time during the 1950s or early 1960s the Council could have decided to move decisively into the field of trade in its relationship to development, with all the powers and terms of reference that the General Assembly subsequently handed to UNCTAD. The fact that it did not do so reflects the inability of its members to see the writing on the wall. Rarely were the key issues of trade and development even discussed by the Council, let alone acted upon. Insofar as there was any awareness of the problem at all, it was seen as something that belonged properly within the competence and responsibility of GATT. In the view of Council members from developed countries, it was not for the Council to make judgments as to whether or not GATT was discharging its responsibilities adequately.

In taking this position they were, of course, evading the responsibility of the Council, under Articles 58, 63 and 64 of the United Nations Charter, for co-ordination of the agencies of the UN system. Council members appeared to be more concerned about co-ordination as a means of preventing the duplication of functions within the UN system than about whether the responsibilities of the system as a whole were being fully discharged. Hence the supreme irony: ECOSOC, the very agency charged under the Charter with the duty of co-ordination, was itself responsible for the further fragmentation of the system through its failure to carry out its co-ordinating functions, making it necessary to set up a new institution for trade and development.

(c) The evolution of developing country views

Despite the shortcomings of existing institutional arrangements in the field of trade from the standpoint of developing countries, it should not be supposed that these countries approached the question of institutional innovation lightly. They were as well aware as the developed countries of the costs and frustrations of multiplying international bureaucracies with overlapping functions. At the 1962 General Assembly, a proposal by Burma to assert "the advisability of establishing a United Nations agency for international trade" was not accepted by the developing countries pending study of the matter at UNCTAD I. They declared their readiness to examine "the effectiveness of the activities of existing international bodies dealing with international trade in meeting trade problems of developing countries", and the possibility of effecting the organizational improvements and changes needed "to maximize the beneficial results of trade for the promotion of economic development."[13] Their overriding preoccupation was that UNCTAD I should concentrate on the substance of their problems without prejudging the institutional issue. Only gradually, and after much hesitation, did they come round to the view that only through the creation of a new institution could they ensure serious and adequate consideration of their trade problems.

In the course of the meetings of the Preparatory Committee and the early stages of UNCTAD I itself, it became clear that there was little common ground between centre and periphery on ways even of approaching, let alone of dealing with, the trade problems of the developing countries. Had such common ground emerged, the industrial countries might well have been more successful in persuading the developing countries that the issues of trade and development could best be handled through GATT. In the absence of a common approach to the substance of these issues, however, the developing countries reached the conclusion that if they were to have any chance of attaining at least some of their objectives, new institutional auspices more favourable to their point of view would have to be created. At any rate there was little inducement to them to compromise on the institutional question if by so doing they gained nothing on the issues of substance with which they were mainly concerned.

Even so, it was only the socialist countries that advocated the immediate establishment of an international trade organization. While the idea of such an organization met with some support among the developing countries, they recognized that the opposition of the OECD countries, and especially of the United States, made it almost certain that the failure of the original plan of 1947 for an ITO would be repeated. Accordingly, they opted for a formula that did not call for legislative ratification by member governments, but could be implemented by the General Assembly through the creation of a Conference, a Trade and Development Board and other subordinate bodies, all operating within the authority of the United Nations under its Charter.

(d) The bias of the Kennedy Round

It is noteworthy that the contention of developing countries at UNCTAD I that GATT discriminated in favour of the trade of industrial countries, and did not provide comparable benefits to developing countries, was strikingly confirmed in subsequent studies on the Kennedy Round of trade negotiations carried out by the UNCTAD secretariat and by Professor Bela Balassa, a consultant to the World Bank.[14]

Professor Balassa's study pointed out that the structure of protection in the industrial countries was biased against imports of processed goods from developing countries. On the one hand, tariffs tended to rise with the degree of fabrication; on the other, manufactured goods of interest to developing countries tended to bear higher duties, both nominal and effective, than the technologically sophisticated products traded among the industrial nations. Nevertheless, tariff reductions undertaken in the Kennedy Round (1964–1967) had been larger on items that were of interest to the industrial nations than on the export products of the developing countries.

The UNCTAD secretariat likewise found that despite a number of major concessions on some items of special importance to developing countries, the products in which the developing countries had expressed particular interest, and in which they had already established some trade, received on average significantly smaller tariff reductions in the Kennedy Round than did other products. This result reflected the fact that those product groups for which industrial countries were the main suppliers, particularly those characterized by advanced technology or capital intensity, received deeper and more widespread cuts. When the tariff averages were weighted to take account of trade importance, the asymmetry of the results were even more apparent. Moreover, little or no improvement in the access of developing countries to the markets of developed countries had been achieved inasmuch as quantitative restrictions and other non-tariff barriers continued to apply to a number of products and there had been no modification by the industrial countries of internal agriculural support policies or fiscal measures. The UNCTAD secretariat concluded that in the light of the foregoing, the Kennedy Round would contribute to a further decline in the share of developing countries in world trade.[16]

V. The role of the secretariat

(a) Malinowski's contribution

If Prebisch was the intellectual leader and master strategist in seeking the basis for a new world economic order, it was his lieutenant, W. R. Malinowski, who supplied the organizational and tactical imagination. Malinowski was certainly among the first, if not the first, to perceive that the effective mobilization of international efforts in support of development would necessitate institutional innovation of at least two kinds. On the one hand, it was not sufficient for nations and people to be intellectually convinced of the need for improving the world environment for development. Those convictions would have to be mobilized in a new institution capable of formulating the requisite programmes and policies and of promoting their execution, with the assistance of a competent and dedicated secretariat. On the other hand, the political will required for the creation of such a new institution would emerge only if Third World countries developed sufficient unity and singlemindedness of purpose to make it impossible for the developed countries to wave them aside, as they had so often done in the past.

Raúl Prebisch himself considers that Malinowski was the single most influential person in bringing about the establishment of UNCTAD, and it is therefore of great interest to consider how he came to exert the influence that he did.

Malinowski had, from the very beginnings of the UN regional economic commissions in 1947, championed their cause against what he regarded as the excessive dominance and conservatism of the Headquarters staff. He foresaw that the commissions for Asia and the Far East, Latin America and later Africa would be much more effective in articulating the needs of developing countries than the economic institutions and staff at UN Headquarters, where the representation of developing countries was much weaker. In his capacity as Chief of the Regional Economic Commissions Section at Headquarters, he was tireless in building up the strength of the regional commissions. In so doing he developed a constituency of his own, gaining the deep respect of many UN delegations as well as of certain senior UN officials, particularly the Executive Secretaries of the commissions, including Prebisch.

This created the basis for his subsequent appointment as Secretary of the Economic and Social Council, and of the Second (Economic and Financial) Committee of the General Assembly, which provided the opportunity for him to put another important building block in place. Operating from the vantage point of these key positions, he established methods of work that gave a parliamentary form to UN debates. The formation of caucuses or groupings of countries within the organizations of the UN family has sometimes been deplored as a source of polarization and rigidity in United Nations proceedings. That there are potential weaknesses in the caucus system cannot be doubted, but the same is true of parliamentary parties and groupings at the national level. The system was nevertheless indispensable in giving shape and order to UN proceedings by concentrating attention on fundamental points of agreement and disagreement among countries. Through this system alone was it possible to overcome the disorder and fragmentation that would have been inevitable if each and every member of the world body had insisted on its own priorities and had been unwilling to make common cause with other countries having similar, though not identical, views and interests. It was also apparent that unless the developing countries were able to unite on a common platform, they would be at a severe disadvantage in negotiations with the industrial countries of the OECD, which had acquired the habit of acting together ever since Marshall Plan days.

By 1963, immediately before UNCTAD I, Malinowski's influence, and the constituency underlying that influence, had grown to the point at which he was able to play a decisive role in the selection of a Secretary-General to take charge of preparations for the first Conference. Despite the reputation that Prebisch had gained as Executive Secretary of the Economic Commission for Latin America and as a development theorist, it was by no means a foregone conclusion that the task would fall to him. Nor was Prebisch the kind of man to press his own claims in this regard: on the contrary, he stood completely aloof from the lobbying that preceded U Thant's decision, not only because it was not in his character to do otherwise, but because of his unwillingness to put pressure on the Secretary-General.

Malinowski's contribution in this situation, as on many other occasions, was to assist the developing countries in reaching a common position. It soon became clear that the great majority of the countries that had pressed for the Conference to be held wished Prebisch to lead it. Secretary-General U Thant had himself been deeply impressed by Prebisch, and therefore welcomed the choice that developing country delegations urged upon him.

(b) Neutrality and impartiality

The activities of the UNCTAD secretariat in support of the changes, institutional and otherwise, that were needed to promote world development became a subject of intense controversy, a controversy that has continued, off and on, ever since. The main question at issue is whether it is proper for international civil servants to render assistance to one particular group of countries by helping it to define its objectives, and subsequently to bring pressure on other groups for co-operation in achieving those objectives.

It should be borne in mind that the developing countries before and during UNCTAD I were at a severe tactical disadvantage in that they lacked the political and technical support that was afforded to the developed countries by the highly skilled and well staffed OECD secretariat. It was the considered view not only of Malinowski but of his superiors Raúl Prebisch and Secretary-General U Thant, both of whom had complete confidence in him, that while the Secretariat should always act in full conformity with the Charter, and "not seek or receive instructions from any government or from any other authority external to the Organization", the Secretary-General was endowed by the Charter with a certain initiative and independence. There would, in their view, be no derogation from either the letter or the spirit of the Charter if the Secretary-General and his staff took due account of the fact that some nations were much weaker than others, and much less well equipped to argue their own case before the organs of the United Nations. Any countries requesting assistance in elaborating their case, or in organizing themselves for that purpose, were entitled to expect a helpful response from the Secretariat, within the limits of its authority and capabilities.

U Thant himself, in a television interview with Ambassador Adlai Stevenson immediately prior to his appointment as Secretary-General of the United Nations, had said that it was very difficult for a UN official to be neutral on the burning issues of the day. Whoever occupied the office of Secretary-General must be impartial, he said, but not necessarily neutral.

Following the lead of Secretary-General U Thant, the UNCTAD secretariat drew an analogy between the tasks of the United Nations in the field of development and those of the World Health Organization in fighting disease: in neither case could the respective secretariats take a neutral position in the face of clear mandates to solve the problems of ill-health and under-development.

The UNCTAD secretariat recognized its obligation to show the maximum of objectivity in dealing with development problems. Impartiality, coupled with the required sense of initiative, should express itself at all stages of international action and work: in the analysis and diagnosis of a problem, in the formulation of specific remedies and measures and in proposing new measures or compromises in cases where governments were not able to reach agreement or find a solution. The secretariat appealed for governments to understand the difficulty and delicacy of its role, and the distinction to be drawn between neutrality and impartiality.[17]

There is no doubt that the fierce opposition of the OECD countries to this view of the role of the secretariat made it very difficult at times for the UNCTAD staff to retain the confidence of these countries and hence to function as effectively as they might as mediators in the clash of views between North and South. And yet there was a sense in which the technical support provided to the developing countries by the UNCTAD secretariat, which was never sufficient to offset more than a small fraction of the resources that the OECD delegations commanded, jointly and severally, was in the highest interests of the Organization as a whole, including those of the developed as well as of the developing countries. It would, quite simply, have been against the best interests of the OECD countries themselves if the developing countries had been unable to articulate their own case in the most effective terms possible. It was difficult and frustrating enough for the developing countries that so little common ground could be established with the industrial world. If they had not even been able to find or create an institution willing to take their case seriously, the confrontation between the two groups might well have taken a much more dangerous and explosive form than occurred in fact.

Equally, however, the UNCTAD secretariat has had at all times to keep in mind the full implications of the duality of its role. This implies that the utmost care has had to be taken to avoid damaging its own credibility in fulfilling the functions required of an impartial secretariat in a negotiating forum. Examples of the occasions on which successful negotiations have been carried out in UNCTAD will be found elsewhere in this volume.

VI. The Group of Seventy-Seven

The capacity of the developing countries to mobilize the political momentum required for the creation of a new institution to promote trade and development depended on another and prior institutional innovation of the highest importance, the establishment of the Group of 77. As has been mentioned, the OECD countries had already been meeting as a group since the Marshall Plan years to concert their views and policies. Moreover, they had established a secretariat in Paris to provide them with the necessary political and technical services and support. The developing countries, on the other hand, many of which had only recently acquired political independence, were slower to seek an understanding with one another. This was partly because of their much greater heterogeneity, both culturally and in terms of development levels, but partly also because one of the features of the colonial period had been the creation of much stronger ties between the industrial centres and their associated dependencies than among the dependencies themselves.

Whatever differences they may have had as regards language, levels of living, and social and cultural characteristics, the developing countries could readily make common cause in relation to the unfavourable world conditions for their trade, and the various forms of direct and indirect discrimination that they were encountering at the hands of the industrial countries. Consequently, the emergence of trade problems as the main issue between developed and developing countries facilitated the building of Third World unity.

In July 1962 a Conference on the Problems of Economic Development was held in Cairo, attended by thirty-six non-aligned developing countries, of which five had the status of observers. The Conference adopted a Declaration that set out the main features of a common programme, concerned with internal as well as with external problems of development, and expressed itself as being "resolutely in favour" of the holding of an international economic conference to deal with "all vital questions relating to international trade, primary commodity trade, and economic relations between developing and developed countries."[18]

There followed a series of regional meetings of developing countries—of Latin American countries at Brasilia and Alta Gracia, of African countries at Niamey and of Asian countries at Teheran.[19] All these meetings culminated in resolutions which, though they differed in detail, expressed an essentially common purpose: to bring about basic improvements in the international environment for development, and particularly in the framework and conditions of world trade.

It was in the light of these events that the Brazilian Minister of State for External Relations, in his statement in UNCTAD I on 24 March 1964, was able to say that "For the first time in the history of economic conferences, the under-developed nations come here as a united front".

The significance of this development was, of course, not lost on the industrial countries, and was clearly and realistically set forth after the Conference in a report submitted on 1 July 1964 by Ambassador P. Forthomme, of Belgium, to the OECD Working Party on UNCTAD questions, of which he was chairman. Ambassador Forthomme said, among other things, that:

> ...in any event UNCTAD I has worked a change, and probably an irreversible change, in the nature of the relationships between the developed and the developing countries. In the past, the developed countries individually and collectively found themselves in a strong position in relation to the less-developed countries, because of the political fragmentation of the latter. At the Conference, the traditional position became changed by the appearance of a new fact, namely the unity of manoeuvre and action of the less-developed countries. That is unquestionably the outstanding feature of the Conference, which dominated the whole of its proceedings.

Ambassador Forthomme's perceptive judgment was fully borne out by subsequent events. It was at UNCTAD I that the Group of 77 emerged as a force to be reckoned with, a force that would gradually extend its sphere of interest far beyond UNCTAD to all other international organizations, and far beyond trade and development to every issue of international concern.

---

1. *Proceedings of the United Nations Conference on Trade and Development,* Preamble, para. 9.

2. *Ibid,* para. 53.

3. The term UNCTAD I is used to denote the first United Nations Conference on Trade and Development (Geneva 1964).

4. John Spraos, *Inequalizing trade?,* Oxford University Press, 1983.

5. Raúl Prebisch, *Towards a New Trade Policy for Development,* United Nations Sales No.: 64.II.B.4. p. 113

6. *Ibid.*

7. Raúl Prebisch, Statement to Consultative Meeting on Trade Policy, Economic Commission for Latin America, 9 October 1963.

8. Prebisch, *Towards a New Trade Policy for Development, op. cit.,* p. 124

9. UN document A/PV/589, para. 125

10. UN document A/C. 2/L.319, A/3545, para. 15

11. Prebisch, op.cit., p. 92

12. This concern was later voiced explicitly in the Algiers Charter of the Group of 77, TD/38, 3 November 1967.

13. UN document A/C.2/L.648/Rev.1 and Add.1, draft resolution sponsored by 25 developing countries.

14. Both studies are contained in a volume entitled *The Kennedy Round: estimated effects on tariff barriers*, United Nations Sales No. E.68.II.D.12.

15. *Ibid.*, p. 189.

16. *Ibid.*, pp. 3–5.

17. For further discussion of this issue see Diego Cordovez, "UNCTAD and Development Diplomacy", *Journal of World Trade Law*, 1971, pp. 131–2.

18. UN document A/5162, para. 59.

19. *Proceedings of the United Nations Conference on Trade and Development*, Vols. VI and VII, New York, 1964.

UNCTAD AS A NEGOTIATING INSTRUMENT ON TRADE POLICY: THE UNCTAD-GATT RELATIONSHIP

by R. Krishnamurti

I. Introduction

The emergence and evolution of UNCTAD as an instrument of negotiation in the field of trade policy can be traced through the changing pattern of its relationship with GATT.[1] Of the trinity of post-1945 international economic institutions (the others being the IMF and the IBRD), the General Agreement on Tariffs and Trade was the element to which was assigned the prime responsibility for determining the rules and procedures for international trade. The decision to establish UNCTAD as a permanent institution in the field of trade and development[2] was, it should be recalled, a compromise between conflicting views: on the one hand were those who sought to establish a universal, comprehensive and dynamic United Nations institution in this field, to fill the void left by the absence of the International Trade Organization and, in particular, to promote the trade and development of the developing countries; and on the other were the defenders of the institutional *status quo*, i.e. the GATT. In the negotiations which led to this compromise, at UNCTAD I and the subsequent session of the UN General Assembly, a comprehensive international trade organization was retained only as a possible goal, presumed to be a distant one at that, which might in time transcend existing international trade institutions and bring about their merger into one. For the foreseeable future, however, the compromise consisted of the addition of a new institution, UNCTAD, to an existing one, GATT. This uncomfortable institutional duality was the context in which UNCTAD had to struggle for recognition as a forum for serious South-North negotiation on trade policy matters, always overshadowed by the presence of the longer-established institution which was the preferred forum of the most powerful trading countries. The UNCTAD-GATT relationship has therefore been a crucial, complex and problematic factor in UNCTAD's institutional evolution and is likely to remain an important determinant of its future negotiating responsibilities in the trade policy field.

Before venturing to describe and analyze that relationship, however, it is

33

fitting to pay tribute here to the signal contributions, at both the conceptual and the operational levels, made by Wladek Malinowski to ensure that UNCTAD emerged as an institution with a mandate to negotiate and not only as a forum for debate.

From the early preparatory stages for UNCTAD I, Malinowski realized the importance and necessity of UNCTAD being endowed with broad and comprehensive negotiating responsibilities, including the authority to draw up legal instruments in the field of trade and development. He never accepted for a moment the view, then commonly held even in some high United Nations circles, that such mandates could be withheld from a universal United Nations organ, though he recognized the need to take into account those of existing agencies. His firm conviction on this issue derived basically from his dedication to the United Nations and his passionate desire to strengthen the Organization. His thinking had an important impact on the attitudes and proposals of developing countries at UNCTAD I, on Raúl Prebisch, who shared this conviction, and on their colleagues in the Conference secretariat. As has already been mentioned in this volume,[3] Malinowski was instrumental in defining the decision-making process in UNCTAD so as to exclude any veto powers or an entrenched consensus requirement. It is also of interest that he was largely responsible for the designation of the final document of UNCTAD I as the 'Final Act' of the Conference, a designation intended to strengthen the institution's legal basis, even though the Final Act was not itself a legal instrument.

If UNCTAD's subsequent strength as a negotiating organ is derived from the existence of the 'Group of 77' and the concerted action of this caucus of developing countries in utilizing UNCTAD machinery (its critics notwithstanding), it must be recognized that Malinowski played a crucial part in the evolution and functioning of that Group. This too was a contribution he made to strengthening UNCTAD's negotiating functions. True, the emergence of the Group of 77 was the result of the political and economic conjuncture then shaping up, and was particularly due to the failure of the existing United Nations institutions to take account of development needs, to disillusionment with their record in the post-war years, and to the leadership of a number of developing countries to that end. Nonetheless, it was during UNCTAD I that the three regional groups of developing countries, and the Group of 77 as a whole, emerged in an organized and coherent form, and started working out their own consultative, co-ordinating and negotiating mechanisms both among themselves and with the other groups, especially the OECD. The considerable cohesion, political will and speed which the Group of 77 demonstrated in getting into action caused chagrin if not shock to some of the Western powers, notably the USA, which started to realize how, by united action, the United Nations machinery could be utilized to advance economic development. The advice and assistance rendered by Malinowski to the member governments, regional groups, and secretariat colleagues who were involved in this process of growth of the Group of 77 merits special mention, as a matter both of historical record and of historic significance. Looking back today at those distant times of 1963–64, with no archives to draw upon, and deprived of the testimony of those who were involved in that process either because they have departed from the scene or because for whatever reasons they have not found it feasible to narrate their experiences, it is up to the survivors to give a true perspective on Malinowski's vital role in these historic developments.[4]

With UNCTAD and the Group of 77 set up and functioning, Malinowski continued to play a key role as a negotiator, which extended far beyond his official position as Director of the Division for Invisibles. There was hardly any important decision whether institutional, legal, or political, taken by the UNCTAD Secretary-General or the Trade and Development Board and its committees, especially in the first five to six formative years, which did not bear his imprint.

II. The formative years of the relationship

The Western powers, which after great resistance agreed in 1964 to the establishment of UNCTAD, continued their efforts immediately thereafter to preserve and strengthen GATT as the principal negotiating and legal instrument in the field of international trade, and to limit UNCTAD's role and its growth. GATT's operations and programmes in regard to developing countries were therefore stepped up, Part IV of the General Agreement was adopted, the GATT Committee on Trade and Development established, and sustained efforts were mounted to enlist developing country membership of GATT. A great deal of rivalry, vagueness of mandates, and overlapping in work programmes became evident in those early formative years of the UNCTAD-GATT relationship, to the point that the Secretary-General of UNCTAD and the Director-General of GATT considered it necessary to bring this to the attention of their respective governing bodies in 1966.

At the twenty-third session of the GATT Contracting Parties in April 1966, the Director-General of GATT (then Sir Eric Wyndham White) made the first concrete proposal, i.e. to set up a programming committee composed of senior officials of both bodies, with responsibility for guiding the study of matters such as projects and proposals under consideration in the two institutions relating to developing countries, "with a view to ensuring complementarity, harmonious co-operation, avoidance of duplication and co-ordinated results". The membership of the programming committee, he suggested, would consist of the chairmen of the legislative bodies of UNCTAD and GATT, and of the two secretariat heads. This proposal came up before the fourth session of the Trade and Development Board and the Secretary-General of UNCTAD (Dr. Prebisch) urged that a decision be quickly made. The Board did not respond, however, partly because scepticism prevailed among developing countries, though it was not made explicit, about the wisdom of starting co-ordination efforts even before UNCTAD had had at least a few years to develop and elaborate its incipient mandates; and partly because there was a change in the attitude of some major trading nations, again not openly stated, which had earlier supported the proposal in GATT but had second thoughts by the time it came before UNCTAD.[5] After consultations between the heads of the two secretariats, it was agreed to set up a sub-committee under the UN Administrative Committee on Co-ordination (ACC), this being considered an appropriate way of dealing with such problems. The ACC sub-committee was ineffective and short-lived, which is not hard to understand, given the ACC's poor overall record in inter-agency co-ordination in the face of the support by member governments for duplicating and parallel mandates in different bodies, and of the independence and autonomy of the specialized agencies of the United Nations system.

This is not to overlook the efforts that were pursued during 1966–68 to promote joint projects and operations by the two organizations, which produced agreements on the joint sponsorship of the International Trade Centre and on joint servicing by the two secretariats of the trade negotiations among developing countries (see section IV below).

There were doubts and fears on the part of Prebisch and his senior colleagues at the time[6] that, given the Western efforts to strengthen GATT *vis-à-vis* UNCTAD, the establishment of a programming committee of the type proposed would cause serious obstacles to UNCTAD's evolution and growth, at both secretariat and inter-governmental levels. It was feared that UNCTAD would be stunted and stifled in the name of co-ordination and harmonization and inhibited in putting forward new and dynamic ideas and approaches in several areas either not covered or only partially covered by GATT. Looking back over the years, such fears would not appear to have been ill-founded.

Over the years, the two institutions have developed and carried out their work and negotiating programmes largely without formal co-ordination, essentially on an *ad hoc* basis, as determined by the pulls and pressures of member governments. As for UNCTAD, suffice it to say in this context that in its two decades of existence it has developed ideas and policies, as well as competence and negotiating mechanisms, covering a broad range of trade, finance and development issues, programmes and instruments, including: the Integrated Programme for Commodities and the Common Fund, the Generalized System of Preferences, the Code of Conduct for Liner Conferences, the Convention on Multimodal Transport, restrictive business practices, insurance problems, the proposed code on transfer of technology, reverse transfer of technology, economic co-operation among developing countries, 'East-South' economic co-operation, development finance, aid, debt problems, monetary reform, and problems of the least-developed countries. These tasks have given impressive dimensions to UNCTAD's operations, going far beyond the international trade sector, though not wholly divorced from it, and giving it developmental orientations. This was an evolution expected of UNCTAD by the founding developing countries and accelerated after 1974 by the impetus of the quest for a New International Economic Order.

For its part GATT, which is both a legal agreement embodying rights and obligations and an operational institution, has accumulated enormously increased responsibilities deriving from its tasks of consultation, surveillance and dispute settlement, and from its recurrent 'rounds' of multilateral trade negotiations (MTNs) and their continuous follow-up.

These developments have led to the realization by member governments, and it should be noted here that all the members of GATT are also members of UNCTAD, of the importance if not the inevitability of the distinctive and independent co-existence of the two institutions, with a certain concomitant lack of clarity in respect of their mandates, and differences if not conflicts in regard to the ideologies, principles and policies which should govern international economic and trade relations. UNCTAD has been stressing developmental approaches whereas GATT has been promoting a liberal international trading system. This philosophical distinction entails areas of overlap, as well as conflicts of policies.

Neither UNCTAD's authority nor its skill in concluding international legal instruments and rules has, however, been fully commensurate with the breadth of its development-oriented work programmes and negotiation efforts. Western countries have accepted modifications of the principal rules of an essentially liberal trading system only in select cases, and again as derogations to them rather than as basic new principles and rules.[7] Even in so doing, they have either sought legal sanctions in the GATT framework or ensured compatibility with that framework or others supportive of Western concepts and practices. The battle of ideas in UNCTAD is therefore constant and dynamic.

The following sections analyze briefly the work undertaken by UNCTAD and GATT in a number of areas of interest to both institutions, including commodity negotiations, ECDC, East-West and East-South trade, restrictive business practices, textiles, technical co-operation, and last but not least the Kennedy and Tokyo rounds of trade negotiations. Reference is also made to the results of the most recent ministerial gatherings in GATT and UNCTAD. And, in conclusion, an examination is made of possibilities for improving co-ordination and co-operation between the two bodies.

III. Negotiations on commodity issues[8]

UNCTAD's responsibilities with respect to international commodity agreements have been generally recognized by member States under General Assembly resolution 1995 (XIX), after which UNCTAD took over the functions of the Interim Co-ordinating Committee for International Commodity Arrangements (ICCICA). It has also been given the task of co-ordinating the activities and operations of international commodity councils.

The record of international commodity arrangements and stabilization efforts has been admitted to be dismal, largely on account of the negative policies of the major industrialized nations, in particular the USA. However, UNCTAD deserves credit for successfully focusing on an integrated approach to commodity problems, and for negotiating the Integrated Programme for Commodities (IPC) and the Common Fund as instruments for implementing that approach. Since 1979, the momentum for action in this area has regrettably been lost and an acute crisis in commodity markets has developed showing the programmes as well as the results so far obtained to be meagre and ineffective.[9]

None of the main elements of the IPC: the Common Fund, arrangements for core commodities, the framework for processing, marketing and distribution of commodities, and compensatory financing arrangements, has yet taken off. The Common Fund has not been established as an operational institution, largely owing to lack of adequate ratification by member States, including a large number of developing countries. Even allowing for the fact that the Common Fund was never envisaged as a panacea for all commodity ills, the institution which has emerged from the negotiating process is not likely to be able to cope adequately with—much less to overcome—the problems before it, given the modest resources of its first and second windows (especially in relation to the initial negotiating proposals and targets), the limitations on its borrowing and other financial operations, its still basically conservative and traditional terms of reference (in contrast to the NIEO-oriented proposals) and its decision-making structure. It must nonetheless be emphasized that, had the Common Fund been operational now, it would have provided political and financial support for the negotiation of additional international commodity arrangements, as well as assistance to efforts in commodity development, though in the latter case its own modest resources would have had to be supplemented to a very considerable extent by other international, bilateral and national sources.

Progress in negotiating international arrangements for individual commodities in the IPC has been most disappointing, for reasons often cited, such as the lack of commitment of important producer and consumer countries, genuine divergences of national interests, the lack of a unified position amongst developing countries, the attitude of transnational companies in certain basic commodity areas, and technical difficulties.

In its task of co-ordinating the activities of the various international commodity councils, UNCTAD's record cannot be considered much of a success. However, its reviews and assessments of the problems, and its consultations and working arrangements with other agencies (which have improved over the years) provide some overview and co-ordination. The commodity councils enjoy virtual autonomy under their respective terms of reference, and their negotiations on individual commodities have conformed largely to the traditional bargaining and negotiating modes, reflecting the national interests of producing and consuming countries. UNCTAD's philosophy and ideas have in some measure permeated these bodies; developing countries have often worked together for common objectives, and producers' associations have been formed for some commodities. Given the character of the technical issues and the primacy of national interests in commodity negotiations, however, it would perhaps be unrealistic to expect a greater measure of concertation by developing countries or of co-ordination by UNCTAD.

When it comes to processing, marketing and distribution, which form part of the IPC and for which the objective of a 'framework' was agreed under UNCTAD resolution 124 (V), considerable secretariat work has been carried out, including studies on several commodities and a policy document containing suggestions *inter alia* for redeployment of production capacities, improved competitiveness of natural products, elimination of tariff escalation in developed countries against processed products and reduction of non-tariff barriers.[10] Study has also been made of the feasibility of drawing up the principal guidelines and principles of an overall 'framework' for increasing developing countries' participation in processing, marketing and distribution, which would be applied at the level of specific commodities or commodity sectors. Little progress has been achieved in developing the elements and modalities of this 'framework'.

Clearly there are major differences between developing countries and developed countries on the approaches to this set of issues, and on what really constitutes a 'framework'. If by the latter is meant a system of commodity arrangements which would not only consist of the traditional elements relating to prices, quotas and buffer stocks but also contain commitments in respect of larger shares for developing countries in processing, marketing and distribution of the products, as well as measures for the reduction of tariff and non-tariff barriers, then the difficulties of negotiating such a 'framework' would be multiplied to the point of rendering agreement impossible. The number, variety and complexity of the issues which would arise in the negotiations do not easily lend themselves to the conclusion of concrete commitments under one umbrella. Processing, marketing and distribution involve ecomonic, legal and contractual issues relating to activities of private enterprise in countries and across national frontiers in respect of private capital investment and technology transfer. Existing systems are undoubtedly unfair and need correction, but such corrective measures cannot be fitted into international commodity arrangements. National laws and policies in developed and developing countries will seldom make it possible to impose such commitments on private corporations or to oblige such companies to carry them out. Differences and conflicts of national interests among developing countries themselves would make it extremely difficult to negotiate commitments for granting advantages to developing countries, seeing that large numbers of private firms are required to accept such decisions. Problems and difficulties of this kind have been abundantly experienced in the industrial sphere, in the UNIDO sectoral consultations and in the regional and sub-regional integration and complementarity agreements of developing countries. What is perhaps both workable and desirable to aim at in the UNCTAD 'framework' on processing, marketing and distribution is to reach agreement on overall guidelines and principles, supplemented if at all possible by targets on quantitative goals in certain sectors which would not constitute binding legal commitments but provide signposts for forward movement.

Furthermore, the negotiations themselves will have to take place through a multiplicity of channels: governmental, private, national, regional and international. GATT, UNIDO and FAO would all be involved. Reductions of tariff and non-tariff barriers, for example, could be negotiated in the GATT pursuant to IPC recommendations or guidelines. But the UNCTAD 'framework' could be the focal point for overview and assessment of trends and progress from time to time, in such particular product sectors as might be agreed upon.

UNCTAD's competence and ongoing activities in commodities are broad, but do not confer exclusivity on it. GATT has continued to exercise important functions in this area with regard to agricultural and tropical products. These relate to tariff and non-tariff barriers, access to markets, export subsidies, persistent protectionism, and generally to rules applying to agricultural trade, all aimed at trade liberalization and mitigation of barriers.

During the 1964–67 Kennedy Round, unsuccessful attempts were made in GATT to negotiate international agrements on cereals and sugar, and these were later on brought to commodity conferences under UNCTAD auspices.[11]

In the 1973–79 Tokyo Round, agreements were reached in respect of bovine meat and dairy products, in addition to a decision to continue the negotiations for the establishment of an agricultural framework. These agreements provide *inter alia* for the establishment of an International Meat Council[12] and an International Dairy Products Council, with informational and consultative functions, as well as the promotion of measures by governments for dismantling trade barriers and liberalizing world trade in the products concerned. As regards grains, some proposals were tabled and considered in the Tokyo Round. One was for an international agreement on grains, based on a system of minimum and maximum prices, stock reserves, and provisions for consultations and certain obligations between members at agreed 'trigger prices'. Developing countries proposed measures for a two-price system offering favourable and differential treatment in their own favour. No progress was made in these negotiations and it was finally decided to let the matter be handled by the International Wheat Council, which was concerned with the negotiation of the International Wheat Agreement, and to request the Secretary-General of UNCTAD to fix a date for reconvening the negotiating conference on wheat, which had twice met inconclusively, in 1978 and 1979.[13]

Trade in agriculture was probably the most contentious item on the GATT ministerial agenda of November 1982. The Ministerial Declaration includes a number of provisions calling for further study of trade policies and measures affecting agriculture, as well as for consideration of action to liberalize agricultural trade, to bring it more fully into the multilateral trading system, and to improve the application of GATT rules and disciplines to such trade. A Committee on Trade in Agriculture has been established with a two-year work programme.

A number of agricultural products such as wheat, meat, dairy products and sugar, are likely to be the objects of very difficult negotiations involving the USA, the EEC, Canada, Japan and Australia, but the interest of many developing countries are also involved both as exporters and as consumers or recipients of food aid. Close co-operation between GATT and UNCTAD is both desirable and necessary in these commodity areas, especially those involving international commodity agreements.

IV. Trade relations among developing countries

In the ECDC area, the roles of UNCTAD and GATT have so far remained largely complementary. In its early years, and almost up to the mid-seventies, UNCTAD's principal work on ECDC consisted in providing technical assistance and advice to regional and sub-regional groupings of developing countries in their co-operation programmes, in association with regional economic commissions. Since then, with the adoption of the ECDC programmes of the Group of 77 at Mexico City and Manila in 1976, Arusha in 1979 and Caracas in 1981, and with the establishment of the UNCTAD

Committee on ECDC, UNCTAD's mandates and work programmes have taken on impressive dimensions.[14]

The highlight of GATT's rather limited activities in the area of ECDC at the global or interregional level was the adoption in November 1971 of the Protocol on Trade Negotiations among Developing Countries, the result of a round of negotiations initiated in 1967. Under this Protocol 16 countries, considered to be 'developing' in the GATT context, exchanged tariff concession among themselves; a GATT waiver was obtained to provide the legal basis for this programme.[15] The Protocol was left open to other developing countries. It entered into force in February 1973, at which time 17 countries had ratified it.[16] The Protocol provides for an annual review of the working of the arrangement, on the basis of reports to be furnished by the participating countries. It also provides for the establishment of a Committee of Participating Countries for joint action to give effect to the provisions of the Protocol and generally to facilitate its operation. This Committee has been meeting from time to time as necessary.

The results of the programme have been rather modest.[17] In 1979, the aggregate value of trade in products included in the agreement was US $329 million, compared to US $40.4 million in 1976, and US $155 million in 1978. The item-by-item method of negotiation has not proved very effective.

Despite the meagre results and lack of dynamism of the arrangement, it is important for two reasons. First, it provides a legal basis in GATT for preferential trade agreements among a number of developing countries on a global or interregional basis, as distinguished from regional and sub-regional arrangements among geographically contiguous countries.[18] Secondly, the experience gained in its negotiation and operation, including experience of negotiating modalities, operative provisions and consultations, has been valuable in both a positive and a negative sense: the negative lesson being the limitation of item-by-item negotiation and the positive outcome being the acquisition of expertise in negotiating techniques. Also worthy of mention in this context is the early agreement of the executive heads of GATT and UNCTAD on the joint servicing of these negotiations. In practice, however, although the UNCTAD secretariat participated to some extent in this exercise, it remained basically the responsibility of the GATT secretariat.

The 'Enabling Clause' adopted in November 1979, in the context of the Tokyo Round of MTN's, providing for differential treatment for developing countries, dispenses with the need for a special waiver for regional or global preferential arragements among developing countries "for the mutual reduction or elimination of tariffs, and, in accordance with criteria or conditions which may be prescribed by the Contracting Parties, for the mutual reduction or elimination of non-tariff measures, on products imported from one another". It is not clear from this whether preferential non-tariff arrangements can be implemented without prior consideration by GATT, even if a waiver is considered superfluous. Interpretation of this provision would be important in connexion with the UNCTAD programmes for a Global System of Trade Preferences among developing countries (GSTP) and preferences among State Trading Organizations (STOs), now under consideration.

At the conclusion of the Tokyo Round, consideration was given to initiating another round of trade negotiations among developing countries in GATT. The item is included in the current GATT work programme drawn up by its Director-General, and technical work by the GATT secretariat and informal consultations within the Committee of Participating Countries have been undertaken. It does not seem likely, however, that such a negotiating round will be initiated in the near future.

UNCTAD's current work programme on ECDC comprises three major trade components, the GSTP, STOs, and multinational industrial and trading enterprises, as well as a number of non-trade components. The three trade programmes (which are relevant in the present context) are complex and ambitious, the GSTP perhaps most of all. The Group of 77 has adopted a declaration outlining the aims, principles, elements, and modalities of the proposed negotiations on the GSTP. The objects of negotiation are to include tariff and non-tariff measures, direct trade measures, long-term contracts and rules of origin. The declaration provides that the GSTP will be reserved for the participation of member States of the Group of 77; that rather than replace, it should supplement and reinforce the existing regional, sub-regional and interregional economic groupings; that the special needs of the least developed countries should be clearly provided for; and that linear, product-by-product and sectoral approaches or combinations of these approaches, as well as direct trade methods, will be explored. A GSTP Negotiating Committee has been established, open to the participating members of the Group of 77. This Committee is charged with establishing the necessary mechanisms and procedures for the various negotiations and for conducting and overseeing them. The UNCTAD secretariat is requested to provide technical, logistical and other support for the Committee.[19] Other competent bodies, such as GATT, ITC, FAO, UNDP and UNIDO, are also requested to provide support for the negotiations.

Clearly, the GSTP will be massively complex, both technically and logistically, and will call for considerable expertise and resources from governments and the UNCTAD secretariat. Even the gradual, step-by-step process of negotiation envisaged in the programme will be far from easy to organize, given the intricacy of the issues and the need to reconcile divergent national and regional interests. It is not realistic to expect that the type of UNCTAD-style group meetings so far convened on the GSTP, even with adequate secretariat support, would provide effective mechanisms for the negotiations. Apart from formal multilateral meetings, the need would arise for an almost continuous process of informal plurilateral and bilateral consultations and negotiations, involving member governments and regional and sub-regional groupings. Already over forty Group of 77 goverments have signified their intention to participate in the GSTP negotiations, which is a good indication of their interest, and more will join as the work picks up momentum. These governments therefore need to consider rather urgently how best they can mobilize their own technical expertise and resources, besides tapping those of UNCTAD and other secretariats.

The formation of a 'core' of their own experts, contributed by governments on an agreed regional basis, would be a significant way of effectively preparing for the GSTP negotiations and of mobilizing support. A similar measure has already been adopted by the Group of 77 in connexion with the negotiations on the Multi-Fibre Arrangement in GATT. Such an informal technical core need not give rise to institutional debate and doubt among the Group of 77, if it is strictly agreed that the core would be *ad hoc* and restricted to GSTP objectives, and would not give rise to any implications for longer-term Group of 77 secretariat facilities.

The GSTP should provide a useful opportunity for UNCTAD-GATT co-operation. Formal agreement on joint handling of the GSTP by the two institutions may have to be ruled out for many reasons including the unresolved issue concerning countries that can participate and the central role assigned to UNCTAD in this project by its initiators, as well as the practical difficulty of 'joint' arrangements. This should not, however, prevent GATT from offering its expertise and assistance, nor UNCTAD from strengthening its contacts with the GATT secretariat to that end. The suggested Group of 77 technical core would make it easier to achieve this objective.

V. East-West and East-South trade and economic co-operation

UNCTAD, set up as a universal trade organization to deal with all flows of trade, has not lived up to its responsibilities in regard to East-West trade, as envisaged in General Assembly resolution 1995 (XIX) and as sought at successive sessions of the Conference. This failure is attributable to two principal factors: the firm stand taken by the Western countries against dealing with East-West trade and economic issues in UNCTAD; and the position of the developing countries themselves, which have been preoccupied with their own trade and aid demands on the socialist countries of Eastern Europe, analogous to their demands on the Western countries, and have not concerned themselves overly with East-West issues. The pressure for debating these issues in UNCTAD has consequently come only from the Eastern countries themselves.

On the other hand, GATT has strengthened its role in East-West trade and economic exchanges, mainly through its legal framework. Socialist countries (other than the USSR) were either early members of GATT or have acceded to it over the past 10 years or so. They have participated in the MTNs and other GATT negotiations, mainly to secure and improve most-favoured-nation (MFN) benefits, to gain better access to Western markets, credit and technology, and to reduce or eliminate discrimination against them.

Under the accession agreements, the socialist countries have assumed GATT obligations and have presented relevant information in connexion with the GATT reviews under their protocols of accession.[20] These documents indicate that GATT has been pragmatic in dealing with the socialist countries, and in adapting principles and rules to their state trading systems by devising appropriate yardsticks or criteria. These have included, for example, commitments to increase imports from contracting parties by a certain rate annually or to increase imports from them by a rate not less than the rate of increase of total imports, and also comparisons of import growth from other centrally-planned economies with that from market-economy countries. In regard to the licensing and quota systems of the socialist countries, as well as the pricing of their exports and export subsidies, it is clear that GATT provisions have been applied with a significant degree of pragmatism. Also deserving of note is GATT's acceptance of tariff concessions without import yardsticks in connexion with Hungary's accession to the General Agreement, because Hungary had then introduced a number of market mechanisms in its economic structure and foreign trade, and only generally indicated its intention to increase imports. The socialist countries have presented relevant data to the GATT for scrutiny and surveillance in a multilateral framework. In turn, they received the benefit of MFN concessions (even if these are not considered fully satisfactory) and of consultation, negotiation and mediation in the GATT. The recognition of the compatibility of the socialist foreign trade system with the GATT principles of liberal, non-discriminatory and multilateral trade is very important in providing an international legal framework for the socialist countries, even if a large volume of their foreign trade is conducted under bilateral arrangements.

There is however a major limitation: the US regulations governing East-West trade (under the US Trade Act, as well as the Export Administration Act) do not grant MFN treatment automatically to the socialist countries on their accession to GATT, but contain political, defence and foreign policy objectives (e.g. freedom of emigration). GATT, like other international institutions, has had to accept the force of these non-economic considerations.[21]

Even so, socialist countries' membership of GATT has increased its universality, as has the fact that most developing countries are already in it.

That China is now an observer is also of considerable political significance from the institutional point of view. However, the non-participation of the USSR in GATT is still a major factor limiting its universality.

In the area of East-South trade, GATT's role has been slight, though in contractual terms these relationships come theoretically within the scope of GATT. For its part, UNCTAD has developed, after a slow start, a steadily growing contribution in terms of inter-governmental study and recommendations, bilateral and multilateral consultations, and technical co-operation programmes. UNCTAD resolutions 15 (II), 53 (III) and 95 (IV) embody the main measures, including medium-term and long-term agreements, bilateral and tripartite industrial co-operation arrangements, provisions in national development plans co-ordinated by CMEA for increased imports from developing countries, improved payments and convertibility facilities, etc. The consultations on East-South trade held in the framework of the sessions of the Trade and Development Board, and UNCTAD technical co-operation efforts in the form of seminars and advisory services, have also been helpful. Yet there is still considerable untapped potential in this area, and UNCTAD can significantly increase its contribution, given more dynamic and open policies by both the developing and the socialist countries.

VI. The Generalized System of Preferences

The Generalized System of Preferences (GSP) is among the earliest important successes of UNCTAD in the field of negotiation. The Group B (OECD) countries have invariably emphasized the unilateral character of the GSP, implying that it was a concession granted by them, not a negotiated instrument. It remains nevertheless a fact that the acceptance and implementation of the GSP, in face of strong initial opposition (especially from the USA) to the departure from the MFN principle which it involved, called for concerted and intensive consultations and negotiations in the UNCTAD machinery.[22] UNCTAD's responsibilities for the continuing review and monitoring of GSP implementation have been accepted all round and have been exercised with a high degree of efficiency and seriousness.

The UNCTAD Special Committee on Preferences was established and charged with annual and triennial reviews of the scheme and with a comprehensive review before the end of the first ten years, with the objective of reviewing the operation of the GSP and securing improvements in a variety of respects. These reviews have brought forth a wealth of analytical and statistical material from the UNCTAD secretariat and have served to bring about improvements in product coverage over the years. UNCTAD resolution 96 (IV) embodied by far the best recommendations negotiable for improving the GSP at the time (1976), but the years that followed have witnessed an increasing reluctance and restrictiveness on the part of preference-giving countries, coinciding with adverse world economic conditions.

After the GSP became fully established and operational, the demands of developing countries focused in particular on improvement of product coverage, liberalization of ceilings and maximum amount limitations, zero-duty admission for all covered products, relaxation or elimination of the 'competitive need' criteria, elimination of discretionary and discriminatory elements applied on the principle of 'graduation', compensation for erosion of preferential tariff margins by MFN tariff cuts, non-discriminatory treatment of all developing countries, prior consultations on the basis of agreed criteria and procedures with respect to safeguard measures which reduce or suspend preferential treatment and, last but not least, the strengthening of the legal status of the GSP in the form of a binding legal instrument, or through other action in GATT.

Recent record shows that while developed countries have accepted the GSP as a long-term measure extending beyond the first ten years and are prepared to keep it going with minor improvements, they are progressively impairing its generalized and non-discriminatory character by introducing unilateral and discriminatory provisions, as well as differentiation and graduation among developing countries. It would seem that the developing countries as a group and the affected developing countries in particular, while rejecting these measures of graduation in principle, have had no choice but to tolerate them in practice.

In the post-MTN phase, consideration of the GSP in the Special Committee on Preferences has focused on the issues of graduation and differentiation, on the improvement of the GSP, and on implementation of the GATT 'Enabling Clause' (see below). Commitments to improve GSP have been reaffirmed in the Committee. The Group of 77 tabled a resolution in 1982 calling for a number of measures: the GSP to be instituted as a legal and permanent instrument; graduation and differentiation to be eliminated; the GATT Enabling Clause to be strictly adhered to, so that GSP modifications may respond positively to the development, financial and trade needs of developing countries; and multilateral consultation machinery to be set up under the auspices of the UNCTAD Special Committee, to review and examine all restrictive measures including graduation and safeguard action.[23]

GATT has played a relatively limited role in the negotiations and implementation of the GSP. The waiver granted by the GATT decision of 25 June 1971 was, to be sure, an essential condition for the implementation of the GSP. Once the agreement on the GSP had been unanimously negotiated in UNCTAD, the waiver became more or less a formal ratification. The waiver provided for reviews by GATT, which it has undertaken principally through its Committee on Trade and Development, but also through other bodies as necessary. Basically, however, GATT has so far left it to UNCTAD to study, review and manage the GSP. Developing countries continued to press in GATT Bodies to secure a firmer and more durable legal basis for the GSP. This pressure increased after 1973 during the MTNs, when they presented many demands for GSP improvement there, as in UNCTAD. The adverse world economic situation and protectionism apart, once the MTNs started the industrialized countries virtually halted all but minor improvements to the GSP, reserving any concessions for the final MTN package for tactical reasons.

In the event, apart from a number of tariff cuts in either GSP or MFN form (which were by no means claimed as satisfactory even by the developed countries themselves), the principal advantage from the MTNs in regard to the GSP was the Enabling Clause embodied in the GATT decision of 28 November 1979 providing for derogation of GATT's article 1 on MFN, so that developed countries could accord preferential treatment to developing countries without obtaining specific waivers for the purpose. At the same time, GATT's role in GSP review and surveillance was strengthened by paragraph 4 of that decision, whereby any contracting party introducing a preferential arrangement in favour of developing countries but subsequently modifying or withdrawing it, "shall notify the Contracting Parties" and furnish them with all the information they may deem appropriate relating to such action, and afford adequate opportunity for prompt consultation at the request of any interested contracting party. Further "the Contracting Parties shall, if requested to do so by such contracting party, consult with all contracting parties concerned with the matter, with a view to reaching solutions satisfactory to all such contracting parties". It is not known whether any developing countries have tried to resort to these provisions of the Enabling Clause in the last few years, during which discriminatory and restrictive measures have been unilaterally introduced in the name of graduation and differentiation.

The GATT Ministerial Declaration of November 1982 contains important commitments to ensure differential and more favourable treatment for developing countries by effective implementation of Part IV of the Agreement, and calls upon the Committee on Trade and Development to review the operation of the Enabling Clause, as provided for in its paragraph 9, "with respect to objectivity and transparency of modifications to GSP schemes and the operation of consultative provisions relating to differential and more favourable treatment for developing countries."[24]

It will be interesting to observe how developed countries respond to this review requirement and in particular whether they are prepared to implement the mandatory consultative provisions of paragraph 4 of the Enabling Clause. It would be no surprise if they were to use this review process to justify, buttress and legalize differentiation and graduation in the GSP on the basis of the general formulation contained in paragraph 9 of the Enabling Clause. Time will show whether the GSP will be strengthened as an aid to development or legitimized as a tool of discrimination in applying these provisions. If developing countries turn to these GATT procedures simply because they are contractual, they could leave themselves open to such risks. Moreover, in doing so, they could steadily erode the review, surveillance, consultation and implementation functions of UNCTAD with respect to the GSP.

A noteworthy development in the GSP was UNCTAD resolution 159 (VI) which reaffirms the generalized, non-discriminatory and non-reciprocal character of the GSP;[25] it also provides that "any preference-giving country taking action to modify its scheme shall afford adequate opportunity for prompt consultations, upon request, with respect to any difficulty or matter that may arise". It is to be hoped that these commitments will be implemented through the UNCTAD machinery.

VII. Restrictive business practices

The Havana Charter had a chapter dealing with restrictive business practices (RBPs) but this was not included in the GATT. ECOSOC took up this subject in the early 1950s and an *ad hoc* committee drafted an international code; this was not adopted by ECOSOC, largely for lack of support by the major industrial nations. This ended ECOSOC's efforts. GATT took up the subject in 1955 and the Contracting Parties in 1960 adopted *ad hoc* notification and consultation procedures for dealing with conflicts of interest between contracting parties in this area.[26] These procedures have not been used by the Contracting Parties so far.[27]

UNCTAD's work in this area was initiated in 1968 by Conference resolution 25 (II), the developed countries voting against the project. The work was, however, steadily pursued and developed over the next twelve years, through secretariat studies and expert and inter-governmental discussion, to the point that a negotiating conference held in UNCTAD in 1980 unanimously adopted the Set of Multilaterally Agreed Equitable Principles and Rules for the Control of RBPs, which was approved by the UN General Assembly later the same year.

The Set of Principles and Rules is not a binding legal instrument. It is a set of voluntary recommended norms, but with some kind of commitment on the part of governments to implement them and with provision for some kind of monitoring and implementation by UNCTAD. Governments which have accepted the Set have agreed to meet their commitment by suitable action.

The Set enjoins States to curb a certain number of restrictive business practices at the national, regional and sub-regional levels. A high degree of vagueness and uncertainty about the meaning and interpretation of the provisions is likely to render their practical application very difficult and evasion rather easy.[28]

The provision of special and preferential treatment for developing countries is more or less similar to that under the GATT Enabling Clause which emerged from the MTNs, i.e. it is couched in general terms and is not as specific and comprehensive as proposed by developing countries. Given the nature of the instrument, however, developing countries need have no serious apprehensions that their national developmental or ECDC programmes will be hampered.

A number of recommendations in the Set of Principles and Rules are addressed to enterprises (section D). Member governments are to disseminate information on the Set and to establish mechanisms for information, investigation, consultation and compliance. It remains to be seen, however, whether enterprises will go far in complying with the recommendations. Already at its first and second sessions, the UNCTAD Intergovernmental Group of Experts on RBPs, set up to monitor the operation of the Set, has expressed concern at persistent resort to restrictive practices, and called upon countries to institute effective legislative and administrative action for controlling them. This would seem to point to the slight possibilities of voluntary response by enterprises to the Set's recommendations.[29]

The Principles and Rules are universal in character and therefore applicable to the socialist system. The socialist countries accepted the Set by consensus and without entering any formal reservations. They have however invariably pointed out that UNCTAD resolution 25 (II), which still forms the basis of UNCTAD work in this area, relates to "restrictive business practices adopted by private enterprises of developed countries", and that the restrictive business practices known in the market economies are alien to the socialist system. This view is not accepted by developing or Western industrialized nations.

Implementation of the Set of Principles and Rules is to be achieved through the work of the inter-governmental monitoring group in UNCTAD and by collection of information, reporting, and consultation. A member State may request consultations about the control of restrictive business practices with other States concerned, who should accord full consideration to such a request. The Secretary-General of UNCTAD, if requested, may provide conference facilities for such a consultation and the States concerned may prepare a report on the consultation for inclusion in the Secretary-General's annual report. The process of information-gathering and implementation will further be developed by means of seminars, conferences, technical assistance and exchange of personnel.

The UNCTAD Intergovernmental Group is to provide a forum and channels for mulilateral consultations and for exchanges of views between member States on matters related to the Set of Principles and Rules, its operation and experience gained in its application, with a view to making it more effective. The Group is also called upon to collect and disseminate information, make recommendations to member governments on matters pertaining to the application and implementation of the Set, and submit reports at least once a year on its work. Five years after the adoption of the Set, a UN Conference will be convened under UNCTAD auspices for the purpose of reviewing all aspects of the Set of Principles and Rules, and to consider possibilities for improvement and further development. The Intergovernmental Group and its subsidiary organs cannot function as a tribunal or pass judgement on the conduct of individual governments or enterprises in connexion with any specific transaction, nor become involved when parties to a specific business transaction are in dispute; these limitations are reasonable and legitimate.

The foregoing provisions concerning information, consultation, review and implementation are fairly far-reaching. It has to be admitted that they could have offered a stronger monitoring and enforcing role for UNCTAD, and an 'honest broker' or mediating role for its Secretary-General. They also lack provision for panels of study and investigation or for dispute settlement. Nevertheless, they offer considerable scope for practical, realistic and highly useful ways of monitoring and implementation, building up case law, evolving habits of inter-governmental co-operation (both bilateral and multilateral) and stimulating further development of existing national and regional control systems. The magnitude, complexity and range of tasks involved in follow-up and implementation are quite considerable and it is up to member governments, of both developed and developing countries, to take action to give genuine effect to the Set of Principles and Rules through their own policies and laws. The UNCTAD secretariat also has an important responsibility and scope for exercising its initiative, if the momentum gained by the adoption of the Set is not to be lost. Dramatic and quick results are not however to be expected.

GATT still avoids the area of restrictive business practices, though the Ministerial Declaration of November 1982 adopted a decision on services which could lead to a possible resumption of GATT activity. If this were to occur UNCTAD's incipient legislative and implementing programmes might run into considerable difficulties, especially if UNCTAD's initiative and momentum are not maintained in the meantime.

VIII. Trade in textiles

Before UNCTAD came into existence, international trade in cotton textiles was subjected to restrictions under a short-term arrangement, and later a long-term arrangement (LTA) under the GATT, as a temporary departure from its provisions. Subsequently, the GATT was the forum for negotiations on the Multi-Fibre Arrangement (MFA). The GATT continues to be concerned with the review and administration of textile trade arrangements and related consultations and negotiations. UNCTAD has consequently always lacked a negotiating role in what is regarded as one of the most important export sectors of interest to developing countries.

From the beginning, the UNCTAD Committee on Manufacturers provided a forum for study, discussion and continuing review of international trade in textiles, especially the LTA and the MFA over their successive phases. From time to time, Group B countries, while objecting to the inclusion of this subject on the UNCTAD agenda because it was under negotiation in the GATT, conceded a discussion and review. UNCTAD secretariat studies on textiles were an important contribution to the analysis of the economic and trade aspects of these arrangements and put forward suggestions for improving them. The secretariat also assisted Group of 77 countries in preparing for the textile negotiations. The Group of 77 tabled draft resolutions on textiles in UNCTAD from time to time, often coinciding with the continuing GATT negotiations, but Group B would not negotiate on them, holding that GATT was the proper place for such negotiations. On only one occasion was a proposal on textiles successfully negotiated in UNCTAD, at the seventh session of the Committee on Manufacturers in July 1975 (decision II (VII)). That decision was thin in substance and simply called for strict adherence by the developed countries to the provisions of the LTA. At the time, even this was considered important for the recognition of UNCTAD's role in the matter. When the later negotiations on the MFA were in progress in the GATT, UNCTAD secretariat studies and discussions helped to clarify the issues, especially for the benefit of developing countries.

In the renewed MFA, which is to extend to July 1986, the growth provision has been dropped, and the larger exporters have had to accept restraints, while the new entrants and smaller producers have been promised better deals. The bilateral agreements which have been negotiated under the MFA have not been satisfactory, and given the large number of exporting countries competing for limited market opportunities, the industrialized countries have had very little trouble driving hard bargains and playing off one exporter against the other.

In response to the pressure of developing countries, the 1982 Ministerial Declaration contains a decision to give priority to a study of trade in textile and clothing, which is to examine the feasibility of liberalizing the MFA restraints and of applying GATT provisions fully to this sector of trade. The study would also cover the implications for importing and exporting countries of phasing out or maintaining the restrictions. One should not be over optimistic about the results of such a study, taking into account the lessons of the last twenty years. Meanwhile, it is to be hoped that the UNCTAD secretariat will continue to assist the developing countries in this area and that issues related to textile arrangements will be discussed in the Committee on Manufactures and in the Trade and Development Board.

IX. Technical co-operation

UNCTAD's technical co-operation programme covers several areas: ECDC, GSP, RBPs, MTNs, technology, East-South trade, trade facilitation, insurance, maritime transport and least developed countries. These areas constitute a dynamic and growing set of operations which has brought UNCTAD and its ideas closer to governments in the field.

GATT has its own programme of technical co-operation. For many years, it has been conducting commerical policy courses for officials from developing countries, and has invited UNCTAD officials to contribute to them in selected areas of UNCTAD work. GATT provided assistance and advice to developing countries during the Tokyo Round for their more effective participation in the MTNs, and is continuing similar assistance in the follow-up phase. Specific provisions for technical co-operation have been incorporated in a number of MTN codes and decisions, for example those on technical standards and on dispute settlement procedures. The recent GATT Ministerial Meeting decided to strengthen the GATT technical co-operation programme "with a view to facilitating the more effective participation of developing countries in the GATT trading system", and to give special technical assistance to the least developed countries.

The programmes of the two institutions have grown largely in response to their substantive work programmes, and on a pragmatic basis. There is an overlap in some areas (e.g. MTNs, trade policy) but not in others (e.g. shipping, insurance, technology). No deliberate efforts seem to have been made to co-ordinate the technical co-operation programmes. However, there are working contacts and exchanges of information at staff levels, while some measure of co-ordination is introduced through the allocation of UNDP funds and of voluntary contributions by governments.

An early and continuing case of successful UNCTAD-GATT collaboration is the International Trade Centre (ITC). This Centre was created in 1964 by GATT, but became a joint enterprise of the two institutions in late 1967. Credit for this goes to the two secretariat heads at the time (Prebisch and Wyndham White). In the first two years or so following the decision on the joint operation of the ITC, a liaison committee of officials of the two bodies met fairly regularly, with the Director of the ITC also participating. This helped to iron out substantive and administrative problems on which the ITC Director sought advice.

The ITC has proved itself a valuable instrument of technical assistance to developing countries in a varied range of technical trade promotion activities, mobilizing substantial voluntary contributions from developed countries as well as UNDP funds. At present an UNCTAD-GATT Joint Advisory Group and its Technical Committee supervise and guide the ITC at the inter-governmental level. It should be recalled also that for many years, until the mid-seventies, the ITC annual report of activities was on the agenda of the UNCTAD Committee on Manufactures and was reviewed by it.

Technical assistance in commercial policy areas, as distinct from technical trade promotion questions, does not form part of ITC's functions. This was jointly decided by the heads of UNCTAD and GATT at the time they negotiated the terms of reference of the joint operation, for two reasons. First, commercial policy issues entailed substantial differences in views and policies among member States and even between the respective UNCTAD and GATT philosophies and approaches. Secondly, it was felt that the ITC was not adequately equipped to deal with commercial policy issues and should not be burdened with additional tasks. This delimitation of the ITC's functions seems by and large to have been maintained over sixteen years of its operation under UNCTAD-GATT auspices.

X. The Kennedy and Tokyo Rounds of trade negotiations

GATT as an institution has derived its strength not only from its contractual character and the strong backing of Western countries, but from the prospects of tangible benefits offered by participation in its major negotiating rounds and their follow-up, even though these prospects have generally failed to materialize to a degree which would satisfy the weaker trading countries.

GATT has completed two major rounds of trade negotiations since the establishment of UNCTAD, the Kennedy and Tokyo Rounds. The interface and interaction of the two institutions regarding these rounds have been extensively documented, more particularly with respect to the Tokyo Round,[30] and only the more important points pertaining to the authority and performance of the two institutions need be cited here.

The Kennedy Round (1964–67) coincided with the first years of UNCTAD. The newly-established institution, preoccupied as it was with setting up its principal committees and elaborating its work programmes, had little time to devote to the negotiations in GATT. Nevertheless, the UNCTAD secretariat followed the negotiations; staff members designated by the Secretary-General attended a number of meetings of the Kennedy Round negotiating groups and received some of the relevant GATT documentation, though their access to the more confidential and restricted negotiating groups and to related documentation was limited. Furthermore, the UNCTAD secretariat was probably the earliest to come up with a provisional evaluation of the results of the Kennedy Round for the developing countries, which it submitted to UNCTAD II in early 1968.[31]

The years following the Kennedy Round fall roughly into three phases: the period up to the launching of the Tokyo Round, the Tokyo Round itself (1973–79) and the post-Tokyo Round phase, leading up to the GATT Ministerial meeting of 1982.

The first phase witnessed the continuation and in some cases the intensification of technical work in a number of GATT bodies on issues such as tropical products, non-tariff barriers, safeguards and export subsidies. This work was not necessarily aimed at launching another round of negotiations, but was the follow-up to the Kennedy Round. Efforts in the UNCTAD machinery, initiated and pressed by developing countries principally through the Committee on Manufactures, to bring about the liberalization of non-tariff barriers and improve market access, met with a strong negative response from Groub B countries. Despite successive decisions adopted unanimously by that Committee (decisions 2 (III), 1 (IV) and 1 (V)), calling upon the UNCTAD secretariat not only to carry out studies on these subjects but also to provide a forum for consultations and to formulate suggestions and recommendations, there was hardly any advance in trade liberalization. Even when the industrialized countries accepted certain recommendations in UNCTAD concerning adjustment assistance and standstill on further trade restrictions, they omitted to adhere to them and utilized the GATT machinery to maintain or even, as was the case of textiles, to intensify trade restrictions which were both unjustified and inconsistent with GATT provisions.

In the second phase, i.e. when the Tokyo Round of MTNs had been officially launched and was in progress from September 1973 till December 1979, the UNCTAD machinery was precluded from any meaningful negotiating role on issues arising in the MTNs. Developing countries, with the support of the UN General Assembly, worked and negotiated hard to ensure a clearly defined role for UNCTAD in the MTNs, without prejudice to the negotiations being held under the GATT umbrella. Their modest success in these efforts was seen in the consensus on assigning a number of MTN-related responsibilities to UNCTAD. The Trade and Development Board and its subsidiary bodies were to follow the MTNs closely from the point of view of developing countries and in that context to put forward proposals and facilitate consultations;[32] the Secretary-General of UNCTAD was to have access to the relevant meetings and documentation of the MTNs, and prepare appropriate studies for UNCTAD bodies; and finally the Secretary-General was also to provide technical assistance to developing countries individually and collectively at regional and global levels, to facilitate their effective participation in the MTNs.

To carry out the last task, the UNCTAD secretariat obtained UNDP finance for a special technical assistance team at UNCTAD headquarters and for related regional teams, and provided substantive support to these teams from its competent divisions. The UNCTAD Secretary-General's access to MTN meetings and documentation was less than perfect, being subject to constraints most of which were related to the necessary confidentiality of the issues under negotiation. Subject to these constraints, the UNCTAD secretariat presented several studies over the years to UNCTAD bodies, including the Board and some of its committees.

However, the first function, which related to inter-governmental action in UNCTAD, could not be carried out effectively. The MTNs indeed appeared regularly on the agenda of many UNCTAD bodies, and during the years between 1973 and 1976 developing countries presented a number of proposals for negotiation in those bodies. But the Group B countries would not enter into such negotiations, since the same issues were under negotiation in GATT, and these countries were not prepared to prejudge or prejudice the outcome of that process. However, the UNCTAD studies and the draft resolutions submitted by developing countries were, by consensus, remitted to the appropriate GATT bodies.[33] In 1977–78, as the Tokyo Round approached a conclusion, the deliberation of these issues in UNCTAD, already so limited, became less and less meaningful owing largely to the lack of transparency of the GATT negotiating process itself and to the priority given by developing countries to action in GATT. When UNCTAD V convened in May 1979, at a very critical and decisive final phase of the Tokyo Round, it was regarded by developing countries as probably their last chance to utilize UNCTAD machinery to obtain support for their positions in the MTNs. Determined efforts and intensive negotiations in Manila centred round a comprehensive draft resolution tabled by the Group of 77; Group B also tabled their own proposal. These efforts failed to produce an agreed resolution, and all that UNCTAD V could agree upon was to request the Trade and Development Board to make a global evaluation of the MTNs on the basis of a report by the Secretary-General of UNCTAD (Conference resolution 132 (V)). The developing countries adopted a declaration expressing their disappointment and listing the proposals they still were determined to pursue in the MTNs. But the final results of the Tokyo Round which emerged later that year fell lamentably short of the commitments made in the 1973 Tokyo Declaration on most issues of interest to developing countries.[34]

In the post-Tokyo Round phase, since the beginning of 1980, the UNCTAD secretariat has continued to follow action on MTN decisions and codes and on the unresolved issues. It has presented some excellent analyses and evaluations.[35] The Trade and Development Board and the Committee on Manufactures have kept the MTN follow-up under review. The Board has asked the competent UNCTAD committees to examine developments in international trade arising from the implementation of the MTN results, and to transmit to GATT Bodies the relevant UNCTAD documentation. In July 1980, the Committee on Manufactures adopted Agreed Conclusions calling for action to implement MTN decisions for the benefit of developing countries, and stressing the importance of the MFN principle and of transparency in the work of GATT bodies. In the following section of this paper, we shall more closely examine the role which UNCTAD could play in respect of the follow-up to the Tokyo Round decisions and to the GATT Ministerial Declaration of November 1982.

XI. The 1982 GATT Ministerial Declaration

Attention has already been drawn to important decisions taken by the GATT Ministerial Meeting of November 1982 in the various areas dealt with, and to their possible implications for UNCTAD. In this section we shall attempt to consider briefly some other aspects of the Ministerial Declaration not dealt with earlier, and to make some general comments on the possible overall impact of the Declaration on UNCTAD and its negotiating and work programmes, as well as on the developing countries themselves.

In response to the pressure exerted by developing countries to obtain commitments from the developed countries in respect of their major concerns, which had received only scant attention in the Tokyo Round, the Ministerial Declaration includes several references under the various headings to the need to take into account the interests of the developing countries. Special attention is paid to the least developed countries. An annex to the Declaration deals with "GATT rules and activities relating to developing countries". Among the specific decisions made are: the GATT Committee on Trade and Development is to review how contracting parties individually and collectively have responded to the requirements of Part IV, hold necessary consultations, and suggest improvements to Part IV; the same body is to review the application of differential and more favourable treatment to developing countries; improvement of the GSP is to be sought; consultations and negotiations are to be held aimed at the further liberalization of trade in tropical products, the relaxation of quantitative restrictions, and reducing tariff escalation; special attention is drawn to the terms and conditions of export credits for capital goods; the MFA is to be reviewed. This is an impressive list indeed, including many items which have lingered on GATT liberalization agendas and action programmes for over twenty years, with a lack of results which is painfully obvious. Time has still to show whether these new commitments are any different from preceding ones.

Special comment is required on two new areas of work referred to in the Ministerial Declaration, namely, services and "an examination of the prospects for increasing trade between developed and developing countries and the possibilities in GATT for facilitating this objective", the latter to be undertaken by the Committee on Trade and Development.

On services, the Declaration recommends that interested contracting parties undertake a national examination of the issues in this sector, exchange information among themselves, " *inter alia,* through international organizations such as the GATT", and "review the results of these examinations, along with the information and comments by relevant international organizations, at their 1984 session and ... consider whether any multilateral action in these matters is appropriate and desirable". This decision falls far short of the ambitious proposals advanced by the USA to bring the services sector under the purview of the GATT and to extend and reinforce the GATT articles to that end. The developing countries have taken a firm position that rules applicable to trade in goods are not necessarily applicable to services; that GATT's scope and competence should not be enlarged; that UNCTAD is the appropriate organization where a great deal of work is already being carried out in the services sector; and that their developmental policies and national interests would be seriously injured by the extension of GATT-type principles and rules to the services sector.

One has only to recall the developmental content being injected by UNCTAD into such service-related issues as restrictive business practices, transfer of technology, the brain drain, shipping practices (including most recently ship-registration and maritime fraud) and insurance, not to mention other issues where the service content is less marked though still important, to realize how adversely this developmental approach could be affected if the GATT, under pressure from the USA, were to embark on 'liberalization' measures in the services sector.

Concerning the proposed GATT study on North-South trade, it is worth recalling that this was included in the Ministerial Declaration after the developing countries had decisively rejected a proposal by the USA for a round of North-South trade negotiations in GATT, involving particularly those developing countries considered by the USA to have 'graduated' and designed to introduce 'intermediate' preferential tariff rates (i.e. intermediate between MFN and GSP rates) in exchange for tariff and non-tariff concessions and for the increased assumption of GATT obligations by the 'graduates'. The effect of that proposal, if accepted, would have been to legalize 'graduation' in a contractual framework, to dilute non-reciprocity in law as well as in fact, and to divide 'graduates', whoever they may be, from the other developing countries with a consequent weakening in the solidarity of the entire group.

The GATT study by the Committee on Trade and Development will not, however, be limited to the US proposal. It may be comprehensive and include many areas of policy at the core of economic development. By all tokens, UNCTAD is the pre-eminent institution for North-South trade and would need to watch the possible implications of the GATT initiative very closely.[36] This could be a source of fruitful co-operation, or of its opposite.

On the more general outcome of the GATT Ministerial Meeting a surprising measure of consensus prevails: that it was a failure—or only 'a C plus' in the words of the US representative; that the commitment to the disciplines of the GATT system and to rolling back protectionism was half-hearted and weak; and that it did not launch another round of GATT negotiations as earlier GATT Ministerial Meetings had done, and as the USA had planned this time. It may be judged the first time in GATT's history that the USA did not succeed in getting the Contracting Parties to accept some of its major proposals which, apart from those already mentioned, also included phasing out agricultural subsidies. The success of the concerted action by the developing countries (operating as the Group of 77) in warding off the services issue and the North-South trade round may also be marked up as another 'first'. Given the weak negotiating power of developing countries, however, and the character of GATT modalities, nothing can be taken for granted.

The Ministerial Declaration decided that the rules and procedures of the GATT 'system' would be effectively and fairly applied, "on the basis of agreed interpretations, for the economic development and benefit of all". Furthermore, it reaffirmed that "consensus will continue to be the traditional method of resolving disputes [and] it is understood that decisions in this process cannot add to or diminish the rights and obligations provided in the General Agreement". In addition, the Contracting Parties have reaffirmed their decision "to preserve, in the operation and functioning of GATT instruments, the unity and consistency of the GATT system". These statements should be read in conjuction with the decision of the Contracting Parties in December 1979, in connexion with the MTN codes and conventions (to which a large number of developing members of GATT have not acceded), that the existing rights and benefits under the GATT of countries not parties to those agreements will not be affected by them. These reaffirmations are of critical importance since developing countries are often subjected to heavy pressure to accept a 'consensus' which denies their interests and legal rights. Regrettably, the MTN codes and decisions are already being applied on a 'conditional MFN' basis, and the basic principles of MFN, multilateralism and GATT disciplines are being seriously eroded.

Following the GATT Ministerial Meeting, the US Administration is reportedly considering additional initiatives to alter the GATT.[37] The options considered are known as: 'GATT plus', i.e. a group of countries which would agree to engage in freer trade than called for under the GATT, for example, two-way free trade among themselves; 'super GATT', i.e. a group of countries which would exercise leadership in GATT and persuade others to join them; and 'GATT of the like-minded', i.e. a group of countries agreeing to cut trade barriers among themselves, and inviting other nations to join in. Any of the three proposals would undermine the MFN principle and MFN-based bilateral and multilateral agreements. They highlight the chronic problem arising from the gap batween the GATT principles on paper and their breach in practice, between the GATT decision-making rules and the established practice of the weighty trading nations working out their 'deals' and subsequently securing GATT legality.

XII. Developments at UNCTAD VI

The decisions adopted by the sixth Conference of UNCTAD at Belgrade in June 1983 do not appear to imply any significant change in the UNCTAD-GATT relationship so far considered. It is not the intention here to evaluate the substantive results of the Conference; it is generally recognized that they are slight indeed. The expression 'missed opportunity' has been frequently used in this respect. However, UNCTAD VI reaffirmed and in some areas strengthened UNCTAD's work programme and negotiating potentials. Of course, the technical studies and consultations in such areas will take time to complete, after which real negotiations could begin. Only then would it become evident whether any new problems would arise in relation to GATT's work programmes and negotiating processes.

The Belgrade decision on international trade in goods and services, and the related one on the UNCTAD work programme on protectionism and structural adjustment (resolutions 159 (VI) and 160 (VI)) are important in the context of the UNCTAD-GATT relationship. They reaffirm and somewhat strengthen the role of the Trade and Development Board in reviewing relevant developments in protectionism and structural adjustment, monitoring implementation of past recommendations on these subjects, and where necessary making recommendations concerning the "general problems of protectionism". In respect of the GATT work on an improved and more efficient safeguard system, the Board is enjoined to "follow closely the work with a view to assisting developing countries to participate in this process fully". On structural adjustment, UNCTAD's role has been enhanced, the Board being called upon not only to continue its annual review of patterns of production and trade in the world economy, and to provide a forum for exchange of information and experience, but also to "make general policy recommendations", *inter alia* with a view to encouraging the movement of factors of production into lines of production in the light of the dynamics of comparative advantage and the attainment of optimal overall economic growth".

Another significant decision on the international trading system, embodied in resolution 159 (VI), envisages that the Board "could while fully respecting the principles of MFN and non-discrimination, make recommendations on principles and policies related to international trade, and make proposals as to the strengthening and improvement of the trading system with a view to giving it a more universal and dynamic character as well as making it more responsive to the needs of developing countries and supportive of accelerated economic growth and development, particularly of developing countries".

The same resolution refers to the issues of North-South trade expansion and services, arising from the GATT Ministerial Declaration. In provisions on services which attracted the sole negative vote of the USA, the resolution recognizes the need for and importance of further activities by international organizations in this field, desires the Secretary-General of UNCTAD to continue studying the issues involved and states that "UNCTAD will, *inter alia*, consider the role of the services sector in the development process", under a work programme to be adopted by the Board. The USA voted against this part of the resolution on the ground that it dealt inadequately with the complementarity of UNCTAD and GATT. It further disagreed with the Group of 77 view of the role of the GATT in the services sector. It is to be expected that the US will continue to promote GATT activities in this sector, while developing countries will attempt to check the extension of GATT jurisdiction.

It remains to be seen how far UNCTAD will be able to avail itself of these mandates on the subjects of the international trading system, protectionism, structural adjustment and services. Although the Board recommendations are to relate to 'general policy' and 'general problems', formulations intended by Group B to exclude UNCTAD from concrete operations and negotiations, especially those on specific products or sectors, it cannot be denied that policies and recommendations will need to be based upon concrete case studies, as well as on innovative and development-oriented ideas and approaches. They cannot be conjured out of thin air. Nor should "full respect for the principles of MFN and non-discrimination" inhibit dynamic interpretation of the rules and principles of international trade. The Group of 77 and the UNCTAD secretariat are therefore set to continue the battle of ideas and of negotiations to another stage.

XIII. Institutional evolution, co-ordination and co-operation

Suggestions have been made from time to time, in the United Nations context and outside, for bringing UNCTAD and GATT closer together.

These suggestions have ranged from improved secretariat collaboration and the creation of a joint co-ordinating or programming committee to the establishment of a comprehensive international trade organization in which both UNCTAD and GATT would be merged.

At UNCTAD III in 1972, interest in the ITO idea was revived by the developing countries. Against Group B opposition, the Conference adopted a resolution on further evolution in the institutional machinery of UNCTAD, which called upon the Trade and Development Board to give consideration to the question of establishing a comprehensive trade organization, invited views and suggestions of member governments, and requested the Secretary-General of UNCTAD to present a study (resolution 80 (III)). Over the next few years, the matter received rather perfunctory consideration by the Board, but there was no substantive progress, and the subject was dropped.

In a 1975 report on "A New United Nations Structure for Global Economic Co-operation,"[38] a United Nations Group of Experts recommended consideration of the possibility of establishing an international trade organization which, in effect, would incorporate UNCTAD and GATT. The new organization would have two 'chambers', one concerned with broad policy and the other with trade negotiations, but would have a common secretariat. Among other issues listed for examination in the same context were the possibility of setting up an umbrella commodity organization, either by itself or as a 'third chamber' in a new ITO, and the question of whether a new ITO should ultimately deal not only with trade issues but also with other issues such as restrictive business practices, transfer of technology, private investment and transnational companies. These possibilities were to be viewed in the context of evolution toward an ITO over a transitional period. But nothing came of these ideas. Nor does the ITO appear to have received any particular attention from the *Ad Hoc* Committee on Restructuring of the Economic and Social Sectors of the United Nations System,[39] which was set up by the seventh special session of the General Assembly in September 1975.

Following the decisions of the General Assembly in 1974–75 on the NIEO and related subjects, deliberations and negotiations in UNCTAD assumed new dimensions and concerns, delving deeper into fundamental developmental issues and structural problems of the world economy. By its successive resolutions on institutional questions, endorsed by the General Assembly, UNCTAD is characterized as "a principal instrument of the General Assembly for negotiations on relevant areas of international trade and related issues of international economic co-operation, particularly in the context of negotiations on the establishment of the New International Economic Order" and one of the major instruments of the United Nations for reviewing the above problems and their implementation as appropriate.

This evolution is not inconsistent with the future emergence of a new ITO, but it definitely includes elements which go well beyond the mandate of an institution dealing solely with trade issues.

At UNCTAD VI, the Group of 77 revived its proposal of earlier years to establish "a comprehensive international organization to deal, in an integrated manner, with all aspects of trade and development and related matters". It suggested that the Board should undertake in 1985 "an in-depth study of the ways and means of bringing into existence such an organization" and that UNCTAD VII should consider the subject. In the meantime, according to this proposal, "the UNCTAD permanent machinery should be adapted as necessary to cope with the new requirements stemming from the need to strengthen inter-governmental consideration of developments in the world economy and in international economic policies in the context of interdependence".[40] The Conference, as expected, did not take substantive action on this proposal but remitted it to the Board for "further consideration". It would call for a high degree of optimism indeed to believe that a formal decision would be made in UNCTAD to establish such an organization, given the basic opposition of Group B and taking into account the disappointing results of the efforts over the last ten or so years to secure for UNCTAD such modest institutional aims as a measure of rationalization and streamlining, and a larger degree of administrative and budgetary autonomy and flexibility.

As for GATT, in preparation for and during the Tokyo Round, several ideas and proposals for its reform were put forward by developed and developing countries. The USA's objectives were to strengthen the GATT articles and provisions, particularly those pertaining to consultation, notification, surveillance and dispute settlement, and to modify GATT operations so as to reflect more adequately the economic and trading importance of industrialized countries. The US Trade Act of 1974 had embodied several provisions to this end. The larger questions of an ITO or a more comprehensive institution were not brought up by any country, presumably because discussion of such questions was considered unrealistic. However, the GATT was developed and reformed in a number of respects by the MTN codes and decisions. The ministerial decisions of November 1982 aim at more effective and transparent application of the multilateral disciplines embodied in GATT. In addition, as indicated earlier, the Ministerial Declaration provides for important new areas of work for GATT: trade in services, North-South trade expansion, trade in certain natural resource products, structural adjustment and trade policy, besides the pursuit of MTN follow-up on tariffs, tropical products, special and differential treatment of developing countries and trade in textiles.

The need for UNCTAD-GATT co-ordination has been stressed by the Brandt Commission in both its reports. In the first of these, after reviewing the negotiating mandates and progress being made in the two institutions, the Commission stressed "a definite need in the short term to co-ordinate these two bodies more closely, and to prevent duplication. This could be achieved by a small co-ordinating body, the creation of which should not be difficult since both organizations have an interest in concerting their negotiations and research." It also considered that in the longer term a new attempt should be made to create an ITO which would encompass the functions of both UNCTAD and GATT. In its second report, the Commission reiterated the latter recommendation, in addition to emphasizing the need for closer consultation and co-operation between GATT, UNCTAD, IMF, and other bodies, and for more joint and co-ordinated efforts in their activities.[41]

A Commonwealth Group of Experts, reporting in 1982 on the North-South dialogue and the obstacles to the negotiating process, refers to the compartmentalization of institutions, which has prevented linked issues from receiving co-ordinated treatment and inhibited the rational development of the whole negotiating process.[42] As a case in point, it cites the paucity of joint and co-ordinated efforts between UNCTAD and GATT, and describes their experience as one more of rivalry than of co-operation. The Commonwealth report attributes this in no small measure to the different levels of political support for the two organizations. It calls for further substantial efforts to clarify the responsibility and competence of the institutions, and to avoid duplication and institutional proliferation.

In a recent study making the case for a 'New Global Trade Organization'[43], Miriam Camps proposes a new organization in which membership would be open to any State accepting a few common principles, and work would largely be done in subsidiary bodies which would operate with considerable autonomy. These bodies would include one to deal with a code on tariffs and trade (taking over GATT), another to deal with trade among developing countries with membership limited to them only, and a Trade Policy Review Board to deal with matters of concern to all members. The author's main focus is on maintaining an open trading system of the Western liberal conception, with urgent attention to policies and problems of structural change and adjustment.

It is therefore clear that UNCTAD and GATT are pursuing continuing and new mandates and activities on parallel lines, overlapping in some though by no means all areas, without sufficient clarity and definition between their respective functions of secretariat study, technical assistance, inter-governmental deliberation, consultation, recommendation, and finally formulation of legal instruments. Developing countries' initiatives and efforts in UNCTAD have been fairly successful with respect to secretariat study and inter-governmental deliberation, less so in consultation and recommendation, and least so in drawing up legal codes and conventions.

There is also a continuous process of mutual interaction, with UNCTAD's deliberations, proposals and recommendations influencing GATT decisions and actions, which in turn have an impact on UNCTAD. This duality is untidy and it breeds institutional rivalry which can become wasteful and unhealthy to the point of outweighing the perceived advantage. It would seem, however, that in the judgement of member States the situation has not reached that stage, while, given the aspirations and strivings of developing countries to restructure the international economy, UNCTAD's comprehensive role remains of critical even if not of decisive significance to them.

Furthermore, there seems no alternative to this duality in the short run. However desirable from the standpoint of neatness and elegance, as well as of institutional effectiveness, the practical prospects of merging UNCTAD and GATT or of establishing an ITO can only be regarded as dim. The political, ideological, economic and legal issues and difficulties involved in negotiating an ITO or a merger are too formidable, even were governments to agree in principle to consider the proposition. Attention will therefore need to be turned to methods of achieving a greater degree of co-operation and perhaps of co-ordination on a pragmatic basis. The desirability of increased co-ordination and co-operation could hardly be open to question at this stage in the UNCTAD-GATT relationship, but the practical methods of achieving it are none too easy to devise.

The earlier idea of a joint co-ordinating or programming committee could be reconsidered.[44] It could be composed of elected governmental officials of both bodies: for UNCTAD, the President of the Trade and Development Board and the Chairmen of two committees concerned with GATT-related issues (chosen by rotation), and on the GATT side, the Chairmen of the Contracting Parties, of the Council, and of the Committee on Trade and Development; the two executive heads would also be members. Such a committee could provide for useful exchange of views on programming studies, meetings and negotiations. It would not have the authority to modify or depart from decisions already taken in either of the two bodies on these matters, nor to prejudge future decisions on these issues, given the difference in views, ideologies, legal frameworks, and sources of political support. Nevertheless, the committee could be helpful in promoting co-operation on an informal basis. After all, chairmen of inter-governmental bodies are often called upon to use their good offices in informal consultations to promote consensus solutions, as are the heads of secretariats. It would be essential, of course, that the establishment of a committee of this kind, and its terms of reference (formulated so as not to prejudice the legislative mandates of either institution), should be approved by the Trade and Development Board, on the one hand, and the Contracting Parties or the GATT Council, on the other, thus ensuring the transparency of these decisions.

Substantially improved contacts between the two secretariats would offer advantages in a better exchange of data, of information on continuing programmes and of views on outstanding issues. These could be fostered by an informal understanding between the heads of the two secretariats and by reviving the idea of a joint secretariat group composed of senior officials.[45] Moreover, the heads of the two secretariats could meet more often than has been the case during the past 10 years or so. These meetings could be prepared by the joint secretariat committee. Joint studies by the two secretariats are possible but difficult and perhaps not likely. It would be hard to expect the Secretary-General of UNCTAD not to put forward bold and innovative ideas and proposals; it would be just as hard to expect the Director-General of GATT to accept them all.

The probable results of such mechanisms should not be over-estimated. But the increased contacts would be conductive to improved knowledge of each other's programmes and to a mitigation of some psychological 'hang-ups', and might gradually promote better co-operation.

XIV. Concluding remarks

The foregoing notes, observations and opinions may convey some impression of the density and complexity of the pattern of UNCTAD-GATT relations which this paper set out to describe and analyze. Yet clearly visible in this pattern, and hopefully discernible too in the preceding sections, is one thread which runs through it and determines its overall form.

This central element is the difference between the heavy bilateralization and lack of transparency of GATT modalities and the openness of UNCTAD's, which better enable the developing countries to make their interests known and felt. This difference between the two institutions, rooted in their different philosophies and political constituencies, remains the determining factor in their future evolution as instruments of negotiation on trade policy questions.

Taking into account the experience of the past years and the persistence of these deep institutional and philosophical differences between UNCTAD and GATT, one clear lesson may be drawn. It would be unrealistic to expect governments, especially those of industrialized countries, to use UNCTAD bodies to engage in negotiations involving legal or contractual commitments on the very issues which are the subject matter of concrete and specific negotiations in the GATT framework, and all the more so if GATT negotiations have advanced to a sensitive and complex stage and governments do not want to show their hands except in a final package.

It does not by any means follow that UNCTAD should stand back from trade policy issues. That would be disastrous for the developing countries. It would be desirable for UNCTAD to pursue these issues, with a view to providing a truly multilateral and transparent machinery, to the benefit not only of developing countries, but of others as well including smaller, weaker developed countries. In some of these areas UNCTAD may not be able to negotiate decisions of a contractual character, but it can articulate issues, promote consultations, formulate proposals and suggestions, and make recommendations.

It is further necessary to stress that UNCTAD's acceptance of a deliberative and recommendatory mandate on some trade policy issues from time to time should not lead to the permanent freezing of its mandate to draw up legal instruments in their regard. UNCTAD's negotiating mandates should remain open and UNCTAD, as a multi-dimensional institution, should maintain its competence to make international laws when conditions are right. Developing countries should continue to strengthen UNCTAD to this end and to utilize its substantive resources.

---

1. A comprehensive treatment of UNCTAD as a negotiating instrument would have to deal with several other dimensions—political, institutional, legal and substantive—some of which are taken up in other contributions to this volume. In a paper entitled "UNCTAD as a negotiating institution" (*UNCTAD Reprint No. 12;* originally published in the *Journal of World Trade Law* (JWTL) Vol. 15, No. 1, Jan/Feb 1981), this author dealt with some other aspects of the subject, including the growth of UNCTAD's mandates, the impact of the group system on UNCTAD and the role of the secretariat. The present paper may be read in conjunction with that earlier study.

For an authoritative analysis of the establishment of UNCTAD, and of its development up to about 1970, see Diego Cordovez, "The making of UNCTAD", JWTL, May–June 1967, and "UNCTAD and Development Diplomacy", JWTL, 1971. Cordovez treats the political and substantive issues as well as details of negotiations at UNCTAD I and up to UNCTAD II with insight and thorough knowledge. See also Sidney Dell's contribution to this volume, *The Origins of UNCTAD.* For an analysis from the US point of view at that time, see Richard Gardner's article on UNCTAD in *The Global Partnership,* edited by R.N. Gardner and M.F. Millikan, Praeger, 1968. Mr. Gardner was deputy leader of the US delegation at UNCTAD I.

2. General Assembly resolution 1995 (XIX).

3. In the biographical note on Malinowski by Zenon Carnapas.

4. The present author was closely associated with Dr. Prebisch and Malinowski in Group of 77 affairs during UNCTAD I and thereafter for several years till Dr. Prebisch retired in March 1969. Among others of the secretariat, noteworthy associates in this work at the time were: Diego Cordovez, Jorge Viteri, Eugene Adoboli, Erling Nypan and, from 1966, Paul Berthoud.

5. See in this connexion UNCTAD document TD/B/89, paragraphs 35–37, and GATT document L/2642; also Diego Cordovez, "UNCTAD and Development Diplomacy", *op. cit.,* chapter on UNCTAD-GATT relations.

6. The writer, who participated in the internal secretariat discussions on this range of issues, can testify to Malinowski's crucial role in them.

7. For a valuable analysis, see Stein Rossen: *Notes on Rules and Mechanisms governing International Economic Relations,* the Chr. Michelsen Institute, Bergen, Norway, 1981; Rossen's contribution to the present volume draws on that study.

8. For a fuller treatment of commodity issues, see Alfred Maizels' contribution to this volume.

9. This commodity crisis led the UNCTAD secretariat to propose an immediate action programme of provisional commodity agreements to arrest and reverse the disastrous downward trend in commodity prices, and thus pave the way for longer-term, more comprehensive agreements for commodities, as soon as market conditions allow. The immediate action programme was said not to replace the IPC, but to be regarded as a new element in it. For financing, the immediate programme looks to the Common Fund as one of the sources, thus rendering the Fund's establishment even more urgent. See "Commodity Issues: a review and proposals for further action", UNCTAD document TD/273, Jan. 1983.

10. Policy document TD/B/C.1/PSC.27; studies on cocoa, bauxite/alumina, manganese, hard fibres, phosphates, tea, sugar, copper, coffee and jute.

11. These GATT efforts, conducted without reference to or consultation with UNCTAD, aroused a courageous protest from the then UNCTAD Secretary-General Dr. Prebisch.

12. The UNCTAD Preparatory Committee on Meat, which was considering international meat trade questions, has now decided to leave them to the GATT International Meat Council, and to deal with developmental projects and problems.

13. A call for resuming this conference has been made by UNCTAD in its resolution 154 (VI).

14. See Moses T. Adebanjo's contribution to this volume.

15. GATT *Basic Instruments and Selected Documents* (BISD), 18th Supplement, p. 11.

16. These included Israel, Spain, Turkey and Greece, which are not members of the Group of 77. Greece withdrew from the Protocol in June 1980.

17. GATT, BISD, 26th Supplement, pp. 337–340 and 27th Supplement, pp. 172–173.

18. By its decision of 14 November 1968, GATT approved a trade expansion and co-operation agreement concluded by three countries in different regions: Egypt, India and Yugoslavia.

19. This request ran into opposition from most of the developed countries in UNCTAD, on the grounds that secretariat support for the GSTP would go against the principle of universality of the United Nations and the right of all member States to attend UN meetings, except when direct negotiations of a contractual nature were taking place. This opposition was expressed in a negative vote by most Group B countries in the Trade and Development Board in October 1982. Subsequent decisions on this matter have opened the way for the provision of UNCTAD secretariat support for the negotiations, though the opposition remains.

20. This is not the place to enter into even a brief discussion of the substantive and legal issues arising in connexion with GATT membership for socialist countries. Reference should be made to the relevant issues of the GATT BISD for the reports on their accession agreements and on reviews of protocols.

21. By the 1982 GATT Ministerial Declaration, however, the Contracting Parties individually and collectively undertake "to abstain from taking restrictive trade measures, for reasons of a non-economic character, not consistent with the General Agreement" (paragraph 7 (iii)).

22. It was agreed in 1970 that the GSP would be implemented in the course of 1971. Starting with the EEC in July 1971, nearly all the other preference-givers introduced their schemes in 1971 and 1972, the exceptions being Canada (July 1974) and the USA (January 1976). The prolonged delay by the USA was the subject of recurrent comment and appeal in various UNCTAD bodies by the Group of 77 as well as by other countries.

23. Report of the Special Committee on Preferences, 11th session (TD/B/906), Annex I. See also the sixth general report on the GSP (TD/B/C.5/73) and "Differential treatment in the context of the GSP" (TD/B/C.5/74).

24. See the Annex to the Declaration which deals with "GATT rules and activities relating to developing countries".

25. This reaffirmation is to be seen in the light of the US Administration's proposal in 1983 to extend its GSP scheme for a further ten years, with provisions for reinforced differentiation and discrimination, as well as reciprocity of access to developing country markets.

26. GATT, Decisions of the 17th session, document L/1397, December 1960.

27. One reason could possibly be that action was taken in OECD. In 1967 OECD adopted a

recommendation concerning co-operation between member countries on restrictive business practices affecting international trade. This provided for notification, consultation and mutually acceptable solutions to problems which might arise. This was followed by the OECD Guidelines for Multinational Enterprises, adopted in June 1976, which also deal with some of the issues in question.

28. See in particular paragraphs 3 and 4 of section D of the Set. Paragraph 3 of Section D exempts subsidiaries and similar entities, dealing with each other as economic entities under common control, from the obligation to refrain from a number of practices. Paragraph 4 of section D, dealing with the abuse of dominant market power, is hedged with several qualifying and interpretative footnotes so as to throw the entire provision into obscurity and open it to any convenient interpretation.

29. Considerable scepticism on this point has also been expressed by the US delegate to the 1980 negotiating conference. See "International anti-trust codes: the post-acceptance phase" by Joel Davidow, in *Anti-Trust Bulletin*, Feb. 1981.

30. See reports by the Secretary-General of UNCTAD: TD/B/778 and Add.1, TD/187 and 227, TD/B/762, TD/B/C.2/120 and Supp.1, TD/B/C.2/146 and TD/B/C.2/177.

31. See *The Kennedy Round: estimated effects on tariff barriers* (UN Sales No. E.68.II.D.12), discussed in this volume by Dell.

32. See General Assembly resolution 34/199 and Conference resolutions 76 (III) and 96 (IV).

33. These proposals covered the principal items of interest to developing countries in the MTNs: strengthening the GSP, eliminating tariff and non-tariff barriers, safeguards, export subsidies, tropical products, government procurement, special and differential treatment, strengthening of Part IV of GATT, etc.

34. For an account of the difficulties faced by developing countries in the MTNs, see "Multilateral Trade Negotiations and the Developing Countries" by R. Krishnamurti, in *Third World Quarterly*, April 1980.

35. See the following secretariat reports and notes: *Assessment of the results of the multilateral trade negotiations*, (TD/B/778/Rev.1); *Multilateral trade negotiations: Implementation of the results and negotiation of unresolved issues* (TD/B/838); *Multilateral trade negotiations* (TD/B/913); *Implementation of the results of the Tokyo Round* (TD/B/C.2/R.8).

36. The USA Trade Representative, William Brock, in his testimony to the US Congress after the GATT Ministerial Meeting, stated that, though the GATT had not endorsed the US proposal for North-South trade negotiations, the US would pursue it in bilateral channels. Recent reports indicate that this aim is also being pursued in informal contacts with small selected groups of developing countries.

37. *International Herald Tribune*, 17 March 1983, report by Stuart Auerbach. The USA is reported to have established informal contact with a number of nations: Canada, Japan, Finland, Norway, Sweden, Brazil, South Korea, and the ASEAN countries.

38. The Group was set up by General Assembly resolution 3343 (XXIX) (Dec. 1974). See its report (E/AC.62/9, May 1975), pp. 53–55; see also Annex II for detailed background material.

39. The *Ad Hoc* Committee recommended the strengthening of UNCTAD on the basis of UNCTAD resolution 90 (IV), adopted at the Nairobi Conference in 1976, as an organ of the General Assembly for "deliberation, negotiation, review and implementation in the field of international trade and related areas of international economic co-operation". As regards GATT, as with the United Nations specialized agencies, the Committee called for its co-operation with the Assembly and ECOSOC (UN document A/32/34).

40. TD(VI)/C.4/L.17, draft proposal of the Group of 77.

41. *North-South: A Programme for Survival*, London, 1980, pp. 183–185; *Common Crisis North-South: Cooperation for World Recovery*, London, 1983, pp. 115–117.

42. *The North-South Dialogue—Making it Work*, Report by a Commonwealth Group of Experts, Commonwealth Secretariat, London 1982, paras. 4.17 and 4.18.

43. See Miriam Camps, with Catherine Gwin, *Collective Management: the Reform of Global Economic Organizations*, New York, McGraw Hill, 1981. See also *Handmaiden in Distress: World Trade in the 1980s*, by Carlos F. Diaz-Alejandro and Gerald K. Helleiner, North-South Institute, Ottawa, 1982. The last two authors, while visualizing a more comprehensive

organization covering services and direct foreign investment as well as trade, call for immediate priority action to restore the authority, credibility and transparency of GATT rules and disciplines.

44. See section II above.

45. In the first years of UNCTAD, an informal joint secretariat liaison group of six senior officials, three from each side, met from time to time. (The writer of this article was a member of the group.) In the present context, such a group could also consist of six senior officials, with each side being led by a deputy executive head.

UNCTAD AND THE EMERGENCE OF INTERNATIONAL DEVELOPMENT LAW

by Paul Berthoud

The thinking which nurtured the political forces that led to the creation of UNCTAD; the dialogue, oscillating between confrontation and negotiation, instituted within UNCTAD once it was created; the achievements of UNCTAD, both in terms of the evolution of ideas about trade and development and in the form of concrete results in many areas; its frustrations in face of so little progress in meeting the challenge of establishing a New International Economic Order: that thinking, that dialogue, those achievements and those frustrations were essentially economic in nature. Their resonance in the realm of law has however been profound. International development economics has had so important a bearing on legal science and legal practice as to have led to the emergence of international development law as a new juridical discipline.

Like international development economics, international development law has emerged as a challenge to a well-established body of doctrine and practice. Traditional international law was no better prepared than traditional international economics for the onslaught on some of its most fundamental concepts and tools of analysis that was to take place in the present generation. But perhaps paradoxically, it is probably true that international development law, which emerged later than international development economics and decidedly under the influence of the latter, has more quickly gained wide, if not general, acceptance in legal science—as if, as a whole, jurists were more readily receptive than economists to the idea that the international dimension of the development process calls for an adjustment of their previously accepted framework of concepts, instruments and procedures.

Our purpose here will be to outline the main features of this new legal discipline referred to as international development law and to point to the way in which UNCTAD has been centrally involved in this novative process, even being the main agent of such novation for a while, until the South-North dialogue had spread across the whole spectrum of multilateral diplomacy.

71

I. The setting

As intimated above, it is with economics that we have to start our *démarche*, and specifically with international trade, as trade has been the trigger of a process that has challenged the existing international economic order and led to the claim for a New International Economic Order, with its consequences for the international legal order.

Development economists have analyzed the free trade system, from the point of view of the developing countries and demystified the concept of the so-called market economy, on which international economic co-operation had been built after World War II. In a nutshell, this system amounted to applying the premises of liberal economics to international economic relations: the free play of market forces would lead to the optimum allocation of resources, which would in turn lead to an equitable distribution of income among economic partners. It was the principle of mutual advantage in freedom of trade applied to international economic relations.

The legal envelope for such a system would be both simple and natural, slotting into the framework of classical international law: it applied the principle of the sovereign equality of states to international economic relations. International law was based on legal principles that were to apply to every situation, with no more reference to the level of development of the parties than to their level of power. It was a legal order in which sovereign equality ignored inequality of power and, by the same token, ignored inequality of development. At such a level of abstraction, the principle of juridical equality of states offered for the conduct of international economic relations a fundamental guarantee of unlimited competition and free movement of goods. Specified in normative terms, this principle of equality found concrete expression in particular in the two derived concepts of reciprocity and non-discrimination. Thus we had the famous trilogy, the three legal pillars of the international economic order: equality, reciprocity, non-discrimination. In concrete terms, this system took in international public law the form of the General Agreement on Tariffs and Trade. Its perfect expression was the most-favoured-nation clause.

The analysis put forward by development economists, in tearing down the mystique of liberal economics as it applied to relations between countries at different levels of development, was consequently bound to have a profound effect on the international legal order that underwrote the existing international economic order. This is not the place to discuss that analysis. Suffice it for our purpose to recall that it entailed a basic questioning of the working of the market economy in relations between developed and developing countries, pointing out that differences in the level of development and in the economic structures of the partners had as consequences that their markets were not really competitive, their resources not really mobile, and that equitable distribution of income between partners was thus made impossible. The demonstration was founded in the analysis of the 'double dependency' of the developing countries, which in a system of free trade had as a consequence that developing countries had a secular propensity to import more than they could export. Development economists called this the structural asymmetry of international demand, a concept which incidentally is of particular interest to the jurist in so far as it was later to lay the foundation, at the level of legal principles, for the notion of implicit reciprocity.

The legal consequences of the analysis of the development economists were to be quite far reaching. To challenge the post-war liberal international economic order entailed at the same time challenging the basic legal principle of sovereign equality as it had previously been accepted in international public law, i.e. conceived in the abstract and ignoring the real inequalities and the structural aspects of international economic relations. In its operational dimension, it was pointed out, this principle had proven ineffective for the weaker countries, which had been largely excluded from sharing in the benefits of international economic activity and only marginally able to influence the course of world economic events. Sovereign equality had given them presence, but not participation. Developing countries were thus to denounce at the level of legal principles the unfair and unjust nature of the trilogy: equality, reciprocity, non-discrimination. The three pillars of the international order came to be seen as three obstacles to development, and denounced as such: equal treatment among unequals is inequitable towards the weaker partner; reciprocity among unequals breeds injustice; non-discrimination among unequals is in effect discrimination in favour of the stronger partner.

The principle of sovereign equality of states was in no way to disappear in this argument. On the contrary, it was to be forcefully re-affirmed and in particular to be used by the developing countries as a group, as a basic parameter to assert their strength in international fora. Sovereign equality was to be redefined, however, as a principle involving the evaluation of equality in real and functional terms, giving it its full meaning and *raison d'être* through an economic content and a true reflection of the concepts of justice and equity in international economic relations. It followed that real equality of opportunity implied the acceptance of unequal treatment to correct inequalities in real terms, and there was in this neither contradiction nor paradox, but rather the true expression of sovereign equality as a fully meaningful principle.

At the level of international public law, the New International Economic Order that is being sought and advocated by the developing countries will therefore entail the recognition in legal terms of the existence of an external and structural disequilibrium between the economies of the industrial centres and the economies of the peripheral countries, to use Raúl Prebisch's terminology, and the adoption of specific rules reflecting the unequal economic and social structure of the international community. In other words, the point is to introduce into international law a variable representing the economic inequality of states, with the explicit objective of ensuring the equality of economic opportunities, benefits and advantages through measures that are adjusted to the different economic capacities of the partners. This ultimately means that the rights and duties of states are to be determined in accordance with the degree of development of their economic structures. For that purpose, countries are to be classified as developed countries and developing countries, a distinction that calls for new principles of international co-operation and new legal rules to regulate that co-operation. This is how one would move, as Dean Colliard so well stated, from an international law of indifference to an international law of finality; or, to use W. Friedmann's terminology, from an international law of co-existence to an international law of co-operation, i.e. from a legal order underlying society in which each state pursues its own finality and objectives, to a legal order which is concerned with the fate of international society as a whole.[1]

Such is the setting for the emergence of international development law. In the field of international trade, the main demands of the developing countries are well known: a network of commodity agreements, with a system of reinsurance in the form of a Common Fund; the granting of tariff preferences; access to markets; the elimination of non-tariff barriers; the elaboration of codes of conduct in the fields of restrictive business practices and the transfer of technology; a fair share in the benefits accruing from the transport of goods by sea. These demands are all direct consequences of economic observation and analysis, and they must all find their concrete expression and become a tangible reality in economic terms. They all however also require the construction of appropriate legal instruments to give operational shape to the measures to be adopted and ensure their proper functioning in practice.

This is essentially a dynamic process, taking place in an international society that is in constant change, in which concepts and precepts are under daily scrutiny at the front-line of multilateral confrontation and negotiation. It is thus difficult to make a firm assessment of the state of affairs at any point in time. It is however already possible to identify two main legal dimensions of the New International Economic Order pursued by the developing countries. On the one hand, a number of new legal principles have taken shape that impart to a redefined legal system a very novel and distinct character. On the other hand, the very fabric of the international legal order is being seriously strained and new normative values are emerging that evoke a drastic departure from conventional juridical thinking and practice. It is largely within UNCTAD that those dimensions have appeared, developed and acquired their dynamic importance. They will be the object of the two main sections of this paper.

II. New legal principles

As for the content of the emerging international development law, we shall identify a number of situations that point to the acceptance of new legal principles and norms to regulate international economic relations between developed and developing countries. Those principles partly overlap, but each deserves to be analysed separately as they are all conceptually important from a juridical point of view.

The first aspect of this evolution which we shall consider is a trend towards the principle of the duality of norms. We shall then review the progressive acceptance of a new trilogy of principles to regulate international trade relations between developed and developing partner states: equality, reciprocity and non-discrimination tend to be substituted by compensatory inequality, non-reciprocity and differential treatment. Finally, though here the problem is rather broader in nature, the trend towards the adoption of instruments for regulatory intervention should also be mentioned in this context.

(a) The duality of norms

The traditional view of sovereign equality had led quite naturally to the unquestioned acceptance of the fact that the international society of equal sovereign states should be regulated uniformly by one set of norms. The set of norms thus applicable to international trade after World War II, i.e. the General Agreement on Tariffs and Trade, functioned for a long time in the overall interest, generally speaking, of the community of developed market-economy countries, whose reciprocal trade continued to represent the greater part of world trade. It has therefore been barely conceivable that this system, to which the biggest trading nations of the world are in any case staunchly attached, might in the foreseeable future be deprived of its role as an instrument to regulate trade among those developed countries. What developing countries have striven for in UNCTAD is the recognition of the necessity to set up a parallel system for regulating international economic relations between developed countries and developing countries, thus giving concrete expression to the principle of the duality of norms: one set of rules would apply to economic and trade relations among developed countries, and another new set of rules would be designed to regulate economic and trade relations between developed and developing countries.

The principle of the duality of norms was already implicit in General Principle Eight adopted by the first UNCTAD Conference in June 1964, both in the concept of non-reciprocity and in that of preferences, presented as they were as advantages that should be granted to all developing countries, and only to developing countries. The emergence of this principle in positive law was to follow shortly in the form of the adoption of unilateral commitments by developed countries. The GATT, in the aftermath and very much under the influence of UNCTAD I, adopted Part IV of the General Agreement in November 1964, accepting the principle that developing countries in general must receive special treatment to compensate the disequilibrium of their external sector. In this framework, Article XXXVII, in particular, under the heading of 'commitments', provides for a series of unilateral commitments that will be undertaken by the developed Contracting Parties. The wording of the article is prudent and filled with restrictions and escape clauses. It nevertheless remains a fact that, in juridical terms, it offered for the first time a binding legal framework which set individual and collective trade objectives and determined in pursuance of these objectives a unilateral action on the part of some countries, the developed countries, in favour of other countries, the developing countries.

The General Agreement had not of course totally ignored the situation of the developing countries before then. Their circumstances had, however, been dealt with as an exception to the legal system by having recourse to escape clauses. Article XXXVII, on the other hand, set out to move away from the exception and towards the rule by establishing separate and different norms for the regulation of trade relations between developed countries and developing countries.

Explicitly or implicitly, the principle of the duality of norms in international economic relations has since then been very broadly accepted at the level of the resolutions, declarations and recommendations of UNCTAD and later of other multilateral fora. Preferences and non-reciprocity, to which we shall next turn our attention, reflect a system of dual norms in relation to the level of economic development of the partners to the transaction or the negotiation.

One finds again an application of this principle in the agreed provisions of the draft International Code of Conduct on the Transfer of Technology. On the one hand, article 1.5 of the draft states that "the Code of Conduct is universally applicable in scope and is addressed to all ... countries and groups of countries, irrespective of their economic and political systems and their level of development". On the other hand, chapter 6 of the draft, under the heading "special treatment for developing countries", contains a long list of detailed provisions expressly directed at governments of developed countries and outlining measures to be taken by those governments. It thus presents another example of a system of duality of norms to be introduced through a set of unilateral commitments.

Finally, though unforeseen in the negotiating process and coming from somewhat unexpected quarters, another case of duality of norms arising from the work of UNCTAD might be mentioned here. The Convention on a Code of Conduct for Liner Conferences is a typical example, to which we shall return, of an interventionist and regulatory mechanism which reflects an explicit concern for the development of developing countries. The European Economic Community, prepared to accept the Convention as the developmental instrument that it is, but determined not to allow its effects to be extended to maritime trade among developed countries, has in effect established in this respect a system of duality of norms: the Community decided, through a Regulation made by the Council, that the ratification of the Convention by its Member States would be entered with a reservation to the effect that the Convention shall not apply to trade carried by liner conferences between States Members of the Community and, on the basis of reciprocity, between States Members of the Community and other States Members of the OECD that are parties to the Convention.

The work of UNCTAD has thus accredited the principle that different sets of norms must apply to international economic relations among developed countries themselves on the one hand, and between developed countries and developing countries on the other. The legal significance of this principle cannot be over-estimated. It marks the erosion of the fundamental tenet of classical international law that the principle of sovereign equality of states is to be expressed in the practice of international relations in the form of a single uniform set of norms that will be applicable equally to all states. The principle of the duality of norms should consequently be singled out as an important landmark of international development law.

(b) Compensatory inequality

Equality, reciprocity and non-discrimination featured as basic principles in the design of the legal instruments aimed at regulating international trade relations in the post-war period. The challenging of these principles and the emergence of the alternative and antithetic trilogy of compensatory inequality, non-reciprocity and differential treatment, represent in concrete terms the most significant feature of the transposition into the legal sphere of the demands of the New International Economic Order.

The most important institution of compensatory inequality that emerged from the work of UNCTAD is, of course, the Generalized System of Preferences (GSP), which is also possibly the most spectacular institution of international development law inasmuch as it embodies all major premises of a new international legal order designed to regulate North–South relations.

We have already mentioned that the most-favoured-nation clause was the corner-stone of equal, reciprocal and non-discriminatory commercial treatment. Symbolically enough, it was embodied in Article 1 of the General Agreement on Tariffs and Trade. In the GATT, the clause was to be unconditional, automatic and multilateral. It was the perfect and absolute expression of equality and non-discrimination. Exceptions to the clause were foreseen, but they were handled strictly as such and circumscribed in precise terms: pre-existing preferential arrangements, schemes of regional economic integration in the form of customs unions or free trade areas, and frontier traffic. Those exceptions notwithstanding, the most-favoured-nation clause remained the legal instrument of equal treatment in international trade law, and as such it would be at the centre of the controversy that developed around the question of the need for a new international economic policy more responsive to the needs of the developing countries.

There is no need to recall here the merits of the most-favoured-nation clause: its positive effect on the trade of developed countries is fully acknowledged. It has prevented the adoption of arbitrary discriminatory measures, the constitution of trading blocs and the spread of economic tension. In relations between unequal partners, on the other hand, it has been denounced as a deficient and inappropriate instrument because it equalizes only in legal terms, and not in real terms, the conditions governing commercial competition. It was challenged head on by demands for tariff preferences for developing countries, which would introduce in their favour a positive discrimination that was necessary to compensate for the economic inequality from which they suffered.

The principle of the granting of preferences to developing countries was reflected in the conclusions of UNCTAD I in 1964 in spite of the staunch opposition of some developed countries. Four further years of arduous negotiations were necessary to ensure the general acceptance of the principle. The objective of the developing countries was the adoption of an instrument of general applicability within the framework of an international development policy. On the other hand, the developed countries insisted all along on having the GSP inserted into the existing legal international order regulating commercial relations, i.e. the GATT, and they strongly resisted the creation of a new permanent legal system. They opposed giving the GSP the form of an amendment to Article 1 of the General Agreement and thus ensured the maintenance of the juridical *status quo*. They also opposed founding the GSP on Part IV of the General Agreement, which in legal terms would have been both possible and coherent. The only solution which was found acceptable by them was for the GSP to be inserted in the existing legal order through the granting of a waiver to the obligations of the General Agreement in pursuance of Article XXV, paragraph 5.

The GSP in fact emerged as a compromise from very difficult negotiations between developed and developing countries, but also among developed countries themselves within the OECD. It is certainly a rough and
ready compromise, from the point of view of legal principles, a system
which is surprising for the importance it has acquired in spite of such
juridical fragility. In terms of law, the GSP is characterized by its unilateral,
voluntary (i.e. non-compulsory) and temporary nature, and by the fact that
it does not ensure the consolidation of the preferential margins that it offers.

As for its unilateral nature, the GSP consists in effect of a set of general
provisions adopted by a resolution of the UNCTAD Trade and Development Board in the form of Agreed Conclusions, offering a framework for
the introduction of individual preferential schemes by preference-giving
countries. What is called a 'generalized system' is actually an assemblage of
sixteen individual schemes, eleven of them of market-economy developed
countries (one of which applies to the EEC as a whole) and five of socialist
countries of Eastern Europe, all unliaterally adopted and put into force by
the preference-giving countries.

The non-compulsory nature of the GSP is affirmed by the Agreed
Conclusions, which expressly state that the granting of preferences does not
constitute a binding commitment, and in particular does not in any way
prevent their subsequent withdrawal in whole or in part. The temporary
nature of the system, in turn, is linked in the position of the preference-
giving countries to the exceptional character of preferences, which are seen
as a derogation from the general principles regulating international trade.
The duration of the GSP was originally set at ten years. The prolongation of
the system has been universally accepted, but preference-giving countries
insist on the fact that the GSP is an institution that is limited in time.

The non-consolidation of preferential margins obtained under the GSP
is embodied in a provision in the section on 'legal status' of the Agreed
Conclusions, by which preference-giving countries reserve their right to
reduce their tariffs within GATT, on a most-favoured-nation basis,
whether unilaterally or following international tariff negotiations. This is
an important point: the comment has been made that the incapacity of the
developing countries to protect their margins of preferential advantage
demonstrates that they have not succeeded in attaining their objective of a
genuine right to more favourable treatment. This issue has taken on
renewed importance as a result of the conclusion of the Tokyo Round of
Multilateral Trade Negotiations, the effect of which has been a partial
erosion of the advantages gained by the developing countries through the
GSP.

Our overall judgement about the GSP must thus be a qualified one. The
best possible compromise issuing from a long and arduous negotiation has
produced a system that is in strictly legal terms weak and limited, not to say

precarious. On the other hand, it remains a fact that it is a system that has had a great resonance in international economic relations, the importance of which at the level of principles cannot be overstated. Applied by all developed countries in their trade relations with developing countries, the GSP has provided solid roots within trade relations between countries at different levels of economic development for the principles of compensatory inequality, non-reciprocity and differential treatment, thus responding to a very profound aspiration of the developing countries. In spite of its innumerable weaknesses, it represents for them a legal acquisition of paramount importance, and it has been acknowledged as such in theories of jurisprudence. For the classical legal scientist, the fragility of the construction raises most serious problems as to whether one can really describe the GSP as an international legal instrument. For the observer of the effects on the legal field of the changes in international relations resulting from the emergence of the developing countries as partners in the community of nations, the GSP will for a long time offer a remarkable case study of the adjustment of legal instruments to a complex reality, reflecting both the convergence of political will and the persistence of acute conflicts of interests.

The International Law Commission of the United Nations itself has not been insensitive to the significance of this development, in spite of the weaknesses of the GSP system from a formal point of view. In 1978, the Commission introduced in its proposed articles on the most-favoured-nation clause, which it was considering in the context of its work on the law of treaties, an article 23 providing that "a beneficiary State [of the most-favoured-nation clause] is not entitled under a most-favoured nation clause to treatment extended by a developed granting State to a developing third State on a non-reciprocal basis within a scheme of generalized preferences established by that granting State, which conforms with a generalized system of preferences recognized by the international community of States as a whole or, for the States members of a competent international organization, adopted in accordance with its relevant rules and procedures". Incidentally, an article 24 of the text of the International Law Commission provides for a similar exception for preferences that would be granted by a developing State to other developing States.[2]

(c) Non-reciprocity

Reciprocity in trade negotiations is a reflection at the level of international economic relations of the concept of the equality of states. It was one of the pillars of the economic and legal order instituted after World War II, in which trade negotiations were dominated by the search for reciprocity in the form of equivalent advantages. The situation thus created for the developing countries soon revealed the weight of the inequality of economic forces.

The crudest manifestation of the tariff concessions made by these countries was an erosion of fiscal revenue, tariffs being for them a much more important source of fiscal income than in developed countries. Their need to protect their infant industries was also much greater, and in this respect too reciprocity in the granting of concessions was bound to lead to dramatically different and unequal effects among partners. Consequently, development economics would rapidly point to the need for non-reciprocity in relations between developed and developing countries as one of the means to ensure an equalization of opportunities in real terms among the partners in trade negotiations.

It is this analytical context, incidentally, that gave birth to the theory of implicit reciprocity. This theory starts from the premise that the problem of reciprocity cannot be boiled down to the actual elements of the negotiation and of the exchange of concessions. It must be seen as a structural problem. North-South trade is characterized by a structural asymmetry of demand, because of the 'double dependency' of the developing countries. Any trade concession by a developing country results in a tendency for it to increase its imports, to accentuate the propensity to disequilibrium of its external trade. The theory of implicit reciprocity expounds on this fact: because of the asymmetry of international demand, developing countries are always in a situation of implicit reciprocity since they always have a tendency to import more than they can export.

The principle of non-reciprocity was embodied in General Principle Eight adopted at UNCTAD I: developed countries should grant concessions to all developing countries and should not require any concessions in return from them. At the same time, the Conference expressly noted, in paragraph 5 of resolution A.III.4, "that there is general acceptance of the principle that developed countries should not expect reciprocity for measures taken by them in trade negotiations to reduce or remove tariff and other barriers to the trade of developing countries". Ever since its establishment, UNCTAD was to be the guardian of the principle of non-reciprocity, the practical meaning of which was to be tested essentially in the multilateral trade negotiations conducted within the framework of GATT. Thus UNCTAD Conference resolutions 82 (III) (Santiago-de-Chile, 1972) and 91 (IV) (Nairobi, 1976) both forcefully underlined the importance of non-reciprocity in multilateral trade negotiations, while this principle was reaffirmed in general terms in such pronouncements as resolution 46 (III) on steps to achieve a greater measure of agreement on principles governing international trade relations and trade policies conducive to development (see paragraph 1, principle III).

In the General Agreement itself, non-reciprocity was accepted as a legal principle in 1964, with the adoption of Part IV of the Agreement. Article XXXVI, paragraph 8, provides that "the developed contracting parties do not expect reciprocity for commitments made by them in trade negotiations to reduce or remove tariffs and other barriers to the trade of less-developed contracting parties". This provision was conceptually important inasmuch as it represented a radical departure from the principle of mutual advantage which had from the beginning presided over the conduct of negotiations within the GATT.

One must recognize, however, that the application of the principle of non-reciprocity gave rise to numerous difficulties in practice, and that it has not proven easy to use it as an effective instrument of development policy. In the multilateral trade negotiations as conceived in the GATT, the fundamental problem was that of balancing concessions, and this by the very definition, so to say, of the system of negotiation. Developed countries often expressed their dissatisfaction at what was, in their view, the unduly low value of the concessions offered by the developing countries, to the point of sometimes arguing that those concessions did not offer any real basis for negotiation. To this, developing countries reacted by pointing out that they, and only they, could judge the importance and the value of the concessions they were prepared to offer and appreciate the compatibility of their offers with their financial, commercial and developmental needs. Some developing countries undoubtedly went so far as to interpret non-reciprocity as reflecting the principle of unilateral concessions on the part of the developed countries, in the same way as in the GSP, whereas the developed countries insisted on being offered some concessions by the developing countries, even if these were to be non-reciprocal. In the absence of explicit procedures or jurisprudence to regulate non-reciprocity, the multilateral trade negotiations never overcame the difficulties to which this principle gave rise. It is those difficulties, indeed, that explain the importance attached to the reiteration in UNCTAD, through the years, of the principle of non-reciprocity.

Be that as it may, the principle of non-reciprocity was at least re-affirmed in a formal sense at the end of the Tokyo Round of multilateral trade negotiations. Among a number of texts that were then adopted concerning the legal framework for the conduct of international trade, a decision on "Differential and more favourable treatment, reciprocity and fuller participation of developing countries" does restate and expand upon the above-mentioned provision of Article XXXVI, paragraph 8, of the General Agreement.[3] Two additional provisions of that decision, however, give cause for reflexion as to the scope of the principle of non-reciprocity as stated in the document. A paragraph dealing with the least developed countries states that the developed countries will exercise the greatest moderation towards those countries when seeking to obtain concessions or contributions as counterparts to their own commitments to reduce or eliminate customs duties and other obstacles to the trade of those countries. The call for "greatest moderation" on the part of the developed countries in the specific case of trade relations with the least developed countries is an implicit confirmation of the principle of non-reciprocal concessions on the part of the developing countries and a rejection of the principle of unilateral concessions. More important still, and more controversial, is the next provision of the decision, according to which the less-developed contracting parties are deemed to expect that their capacity to make contributions or negotiated concessions would improve with the progressive development of their economies and the improvement of their trade position and that they would accordingly expect to participate more fully in the framework of rights and obligations under the General Agreement. This is the notorious 'graduation clause', considered by the developed countries to represent an indispensable complement to their acceptance of the principle of non-reciprocity, and only accepted with the greatest reticence by the developing countries. In fact, a few months before the conclusion of the Tokyo Round, the Group of 77 issued a declaration on multilateral trade negotiations at UNCTAD V in which they expressed their "rejection of the concept of 'graduation', sought to be introduced by developed countries in the trading system and which would allow developed countries to discriminate among developing countries in a unilateral and arbitrary manner".

(d) Differential treatment

The principle of differential treatment in favour of developing countries underlies much thinking in development economics, and it has been implicit from the very beginning in some of the demands formulated by the developing countries in their efforts to reshape international economic relations so as to take account of their position and of their needs. The duality of norms referred to above expresses in a formal legal sense the principle of differential treatment. The concept of differential treatment, as such, also gradually emerged in the deliberations of UNCTAD, and Conference resolution 96 (IV) reflected it in its recommendations on non-tariff barriers.

More recently, the Set of Multilaterally Agreed Equitable Principles and Rules for the Control of Restrictive Business Practices formally embodied the principle of differential treatment. In its section on scope of application, the Set of Principles and Rules states that it "shall be universally applicable to all countries . . ". It contains, however, a section C (iii) entitled "Preferential or differential treatment for developing countries". The wording of the single provision in that section is of particular interest: "In order to ensure the equitable application of the Set of Principles and Rules, States, particularly of developed countries, should take into account in their control of restrictive business practices the development, financial and trade needs of developing countries . . . ". It should be noted that, in contrast to the approach adopted in the draft Code of Conduct on the Transfer of Technology discussed above, the Set of Principles and Rules does not embody alternative provisions to regulate the differential treatment foreseen for the developing countries, but only requires that their special position be taken into account in the application of the Set of Principles and Rules. It is therefore a case of differential treatment without a system of duality of norms.

It would appear that general recognition and acceptance of the principle of differential treatment has been slower than was the case for the principle of non-reciprocity. It is true that the concept of differential and more favourable treatment has been embodied in both the title and the first provision of the decision referred to above, adopted by the Contracting Parties of GATT at the end of the Tokyo Round, concerning the legal framework for the conduct of international trade: "The provisions of Article 1 of the General Agreement notwithstanding, the Contracting Parties can grant a differential and more favourable treatment to developing countries without extending it to other contracting parties". This is the celebrated "enabling clause", about which there was so much talk in the final phase of the Tokyo Round. The provision does, however, explicitly list the specific and limited cases to which the clause may apply: tariff preferences accorded under the GSP; non-tariff measures governed by codes negotiated under GATT auspices; tariff preferences and, subject to conditions that may be prescribed, non-tariff preferences granted to one another by developing countries in the framework of regional or global trade arrangements; and special treatment for least-developed countries. The limitative nature of the clause is underlined by a note to the paragraph which states that it will remain possible for the Contracting Parties to examine any proposal for differential and more favourable treatment that does not fall under the provisions of the paragraph. The decision provides in addition for a procedure of notification, as well as of consultation at the request of any interested contracting party.[4]

The developing countries have stressed the unsatisfactory nature of this clause, which provides for a principle of differential treatment of limited scope of application and whose expansion shall have to be the object of further negotiations among the Contracting Parties. Fundamentally, an enabling clause, i.e. a provision that was only permissive, fell far short of the aspirations of the developing countries to the affirmation of a legal norm that would fully reflect the principle of differential treatment.

Here also, it is the International Law Commission of the United Nations that can provide us with the measure of the state of evolution of the legal principles governing international economic relations. Whereas in 1978 it accepted as a general principle, as we have seen above, an exception to the most-favoured-nation clause in relation to treatment under a generalized system of preferences, the Commission took a much more cautious approach in respect of differential treatment in general. It declared itself conscious of the fact that promoting the trade of developing countries with a view to their economic development was being pursued in areas other than that of preferences. It referred in this regard to the multilateral trade negotiations, in the context of which a concept of differential measures had been formulated as distinct from that of preferences, and it made specific reference to pronouncements at the third and fourth sessions of the UNC-TAD Conference, as well as to Article 18 of the Charter of Economic Rights and Duties of States. The International Law Commission went on to say, however, that "while all these developments may show that there might be a tendency among States to promote the trade of developing countries through 'differential treatment', the conclusion of the Commission is that this tendency has not yet crystallized sufficiently to permit it to be em-bodied in a clear legal rule which could find its place among the general rules on the functioning and application of the most-favoured-nation clause ... What has been said of 'differential treatment' can also be said of other concepts evolving with the aim of promoting the trade of developing countries. Under these circumstances it seemed to the Commission that at least at the present stage of development there is no agreement discernible which would warrant the inclusion, in the articles of the present draft, of rules other than those contained in articles 23 and 24 in favour of the developing countries". The Commission noted in particular that UNCTAD at its fourth session in Nairobi in 1976 had not provided the Commission with a definitive text upon which it could have based the adoption of a new rule. With a view, however, to the possibility of such new rules being developed, the Commission decided to include in its draft articles a general reservation that was embodied in draft article 30: "The present articles are without prejudice to the establishment of new rules of international law in favour of developing countries". The International Law Commission did not therefore feel it was in a position to give recognition to the concept of differential treatment as a general legal principle, and one may legitimately regret this *opinio nec juris*. To be fair, one has however to recognize that its article 30 shows some sensitivity to the dynamics of the concept of inter-national development law.[5]

(e) Regulatory intervention

The search for translating the tenets of development economics into practice has led to the emergence of legal instruments of an interventionist and regulatory nature. These aim at establishing rules of the game to ensure a more equitable share of the benefits of international economic activity for the developing countries and, more recently and more generally, to contribute to the development of these countries. Such instruments are particularly unpopular with the partisans of free trade, because they specifically seek to interfere with the 'free play' of market forces with a view to favouring one group of economic partners, i.e. the developing countries.

It is the regulation of commodity trade that provides the most significant and the most striking example of measures of this nature, and it may be said that the international commodity agreement is to regulatory intervention what the Generalized System of Preferences is to compensatory inequality. It is therefore of considerable interest to examine the evolution of the very concept of the commodity agreement, of its finality and of the principles that govern its application.

The still-born Havana Charter adopted in 1948 by the United Nations Conference on Trade and Employment had attempted, in a narrow and closely defined context, to produce a codification of some fundamental principles that should govern international commodity agreements. The general tone of the Charter was clearly that commodity agreements were short-term corrective mechanisms which should interfere with the normal play of market forces only in certain specific circumstances. The very wording of the draft Charter makes this wholly clear. Its Article 57, dealing with the objectives of inter-governmental commodity agreements, states: "The Members recognize that intergovernmental commodity agreements are appropriate for the achievements of the following objectives: (a) to prevent or alleviate the serious economic difficulties which may arise when adjustments between production and consumption cannot be effected by normal market forces alone as rapidly as the circumstances require;...".[6] Commodity agreements were clearly conceived in a strictly limitative spirit as exceptions to the 'rules of the game' incorporated in another chapter of the Havana Charter, a chapter that later became the General Agreement on Tariffs and Trade. Commodity agreements were therefore in a sense unwanted instruments, tolerated as a necessary evil; they were strictly circumscribed, with precise provisions defining the conditions under which they could be negotiated and operate. In particular, the Havana Charter made no mention of the question of the benefits that could accrue to the national economy of the parties to a commodity agreement. Its preoccupation was centred on the question of the equilibrium between supply and demand and, in respect of the producers, with ensuring an acceptable position for the efficient producer.

Progressively, through the years, the developing countries have been able to challenge this conceptual framework and they stressed in UNCTAD the need for inter-governmental control of commodity markets as a means to improve their economic performance and to assist them in their development. One can clearly trace this process in the evolution of the declared objectives of the commodity agreements negotiated during the past twenty years, in which provisions reflecting an adherence to the principles of the market economy slowly give way to objectives that reflect a concern for the development of the developing countries. This is evident not only in the importance attached to the trade-stabilizing effects of commodity agreements, allowing producing countries to rely on stable and predictable external revenues. Today, in addition, international commodity agreements embody objectives aiming at creating trade with a view to ensuring the growth of external income. Thus the first objective mentioned in the International Sugar Agreement, 1977, in paragraph (a) of Article 1, is: "to raise the level of international trade in sugar, particularly in order to increase the export earnings of developing exporting countries". The most recent of the price-stabilizing commodity agreements, the International Natural Rubber Agreement, 1979, which is far from insensitive to the reluctance of partisans of the market economy to accept regulatory mechanisms, nevertheless states as an objective, in paragraph (c) of Article 1: "to help to stabilize the export earnings from natural rubber of exporting members, and to increase their earnings based on expanding natural rubber export volumes at fair and remunerative prices, thereby helping to provide the necessary incentives for a dynamic and rising rate of production and the resources for accelerated economic growth and social development".

There is hardly any need to recall that this evolution of international commodity agreements towards becoming instruments of international development policy has been systematically spearheaded and stimulated by the pronouncements and recommendations that mark the work of UNCTAD in the field of commodity trade.[7]

In an altogether different field, UNCTAD made another important contribution to the principle of regulatory intervention. The Convention on a Code of Conduct for Liner Conferences, adopted in 1974, offers a striking example of an interventionist instrument clearly designed to favour the development of developing countries through a strengthening of their trading position. This Convention regulates the question of establishing equality of opportunities between trading partners in a particularly visible and dramatic way, inasmuch as it establishes the principle of the equal rights of the national shipping lines of two countries, the foreign trade between which is carried by a liner conference, to participate in the freight and volume of traffic generated by their mutual foreign trade and carried by the conference. It is provided that third-country shipping lines, if any, shall have the right to acquire a significant part, such as 20 per cent according to the Convention, in the freight and volume of traffic generated by the trade. This is the famous 40:40:20 formula, scorned by liberal economists as sanctioning a regime of 'flag preferences', but welcomed by the Third World as a whole as an extrapolation into the international legal order, in a specific case, of the principle of real equality of opportunity for the developing countries in international economic activity.[8]

Another set of provisions in this Convention, of perhaps more immediate importance for the developing countries and which are certainly no less interventionist in spirit, establishes a general framework of international regulation for the procedures governing the determination of freight rates. Finally, a chapter on "Provisions and machinery for settlement of disputes" that may arise in respect of participation in conference trade or in establishing freight rates, provides in particular for international mandatory conciliation in case of failure of direct negotiations between the parties, as well as for the creation of a permanent 'Conciliation Registry'. The Convention on a Code of Conduct for Liner Conferences thus sets up a relatively sophisticated regulatory system that ensures the 'publicization' of an important segment of international economic activity, entirely conceived and designed with a view to favouring the position of developing countries in their capacity as maritime traders.

At various levels of 'legal content' and in various degrees of material specificity, other regulatory micro-systems have recently been established or are being negotiated within UNCTAD, in respect of such subjects as restrictive business practices or the transfer of technology. Regulatory intervention with a view to strengthening the position of developing countries in international economic activity can thus be identified as an important trend giving substance to the concept of international development law.

III. New normative values

(a) De-stabilizing the old legal order

The work of UNCTAD over two decades has played a major role, as we have seen, in the emergence of new legal principles that represent an important contribution to international development law. No less important, however, has been the impact of UNCTAD's work on the very concept of law as the instrument for regulating international relations. One of the salient features of international development law today, and one which is still controversial, is its receptivity to a broader approach than has been the case in traditional international law to the legal significance and function of norms entailing various degrees of binding force.

This 'opening up' of the legal significance and function of norms of various types has been largely the result of the search for a transformation of international economic relations to provide for a more equitable position for the developing countries. UNCTAD has been the setting in which this process has taken place in a dialogue between developing and developed countries, for a long time largely in isolation from more conventional thinking elsewhere about the significance and scope of 'informal' normative work. In more recent years, however, this dialogue has also been pursued in a number of other fora, without in any way detracting from the central and crucial role that has been and continues to be played by UNCTAD in the matter.

It is important for an understanding of this legal phenomenon not to lose sight of the nature of the quest for a New International Economic Order in which the jurist eventually finds himself involved. This process was triggered in the economic sphere by the rejection of the classical theory of free trade. In such a venture, general principles arising from the need for economic change invariably precede the development of the legal rules that will be necessary to translate those principles into the concrete reality of inter-state relations. The search for change in the existing economic order therefore tends to lean more on principles of economic equity than on the legal norms that will eventually provide the envelope for those principles. Those legal norms will follow; they will emerge as the crystallization of a process that takes place at the level of economics and politics.

As a consequence, we are today faced, in respect of the international dimension of development, with an evolving and unsettled international order. Next to the old order, whose legal structures are still largely intact, a new order is emerging that draws nourishment essentially from the confrontations and negotiations that take place between developing and developed countries at the level of multilateral diplomacy. This new order has its foundations in the principles and directives of international economic policy embodied in innumerable resolutions, recommendations and decisions adopted in UNCTAD and in other multilateral fora.

Those resolutions, recommendations and decisions are no more legal rules, in a classical juridical sense, than the principles of economic policy they reflect. This point is constantly being made. They nonetheless represent a body of decisions which the international community recommends to governments as measures of economic policy, and it is the view of more than two-thirds of the states that constitute the international community that these decisions must serve as a source of inspiration for the formulation of new legal rules.

Such rules are beginning to emerge, as we have seen in the preceding section of this paper. As rules of law, in themselves, they do not as a whole offer a coherent legal system. They represent, in each case, the end result in the legal sphere of a process of economic adjustment, and they are coherent only in relation to the economic order that has given rise to them. In that framework of coherence, the principle, the directive, the recommendation and the binding legal norm all co-exist, are entangled and support one another.

Faced as we are with an ongoing negotiation, we are dealing with a process which entails uncertain concepts, shifting positions and imprecise instruments. Development diplomacy is thus a melting pot in which principles, declarations, recommendations or binding legal norms emerge at the whim of circumstance, as the result of negotiation. Because they are the result of negotiation, they are largely conditioned by the negotiating power of the parties: hence their variety, their frequent ambiguity and their formal imperfection; hence also the lack of clarity and the contradictions which often beset them.

Most of the time, these pronouncements represent negotiated compromises adopted by consensus. Often, though, they are qualified by reservations or interpretative declarations entered by some of the partners in the negotiation. From time to time, as if in a desperate assault, it is by majority vote that those principles and recommendations are adopted. They will nonetheless be quoted as principles and recommendations adopted by the multilateral body in which the voting took place, giving rise to a deliberate ambiguity in respect of their significance. With the passing of time, however, ideas evolve and positions are adjusted, and examples exist of resolutions, which had been the subject of an abstention or even a negative vote on the part of certain states, being quoted ten years or so later as expressing the consensus of the international community.

The ultimate outcome, the binding legal provision, often remains a difficult last step, an obstacle before which one must show patience and resourcefulness—such as the suggestion made in UNCTAD some time ago according to which the Code of Conduct on the Transfer of Technology should be adopted without further delay, it being understood that the question of the legal nature of the Code would be decided by a review conference to take place five years after the adoption of the Code! Alternatively, ambiguity as to the legal nature of the instrument being adopted may be entertained to the extreme. For example, though it was unanimously accepted that the Set of Multilaterally Agreed Equitable Principles and Rules for the Control of Restrictive Business Practices would have no binding legal force, the developing countries objected most strongly during the negotiation in UNCTAD to the use of the word 'voluntary' to characterize the Set of Principles and Rules, a position which they carried to the point of making the avoidance of that word a non-negotiable requisite of the draft that was then being considered.

What we are therefore witnessing in North-South relations is a process of destabilization, of erosion, of de-legitimization of the established international legal order, sustained and stimulated by the cohesion of the Group of 77 in UNCTAD and in other international fora. This process is deliberately engineered and pursued in the twilight zone of pre-law, of para-law or of peri-law. Let us hear what one of the leaders of the Third World, Shridath Ramphal, has to say about it. He evokes the emergence of new legal rules to regulate the international economic order and, referring to the principles of the New International Economic Order, goes on to say "Meanwhile, in spite of their present evolutionary character, [those principles] cannot be disregarded by States without overstepping the imperceptible line between impropriety and illegality, between discretion and arbitrariness, between the exercise of a legal right to disregard a recommendation and the abuse of that right. Even in such a twilight zone the defaulting State would soon find that it has exposed itself to consequences that follow with all the legitimacy of a legal sanction".[9] One could hardly be more explicit in respect of the utilization of legal instruments for the advancement of economic and political objectives.

This process of destabilization of the old legal order is irreversible, and there is no doubt that with the passing of time there will be a more and more generalized acceptance and a more and more systematic application by states of new principles that will progressively displace and invalidate the traditional legal norms that governed the old economic order, that will replace the international law of indifference by an international law of finality, that will entrust the international community with responsibility for the problem of the development of the developing countries. In the long run, this evolution will have important consequences for the functioning of the international community, in that it will challenge the very foundations of inter-state relationships in respect of states at different levels of development. The Western diplomat perceived it very well who, opposing the adoption of the Charter of Economic Rights and Duties of States, exclaimed at the rostrum of the United Nations General Assembly: "Gentlemen, one does not codify a revolution!".

(b) The Charter of Economic Rights and Duties of States

The Charter of Economic Rights and Duties of States was adopted, nevertheless, by the United Nations General Assembly and this event was greeted by developing countries as a most important political and legal landmark in the search for a New International Economic Order, for an order based on a desire for justice and co-operation in international economic relations. It would be inconceivable, indeed, to deal with the subject of UNCTAD and the emergence of international development law without dwelling for a moment on the Charter of Economic Rights and Duties of States, and this on two counts. From a formal point of view, firstly, it will be recalled that the very idea of the Charter was born in UNCTAD; it was at UNCTAD III (Santiago-de-Chile, 1972) that the President of Mexico launched the initiative that was to lead to the adoption of the Charter by the General Assembly less than three years later. The preparatory work for the Charter was almost entirely conducted within the framework of UNCTAD. This was in essence and spirit truly an UNCTAD venture; while perhaps no other single activity of UNCTAD did as much as the negotiations on the Charter to project the development issue onto the stage of world politics.

Secondly, the Charter is of very particular interest and relevance to us because it represents the epitome of an instrument of international development law. In point of fact, ambiguity as to the legal nature of the Charter to be drafted was seeded in the very first resolution which was adopted on the matter, UNCTAD resolution 45 (III). This resolution, which set up a Working Group within UNCTAD to draw up the text of a draft Charter, recalled in its consideranda that one of the main functions of UNCTAD was "to formulate principles and policies on international trade and related problems of economic development", went on to note "with concern that the international legal instruments on which the economic relations between States are currently based are precarious and that it is not feasible to establish a just order and a stable world as long as a charter to protect duly the rights of all countries and in particular the developing States is not formulated", and noted further "the urgent need in the international community to establish generally accepted norms to govern international economic relations systematically". Those provisions were to be quoted later to point to the fact that the intent and purpose of the initiative was the establishment of a normative system presupposing the existence of clearly determined and enforceable rights and duties.

The fact that the Charter was finally adopted by the General Assembly by majority vote (120 in favour to 6 against, with 10 abstentions) has not basically altered the judgement made by the developing countries as to the legal nature of the Charter. Indeed, it has given cause for a refinement of the doctrinal position of Third World jurists in respect of the international legal order as a whole. Thus, Tomas Polanco Alcántara has pointed out that the very high percentage of States which approved the Charter gives sufficient justificative political support to the legal reforms which the Charter introduces. He speaks of legal realities that are acquiring progressive strength, of the ethico-juridical foundations to the rights and duties embodied in the Charter that are implied in the support given to them by 120 countries, and he states: "It would never have been politically possible to compel the countries which opposed the Charter to accept its new principles as valid and binding for them, and it would have been equally impossible to obtain from the countries which voted in favour that they desist from their objective of instituting this new order which they consider indispensable. It is both incomprehensible and unacceptable to pretend that a resolution adopted by 120 States is only a recommendation of a moral nature because of the fact that six States opposed it. It is evident that there is a point at which the ethical and political importance of such a big majority of sovereign States transforms what they have approved into an authentic legal obligation, whichever are the States that withheld their vote".[10] This is an expression of the basic challenge to the traditional Euro-centric international legal order which is now widespread in legal doctrine in the Third World.

This conceptual framework does not presume that this "authentic legal obligation" is necessarily enforceable at this time—though it would prob-ably be argued that it is binding. It assumes, as we have just seen, the "progressive strength of legal realities" and one finds in analytical com-ments on the Charter expressions such as "framework code" and "revendi-cative law". This very terminology points to an important feature of the thinking in developing countries in respect of the nature of international development law. According to a view that is now fairly generally held in legal circles in such countries, the function of international development law is not only to provide the normative framework necessary for orderly intercourse in international economic relations. It also has an active role to play in the pursuance and attainment of aims and objectives which it embodies.

The Charter of Economic Rights and Duties of States, perhaps more than any other instrument of international development law, has been conceived and is perceived by developing countries in a perspective of progression towards generalized compliance. It is accepted that many of its provisions are programmatic in nature and not immediately susceptible to complete application. It is expected, however, that the pressure generated by the very existence of the Charter will, in the long run, bring its weight to bear on those states which opposed it in full or in part, ensure a larger and ultimately full compliance with its precepts and principles, and give its provisions the nature of true legal norms of a binding nature. It is in the context of an analysis of the Charter of Economic Rights and Duties of States as the principal normative instrument of the New International Economic Order that Hector Gros Espiell forcefully emphasizes this essen-tial feature of international development law: "The term international development law should be understood not only as a new discipline, but also as a legal technique aimed at providing the normative instruments of the struggle against under-development ... Development law cannot be conceived only as a set of norms dealing with a specific matter, i.e. development. On the contrary, it constitutes a legal system aiming at stimulating and accelerating development. In the final analysis, it is a law that is essentially finalistic and teleological, whose characteristics are deter-mined by the mission that is assigned to it".[11]

The Charter itself, it may be pointed out, contains provisions which are very much in keeping with this approach, in particular Article 33, para-graph 2, on the interrelated nature of the provisions of the Charter in their interpretation and application, and Article 34 on the periodic "systematic and comprehensive consideration of the implementation of the Charter, covering both progress achieved and any improvements and additions which might become necessary . . . ".

It should finally be noted that the Charter attaches fundamental importance to the basic principles of international public law, sovereignty, territorial integrity, political independence and sovereign equality of all States, listing as it does those principles in Chapter I on the fundamentals of international economic relations. We may refer here to our introductory observation on the place of the principle of sovereign equality in international development law. The economic rights and duties proclaimed by the Charter have been described as a modern and up-dated expression of those basic principles of international public law. As Hector Gros Espiell points out: "In effect, one is today conscious of the fact that without the recognition of these economic rights, it is impossible for the rights that are classically called 'fundamental', that derive from the very existence of States, to have a true, realistic and integral projection, capable of ensuring an international order based on justice, equity and co-operation".[12]

(c) International law revisited

In the search for the establishment of a New International Economic Order, the lawyer is thus put on trial. He is dragged into an adventure which has not been of his making and over which he has no control because its fundamentals belong to the realm of economics and politics. He is nevertheless harassed, the time-honoured tools of his trade are taken from him, he is confronted with a reality that tends to disregard the traditional distinction between law and non-law, between the legal norm that has a binding character and the non-binding pronouncement that rests outside the sphere of law. Legal science was not slow in perceiving the dilemma thus facing the lawyer. Michel Virally wrote in 1973: "The lawyer, who is fond of clarity, is led to move into a twilight zone in which it is difficult to distinguish dog from wolf and to recognize at first sight whether one is facing the familiar and reassuring silhouette of the legal norm, or on the contrary the untamed and intractable form of a norm the real nature of which escapes us".[13] At about the same time, Maurice Flory noted that "pressures combining with imagination have succeeded in acclimatizing new techniques leading to new types of recommendations over which the lawyer bends with curiosity without being able to detect whether one faces a non-legal, a pre-legal or a quasi-legal pronouncement".[14]

We are here facing an important aspect of the reality of international life, and legal science could hardly maintain a purely formal view of its scope and function, ignoring the weight which development thinking as it has already taken shape carries at the level of States. International development law had therefore to take cognizance of the process of progressive evolution towards an *opinio juris* that is involved in the diplomatic activity taking place in search of a New International Economic Order.

There is no doubt that such a venture does violence to the classical canons of juridical rigour. We should not forget, however, that we are moving in the realm of international public law whose very foundations are themselves rather fragile in scientific legal terms. Maurice Flory made the point very well in describing the features that make international development law particularly unsatisfactory for the traditional jurist: "(1) An integral part of international public law, it embodies all the well-known weaknesses of the latter: law of co-ordination and not of subordination, law without a legislator, without enforcement and without judge, law beset with lacunae. (2) A branch of economic law, it must take into account the two concepts of conjuncture and of prospective, which largely make it a law of the uncertain. (3) Fruit of the marriage, finally, between international public law and economic law, international development law is the youngest branch of international law, thus the most incomplete, the least elaborated, while dealing with one of the most controversial aspects of economics, inasmuch as there are few areas in which the economists have done so much work and ended with so many queries."[15]

If the distinction between law and non-law truncates reality and threatens to marginalize the lawyer and to remove him from real life, if the coherence of the process of evolution of the relationship between States at different levels of development can only be apprehended in a complex web of norms, of principles and of pronouncements of varying nature, then we must enlarge our horizon to take a new look at the non-binding norm, and to reflect on the legal value of resolutions, recommendations, principles and directives adopted in the framework of multilateral diplomacy.

It is generally accepted that an agreement which has no binding legal value does not commit the legal responsibility of the parties, however seriously they view the agreement. This means that the non-observance of this agreement cannot be a cause to claim reparation; which is very different from saying that the agreement need not be observed, or that the parties are free to act as if such an agreement did not exist. In fact, agreements of a non-binding nature do have undeniable internal effects for the parties. Their existence will influence national positions and practice and we must presume that they carry instructions to the representatives of the parties to act in conformity with them. A party will also be in a position to invoke the existence of the agreement with a view to justifying a measure that it has taken. As for external effects, they will be still clearer, at the level of the reaction of a party, or of a group of parties, to the behaviour of another party or of another group of parties. In particular, a party will be in a position to make representations to another party in respect of the fulfill-ment of those commitments. It is clear that the conduct of the State that is party to the agreement is no longer discretionary, that it is no longer within the realm of exclusive national competence.

Should the non-observance of the agreement be manifest, this would of course raise the question as to whether the agreement is still in force or whether we face a situation of annulment or termination through non-observance. But as long as it is in force, it wields its power over the behaviour of the parties. In practice, the party that complains about the non-observance of a non-binding agreement by another party is likely to launch an exhortation that the agreement be complied with, rather than calling for its denunciation, in the hope of generating enough pressure to force compliance. Non-binding agreements thus create a framework of pressure; they embody norms that are pressing, if not legally binding. This is the nature of what has come to be known as 'soft law', which is today a very important instrument in international relations between countries at different levels of development. One may recall here the considerations adduced above about the serious legal weaknesses of the Generalized System of Preferences, and its fundamental importance nevertheless in practice. The GSP offers a perfect illustration of the way in which non-binding commitments can generate definite and tangible effects.

There are few today who continue to argue that this is a perversion of legal science. In a world undergoing a fundamental change, the lawyer must remember at all times that his role is not to attempt to recognize what he knows, but rather to attempt to know the reality. The point is not to ask him to abandon his conceptual tools or to introduce disorder in juridical thinking. The lawyer must however make a serious effort to understand a moving reality, to accept new concepts and to adjust his framework of analysis.

We could thus outline the normative values of international development law as a new branch of international public law, and indicate its specific characteristics. From a formal point of view, it is a law that takes shape in the dialectic of the South-North dialogue, a dialogue nurtured by the questioning of a system of international relations based on the principle of formal equality. It is a law that takes shape on the multilateral plane, presupposing a categorization of groups of countries in accordance with their degree of development. It is a law that takes shape through a political process, and is consequently subject to ambiguity, imperfection, sometimes contradictions, at the whim of the relative power of the partners in the negotiation. As a corollary, it is a law whose shaping presupposes the existence of a multilateral institutional framework.

From the point of view of its nature, the essential feature of international development law is its progressiveness. It is the object of a slow evolutionary process in which general principles and abstract rules play an important part, in which a large role is played by non-binding normative activity and which is characterized by normative flexibility. It embodies aims and objectives, principles and precepts that are to acquire strength gradually and to evolve into enforceable legal norms.

★   ★   ★

The work of UNCTAD has entailed visible activities of a legal nature which have attracted considerable attention. This is the case of the negotiation of legally-binding instruments such as commodity agreements and the Convention on a Code of Conduct for Liner Conferences, as well as of instruments of a non-binding legal nature such as the Generalized System of Preferences, the Set of Multilaterally Agreed Equitable Principles and Rules for the Control of Restrictive Business Practices, and the Code of Conduct on the Transfer of Technology. Those activities have provided important building blocks for the body of legal discipline that is now known as international development law.

However, the visible part of UNCTAD's contribution to the emergence of international development law represents only one aspect of that contribution. Far beyond its external legal manifestations, the process that has taken place in UNCTAD since its inception to the present day has had a profound influence on the concepts and institutions of the international legal order, both towards the shaping and acceptance of new legal principles and towards an alteration of the very fabric of that order and the acceptance of new normative values. It may thus be said that the effects of the work of UNCTAD on the international legal sphere are in no way second to the impact of its work on the sphere of international economic relations.

---

1. Claude-Albert Colliard, "Cadre institutionnel et techniques d'élaboration du droit" in *Pays en voie de développement et transformation du droit international,* Colloque d'Aix-en-Provence de la Société française pour le droit international, Pedone, Paris, 1974, pp. 99 and 185; W. Friedmann, *The Changing Structure of International Law,* New York, 1964, *passim.*

2. *Report of the International Law Commission on the Work of its Thirtieth Session,* 1978, United Nations document A/33/10, pp. 137 and ff.

3. Paragraph 5 of the Decision, in *Agreements relating to the framework for the conduct of international trade,* General Agreement on Tariffs and Trade, Geneva, 1979, p. 6.

4. *Ibid,* paras. 1 and 4, pp. 5 and 6.

5. International Law Commission, *op. cit.,* pp. 173 ff.

6. United Nations Conference on Trade and Employment, Final Act and Related Documents, 1948, United Nations document E/CONF. 2/78, p. 39.

7. See the article by Alfred Maizels in this volume.

8. The adoption of the Code was a fitting conclusion to Wladek Malinowski's term in charge of UNCTAD's work on maritime transport. It is the subject of a contribution to this volume by M. J. Shah.

9. Shridath S. Ramphal, in his Foreword to Oswaldo de Rivero, B., *New Economic Order and International Development Law,* Pergamon Press, 1980, p. viii.

10. Tomas Polanco Alcántara, "La obligatoriedad y validez de la Carta de Derechos y

Deberes Económicos de los Estados", in *Derecho Económico Internacional,* Fondo de Cultura Económica, Mexico, 1976, p. 131.

11. Hector Gros Espiell, "El Nuevo Orden Económico Internacional", in *Derecho Económico Internacional,* Fondo de Cultura Económica, Mexico, 1976, pp. 99 and 100.

12. *Ibid,* p. 88.

13. Michel Virally, "Conclusions du Colloque", in *Pays en voie de développement et transformation du droit international,* Colloque d'Aix-en-Provence de la Société francaise pour le droit international, p.308.

14. Maurice M. Flory, "Inégalité économique et évolution du droit international", *ibid,* p. 12.

15. Maurice M. Flory, *op. cit.,* p. 39.

PART TWO

Achievements and Assessments

REFORMING THE WORLD COMMODITY ECONOMY

by Alfred Maizels

I. Commodities and the development process

It is not surprising that the commodity problem, in all its various aspects, has been a major focus of UNCTAD's endeavours to accelerate the development process. The great majority of developing countries are still heavily dependent on primary commodities for their export earnings and for the external financing of their development programmes. The domestic economies of most developing countries also retain much of the lopsided structural character inherited from the period of colonial rule, with agriculture or mining occupying the greater part of the active labour force.

Over the post-war period, the primary commodity sector has generally proved unable to provide foreign exchange earnings on a scale sufficient to finance rapid economic growth in most developing countries. Instead of constituting an 'engine of growth', the commodity export sector has rather tended to be a major constraint on the development process. Commodity prices have shown unfavourable trends in real terms, i.e. in terms of the prices of manufactured goods imported by developing countries, while efforts by these countries to expand their export volume have too often led to price reductions as a result of demand inelasticity. Commodity prices, moreover, have suffered from large and unpredictable short-term fluctuations, which have had serious adverse effects on the abilities of developing countries to implement their development programmes.

These and related problems of the world commodity economy and possible international remedial action, had been under inter-governmental discussion even in the inter-war period, but a concerted international trade policy, including policy on commodities, did not emerge until the Havana Charter of 1948. At that time it was widely believed that the post-war recovery of Western Europe and the pursuit of full employment policies in the industrial countries would lead in the long term to an expanding demand for primary commodities on a scale sufficiently large to remove the need for any inter-governmental intervention in the free working of commodity markets, except under temporary or exceptional circumstances. Such circumstances, in turn, were conceived essentially in terms of oversupply and depressed prices, or the development of widespread unemployment or under-employment in connexion with primary commodities, which could not be corrected within a reasonable time by the normal operation of market forces.[1]

The International Trade Organization (ITO) envisaged in the Havana Charter was not established, however, mainly as a result of opposition in the United States to a new international regulatory mechanism with a wide mandate covering market access, commodity problems, economic development and restrictive business practices. The General Agreement on Tariffs and Trade (GATT), set up on a temporary basis in 1947 pending the envisaged establishment of the ITO, had no mandate to consider international commodity policy. The principles of the Havana Charter for regulating commodity markets were, however, accepted by the Economic and Social Council (ECOSOC) which created an Interim Co-ordinating Committee for International Commodity Arrangements (ICCICA) in 1947 to implement and co-ordinate efforts to reach commodity agreements, by establishing study groups and convening conferences to formulate commodity control schemes. The three central principles on which such control schemes were to be based were: that such schemes would be adopted only to deal with severe market disruption; that they were to aim at price stabilization, and not price increases; and that importing and exporting countries would share equally in the control of the schemes.[2] A number of commodity stabilization agreements, for coffee, sugar, tin and wheat, were concluded under the aegis of the ICCICA.

This general approach to international commodity problems, embodied in the Havana Charter and in the operations of ICCICA, implicitly assumed that the free working of commodity markets would normally provide an optimum allocation of the world's resources and that the upward trend in demand in the developed countries for primary commodity exports from the developing countries would provide the required motive force for the economic growth of the latter group of countries. However, neither of these assumptions was soundly based and, in fact, over the period between the Havana Conference and UNCTAD I the developing countries as a group were faced with a persistent trend towards external trade deficits, which acted as a growing constraint on their development programmes.

In his report to UNCTAD I, Raúl Prebisch identified the principal cause of this external constraint on the development process as arising from a secular tendency of the terms of trade of primary commodity exporting countries to deteriorate, a tendency which was accentuated by the protectionist policies of developed countries in the area of agricultural trade.[3] Prebisch concluded that the essential aims of international policy in this field should be to establish commodity agreements in order to improve the trend governing prices of commodities exported by developing countries, and to promote national measures by developed countries designed to improve access to their domestic markets for the commodities produced by developing countries. Prebisch recognized that for many commodities it may not be feasible to improve price trends for developing exporting countries by means of inter-governmental intervention in world markets (e.g. where an upper limit to prices was effectively provided by the prices of synthetic substitutes), and for such commodities he advocated the use of a compensatory financing mechanism to offset any deterioration in the terms of trade.

Dr. Prebisch's report to UNCTAD I was an important milestone in the evolution of international commodity policy, not only for its analysis of the commodity problems of developing countries but also because it placed these problems firmly in the context of the development needs of the developing countries. Moreover, instead of a reliance on the free play of market forces to stimulate development, the logic of Prebisch's argument pointed to the need for positive action by governments, on a common basis, designed deliberately to improve the long-term rate of growth of commodity export earnings, and to reduce short-term fluctuations in those earnings, while taking into account the interests of consumers in importing countries. It is this link between commodity policy and development, established by Prebisch, which has formed the basis for all subsequent commodity analysis and related policy proposals debated in UNCTAD, as well as in other international fora.

While the Final Act of UNCTAD I set out the principles of a new global strategy for development, major reservations were entered by the developed market-economy countries on critical issues. On commodity policy, for example, 12 of these countries opposed the recommendation on the stabilization of primary commodity prices (Special Principle 7), while most of the remainder abstained. The majority of these countries abstained on the recommendation on modification in domestic support policies for primary production by developed countries (Special Principle 5), while the United States opposed the recommendation on the regulation of surplus disposal for primary commodities by developed countries (Special Principle 8).[4]

The opposition of developed market-economy countries to the new approach to international commodity policy adopted at UNCTAD I was generally based on the *laissez-faire* philosophy of the Havana Charter, and particularly on the argument that any regulation of the free play of market forces will inevitably lead to a misallocation of resources and eventual economic catastrophe. As already indicated, even market regulation designed to reduce excessive fluctuations in commodity prices, which later came to be generally accepted as in the interests of both developed and developing countries, was opposed in principle. In creating UNCTAD in 1964, the General Assembly transferred to it the functions performed by

ICCICA[5], so that UNCTAD became the sole agency responsible for negotiating international commodity agreements, as well as for formulating international commodity policy in relation to development. However, the general opposition by the developed market-economy countries to intervention in the free play of commodity markets was from the outset, and has remained, a major constraint on UNCTAD's capacity to negotiate effective regulatory mechanisms designed to improve the position and prospects of developing countries in their commodity production and trade.

An interesting statistical analysis by Javed Ansari of the voting record at UNCTAD I of each of the 'Group B' countries[6] reveals that indicators of 'economic power' were highly correlated with the degree of opposition to UNCTAD principles. His results showed that the higher the GNP of any Group B country, the greater its voting power in the IMF and IBRD, the greater the aid it gave as a percentage of GNP, and the greater its direct private investment in developing countries, the greater the probability that it would oppose the new UNCTAD principles.[7] In short, it appeared that the developed market-economy countries were well satisfied with the existing international economic system and with the institutional mechanisms established at Bretton Woods, effectively under their control, and that they had no wish to make any changes in either.

II. The commodity-by-commodity approach

A comprehensive analysis of the commodity problem was presented by the UNCTAD secretariat to UNCTAD II, held at New Delhi in 1968. That analysis extended Dr. Prebisch's main lines of argument into an integrated strategy, to be applied jointly by developed and developing countries, to deal with both the short-term problems arising from excessive market fluctuations, and the longer-term problems of improving the trend of commodity prices, expanding market access, promoting the consumption of commodities, meeting the challenge posed by synthetics, expanding commodity exports to socialist countries and to other developing countries, and encouraging appropriate diversification away from the production of commodities in persistent oversupply.[8] It is of some interest to note that this report included *inter alia* a proposal to establish a central fund to assist the financing of international buffer stocks.[9] This idea was to re-emerge at a later date in the guise of the Common Fund, discussed below.

At UNCTAD II, the Group B countries successfully avoided any serious discussion of the secretariat's proposals for an international commodity strategy, or of their analytical basis. Instead, they insisted that progress could be made, not by discussing general principles, but only by considering the problems of each commodity separately, since each market was unique and likely to require its own specially-tailored package of remedial policies.

This commodity-by-commodity approach was accepted by the developing countries as a reasonable basis on which to seek appropriate international action, and the Conference identified a range of 'problem' commodities for detailed discussion in the various specialized international commodity bodies, with a view to identifying the problems and agreeing on appropriate remedial measures.[10]

No results of any significance, however, emerged from this procedure.[11] In many cases, the specialized commodity bodies gave little or no priority to the UNCTAD II resolution, there was generally inadequate technical preparation, while conflicts of view concerning the nature of the problems confronting particular commodity markets often resulted in abortive meetings. Moreover, international remedial action to strengthen commodity markets was generally viewed by developed countries purely in terms of their commercial interest in the commodities concerned, rather than as a common endeavour forming part of a broad strategy of development, as Dr. Prebisch had envisaged, while in some cases progress was limited mainly because of conflicts of interest among developing countries regarding the distribution of export quotas.[12]

Similar difficulties arose out of the programme of "intensive intergovernmental consultations" on the problems facing particular commodities which was launched by UNCTAD III at Santiago in 1972.[13] In the event, no agreements of any significance emerged.

III. The Integrated Programme for Commodities (IPC)

A new initiative to improve the position and prospects of the commodity exports of developing countries was launched by the Secretary-General of UNCTAD, Gamani Corea, at UNCTAD IV, held in Nairobi in 1976. This was in response to the resolutions of the United Nations General Assembly on the Establishment of a New International Economic Order which, among other proposals, called for an overall integrated programme of measures relating to commodities of export interest to developing countries.[14]

As summarized in Dr. Corea's report to UNCTAD IV, the new proposal, which took the form of an "integrated programme for commodities", comprised five basic elements:

(a) the establishment of international stocks covering a wide range of commodities;

(b) the establishment of a common fund to make financial resources available for the acquisition of stocks;

(c) the institution, in circumstances which justify it, of a system of

medium-term to long-term commitments to purchase and sell commodities at agreed prices;

(d) the institution of more adequate measures than are at present available to provide compensatory financing to producers to cover short-
term falls in export earnings;

(e) the initiation of an extensive programme of measures to further the
processing of commodities by the producing countries themselves.[15]

The IPC was conceived as a comprehensive attack on the deep-seated
problems of the lagging commodity sectors of the economies of developing
countries. It was to differ from the earlier commodity-by-commodity approach, which had failed to produce significant results, in two major ways.
First, it was to cover a wide range of commodities on which negotiations to
establish stabilization arrangements could proceed simultaneously, so that
individual countries could secure an adequate overall balance of advantage
from a number of different commodity agreements. Second, it would involve
the creation of a new international financial institution, the Common Fund,
which would act as a catalyst in promoting the speedy conclusion of
commodity agreements, as well as being equipped to take an overall view of
the commodity problem and to intervene, under agreed conditions, in
particular commodity markets in emergencies.[16]

The proposals for an integrated programme had been thoroughly prepared over the two years before UNCTAD IV, and there had been intensive
debates on these proposals in the UNCTAD Committee on Commodities in
the course of 1975. Consequently, the negotiations at UNCTAD IV itself
were essentially political, strong pressure being exerted by the Group of 77
which saw the Integrated Programme as a key element of a New International Economic Order and as an important test case of the willingness of
the developed market-economy countries to co-operate with them in practical measures towards that objective.

The resolution, which was adopted without dissent at UNCTAD IV, was
very wide-ranging in character, envisaging the negotiation of agreements or
arrangements for 18 specified commodities,[17] with the aim of avoiding
excessive price fluctuations, achieving price levels 'remunerative' to producers and 'equitable' to consumers, as well as longer-term objectives such
as increased export earnings for developing countries, improvement in
market access and reliability of supply, diversification of production, improved competitiveness of natural products competing with synthetics, and
improvement in market structures and in the marketing, distribution and
transport system for commodity exports of developing countries.[18]

(a) The Common Fund

The proposal to establish the Common Fund as a new international financial institution, with its own substantial capital structure[19], had been strongly opposed by the majority of the developed market-economy countries during the preliminary discussions in the UNCTAD Committee on Commodities. They generally took the view that such a new source of finance was unnecessary, since individual commodity agreements could be expected to provide adequate finance themselves to cover their own buffer stock operations. However, some developed countries acknowledged that considerable savings might be made by operating a central pool of finance rather than having separate financing facilities for each international buffer stock.

At the Nairobi Conference, a number of the smaller Group B countries supported the proposal of the Group of 77 to establish a new international financial institution to finance a series of buffer stocks, and the consequent division within Group B, together with the political pressure exerted by the developing countries, which included strong support from OPEC countries, resulted in a compromise formula being adopted to negotiate the establishment of a Common Fund.

These negotiations proved to be complex and protracted, but an Agreement was eventually signed in June 1980, four years after the UNCTAD IV resolution, on the objectives, functions, capital structure, mode of operation, and organizational and management structure of the Common Fund.[20] It was evident that, compared to the way it had originally been perceived, the Common Fund as provided for in this Agreement had in many respects been emasculated at the insistence of the developed market-economy countries. For one thing, the Fund was not to control a central pool of funds with which to finance the buffer stock operations of international commodity organizations (ICOs). Instead, most of its financial resources would be derived from deposits with it by the ICOs themselves, the Common Fund being endowed with only a modest amount of its own capital, while being authorized to raise additional amounts, as required, by borrowing from its members, from international financial institutions and from private capital markets.

This reversal of earlier thinking concerning the source of funds inevitably diminishes the potential influence of the Common Fund as an independent financial institution. Moreover, the proposal that the Common Fund should itself be empowered to intervene to support prices in emergency situations in commodity markets not subject to agreements was firmly opposed by Group B countries, and has been omitted from the 1980 Agreement.[21] At the same time, a new element was included in that Agreement, consisting of a 'second window' to finance measures other than stocking (e.g., research and development, productivity improvements and diversification programmes), aimed at improving the structural conditions of commodity markets and at enhancing the long-term competitiveness and prospects of particular commodities. The finance for this 'second window' was set at a modest target level of $280 million, to be raised by voluntary contributions from governments.

It is indeed ironic that this 'second window', which was not part of the original concept of the Common Fund, could become its more important operational arm, since the 'first window', the financing of international buffer stocks, is dependent for its activation on the conclusion of agreements for individual commodities based on stock operations. Since the launching of the IPC in 1976, progress in the negotiation of new commodity agreements has been extremely slow and only limited results have been achieved. Indeed, over the eight years up to mid-1984 only one new price-stabilization agreement (for natural rubber) was concluded, though the existing agreements (for sugar, cocoa, coffee and tin) were all renegotiated. For the other 13 major commodities specifically listed in the IPC resolution, protracted discussions, consultations and, for a few commodities, even negotiations failed to result in agreements. At this slow rate of progress it seems highly unlikely that the 'first window' of the Common Fund will, in fact, become a significant factor in international commodity stabilization efforts.

Difficulties have also arisen in regard to the proposed 'second window', since the developed market-economy countries wish its operations to be confined to purely international projects, such as finance for internationally co-ordinated research, while the developing countries see this new facility as a potentially important additional source of finance for national projects, such as the improvement of productivity in particular export sectors. This latter objective is however seen by developed market-economy countries as an encroachment on the activities of the World Bank. It seems unlikely that, if the 'second window' is confined to purely international projects, it will be of more than marginal interest for the majority of developing countries.

Moreover, although developing countries will have a substantial voice in decision-making in the Common Fund as they will hold approximately 45 per cent of the votes, the developed market-economy countries, with some 40 per cent of the votes, will hold the power to block decisions "with significant financial implications" (such as increases in the Fund's capital) which require a three-fourths majority, or other important decisions (such as projects to be financed by the 'second window'), which require a two-thirds majority. It therefore seems unlikely that the Common Fund, when operative,[22] will be able to play the dynamic and catalytic role in strengthening world commodity markets, and in enhancing the benefits accruing to developing countries from their commodity exports, that had originally been envisaged.

(b) Negotiations on individual commodities

As already mentioned, the various international commodity agreements which were already in existence before the launching of the IPC have since all been successfully re-negotiated under UNCTAD auspices, while a new agreement on natural rubber has been concluded. There seems little doubt that the operation of these agreements has brought significant benefits to producing countries, particularly by helping to attenuate the price recession of 1981–82. But for the majority of the 18 commodities listed in the UNCTAD IV resolution, progress towards the conclusion of new agreements has been slow and limited.

It has recently been argued, with some justification, that one general constraint on the negotiations has been the delay in establishing the Common Fund and making it operational. The absence of a central financing institution would have increased the direct financial burden on countries otherwise willing to consider establishing buffer stocks, and was thus likely to have been a disincentive to take such action.[23] Other reasons mentioned include the relatively favourable conditions on export markets in the later 1970s, which provided little incentive to producing countries to give any priority to regulating commodity markets; conflicts of interests among producing countries, and between producers and consumers of particular commodities; the technical complexities involved; and the failure of developing countries to present common proposals, except for rubber, where this was done and an agreement was subsequently concluded.[24]

While most of these factors undoubtedly operated to slow the rate of progress in particular commodity negotiations, a more general underlying constraint seems, as was suggested earlier, to have been the opposition of the developed market-economy countries to any significant extension of the principle of market regulation. This issue is discussed further below. In any event, it appears evident that these countries have largely succeeded in averting what they had regarded as a potential threat to their existing dominance of world commodity markets by insisting on major modifications in the original concept of the Common Fund, and by limiting its scope of operation through their reluctance to conclude new commodity agreements.

(c) Compensatory financing

Since the problem of short-term fluctuations in commodity prices and export earnings was first discussed in UNCTAD, the developed market-economy countries have stressed their preference for an extension of the existing IMF compensatory financing facility as a means of offsetting short-term fluctuations in export earnings, as against international agreements designed to reduce excessive fluctuations in commodity prices. The IPC resolution had envisaged the "improvement and enlargement of compensatory financing facilities for the stabilization, around a growing trend, of export earnings of developing countries",[25] but it was implicit in the resolution that such enlarged compensatory facilities were regarded as complementary to international stabilization agreements for individual commodities, and not as substitutes for such agreements.

It has indeed always been recognized that even if international agreements on a wide range of commodities were successful in substantially reducing price instability, the commodity export earnings of individual countries would still be likely to suffer from excessive year-to-year fluctuations as a result, for example, of variations in agricultural harvests. Large and unpredictable fluctuations in export earnings have been a major constraint on the ability of many developing countries to carry out their development programmes, and compensatory financing is intended to help meet this problem.

The role that could be played by a compensatory financing facility in stabilizing the commodity export earnings of developing countries came under intensive discussion at UNCTAD V, held in Manila in 1979. A resolution was adopted by majority vote affirming the complementary nature of such a facility, and requesting the UNCTAD secretariat to prepare a detailed study, in consultation with the International Monetary Fund, on the operation of such a complementary facility.[26] This was generally opposed by the larger developed market-economy countries,[27] mainly on the grounds that a compensatory facility was already in operation through the IMF, which made it more appropriate to consider improving existing facilities rather than creating a new mechanism. A related argument was that compensatory finance was more appropriately applied to shortfalls in total export earnings of individual countries, as in the IMF scheme, rather than to shortfalls in earnings from commodity exports alone, as envisaged in the UNCTAD resolution.

The developing countries, on the other hand, argued that the IMF facility was inadequate,[28] that its terms of lending were unduly 'conditional' on domestic policy changes, that the IMF took no account of changes in the terms of trade of developing countries in assessing export shortfalls, and that the IMF facility was not specially adapted to the need of the commodity exporting sector of these countries. In their view, what was required was a specifically tailored mechanism which provided funds for developing countries only, so as to offset unexpected shortfalls in their commodity export earnings, taking into account changes in the purchasing power of these earnings resulting from increases in import prices, and the ability of individual developing countries to repay the loans.[29]

The debate carried over into UNCTAD VI, which adopted a resolution authorizing the Secretary-General of UNCTAD to convene an expert group to consider "the need for an additional complementary facility to compensate for the export earnings shortfalls of developing countries", setting the terms of reference of the group and suggesting the possibility of a negotiating conference on such a new facility. The resolution also invited the IMF to expedite its review of its compensatory financing facility and to consider in this context special arrangements for the benefit of the least developed countries. This time, only the USA voted against the resolution.[30] This issue therefore remains to be decided, but the strong opposition of the principal developed market-economy countries to a new international financial facility outside the IMF makes any proposal to establish such a facility unlikely to succeed.

(d) The indexation issue

Another approach to meeting the problem of deterioration in the terms of trade of commodity-exporting developing countries gained prominence following an agreement made in 1971 between OPEC and the international petroleum companies, under which posted prices were to be increased by 2.5% to take account of the effects of inflation on the prices of imports into OPEC member countries. This linking of commodity prices with the prices of imports, most of which were from developed countries, came to be known as 'indexation'.

The indexation issue was considered at UNCTAD III in 1972 on the basis of a secretariat analysis,[31] but no consensus was reached. The issue was, however, pursued by the Group of 77 and at the 1973 session of the General Assembly a resolution was adopted[32] calling for a study on indexation. In the following year, the sixth special session of the General Assembly, in its resolution on a New International Economic Order, called for "efforts to ... work for a link between the prices of exports of developing countries and the prices of their imports from developed countries".[33]

The possibility of creating such a link was taken up in UNCTAD as part of the discussion of the proposals for an integrated programme for commodities. By the time of the Nairobi Conference in 1976, rising inflation in the industrialized countries had already emerged as a serious problem, not only for those countries but also as the mechanism which raised the prices of essential imports of developing countries, eroding the real value of their commodity exports. The indexation issue therefore needed to be considered within the broader context of stabilization of commodity prices and of efforts to improve the real earnings of developing countries from their commodity exports.

In principle, there are two alternative approaches to creating a link between export and import prices of commodity-exporting countries. One approach, usually known as 'direct indexation', makes use of market stabilization mechanisms, such as buffer stock or export quotas, as traditionally introduced into international commodity agreements. These agreements normally aim to stabilize the market price within a specified range. If an indexation principle were applied, then the price range would have to be adjusted upwards in line with increases in the prices of imports of the countries exporting the commodity in question.[34] Clearly, the ability to make such upward adjustments depends on the body operating the agreement exercising effective control over supplies coming on the market, while such adjustments would not be viable if consumers had readily-available alternatives (e.g. synthetic substitutes, in the case of natural raw materials). However, for a limited group of commodities, particularly where demand is relatively price-inelastic, and where production is wholly or mainly in developing countries, indexation would be technically feasible.

A second approach, known as 'indirect indexation', would not involve intervention in commodity markets, but would instead compensate exporting countries for foreign exchange losses incurred as a result of adverse movements in their terms of trade. Indirect indexation was envisaged as a possible mechanism for those commodities for which direct indexation was not feasible.[35]

The indexation concept, however, met with strong and determined opposition from Group B countries, partly on the grounds that it would inevitably lead to further global inflationary pressure, and partly that (in its direct form) it would interfere with the free play of market forces. The advocates of indexation, on the other hand, pointed out that indexation could not be a significant cause of inflation in developed countries, but was rather an element which would strengthen the motivation for controlling inflation in these countries;[36] it should instead be viewed as a protection for developing countries against the adverse effects of that inflation. As regards the free play of market forces, indexation was simply the extension to the international sphere of the 'income parity' concept which lay behind the domestic agricultural support programmes operated by most of the developed market-economy countries themselves.

The UNCTAD IV resolution on the Integrated Programme for Commodities makes no mention of indexation, which was henceforth no longer a 'live' issue as such, reflecting in this way Group B opposition to the concept. However, the idea of establishing a link between commodity prices and the prices of imports by developing countries was not lost, since the resolution called for "... negotiated price ranges, which would be periodically reviewed and appropriately revised, taking into account, *inter alia,* movements in prices of imported manufactured goods, exchange rates, production costs and world inflation, and levels of production and consumption."[37] It remains to be seen, however, whether any international commodity agreement in fact attains this particular objective.

IV. Longer-run development issues

(a) Access to markets

It will be recalled that in addition to international commodity agreements and adequate compensatory financing, Dr. Prebisch had advocated measures to be taken by developed countries to improve access to their domestic markets for the commodity exports of developing countries. These were three complementary lines of action which were, in his view, required to offset the tendency to deterioration of the terms of trade of commodity exporting developing countries. This line of reasoning was generally accepted at UNCTAD I, which recommend that developed countries should not create new barriers to the commodity exports of developing countries; that existing tariffs, internal fiscal charges and quantitative restrictions should be reduced or eliminated; and the policies which support domestic production of primary commodities in developed countries should be modified so as to reduce their adverse effects on imports.[38]

This was, however, only a recommendation and no specific arrangements were made for its implementation in practical terms. Negotiations for the reduction of trade barriers continued in the framework of GATT in the form of 'rounds' of multilateral trade negotiations. However, neither of the major 'rounds' of the 1960s and 1970s, the Kennedy Round and the Tokyo Round, resulted in significant trade concessions for developing countries' exports of primary commodities.

The major trade barriers confronting the commodity exports of developing countries are those imposed by developed countries as part of their systems of domestic farm-income support. These barriers not only reduce the extent of the market in developed countries for imports of primary commodities, but by the same token they increase the available supply in third markets, leading to reductions in world prices.[39] Though this issue has been raised on many occasions in UNCTAD inter-governmental bodies, the developed market-economy countries have consistently maintained that GATT, and not UNCTAD, is the proper forum for any serious effort to reduce trade barriers. However, GATT has so far proved unable to obtain any significant reduction in the level of agricultural protection.

(b) Processing and marketing

The disappointingly slow progress in establishing the Common Fund and in negotiating new stabilization agreements for individual commodities was no doubt an important factor in focusing attention on the other elements of the IPC. Apart from compensatory financing, discussed earlier, these included in particular the expansion of processing of primary commodities in developing countries and the enhancement of the participation of these countries in the international marketing and distribution of their commodity exports.

The need for developing countries to expand their commodity processing industries in order to export higher value products, as well as to serve as a base for further industrialization, has been generally recognized since the foundation of UNCTAD. A major constraint has been that virtually all developed countries impose substantially higher barriers, both tariff and non-tariff, to imports of commodities in semi-processed and processed forms than to imports in crude, unprocessed forms. Estimates by various analysts have indicated that developing countries would attract substantial additional export earnings if these trade barriers were made less discriminatory against processed commodities.[40]

Exports of processed commodities from developing countries are also frequently limited by various restrictive practices of transnational corporations, such as their prohibition or restriction of exports by firms in developing countries which process commodities with the use of technology acquired from these corporations. In addition, there are many internal constraints in the economies of developing countries, particularly the lack of adequate finance for investment in capital-intensive processing plants and in the associated infrastructure, which limit the opportunities for the development of local processing industries.

While some of these constraints can best be dealt with at the national level, or by common policies adopted by the developing producing countries concerned, clearly any substantial acceleration of processing for export will depend heavily on international co-operation designed to reduce existing trade barriers and facilitate the provision of financial and technical assistance for particular processing projects.

The processing issue is related, in many respects, to that of marketing and distribution. A very substantial proportion of the commodity exports of developing countries is handled by transnational corporations, while for a number of important commodities a few large corporations control a high percentage of either the production or exports of developing countries, as well as the principal transport and marketing channels. Vertically integrated market structures often act as barriers designed to protect profit margins, while entry into only one stage provides only limited market access. The dominant market power of many of the transnationals involved therefore allows them to capture a disproportionate share of the benefits of the commodity trade of developing countries.

That UNCTAD has turned its attention to these inter-related problems of processing and marketing is a sign that these fundamental issues concerning market structure and its influence on the prices received by developing countries for commodity exports are now the subject, for the first time, of detailed analysis and policy discussion among governments. It remains to be seen, however, whether such discussion will lead to agreement on general principles, if not on specific measures, to promote processing activities in the developing countries or to enhance the participation of these countries in the international marketing and distribution system.

V. An assessment

Looking back on two decades of UNCTAD's activities on primary commodities, an overall assessment of their effectiveness can now be attempted. It is useful, to begin with, to make a distinction between two different functions of UNCTAD activity, the generation of new ideas, new concepts and new approaches to the problems of trade and development, and the provision of a forum in which consultations and negotiations among States can be held for the conclusion of international conventions or agreements on specific issues. This is not to suggest that the two functions are not closely inter-related—clearly, negotiations must be based on sound concepts and analysis if their results are to be viable—but simply that very different considerations arise when assessing the results of UNCTAD activity in each of these areas.

There seems little doubt that UNCTAD's principal impact so far has been an intellectual one, in effecting a major change in generally accepted views of the nature of the development problem, and particularly of the constraints on the development process arising from the linkage between the economies of developing countries with those of developed countries. While Dr. Prebisch's original analysis, as presented at UNCTAD I, may not have been fully accepted, particularly by developed market-economy countries, it nonetheless provided the conceptual framework within which the "development dialogue" between rich and poor countries was henceforth to take place. The sharp change in the views and attitudes of governments after the creation of UNCTAD was clearly evident in the area of commodity analysis and in proposals for remedial action. After UNCTAD I, the link between international commodity policy and the development needs of the developing countries swiftly came to be the common assumption of both developed and developing countries.

UNCTAD's intellectual contribution has not been confined to a general analysis of the development problem, but has been marked also by a series of very specific proposals for changes in the existing system of international economic relations designed to assist in the evolution of a more efficient and equitable international system. In the commodity area, such proposals include the idea of a Common Fund, the integrated approach to dealing with the commodity problem, the indexation of commodity prices and many others. Though many such proposals were, in the event, frustrated at the political level, they reflected UNCTAD's position as a fount of new and relevant proposals for specific international action.

The 'UNCTAD approach' to commodity issues gradually spread to other international fora, such as the Food and Agriculture Organization, the Councils operating international commodity agreements, the UN Economic and Social Council (ECOSOC) and even the UN General Assembly itself. Whereas previously the problems of individual commodities had tended to be considered in isolation, they came increasingly to be put in the development context, with remedial policies being proposed by relevant offshoots of the 'Group of 77' developing countries, which was born with UNCTAD.

No less important has been the spread of interest in the development problems of poor countries in the world academic community and in the media. The resolution on the Integrated Programme for Commodities, to take a noteworthy example, gave rise to an intense discussion in academic journals of its theoretical basis, desirability and feasibility, while the Programme itself became a focal point for supportive activity by a large number of non-governmental organizations in virtually all the developed market-economy countries.

The IPC also provided the opportunity for UNCTAD to become a major forum for inter-governmental consultations and negotiations, and so to fulfil the second of its twin functions mentioned above. In the three years following the Nairobi Conference in 1976, there was a vast expansion in the number of UNCTAD meetings, reflecting in the main the additional consultations and negotiations on the Common Fund and on the problems of individual commodities.[41] While these intensive efforts did result in an agreement to establish the Common Fund albeit, as mentioned earlier, in an emasculated form, the negotiations on individual commodities proved largely unsuccessful.[42]

The failure to bring the negotiations on at least the majority of the 18 commodities specified in the Nairobi resolution to a successful conclusion has meant that there still exists no international 'safety net' to support the prices of the commodity exports of developing countries at even minimal levels of cost of production in times of general oversupply. The lack of such a 'safety net', which could have been provided by a series of price-stabilizing agreements, has already had very serious adverse consequences for developing countries heavily dependent on primary commodity exports. Prices of these commodities fell sharply in both 1981 and 1982, reflecting the continuing recession in developed market-economy countries as well as the impact of high interest rates. With the prices of their essential imports, particularly oil and manufactures, higher than in the late 1970s, the non-oil exporting developing countries entered the 1980s with a drastic deterioration in their terms of trade and in their capacity to import. As a consequence, a large number of these countries have been forced to cut back on their development programmes or to abandon them altogether.

The difficulties experienced in negotiating price-stabilizing agreements might at first sight appear somewhat surprising, in view of the widely accepted argument that such agreements would be to the mutual interests of both developing and developed countries. As the first Brandt Commission report argued, unstable commodity prices generally have an adverse effect on innovation and on the improvement of productivity in developing countries, while making rational fiscal and economic planning much more difficult.[43] It could also be argued that fluctuations in commodity prices often result in misleading signals for investment decisions, and consequently in a waste of resources.

For developed countries, too, there are avoidable costs resulting from commodity price fluctuations: sudden jumps in commodity prices accentuate inflationary pressures with consequent loss of output and employment following remedial deflationary measures;[44] volatile markets for certain commodities force enterprises in developed countries to hold larger stocks than would otherwise be needed; while the adverse effect of price uncertainty on investment in new capacity and in productivity improvement is likely to lead in the future to shortages of a number of essential raw materials required by developed countries. International price-stabilizing agreements are therefore likely to bring real benefits to developed countries and, in particular, to make the task of economic management less difficult.

Opposition to the conclusion of price-stabilizing agreements by certain developed-country negotiators has, however, been strong on occasions. One reason is the belief that such agreements will eventually become a means for raising prices above the trend, though in practice this does not appear likely since importing countries would have an equal say with exporters in determining revision of agreed price ranges. For commodities with terminal markets, opposition to price-stabilizing agreements has also come from trading interests which fear that reduction in price fluctuations will reduce speculative activity and hence their own profits.[45]

More generally, opposition by developed country negotiators to the establishment of price-stabilizing mechanisms for individual commodities has been based on the grounds that this would interfere with the 'free play of market forces'.[46] Implicit in this argument are the assumptions that actual commodity markets are perfectly competitive, that there is perfect factor mobility and full employment and that there are no market 'imperfections' (such as oligopoly or state intervention). On these and related assumptions, it can be shown that the free play of market forces will result in an optimum allocation of resources and a maximum level of global welfare or real income.

However, actual commodity markets do not conform to these assumptions. Many of these markets have tended to become dominated by oligopolistic or oligopsonistic structures, reflecting very largely the dramatic postwar expansion of the market power of transnational corporations, as well as the intervention of governments in the determination of prices. In fact, a wide range of commodity prices are essentially 'administered', depending on decisions by private corporations or governments.[47] Moreover, when actual markets exhibit large price fluctuations, the price mechanism fails to provide a sure guide to new investment and to rational resource allocation.

The 'free market' philosophy expounded by the developed market-economy countries in the UNCTAD commodity negotiations contrasts sharply, moreover, with their own domestic policies, which in most of these countries are firmly interventionist. The Common Agricultural Policy of the EEC is only an extreme example of governmental regulation of domestic markets for commodities. Yet the same countries strongly oppose regulation of most of the international markets for commodities, even though the objective is merely price stabilization, and not price raising (as under their own national agricultural regimes). It would appear that, as John Cuddy argues, developed country negotiators "will use or discard [particular theories] as fits their purposes in the negotiations".[48] This conclusion has particular force when one considers that where developed countries are major exporters of a commodity (e.g., wheat), then they have been prepared to give serious consideration to international regulatory action.

The UNCTAD commodity negotiations are also beset by other difficulties. In some cases, of which tea is a notable example, the conclusion of a price-stabilization agreement has been held up because the main producing (developing) countries cannot reach a consensus on the division of a global export quota. Difficulties of quota allocation have also resulted in the suspension of operative agreements from time to time. Moreover, there are complex technical problems to be overcome in formulating viable regulatory schemes for a number of commodities, while for others such as perishable foods buffer stock mechanisms would not be feasible.

Another important constraint on the rate of progress in the various commodity negotiations has been that, with the exception of those on natural rubber, the developing producing countries had no common prepared position on key issues. In the conclusive negotiations on natural rubber, the producers not only presented a common set of proposals for early international action, but also elaborated alternative proposals for producer co-operation in the event of a breakdown in the negotiations with developed importing countries.

These various difficulties could all be overcome, given time and goodwill, as well as the willingness to innovate in the use of alternative stabilization mechanisms. However, the general philosophical objection by the developed market-economy countries to commodity market intervention appears to be an abiding one. Their antipathy towards international price-stabilization measures also seems to be the explanation for two recent trends in UNC-TAD commodity negotiations.

First, on the insistence of the developed market-economy countries, the new agreement on natural rubber, as well as the re-negotiated agreement on cocoa, have been limited to using only buffer stocks for stabilization purposes. The cocoa agreement had previously relied on a combination of buffer stocks and export quotas, while for natural rubber the developing countries had also strongly pressed for the use of export quotas. Consequently, these agreements have been considerably reduced in their efficacy in defending a given floor price, as was clearly demonstrated in the price collapse of 1980–82.

Second, the developed market-economy countries have consistently steered the negotiations on new agreements for other commodities away from price stabilization and towards 'development' measures, such as productivity improvement, cost reduction and market promotion,[49] aspects which should yield direct benefits not only to developing exporting countries, but also to developed importing countries in terms of greater certainty of future supplies, at lower cost, than would otherwise be the case.

As a result of these trends, reflecting the 'free market' philosophy of the major developed market-economy countries, one essential element of the original concept of the Integrated Programme, i.e., the stabilization of commodity prices and the improvement of the real income of developing countries through increased exported earnings, has been effectively undermined. At the same time, the omission of the price stabilizing function from most of the potential agreements still under discussion will inevitably reduce still further the significance of the 'first window' of the Common Fund.

It would indeed appear that the conclusions of Javed Ansari's analysis of the voting at UNCTAD I, quoted earlier, still hold good as regards the recent commodity negotiations: the developed market-economy countries are satisified with the existing organization of commodity markets and have no wish to make significant institutional or structural changes. Indeed, though the strengthening of the commodity sector of the economies of developing countries by the mechanisms envisaged in the IPC for the stabilization of prices and export earnings would bring benefits to developed as well as to developing countries, this consideration seems to be outweighed by the fear felt by the developed countries that their present predominant role in world commodity markets might be reduced and that this, in turn, might lead to a reduction in their share of the benefits of world commodity production and trade.

VI. The outlook for the 1980s

The developing countries entered the 1980s in a sharply deteriorating world economic environment, having to cope with a dramatic decline in the prices of their commodity exports by increasing their borrowings at high rates of interest, rescheduling their existing debts or, more generally, by reducing their essential imports and thus cutting back their development programmes.

There is little doubt that the Integrated Programme for Commodities of 1976 contained all the essential elements of a viable strategy for strengthening the commodity sector of the world economy, and particularly that of the developing countries. But in the new situation of the early 1980s that Programme needs to be complemented by a package of immediate measures of financial support for developing countries heavily dependent on commodity exports, including support for the holding of national stocks to avoid further distress sales on a falling market.

For such an emergency support package to be negotiated as a part of a wider strategy incorporating the Integrated Programme, several changes of an essentially political character would seem to be required. Perhaps the most important would be the recognition by the developed market-economy countries that the crisis in international commodity markets is a manifestation of a deep-seated structural crisis in the world economy, and that the required structural readjustments cannot be effected without positive measures to strengthen the commodity sector. This, in turn, would imply the recognition that in a period of continuing recession and inflationary pressures, the 'free play of market forces' by themselves cannot be expected to achieve this objective.

A second essential requirement would be that developing countries themselves adopt common policies and evolve credible alternative policy options in case their negotiations with developed countries continue to be frustrated. As the example of the natural rubber agreement indicates, such alternative policies can enhance the bargaining position of developing countries and speed negotiations on commodity market regulation to a successful conclusion. But producer-country co-operation can go further than this by adopting policies, such as trade preferences for imports from other developing countries, which will accelerate the growth of their own markets for primary commodities and, to this extent, assist in the expansion of the global market.

These requirements add up to major changes in political ideology and attitudes, but they would appear to be essential prerequisites if UNCTAD is to retain its creditability as the central United Nations forum for the negotiation of an effective international strategy to strengthen the position of the world's commodity producers.

---

1. *Final Act* of the United Nations Conference on Trade and Employment, Havana, 1947–48, Chapter VI.

2. ECOSOC resolution 30(IV). A recent survey of the issues involved can be found in Jock A. Finlayson and Mark W. Zacher, "International trade institutions and the North/South dialogue", in *International Journal*, Vol. 36, No. 4, Autumn, 1981.

3. See R. Prebisch, "Towards a New Trade Policy for Development", in *Proceedings of the United Nations Conference on Trade and Development*, Vol. II, United Nations, New York, 1964. For a further discussion of the terms of trade issue, see Sidney Dell's contribution to this volume and *Inequalizing trade?* by J. Spraos, Oxford University Press, 1983.

4. *Proceedings, op. cit.*, Vol. I, p. 23.

5. General Assembly resolution 1995 (XIX), para. 23(a).

6. The developed market-economy countries, so called because of their inclusion in a 'List B' for the purposes of election to membership of UNCTAD bodies. (Similarly, the socialist countries of Eastern Europe are known in UNCTAD as 'Group D').

7. Javed A. Ansari, "Environmental characteristics and organizational ideology: UNCTAD and the lessons of 1964", in *British Journal of International Studies*, No. 4, 1978.

8. See "The development of an international commodity policy", in *Proceedings* etc., second session, Vol. II, United Nations, New York, 1968.

9. *Ibid*, pp. 34–35.

10. Conference resolution 16 (II) listed 19 such commodities.

11. New international agreements on sugar and cocoa were concluded in 1968 and 1972, respectively, but both were the result of a long period of negotiations, rather than of the Conference resolution.

12. For a detailed review of the resolution 16 (II) programme, see *Proceedings etc.*, third session, Vol. II, pp. 61–66, United Nations, New York, 1973.

13. Conference resolution 83 (III).

14. General Assembly resolution 3202 (S–VI).

15. *New directions and new structures for trade and development*, report by the Secretary-General of UNCTAD to UNCTAD IV, United Nations, New York, 1977, p. 22.

16. The need for an overall international commodity institution had been expressed by J.M. Keynes in a Memorandum of April 1942 (published later as "The international control of raw materials", in *Journal of International Economics*, Vol. 4, No. 3, August 1974).

17. Provision was made, however, for additional commodities to be subsequently included in the Programme.

18. Conference resolution 93 (IV). See *Proceedings* etc., fourth session, Vol. I, pp. 6–9, United Nations, New York, 1977.

19. A total capital of $6 billion was proposed, of which $2 billion would be capital contributed by governments, the rest being raised by borrowing.

20. For a useful summary of this Agreement, see I.S. Chadha, "The Common Fund for Commodities", in *Trade and Development: An UNCTAD Review*, No. 2, Autumn 1980, United Nations, Geneva.

21. As Dragoslav Avramovic, writing in 1978, stated: "A financial federation of [individual] agreements ... would not be the common fund the developing countries, as a group, need and have demanded during the last three years. In such a confederation there will be no possibility of taking initiative in markets other than the five or six [subject to international agreements] and therefore no protection for the many producers of other commodities; no catalytic effect; and little change in the present pattern of market finance and therefore market control", *Journal of World Trade Law*, Vol. 12, 1978, pp. 380–381.

22. By mid-June 1984, 77 countries, accounting for 46·4 per cent of the directly contributed capital, had ratified the Common Fund Agreement, whereas a minimum of 90 countries, accounting for at least two-thirds of the directly contributed capital, is required for its establishment.

23. See *Commodity issues: a review and proposals for further action,* report by the UNCTAD secretariat, TD/273, 11 Jan. 1983, Chapter II.

24. *Ibid.*

25. Resolution 93 (IV), Part III, para. 2(f).

26. Conference resolution 125 (V).

27. 12 developed market-economy countries voted against.

28. Over the period 1963 to 1975, total drawings by developing countries under the IMF facility amounted to only 11 per cent of these countries' shortfalls in export earnings ("Action on Export Earnings Stabilization and Developmental Aspects of Commodity Policy," report by the UNCTAD secretariat, in *Proceedings,* etc., fifth session, Vol. III, p. 93, United Nations, New York, 1981).

29. For a detailed review of the limitations of the IMF facility, as well as of the STABEX compensatory financing scheme of the EEC, see the UNCTAD secretariat report to UNCTAD V *Compensatory financing: issues and proposals for further action,* TD/229/Supp. 1; also J.D.A. Cuddy, "Compensatory financing in the North-South dialogue", in *Journal of World Trade Law,* Vol. 13, No. 1, 1979.

30. Conference resolution 157 (VI) adopted by 90 votes to 1, with 10 abstentions (3 from Group B and 7 from Group D).

31. "Pricing policy, including international price stabilization measures and mechanisms", in *Proceedings,* etc., third session, Vol. II, (United Nations, New York, 1973).

32. Resolution 3083 (XXVIII).

33. Resolution 3202 (S–VI), Part I, para. 1(d).

34. A number of variants can be imagined: e.g. linking to prices of manufactures in which the commodity is used; to changes in the cost of production of the commodity; or to changes in the exchange rate of the currency, or currencies, in which trade in the commodity is denominated. For further discussion, see "Pricing policy . . .", *op. cit.*

35. For a detailed discussion of these varieties of indexation, and of their implications, see *The indexation of prices,* a study by the UNCTAD secretariat, TD/B/503/Supp. 1, 30 July 1974; also J.D.A. Cuddy, *International Price Indexation,* Saxon House, 1976.

36. *New Directions . . ., op. cit.,* pp. 24–25.

37. Resolution 93 (IV), Part III, paragraph 2(c).

38. Recommendation A.II.1, which was adopted without dissent (*Proceedings,* etc., first session, Vol. I, pp. 26–30).

39. In addition, where third markets are reduced to a residual character by developed country protectionism, as with sugar, 'free market' prices inevitably become very unstable.

40. For a review of these estimates, see *Processing before export of primary commodities* (TD/229/Supp. 2), in *Proceedings* etc., fifth session, Vol. III, *op. cit.*

41. The number of weeks of official UNCTAD meetings rose from an average of 44 during the period 1971–76 to 115 in 1979, an increase of almost 170% (*Proceedings,* etc., fifth session, *op. cit.,* p. 501).

42. As already mentioned, only one new price-stabilization agreement (for natural rubber) had been concluded by mid-1984. There have also been "commodity development agreements", without price provisions, for jute and jute products and for tropical timber.

43. *North-South: A Programme for Survival,* London, Pan Books, 1980, Chapter 9.

44. For an analysis of the impact of commodity price rises on industrial activity in the developed countries, see Nicholas Kaldor, "Inflation and Recession in the World Economy", in *Economic Journal,* no. 86, December 1976.

45. Such opposition appears to have been a significant factor in the long delay, which lasted over a decade, in negotiating the first International Cocoa Agreement (1972).

46. This opposition to price stabilization for individual commodities appears to be in conflict with the commitment embodied in the IPC resolution, which was accepted by all UNCTAD members in 1976.

47. For a perceptive discussion of commodity market imperfections, see G.K. Helleiner,

"World market imperfections and the developing countries", in William R. Cline, *Policy Alternatives for a New International Economic Order*, Praeger, 1979.

48. For a detailed critique of the arguments in favour of the 'free play of market forces', as put forward by developed country negotiators in UNCTAD, see J.D.A. Cuddy, "Theory and practice in NIEO negotiations on commodities", in G.K. Helleiner (ed.), *For Good or Evil: Economic Theory and North-South Negotiations*, University of Toronto Press, 1982.

49. This is the case in the negotiations on cotton, hard fibres, jute and bananas; for copper, exceptionally, the lack of progress essentially reflects disagreements among the producing countries.

THE TECHNOLOGICAL TRANSFORMATION OF THE THIRD WORLD: MAIN ISSUES FOR ACTION

by Surendra J. Patel

It is commonplace to hear that the world is passing through a period of turbulence, in the economic, social, political and military spheres. Behind these crises is a central challenge: to find an orderly way of accommodating the changing economic and strategic strengths of nations. The powerful and the established are preventing the weak and the new from finding a place for themselves in the comity of nations. There is one feature of these crises which has been less noticed. The problem children of the post-war world were the developing countries. Now the developed countries, both socialist and capitalist, have joined their ranks. The search for a more rational international order has consequently become all the more urgent. It is our very survival which hinges on its attainment.

It is recognized that the international community consists of unequal partners. The Third World, including China, accounts for 75 per cent of its population, but for some 25 per cent of its exports, 20 per cent of its imports and GNP, 15–20 per cent of its industrial output and less than 5 per cent of its capital goods output. Nowhere is this inequality expressed more sharply than in the technological field: the Third World has only a 2 per cent share in worldwide research and development expenditure, 1 per cent in patent holding and nearly no share in development of 'frontier technology'. To remedy this vast discrepancy, to bridge the gap between the promise of technology and its practical impact on Third World development, is undoubtedly the central task of the latter part of the twentieth century.

I. Constraints of the current international technological order

It was only a few hundred years ago that Europe was the recipient of the benefits of scientific and technological advances in the rest of the world. Technology flowed then from east to west. The last two centuries have completely reversed this flow.

The explosive development of technology since 1850 has radically altered the ability of people to produce more and varied goods and services. Productivity per person may be used as a measure of technological change incorporated in the production process. It may have barely doubled between the birth of Christ and 1850. But in the 130 years since then, it has increased 12 to 15 times in the industrially advanced countries. This vast transformation of their technological strength has in the process created a treasure-house of technologies which other nations can draw upon for their progress.

The fundamentally unique character of technology makes it amenable to exchange and diffusion. It is unlike any other commodity. It is the engine of man's capacity to produce all goods and services. It is the genetic code, not of one man, but of all mankind. It has grown cumulatively over the centuries. Most nations have contributed to this growth, but fortunately none has retained predominance over it for long. It can be transferred to persons across national frontiers with little regard for climate, race, religion or sex. Once transferred, both its original owner and the new acquirer have it; the real economic cost of its transfer is zero. Unlike other commodities, it cannot once obtained be worn out by its consumption. Once mastered, it has a long life. Once adapted, it gains in value. It has much that is reminiscent of Shakespeare's description of Cleopatra: "Age cannot wither her, nor custom stale her infinite variety".

And yet, the constraints on exchanges of technology are severe. In this respect its achievements differ fundamentally from those of science, which are universal, free and open to access by anybody. Possession of technology by contrast is jealously guarded as a secret by its owners. Property rights in it give its owners command over the terms, conditions and price for its exchange.

The introduction of such property rights in technology is a relatively recent phenomenon. Private property in goods has a long history, even longer than the appearance of the market. Classical economists, Adam Smith, Ricardo and Marx, centred much of their work on the production and exchange of commodities, but did not concern themselves with private ownership of technology. Perhaps the very recent origin of ownership rights in technology has helped it escape the type of questioning to which property in commodities has been subjected throughout history.

Although technology is so very unlike land, its exchange across nations is reminiscent of practices in the feudal age. It is usually leased not sold. Under the feudal system, tenants and sharecroppers enjoyed neither fixity of tenure or rent, nor independence in planning crops or improving land and methods of cultivation. Nor did they have control over the marketing of their products. A fundamental restructuring of the legal fabric governing land relationships in Europe had therefore to precede the modernization of the techniques both of agricultural production and of farm management. Without it, it would have been impossible to create the necessary social and economic climate for the blossoming of the industrial revolution.

There is a certain structural parallel between lease of land under feudalism and transfer of technology now. When technology is leased, it forms part of a much larger transaction covering provision of capital goods and equipment, often of intermediate products, construction of plant, management, marketing and finance. In short, it is a part of a larger package. Even in the arrangements and agreements dealing more or less exclusively with the transfer of technology, there are several restrictive practices: for instance, exclusive grant-back provisions, challenges to validity of patents, exclusive dealing; restrictions on research, use of personnel, adaptations, export and publicity, as well as on use of alternative sources of technology, goods or services, use of technology after expiration of agreements and use of technology already imported. The draft of the International Code of Conduct on the Transfer of Technology now under negotiation in UNCTAD lists some 20 such restrictive practices.

Such restrictive practices, often illegal or inadmissible under national laws in the developed countries, have been widely imposed in transactions with the developing countries. On the other hand, technology suppliers have accepted only the lowest possible degree of responsibility and obligation concerning the implementation of technology agreements, to guarantee that the developing countries will reap the full benefits of their transactions.

In consequence, the developing countries have been unable to obtain the technology they need at the right price, under the right terms and conditions or at the right time. They have to pay heavy direct and indirect costs. In addition, there are several hidden costs, such as transfer pricing, inordinate delays, wrong choices of technology, which are not even amenable to measurement. The annual recurrent cost of their technological dependence, estimated to range from $30 to 50 billion, is vastly greater than the inflow of external resources they currently receive on public or private account.

It was against this background of heavy constraints imposed by the unequal structural relationship between the developed and the developing countries that the world community addressed itself to a series of urgent tasks: to diminish such dependence, to reduce the inordinate costs incurred, to ensure the developing countries' access to technology at reasonable prices, to overcome the constraints imposed by near monopoly of technology in the hands of powerful transnational corporations, to strengthen the technological capacity of the developing countries and accelerate their technological transformation, to establish a New International Technological Order.

The Declaration on the Establishment of the New International Economic Order (NIEO), adopted by the United Nations General Assembly in

1974, gave a powerful stimulus to the restructuring of existing technological relations among countries. Appropriately, it was adopted on 1 May. It attached key importance to technology (rather than science). Technology is referred to twice in the very opening paragraph of the Declaration. The Declaration underlines that "Technological progress has also been made in all spheres of economic activities in the last three decades, thus providing a solid potential for improving the well-being of all people". Despite this solid potential, its benefits "are not shared equitably by all members of the international community".[1]

At the dawn of human awakening, Aristotle had already concluded: "Enough has been said about the theory of wealth-getting; we will now proceed to the practical side". Over the passage of time, many must have been amused, if not indeed distressed, at Aristotle's cheeky confidence. For the dispossessed nations, the initiative taken towards the establishment of the NIEO represents but a first faltering step in proceeding with the practical side. Restructuring technological relations is, without a doubt, an integral part of this process.

Among the 20 principles on which the NIEO is to be founded, the Declaration included:

> "Giving to the developing countries access to the achievements of modern science and technology, and promoting the transfer of technology and the creation of indigenous technology for the benefit of the developing countries in forms and in accordance with procedures which are suited to their economies."

II. The setting in 1970

Technology has been a relatively new subject for national and international attention. Trade, finance, police, war and foreign affairs had constituted the classical nucleus of government administration. Since the nineteenth century, other areas have been added: agriculture, industry, labour, transport, education, health, social services and so on. But despite the strategic influence of science and technology on all aspects of life and government, these subjects had for long been confined either to the ivory towers of intellectuals or to the crowded attics where the inventors of technology were supposed to be working. No wonder formulation of policies on science and technology remained for long the handicapped, or retarded, child of the public family.

A glance at the world in 1970 provides some interesting insights. Since its hesitant start in the nineteenth century, the joint stock company with limited liability had become the dominant form of economic enterprise. Some family firms held out. But most had adopted the new form. Small enterprises, owned and operated by individuals, had been pushed to the peripheral business of retail, and even there large firms were capturing a dominant share of the market. Adam Smith's famous market place, where 'Queen Competition' ruled with a magic wand, had become a handy fairy tale to disguise the interactions between entrepreneurs and politicians.

The post-1945 economy, dwarfed by the twin disasters of the Great Depression and the second World War, was set on the threshold of its golden age of growth. Empires were crumbling. Tariff barriers were being brought down. Market size was blooming. Research, invention, innovation and development were no longer preserves of isolated individuals. They were organized on a massive scale, mainly financed by the public sector.

Fortified by easy access to finance, technology, capital goods and management, the large transnational enterprises were set to establish a new international business order. It was easy to appreciate the significance of the slogan 'sovereignty at bay'. Its logic seemed impeccable. A few hundred transnationals, protected by shiny steel armour and mounted on white chargers, were to reorganize in the most efficient manner the inter-related systems of world production, trade, capital flow and technology. If some nation states, some of them small and some far from small, obdurately refused to welcome this development, that was indeed unfortunate for them. There was little, it was thought, they could do to stop the powerful movement forward that was under way.

In this setting, the Third World countries were particularly vulnerable. They were poor, many of them starving. They were ill-equipped, bereft of capital goods industry and technological skills, the two elements in which technology is embodied. They had little or no say in forming the international economic institutions or the established framework of policies for economic exchange among nations. Many had just finalized their declarations of independence and some were still drafting their constitutions. Powerful persuasion had made them pass laws, almost immediately after adopting their new flags and constitutions, on attracting foreign investment. "Now that you have gained political independence", they were told, "leave it to the experts in finance, technology and management, and foreign investors will recreate in your unhappy lands the marvels of progress they have created in their own homelands, the countries that are now so developed". The promise was indeed too great, the perception on which it was based too feeble. Nearly all the developing countries fell in line with liberal investment laws, competing with each other in offering incentives to outsiders. The archaic inherited laws on patents and trade marks, guaranteeing in a most perverse manner monopolisitic control of their domestic markets to external enterprises, continued to adorn their statute books and guide their policies. Some of these nation states were so small that one had to put 20 of them together to match the gross sales of just one average transnational corporation.

True enough, some of them had started having doubts about the idyllic promise of progress through external dependence. Others had seen its adverse side in the experience of their own incipient development. This applied particularly to China, India, Iraq, South Korea and the Philippines in Asia, to Algeria, Egypt, Ethiopia, Ghana and Nigeria in Africa, to the countries in the Andean Pact (Bolivia, Chile, Colombia, Ecuador, Peru, with Chile replaced by Venezuela later) Argentina, Brazil, Cuba and Mexico in Latin America, and to Romania and Yugoslavia in Europe. Their own experience had shown the weaknesses and pitfalls of this promise. Its lessons were pertinent, for after all they not only constituted nearly three-quarters of the population of the Third World but also contributed some 90 per cent of its industrial output. They were, in a manner of speaking, the front-line states in the development effort.

The lessons of their experience were assessed. In consequence, there emerged a search for new policies aimed at reducing their technological dependence, strengthening their own research, development and technological capacity and marking the path for their accelerated transformation. Opposition was severe, obstacles often insurmountable. Their paths were to be marked later on with reversals and zig-zags.

But the search was on. This was the setting, in 1970, in which two bodies born in 1964 of the same process heralding the arrival and self-assertion of the Third World on the world stage, the Group of 77 and UNCTAD, began the search for new policies to reduce the technological dependence of developing countries and to increase the pace of their technological transformation.[2]

III. Shaping the main issues

The last decade has been devoted to shaping the main issues. In that process, three forces have combined: the Group of 77 as the spearhead, UNCTAD as the forum and the UNCTAD secretariat as the scribe. The process has drawn upon many sources: individual and collective experience in the developing countries, and the rich inheritance of the many-sided development debate, particularly in its post-war phase when the Third World placed its own spokesmen as protagonists on the world stage: intellectuals, United Nations staff, government representatives.

(a) The emergence of the main issues

Coming to terms with the main issues has proved to be a long, trying and often a tortuous process, as was to be expected in such a novel experience for UNCTAD and its member States. A brief mention is worth making of the stages involved in the process and the forms it took. Attention to a new issue was usually drawn by the Group of 77, basing itself on the individual or group experience of its member States. This was then explored in some depth by the secretariat.[3] Such investigation combined strict standards of scholarship with search for practical solutions. It pointed out future lines of action involving negotiations between South and North and operational action by countries of the Third World individually or in groups.

This was followed by consideration in governmental bodies. The form of one outcome of such consideration was always certain: a report. But it also produced resolutions, containing agreements on several issues which were considered obscure or contentious at the beginning and on directives for the steps ahead for the given issue or for opening up new issues for future discussion.

Ten years is a twinkle in the time span of history, but not so short a period for organizations. A broad spectrum of technological issues has been considered, debated, negotiated and even on some occasions decided by roll call vote in the appropriate UNCTAD forum:[4] the Intergovernmental Group on Transfer of Technology, which was established within UNCTAD on 18 September 1970, and which was later transformed into the Committee on Transfer of Technology on 13 September 1974. UNCTAD's contribution to shaping technology issues flows directly from its unique position. It is the only United Nations body which has inter-governmental machinery exclusively devoted to technology issues. Other UNCTAD bodies have however also made specific contributions: for example, several special expert groups, the Trade and Development Board, Conference sessions in Santiago (1972), Nairobi (1976), Manila (1979) and Belgrade (1983), and the special negotiating machinery, set up under UNCTAD auspices, of the United Nations Conference on an International Code of Conduct on the Transfer of Technology, including the Intergovernmental Group preceding it, and the Interim Committee following the fourth session of the Code Conference in April 1981.

(b) The trinity of issues

It would be vain to look into the agendas of the various bodies mentioned for a quick guide to the main issues. Nor would a careful perusal of dozens of resolutions which have been passed on the subject provide such a guide. Except to the persistently careful scholar, most of these contain veritable UNese tedium, in which quantities of chaff are utilized to hide, often with contrived care, the kernel.

The existing conditions under which technology is being exchanged raise several worrisome questions. How is this flow organized? What are the relative economic, financial and technological powers of the parties to the transactions? On the one hand, we mainly find the powerful transnational corporations of the developed countries, and on the other, the incipient, weak, private or public enterprises in the Third World. How can bargaining between such inherently unequal partners safeguard the real interests of the weak? What role in this process is played by the provisions of the Paris Convention protecting industrial property: patents, trade marks, etc? How are the costs of technology determined? Who determines them? Why do suppliers of technology insist upon imposing restrictive conditions in technology transactions? What are the legal or other bases for these restrictions? What are the visible and invisible limitations on the access of the developing countries to technology? Why are the costs of the technological dependence of the Third World so high? How can they be reduced? Is there a need for new standards and norms and for new institutional directions? What steps should be taken to strengthen the technological capacity of the developing countries and to build the muscle necessary for accelerating their technological transformation?

This is only a sample of the questions raised in secretariat contributions and in debates and negotiations in UNCTAD bodies. These are not questions of idle academic curiosity. They relate to the very bases of the economic and technological power wielded by the already established countries, and to the compelling need of the new nation states to improve their access to the vast accumulation of world technology. Resolution of these questions would have profound implications for changing the current balance of power among nations.

These questions dealing with several facets of the existing technological order can be grouped into a trinity of broad issues: restructuring the existing international legal environment for the transfer of technology; strengthening the technological capacity of developing countries and accelerating their technological transformation; and supplementing national, sub-regional and inter-regional initiatives by technical and operational co-operation. Each of these initiatives, which have taken a long time to mature, deserves to be briefly reviewed here.

IV. Restructuring the international legal environment

It was to be expected that the international legal environment would be among the first subjects to attract the attention of the world community. After all, technological relations among nations reflected the highest degree of structural asymmetry. The need to establish some degree of equilibrium was therefore imperative. The search for such a balance has centred upon two important initiatives by the Group of 77: revision of the Paris Convention on the Protection of Industrial Property and establishment of an International Code of Conduct on the Transfer of Technology.

(a) Revision of the Paris Convention and the industrial
     property system

The Paris Convention was adopted by a bare dozen countries in Paris in 1883. It has formed the basis for granting monopolistic property rights to patent and trade mark holders. In the six revisions of the Paris Convention, these rights were further consolidated. It is only recently, and particularly through the initiative of the developing countries, that a new revision of the Paris Convention has become the subject of negotiations. The main thrust of this revision is to balance the monopolistic rights of patent holders with some semblance of obligations on their part, to safeguard the interests of the developing countries by facilitating use of patented techniques in the production process, and to restrict abusive practices originating from the grant of exclusive rights to the holders of patents.

Of the $3\frac{1}{2}$ million patents currently in existence in the world, only a tiny fraction, amounting to no more than 1 per cent of the world total, is held by nationals of the developing countries. Of all the patents granted by the developing countries, some 80 per cent are held by foreigners, mostly transnational corporations of five developed countries (the United States of America, the Federal Republic of Germany, the United Kingdom, Switzerland and France). Of all the patents granted by the developing countries to foreigners, over 95 per cent are never used in the production process in the developing countries. They are plainly used to secure import monopolies. Of all the inter-relationships between the developed and the developing countries, the industrial property system is clearly the most unequal, and certainly the most inequitable.[5]

In this way, practices concerning patents in the developing countries, following the international standards established by the Paris Convention, have legalized a peculiar, or perhaps 'perverse' would be the right word, situation of reverse preference granted to foreign patent holders in the markets of the developing countries. They protect private profits at public cost.

In many a developing country, patent registration is carried out in the same way as registration of births, deaths and marriages, and often by the same office. The cost of registration does not even cover the cost of administration. The operation of this system, almost exclusively in the interest of external patent holders, requires public subsidies on the same plane as education, health and other social services.

It is against this background that the developing countries have asked for a fundamental revision of the industrial property system. The changes proposed include the introduction of inventors' certificates, granted to applicants of any nationality (as is presently the case in socialist countries of Eastern Europe and in Algeria), exclusion of some products and processes, particularly pharmaceuticals, from patent protection in view of their critical importance to the development of the Third World, a severe limitation of the duration of patents for specific products or processes, a shift in favour of greater recognition of the public interest in the balance between monopoly rights of private patent holders and general public interest, strengthening of disclosure requirements, stricter provisions for compulsory licensing and revocation as remedies for non-use of patents, and strong provisions against abuses in patent licensing agreements.

The negotiations on the revision of the Paris Convention are taking place at the World Intellectual Property Organization. But the main impetus for the revision was furnished by the pioneering work in UNCTAD.

(b) Establishment of the International Code of Conduct on
    the Transfer of Technology

The revision of the Paris Convention is mainly an attempt to improve a bad bargain blindly entered into in the age of dependence. A much more far-reaching initiative on the part of developing countries is their effort to establish a code of conduct on the transfer of technology.[6] The negotiations on the Code, in sharp contrast to the situation at the time of signing of the Paris Convention in 1883, are being carried on by 10 times as many governments, representing 25 times more people, producing 200 times as much income. Their combined research, development and technological personnel is at least 500 times larger, and R and D expenditure over 1,000 times greater, with two-thirds absorbed by the public sector. This may give a measure of the difference in the settings for the original Paris Convention and the UNCTAD Code.

The Code has its origin in resolution 39 (III) adopted at UNCTAD III (Santiago, 1972). Since then, inter-governmental negotiations have been going on in UNCTAD, passing through three phases. The first phase involved three negotiating sessions in 1974–75 and the deliberations of UNCTAD IV (Nairobi, 1976), which finally answered in the affirmative the question whether inter-governmental negotiations should be initiated to formulate, negotiate and adopt the Code. The second phase was signalled by the establishment, by the Nairobi Conference in 1976, of the Inter-governmental Group of Experts on the International Code of Conduct on Transfer of Technology. The Group held six sessions between November 1976 and June-July 1978. A significant part of the text of the draft Code was agreed to by consensus during these sessions. But many of the substantial issues could not be resolved.

The third phase was initiated with the convening in 1977 by the United Nations General Assembly, under the auspices of UNCTAD, of the United Nations Conference on an International Code of Conduct for the Transfer of Technology. The Conference started its first session in October 1978 and assembled four more times between then and April 1981.[7]

The contents of the draft Code, as agreed at the fourth session of the Conference on 10 April 1981, consist of a preamble and ten chapters, which on the basis of their substance may be subdivided into four groups.

The first group contains definitions and scope of application (Chapter 1) and objectives and principles (Chapter 2). The Code is to be universally applicable in scope and is addressed to all parties to transfer of technology transactions (from developed, capitalist and socialist, as well as from developing countries) and to all countries, irrespective of their economic and political system and their levels of development.

The second group of provisions concerns the establishment of universally-applicable standards, regulating technology transactions and the conduct of parties to them. They cover three areas: determination of practices and arrangements on technology which are deemed to be undesirable under certain conditions (Chapter 4); identification of responsibilities, obligations and rights of parties to technology transactions (Chapter 5); and applicable law and settlement of disputes (Chapter 9).

The third type of provisions relates to the steps to be taken by governments to meet their commitments to the Code. These may be classified under three categories: national regulation of transfer of technology transactions (Chapter 3); provisions concerning special treatment for developing countries (Chapter 6), which concern only those transactions in which the acquiring party is a developing country; and provisions concerning international co-operation between States (Chapter 7), on a bilateral, multilateral, regional or inter-regional basis, to facilitate the flow of technology and the strengthening of the technological capacity of developing countries.

The fourth group of provisions relates to the application and implementation of the Code, both at national and at international levels. The steps to be taken at the national level are defined in Chapter 3. The scope of its implementation at the international level is defined in Chapter 8, which would establish institutional machinery on the Code within UNCTAD, to be serviced by the UNCTAD secretariat. Its functions, the procedure for the review of the Code, and guidelines for assistance by the UNCTAD secretariat to States are laid down in that chapter.

The basic text of the Code, comprising around 200 articles and sub-articles, is nearly complete. A number of issues are still outstanding. Some of these are minor. But two issues are of central importance: the application of the Code to 'parent-subsidiary' transactions within transnational corporations; and the regulation of restrictive practices. These issues are critical, and constitute the core of the Code.

The General Assembly, in resolution 36/140 of 16 December 1981, decided to establish "as a special measure to accelerate the finalization of the code, an Interim Committee of the Conference to consider and seek solutions to the outstanding issues and make proposals thereon". The Interim Committee met in three sessions during 1982. It proposed new draft texts for resolving the issues so far outstanding. Intensive consultations with individual governments and with regional groups during 1983 prepared the ground for the fifth session of the Code Conference, which was convened in October-November 1983.

The fifth session of the Conference could not reach agreement on the entire text of the Code, as the General Assembly had requested. In several important aspects, however, the Conference made sufficient progress to create a conviction among all member countries of UNCTAD that, barring a wholly unexpected deterioration in international relations, the Code would definitely be adopted at the sixth session of the Conference, to be convened not later than the first half of 1985. This conviction grew from several advances at the fifth session of the Conference. First, agreement was finally achieved on the whole of Chapter 5 on rights and obligations of parties. In addition, a number of provisions of a certain importance in the Preamble and in Chapters 1 and 2 of the draft Code were also resolved. Of perhaps greater significance were the various proposals considered with a view to resolving the critical issues outstanding in Chapter 4 on restrictive practices and Chapter 9 on applicable law and settlement of disputes; these proposals prepared the ground for future agreement on these most difficult chapters in the Code. The sixth session could therefore draw upon all these advances and successfully conclude UNCTAD's commitment to the establishment of this new international instrument.

V. Strengthening the technological capacity of the Third World

The conclusion of the negotiations on the Paris Convention and the Code will pave the way for the most fundamental reform of technology exchange ever experienced. The framework will be laid for new relations among countries. The exchange of technology will be free from some of its absurd restrictions, almost feudal or semi-feudal in character. The exchange of technology will then take place within an increasingly commercial framework. It will not have removed all the obstacles. It will not have yet freed Prometheus, the ancient equivalent of modern technology, from the fetters that bound him. It will not have yet created the technological muscle with which the developing countries could accelerate their technological transformation. There is, however, little doubt that the construction of a new legal framework will be a big landmark, offering the promise of a vastly greater flow of technology among nations.

Perhaps an order of magnitude may help here. By the end of this century, the countries of the Third World may have undertaken over $10,000 billion of capital formation at 1980 prices. This is indeed larger than the sum total of all the goods exported across national frontiers from the time that tribes began to trade till the eve of the Second World War. The technology content of such an immense volume of investments is, by any standards, big and undoubtedly good business. For the Third World, it is bigger than business itself. It is the very key to their transformation.

A rapid realization of such a transformation will require far-reaching changes at the national level in the developing countries, an area of critical concern in UNCTAD.[8] Third World countries will need new laws, regulations and policies, and appropriate institutions for implementing them. From near obscurity, policies on technology will have to move to centre stage in development planning. The scientific and technological manpower which the countries of the Third World are building with heavy investments will then have concrete tasks to tackle.

There is no need to stress that a restructuring of the international environment governing the exchange of technology among countries could at best only provide a helpful framework for such exchanges. The real change in contractual agreements among parties can only come by strengthening the technological capacity of the countries of the Third World. UNCTAD has devoted considerable attention to this subject. It covers a new framework of policies, laws and regulations and the establishment of appropriate institutional structures to implement them. Attention is now being focussed on the detailed steps necessary for the formulation of technology plans as an integral part of national development plans. All these subjects will create the conditions necessary for formulating and adopting appropriate strategies for the technological transformation of developing countries.[9]

The earlier general discussions on technology policies have begun to give way to consideration of specific sectors of critical importance, e.g. pharmaceuticals, food processing, capital goods, energy and skill exchange.[10] The UNCTAD secretariat has contributed several important studies which provide the groundwork for an intensive discussion of technological options at the national level, the scope for collective self-reliance among the developing countries at the sub-regional and regional levels, and the manner in which these could be supplemented at the international level. Three meetings of governmental experts, dealing with food processing, capital goods and energy, were convened in 1982. Their deliberations, with a decisive accent on action by the developing countries themselves, have furnished operational guidelines for concrete action on these critically important sectors.

In consequence, the framework governing transfer, acquisition, distribution and development of technology has vastly altered over the last decade.

More than 30 developing countries have already established one type or another of national machinery to formulate and implement new laws, regulations and policies on technology. Together they account for around three-quarters of the population and about 90 per cent of the industrial output of the Third World. In some countries, the questions relating to technology have already begun to be dealt with at the ministerial level.

Regional centres on transfer and development of technology have already been set up for the continents of Asia, Africa and Latin America. They are still weak. Close working links with national centres on technology, or their equivalent institutional arrangements, remain to be established. The early post-war period with its open door policy towards external investments, with no questions asked, has come to an end. Its place is being taken by new policies and new structures. They are beginning to produce their effect in strengthening the technological capacity of the Third World. The stage is therefore set for new initiatives.

These developments have altered, perhaps in a decisive manner, the setting for world-wide technology exchanges. We might look back a moment at the naive vision, propagated by certain influential figures in the fifties and sixties, that the sovereignty of the newly independent and the smaller countries was an obstacle to an efficient management of the world economy. They were convinced that the great actors on the world economic stage, three to four hundred transnational corporations, would so effectively reorganize world economic control and management in the next few decades as to make these nation states mostly irrelevant. These advocates of 'sovereignty at bay' are much less vocal now. The new nation states are still weak, and their technological dependence is no doubt extreme. But the practice of treating them as imbecile actors in the 'theatre of the absurd' is fading away as a fashion. They are slowly becoming legitimate actors on the world's political and economic stage.

The idea that the developing countries' growth is indissolubly linked to that of the developed countries also had many advocates in the past. But it is very weak in theory, and poor in support from historical precedent. It is not however surprising that most international organizations have been among its most loyal partisans. In recent years, the old faith seems to be weakening for a wide variety of reasons; its advocates are losing confidence in their pronouncements.

It is edifying to remember that Professor W. Arthur Lewis, in the lecture he delivered in Stockholm in December 1979, on receipt of the Nobel Prize for Economics, had begun to cast doubt on this apparently inevitable linkage.[11] The possibilities of autonomous growth of many developing countries, particularly the larger and more advanced among them which account for over 75 per cent of the population and certainly a much higher share of income of the Third World, are being seriously explored. There is little doubt that, in any such exploration, the key factor will be the reduction of the technological dependence of these countries, and a corresponding increase in their capacity to formulate their own strategies for their technological transformation. That would open up the prospects of a dynamic interpretation of inter-dependence between the various components of the world economy, which must lead to a greater role for the Third World in the management of the world economy, and to a more rational, a more equitable and a more equal world order. This process of accommodation could, however, be quite turbulent.

VI. Operational assistance and co-operation

Since its inception, UNCTAD has been relatively strong in policy formulation. It has brought to world attention a large number of critical issues requiring adjustment of structural relationships between the developed and developing countries. This effort has been inadequately matched by active responses at the national level. Unlike many other international bodies, the operational contacts of UNCTAD with the national level, let alone its capacity to offer technical co-operation, have been limited. One of the central concerns of the development of its work programme on technology was therefore to overcome this weakness as far as possible.

The Group of 77 has consistently stressed the importance of creating an institutional base within UNCTAD to respond to requests from the developing countries for assistance on a wide variety of technological issues. As a result, the Advisory Service on the Transfer of Technology was established in UNCTAD in 1976. It provides assistance in the formulation and implementation of technology policies, plans, laws and regulations, in sectors of critical importance as well as others; in the establishment and strengthening of institutional infrastructures to implement the policies, plans, laws and regulations; and in the traning of personnel and exchange of experience among developing countries.[12]

The Advisory Service has acted as a link between the exploration of issues in UNCTAD leading to the formulation of policies, and their transmission to and implementation at the national level in developing countries. Its activities may be grouped into four major areas.

(a) Formulation of technology policies and plans and their
   implementation

UNCTAD missions have already been sent to some 45 developing countries in response to their requests for an examination of their current technology policies, for a review of the existing institutional structure (or 'disorder', as has often been the case) and to make recommendations on policies and institutions in the light of the specific conditions and requirements of the country concerned. The reports of these missions, containing concrete recommendations, have provided the basis for national action in these countries. In consequence, most of the developing countries have now set up appropriate institutional structures, variously referred to as Centres, Departments, Divisions and even in some cases Ministries, and have begun to lay down the main lines of national policies, plans and strategies aimed at accelerating their technological transformation.

(b) The establishment of regional and sub-regional centres
    for the transfer of technology

The Advisory Service has provided active assistance in the establishment of regional centres, or equivalent institutional structures, for co-operation in the field of the transfer and development of technology. Such centres have now been established for Asia and Africa; the West Asian countries have decided in principle on the establishment of such a centre, but the mechanisms for its operation have yet to be worked out; and the Latin American countries have established a network of technological information (RITLA).

(c) Sectors of critical importance to developing countries

UNCTAD's operational work began with pharmaceuticals, for which the technological dependence of the Third World is most severe. It has examined the pharmaceutical problems of Costa Rica, Cuba, Guyana, the Philippines, the United Republic of Tanzania, Nepal, Venezuela and the Maldives. In several of these cases, UNCTAD's recommendations for new and rational policies on pharmaceuticals have been accepted by these Governments for implementation. UNCTAD has contributed towards initiating technology planning for the pharmaceutical sector in Ethiopia.[13]

UNCTAD has also been actively involved in opening possibilities for co-operation in the pharmaceutical sector at the sub-regional level. The countries of the Caribbean region and of the West African Economic Community have already, with the assistance of UNCTAD and the CARICOM and CEAO secretariats, developed operational blueprints for the establishment of sub-regional centres for pharmaceuticals. These centres, which are to be linked with national institutions, are to organize joint purchases of pharmaceuticals and initiate specialized production of pharmaceuticals in the sub-region.

This type of co-operation is being extended to other critical sectors, e.g. food processing, capital goods and energy.

(d) Training programmes, workshops and exchanges of
     personnel

A series of training programmes, workshops and seminars, organized by the
Advisory Service, have served as important instruments to elucidate policies
and open new avenues of co-operation. Nearly 500 officials from more than
70 developing countries have already participated in these programmes.
They have helped alter the very language used in dialogues dealing with
technology.

VII. The Third World in the 1980s: some reflections on choices for policy

The technological transformation of the countries now considered 'developed' in reality spanned over a century. It involved a rise in productivity per
person of about 2 per cent per year, a fairly modest rate. For most of these
countries the process of transformation was heavily concentrated in shorter
periods, barely half a century.

As the process of technological transformation began to spread, there has
been a big rise in the technological distance between those already transformed and those awaiting to begin. During the 1870s, productivity per
person in Great Britain was not even twice as high as in the new entrants,
e.g. Germany and the United States of America. By the end of the First
World War, the comparable ratio had leapt forward; productivity per person
in the countries already industrialized then was five time higher than in the
new entrants, e.g. Japan and the USSR. By the 1970s, the ratio of productivity per person between industrialized countries and the Third World had
risen to over ten. This technological gap is both a problem and a promise. It
is a problem since much larger advances have to be made to come anywhere
near the current levels of productivity in the developed countries. At the
same time, it is a promise since incorporation of new technological advances
in production processes can now raise productivity to levels vastly greater
than was possible during the period of the technological transformation of
the developed countries. Policy choices in the period ahead will have to
produce a mix which helps surmount the problems and fulfil the promise.
The following reflections may be of some relevance in establishing an
appropriate framework of approach to these choices.

1. The world still remains highly unequal. Great changes have however
taken place. Since 1950 the national product of the developing countries has
increased annually at an average rate of 5.5 per cent and is now five times
higher. Even per capita incomes, despite high rates of net population
growth following very successful reductions in mortality rates, have increased 2.5 times.

2. The combined industrial output of the Third World,[14] including mining, is now seven to eight times its 1950 level and approaching 20 per cent of world industrial output today, or almost two-thirds of the whole world's industrial output in the early 1950s. From textiles and toys, it has now grown to cover a whole spectrum of new and modern industries, including capital goods.

3. Even more impressive is the rise in the two elements which embody technology and therefore act as the spearhead of technological transformation: capital goods and skills. Gross capital formation in real terms has grown tenfold, rising from around 10 per cent to over 20 per cent of their GDP, consolidating the quantum jump needed for a sustained process of growth. The expansion of education has undergone a veritable explosion. Enrolment in institutions of higher learning has increased twelve-fold. One out of every four students in such institutes in the whole world now comes from a developing country. The engine of technological transformation of the Third World is not only on the rails, but has already begun to pull ahead.

4. New difficulties have admittedly arisen. Debt burdens have mounted. Service charges on these debts alone are beginning to absorb more foreign exchange than imports of capital goods and technology. Oil price rises have further accentuated the already precarious balance of payments position of many countries. Protectionist policies in the developed countries are cutting into the little progress that was made in enlarging manufactured exports. In fact, the Third World now faces a very real danger that the developed countries, plagued by unemployment and domestic instability, will launch an export offensive to throttle the industrial base which has been built in the Third World.

5. The evolution of a strategy for steering the process of technological transformation will have to be based on the building blocks of the past, which we outlined earlier, but will also have to explore many new ways of meeting the challenges ahead. There is one consideration which may prove pertinent in this process of search. It is an instructive reflection on the course of the economic development of nations that in most cases the origin of the first stimulant to growth has come during depressed rather than buouyant world economic conditions. It was precisely during the Long Depression of 1872–94 that the big spurt in the growth of the United States, Germany and the Scandinavian countries took place. Again, it was the Great Depression of the 1930s which witnessed the real building up of the two major new entrants to industrialization in the twentieth century, Japan and the USSR.

6. The developed countries may well be set now for very slow growth at best and a long recession at worst over the next two decades. The Third World will have more actively to explore the broad potential of its collective

self-reliance. A strategy centred upon expanding domestic output, utilizing national resources to the maximum, responding to domestic needs and co-operating with other developing countries could form the bed-rock of firmer technological transformation than has been the case with externally dependent development so far.

7. The basis for the formulation of such a strategy is provided by a major contribution from the UNCTAD secretariat in a study entitled "A strategy for the technological transformation of the developing countries", (TD/277). The sixth session of UNCTAD in Belgrade (June 1983), basing its deliberations on this study, adopted the future programme of work of UNCTAD under the title "Towards the technological transformation of developing countries" (resolution 143 (VI)). The Conference directed that the subject be taken up for exclusive consideration at a special session of the Committee on Transfer of Technology which was convened early in 1984. The special session has determined the modalities for the formulation of such a stategy, opening the way for the adoption and implementation of strategies at the national level for the technological transformation of developing countries.

8. UNCTAD's active involvement in technology issues has brought them to the forefront of world attention. The focus of emphasis has shifted from transfer of technology to development of national technological capacity, calling in turn for a decisive shift from *ad hoc* policies to technology planning as an integrated part of national development planning, and to the adoption of long-term strategies aimed at bringing about the technological transformation of the Third World. This, in brief, is the groundwork of a New International Technological Order.

---

1. General Assembly resolution 3201 (S–VI).

2. I should here stress the central contribution which Wladek Malinowski made to the development of UNCTAD's work on technology. It was he who had initiated this work at UNCTAD II in New Delhi in 1968, in the context of his responsibilities as Director of the Division for Invisibles. He had asked me in 1969 to explore the possibilities of what UNCTAD could effectively do in this new area of international concern. From then until his retirement from UNCTAD in 1974, I was granted the unique opportunity of working with him very closely. In the year Wladek retired, technology issues were enshrined in the Programme of Action for the New International Economic Order; the Committee on Transfer of Technology, the first major structural change in UNCTAD's inter-governmental machinery, was established; and UNCTAD's work programme had already grown to include such critical issues as the establishment of a code on transfer of technology, revision of the industrial property system and strengthening the technological capacity of developing countries. A big stride indeed.

3. The secretariat's contributions have played a key role in defining just how far possibilities extend. The mortality rates of United Nations documents are, however, usually high. Most of them reach oblivion very soon after the meeting at which they are considered. This life cycle also applies to several secretariat works on technology. Some which have formed the cornerstone of new initiatives are referred to below at appropriate places. (For a Select Bibliography, see TD/B/C.6/INF.2/Rev.3).

4. Most resolutions on technology have been agreed to by consensus. Only three were decided by vote. The Intergovernmental Group on Transfer of Technology at its third session, adopted on 26 July 1974 resolution 2 (III) on the role of the patent system in the transfer of technology to developing countries, with one vote against (the Federal Republic of Germany). On the same date, it adopted resolution 3 (III) on the possibility and feasibility of an international code of conduct in the field of transfer of technology. The latter resolution was adopted, in a roll-call vote, by 31 votes to 4, with 4 abstentions. (The Federal Republic of Germany, Switzerland, the United Kingdom and the United States of America voted against.) On 9 October 1981, the Trade and Development Board at its 23rd session adopted, in a roll-call vote and by 75 votes to 16 with 9 abstentions, resolution 240 (XXIII) inviting the Secretary-General of UNCTAD to prepare a report on common approaches to legislation and regulation dealing with the transfer, application and development of technology in developing countries.

5. See *The role of the patent system in the transfer of technology to developing countries*, report prepared jointly by the United Nations Department of Economic and Social Affairs, the UNCTAD secretariat and the International Bureau of the World Intellectual Property Organization, United Nations publication, Sales No. E.75.II.D.6 (TD/B/AC.11/19/Rev.1); *The international patent system: the revision of the Paris Convention for the Protection of Industrial Property*, report by the UNCTAD secretariat (TD/B/C.6/AC.3/2); *The role of trade marks in developing countries*, report by the UNCTAD secretariat, United Nations publication, Sales No. E.79.II.D.5 (TD/B/C.6/AC.3/3/Rev.1).

6. For the origin, the first substantive case and the state of negotiations as at November 1983, see: report of the working group on a code of conduct on transfer of technology, of the Pugwash Conferences on Science and World Affairs, May 1974 (TD/B/AC.11/L.12); *An international code of conduct on transfer of technology*, report by the UNCTAD secretariat, June 1974, United Nations publication, Sales No. E.75.II.D.15; *Draft international code of conduct on the transfer of technology*, TD/CODE/TOT/41.

7. The March-April 1981 session was formally its fourth session, however, as the second meeting was known as its "resumed first session".

8. See *Towards the technological transformation of the developing countries*, report by the UNCTAD secretariat (TD/238); *Technology planning in developing countries*, study by the UNCTAD secretariat (TD/238/Supp. 1); *Planning the technological transformation of developing countries* (TD/B/C.6/50); and *A strategy for the technological transformation of developing countries* (TD/277).

9. See *Guidelines for the study of the transfer of technology to developing countries*, study by the UNCTAD secretariat, United Nations publication, Sales No. E.72.II.D.19; *Major issues arising from the transfer of technology to developing countries*, report by the UNCTAD secretariat, United Nations publication, Sales No. E.75.II.D.2; *Technological dependence: its nature, consequences and policy implications*, report by the UNCTAD secretariat (TD/190); *Formulation of a strategy for the technological transformation of developing countries: Proposals for an outline*, note by the UNCTAD secretariat (TD/B/779). In addition, there were several case studies, e.g. on Chile, Ethiopia, Sri Lanka, Spain, Hungary, Iraq, Japan and the USSR.

10. *Inter alia*, see: on pharmaceuticals, *Major issues in transfer of technology to developing countries: A case study of the pharmaceutical industry* (TD/B/C.6/4); *Technology policies and planning for the pharmaceutical sector in the developing countries* (TD/B/C.6/56), *Guidelines on technology issues in the pharmaceutical sector in the developing countries* (UNCTAD/TT/49); on capital goods, *Case studies in transfer of technology: Purchase of capital goods and technology in the iron and steel sector—The case of Bokaro, India* (TD/B/C.6/27); on food processing, *The food processing sector in developing countries: some recent trends in the transfer and development of technology* (TD/B/C.6/66); on energy: *Energy supplies for developing countries: issues in transfer and development of technologies* (TD/B/C.6/31/Rev.1); on skill exchange, *Co-operative exchange of skills among developing countries: Policies for collective self-reliance* (TD/B/C.6/AC.4/8/Rev.1), *The reverse transfer of technology: A survey of its main features, causes and policy implications* United Nations publication, Sales No. E.79.II.D.10; on electronics: *Electronics in developing countries: issues in transfer and development of technology* (TD/B/C.6/34). There are also several country studies on most of these sectors.

11. Professor Lewis had earlier been sceptical about the capacity of the developing countries

to develop at even 4 per cent a year. But after noting the much higher growth rates that were achieved, he concluded: "[The developing countries] have demonstrated beyond doubt their capacity to use physical and human resources productively". See his "The slowing down of the engine of growth", in American Economic Review, vol. 70, No. 4, Sept. 1980, pp. 555–564.

12. Among the most important reports on these topics are the following: *Technology planning in developing countries,* study by the UNCTAD secretariat (TD/238/Supp.1); *Handbook on the acquisition of technology by developing countries,* United Nations publication, Sales No. E.78.II.D.15; *Planning the technological transformation of developing countries* (TD/B/C.6/50); *Guidelines on technology issues in the pharmaceutical sector in the developing countries* (UNCTAD/TT/49); *Advisory Service on Transfer of Technology,* progress report by the UNCTAD secretariat (TD/B/C.6/59).

13. See *Technology and Development Perspectives of the Pharmaceutical Sector in Ethiopia* (July 1983), joint study by the UNCTAD secretariat and the Ethiopian Centre for Technology.

14. Including Yugoslavia, Romania and the socialist countries of Asia.

FINANCE, MONEY, DEVELOPING COUNTRIES AND UNCTAD

by Iqbal Haji*

At the time of UNCTAD's inception, and indeed for several years after, financial and monetary issues[1] did not occupy a major place in its deliberations. The emphasis in UNCTAD's early years was on trade issues, as was to be expected given its perception of trade as the engine of development, a perception embodied in the name of the organization. The trade-oriented approach to development has the rather positive political implication, in the North-South context, that developing countries prefer to earn external resources for their development through the mutually-beneficial mechanism of trade, rather than depending on aid transfers. Accordingly, UNCTAD sought to respond primarily to the dissatisfaction of the developing countries with declining terms of trade, fluctuating commodity prices and restricted access to the markets of the industrial countries, a dissatisfaction which, reinforced by the conviction in the developing countries that GATT did not adequately respond to their needs, had motivated the establishment of the organization.

The emphasis on trade issues also reflected the historical realities of the early sixties. Aid and other transfers were relatively small and, while the developing countries pressed for increased and improved transfers and various schemes were canvassed with these ends in view, finance was not a major issue of contention in the incipient South-North dialogue. Moreover, the international monetary system, based on a gold exchange standard, was relatively stable and, prior to the establishment of UNCTAD, had not come under serious scrutiny from the viewpoint of the developing countries.

By and large the predominant emphasis given to trade issues in UNCTAD has continued to this day, but financial and monetary matters have gained in relative importance.[2] There are several reasons for this. The high growth targets for the developing countries set by the United Nations in its successive Development Decade strategies, currently at 7 per cent, have implied an elevated level of external financial requirements for develop-

---

* The author's thanks are particularly due to Sidney Dell for his incisive comments, and to Helga Hoffmann and Anne Miroux, as well as to Gloria Auditor for secretarial assistance.

ment. The world financial system has become more integrated, thereby giving rise to more North-South issues; the growth of the Eurocurrency markets, outside the purview of any national legislation or control, symbolizes this evolution. The move to a 'managed floating' exchange regime in the early seventies has made for a less stable environment, which developing countries feel unable to influence. And the emergence, after the oil price increases in the seventies, of unprecedented surpluses and deficits raised new problems and changed the political configuration of global financial and monetary issues, at least for a while.

In broad terms, the OECD countries and the Bretton Woods institutions still retain their dominance in deliberations and decisions concerning financial and monetary issues. But UNCTAD is now making an important contribution to international deliberations on money and finance as they relate to development, and to shaping decisions taken in other fora. The present paper attempts to assess this contribution, highlighting the main areas dealt with, the results achieved and the problems related to this now important function of UNCTAD.

It should be pointed out that UNCTAD contributes to international discussions on finance and money at three distinct levels. First, the UNCTAD secretariat conducts a wide range of studies on the relationship between finance, money and development, and convenes expert groups on these subjects. This work is of relevance to the entire international community. Secondly, the secretariat provides much substantive back-up to the developing countries in formulating their common positions on financial and monetary issues and in preparing for their discussions and negotiations with the industrial countries. Finally, UNCTAD's inter-governmental bodies (*ad hoc* groups, the Committee on Invisibles and Financing related to Trade, the Trade and Development Board, and the four-yearly Conference sessions) provide governments with universal fora in which to discuss money and finance issues openly, and eventually to come to concrete agreements.

UNCTAD's stand[3] on finance and money may be presented very briefly in four inter-related and thus overlapping themes which provide the structure for this paper:

(i) In order to accelerate their development, developing countries need large volumes of *external finance* to pay for essential imports and, in some cases, to cover domestic development inputs as well. The terms, conditions and institutional framework for such finance need to be significantly improved to meet the requirements of these countries.

(ii) The *external debt* burden hinders the development process and has a negative effect on the global economy; that burden should therefore be reduced. The international framework in which debt problems are dealt with needs to be geared more closely to development objectives.

(iii) The *balance-of-payments* problems of developing countries are largely external in origin and beyond their control. Their nature is such that large amounts of finance are needed to support long periods of adjustment under terms and conditions which are also geared to the needs of development.

(iv) The *international monetary system* is fundamentally defective, inefficient and inequitable. It is in need of basic reform in the interest of all countries but especially of developing countries.

I. External finance for development

The need for external finance for developing countries arises from their inability to draw exclusively on domestic sources to finance the accelerated process of development envisaged by their national development plans and, since the sixties, by United Nations international development strategies.[4] As stated by Prebisch's 'trade gap' theory, a satisfactory rate of economic growth in developing countries requires greater amounts of foreign exchange than these countries could normally earn through 'free trade'. The growth of their earnings from trade is inhibited by the low income-elasticity of demand in the industrial countries for imports from developing countries and by the long-term tendency for the terms of trade of developing countries to decline. Far-reaching and converging measures in trade and finance are required to counteract these tendencies and fill the 'trade gap'.[5]

Successive statements on development strategy by the United Nations and UNCTAD have insisted that the primary responsibility for development lies with the developing countries themselves. In fact, the overwhelming part of investment in developing countries is financed by their domestic savings. However, this effort is both quantitatively and qualitatively insufficient for rapid development, leading to a need for external finance.[6]

External finance for development comes in many forms and shapes. It may be channelled to developing countries bilaterally or multilaterally. It may come in the form of concessional or non-concessional finance. Concessional flows are normally referred to as 'aid' or official development assistance (ODA). There is now a widely used criterion for distinguishing concessional flows from others; they should contain a grant element of at least 25 per cent at a discount rate of 10 per cent.[7] Non-concessional flows include a large variety of items such as export credits, lending by multilateral institutions on ordinary terms, commercial bank lending, bond issues by developing countries on international capital markets, and private direct investment. In 1983 developing countries received $103 billion of net external finance from all sources, of which $36 billion were concessional. In 1970 the corresponding figures in current terms were $19 billion and $8 billion.[8]

Over the years, there has been a large overall increase in the transfer of finance from industrial to developing countries and there have been significant shifts in its composition. The most important compositional change has been the increase in the share of non-concessional flows in the total, with a consequent rise in the overall cost of external finance to developing countries. As part of this trend, the share of private flows has grown, increasing the volatile element in total flows. The transnational commercial banks have become more active and influential. The role of multilateral institutions in channelling concessional finance also grew for a time, but has now steadied. Finally, a notably new development has been the growth of financial transfers among developing countries themselves, a result of the surpluses in OPEC countries which emerged during the seventies. However, the future of these flows is now in considerable doubt, since the OPEC countries as a group have moved into deficit.

The bulk of UNCTAD's efforts on external finance has gone into putting pressure on the developed countries to make a greater volume of concessional finance available to developing countries, both bilaterally and multilaterally. The principal instrument of pressure has been the '0.7 per cent ODA target', according to which the developed countries should annually consecrate seventy cents out of every one hundred dollars (0.7 per cent) of their GNP as aid to developing countries.[9]

Initially, the ODA target was accompanied by a 1 per cent target for all flows (concessional plus non-concessional), but developing countries have shown a distinct lack of enthusiasm for this concept. Indeed the 1 per cent target has now fallen into virtual disuse as far as the United Nations and UNCTAD are concerned. The OECD, however, continues regularly to publish data on 'all flows' and the 1 per cent target. This is not surprising since the OECD members have a relatively creditable record on this count. These OECD 'all flows' calculations include *gross* private flows into developing countries; profit and interest outflows from developing countries are not deducted from the inflows which give rise to them. In some years, such outflows have been quite considerable.

Another important early objective of UNCTAD with respect to concessional flows was to increase the proportion channelled through multilateral institutions. The Pearson Commission in 1969 recommended that 20 per cent of all ODA be distributed in this way, at a time when the actual ratio was about 16 per cent for the OECD countries as a whole. Pressure emanating from UNCTAD helped to achieve and surpass this objective, and the multilateral share of ODA has for some years been stable at around

30 per cent. This strengthening of multilateral institutions has been one of the more creditable achievements of development co-operation. The present outlook, however, is that there will probably be a downturn in multilateralism in aid. The distinct preference of the United States for bilateral aid in recent years is having a negative impact on the prospects for multilateral aid.[10]

In more recent years, prominence has also been given in UNCTAD to a sub-target of ODA for the 'least developed' countries (0.15 per cent of donor's GNP), but little progress is being recorded on this score. A large part of ODA continues to be allocated to the relatively better off developing countries. It should be noted that the distribution of ODA among recipient countries or categories of them is a particularly sensitive issue in UNCTAD bodies.

Questions relating to the quality of aid have also commanded much attention in UNCTAD, particularly in its early years. As has already been noted, the definition of ODA was determined more or less unilaterally by the OECD. There was much deliberation in UNCTAD, however, concerning the proportion of grants in total ODA, and norms for the terms of ODA loans. Partly in response to pressure in UNCTAD on these two points, OECD aid has improved quite significantly on both counts. In 1982, for example, 77 per cent of all OECD aid was in the form of grants, as against 60 per cent in 1971.

Another important qualitative aspect of aid discussed in UNCTAD was the 'tying' of bilateral aid to expenditure in the donor country.[11] In 1970, almost 80 per cent of bilateral OECD aid was tied. An effort was made within the OECD to respond to the pressure from UNCTAD and also from certain donor countries to reach an agreement to untie ODA. In 1971, the OECD countries came quite close to that aim, before the monetary upheavals of that year scuttled the attempt. Nonetheless, in 1981 the share of tied and partially-tied aid had fallen to just under 60 per cent of all OECD bilateral aid.

Other initiatives within UNCTAD have sought to make aid allocation more responsive to the sectoral preferences of developing countries, to increase the proportion of general programme aid as opposed to aid for specific projects, and to make aid flows more "predictable, assured and continuous".[12] ODA donors have been asked to make longer-term commitments, as against their usual preference for annual programmes.

The concept of 'automaticity' has also been introduced into the UNCTAD debate on finance for development. This concept would apply the principles of national revenue collection and distribution to the international community. It has been suggested that taxes and levies could be raised on specific types of incomes or transactions in the industrial countries or on certain international trade flows. These revenues would be automatically available as aid to developing countries, insulating the aid process from the caprices of national legislatures and administrations. Needless to say, 'automaticity' is still a futuristic idea and its complex technical and political aspects remain to be explored.

How much success can UNCTAD claim in the attainment of its objectives with respect to the volume and quality of aid? There is no doubt that the organization has been instrumental in creating a climate of opinion which is in broad terms favourable to more and better resource transfers to developing countries.[13] The absolute amount of aid has increased in most recent years. However, it has not kept pace with GNP growth. Since the sixties, ODA from the OECD countries as a whole has declined as a percentage of their total GNP. This overall trend has been heavily influenced by the poor performance of the largest donor, the United States, in relation to the 0.7 per cent target—which, it has to be said, its Administration has never accepted.

The ranking of donor performance in relation to that target, with the attendant publicity, has been on the whole a useful tool for influencing political and public opinion. In those donor countries with powerful public lobbies in favour of aid (Sweden, Norway, the Netherlands, and, at times, the UK) the ODA:GNP ratio has played an important part in mobilizing opinion. In recent years, public support has focused on aid for the least developed and other low-income countries. This may be why, during the current recession, overall aid levels have so far held up in the face of severe fiscal problems in many of the donor countries.

Nevertheless, the efforts of UNCTAD and other proponents of ODA have not succeeded in avoiding a rather widespread 'aid fatigue', especially in the United States. That country's posture on aid has a tremendous influence on other aid-giving countries. There is now in some of the donor countries a feeling that aid may be futile in face of the immensity and complexity of the development process, or at least a realization that aid is not and in fact could never be a simple answer to development problems. This reaction against an earlier, rather naïve, optimism is compounded in public opinion by images of wastefulness and corruption in the use of aid in the developing countries. Neither can UNCTAD claim much success in preventing aid from becoming more of a political and commercial tool. Such a trend might have been stemmed had more attention been paid to aid lobbies outside the immediate confines of the governments in the donor countries. A positive image of aid as a necessary and effective input into a mutual effort has yet to be generalized.[14]

Part of the problem on UNCTAD's side may be related to the fact that it has concentrated on making an overall case for aid in broad macro-economic terms. Yet those who matter on aid issues in the industrial countries respond much more to specific arguments for aid, on a sectoral or a geographical basis. This explains the success achieved by United Nations bodies in raising funds for programmes dealing with refugees, children, food, health and education.[15] In more recent years, UNCTAD has emphasized 'inter-dependence' or mutual interest as a motivation for aid. This is an important shift—away from an approach oriented purely to developing countries' needs—and the theme is beginning to find a place in the pronouncements of the industrial countries.

As regards non-concessional flows, which now occupy a central role in the development process of a large number of developing countries, UNCTAD's efforts have concentrated on the following:

—encouraging the industrial countries to increase those non-concessional flows which are directly under governmental control, e.g. export credits and non-concessional contributions to multilateral financial institutions;

—removing obstructions to developing countries' access to commercial banks and capital markets, especially bond markets;

—encouraging recourse to commercial borrowing through, for example, schemes for multilateral guarantees to underwrite such borrowings and interest subsidy schemes.

Developing countries have not yet succeeded in establishing themselves in the bond markets. This has much to do with the general difficulties of those markets in several industrial countries, which in turn are connected to either domestic financial or international monetary considerations. With respect to commercial borrowing, a great deal of effort has been invested by UNCTAD in the design of an 'export credit guarantee scheme' under which developing countries would sell their export paper in private capital markets.

As the international financial situation has developed over the years, especially since the recycling of OPEC surpluses became a critical element in the mid-seventies, non-concessional flows to developing countries have increased quite dramatically. Indeed, at the end of the seventies, the ratio of non-concessional flows to concessional flows in the net transfer of resources to developing countries was 60:40, the reverse of the situation at the beginning of the decade. The commercial banking system has been the lynchpin in this process. But the banks' perceptions of creditworthiness have barred a very large number of developing countries, especially the low-income ones, from access to the funds they distribute.

UNCTAD's ability to influence the course of these events is inherently limited for several reasons. Governments in the industrial countries are reluctant to interfere in private capital flows, or they are at least reluctant to be seen to be so involved. This reduces the scope of inter-governmental deliberations in bodies like UNCTAD. In any event, OECD countries are also reluctant to see an enlargement of the role of UNCTAD with respect to non-concessional flows, which they prefer to discuss, if at all, in the Bretton Woods institutions.

Developing countries have also shown a somewhat ambiguous attitude when these issues have come up in UNCTAD. On the one hand, as has been remarked, the new mix of concessional and non-concessional flows has increased the overall cost and the volatility of external financing to developing countries. Action in UNCTAD has not alleviated these problems. On the other hand, a number of developing countries (mainly Latin American together with some middle-income Asian countries) have benefited from the somewhat chaotic evolution of the international financial system, especially from the growth of the Euromarkets. Any enhancement of governmental or inter-governmental intervention in this field, these countries might argue, would inevitably attract attention to the disproportionate share of commercial bank funds they have managed to obtain. Any subsequent international action would prejudice their privileged access to those funds. There are therefore important obstacles to United Nations bodies' playing a more prominent role in relation to non-concessional finance.

Much concern has been expressed in UNCTAD at the overall incoherence of the system of financial transfers to developing countries, by which is meant the insufficiency, instability and high cost of such finance. Important gaps have been identified as regards the types and quality of finance needed for development. At one time, a proposal was made for a new fund similar to the World Development Fund proposed by the Brandt Commission.[16] No progress has been made on this idea.

A word about socialist countries, to wind up this overview of deliberations on development finance. References above to the developed or industrial countries refer in fact to the developed market-economies, i.e. the OECD countries. The socialist countries of Eastern Europe have recently come under increasing pressure from the developing countries to subscribe to the 0.7 per cent ODA target. They have strongly resisted this pressure, indeed have resented it, suspecting it to be a Western-inspired diversion. Their general line is that they are responsible neither for the state of underdevelopment in the Third World nor, consequently, for making up for it by giving aid. They imply that Western aid is simply compensation for past exploitation. They also point a finger at the private flows from the Western countries to developing countries, considering them powerful generators of resource transfers in the opposite direction, from the South to the West. They have repeatedly called for studies on such 'reverse transfers'.

At the 1982 session of the United Nations Economic and Social Council, the delegate of the Soviet Union, in an unprecedented step, announced that the ODA ratio of the USSR was 1.3 per cent of GNP, far surpassing that of the highest-performing OECD donor country. OECD sources have cast doubt on this estimate; the OECD calculation of the Soviet Union's aid shows a 0.15 per cent ratio to GNP, equal to that of the lowest-performing OECD member.

An important new participant in the discussions on finance for development is China. Now a member of both the World Bank and the IMF, China has consistently supported the developing countries' positions on financial and monetary issues. However, even while expressing interest in funds from external sources like the World Bank, China has carefully avoided any significant dependence on such finance for development. It has virtually no external debt to speak of and consistently maintains a healthy level of reserves. At least in the present early stage of its transition to a more open policy, China has weathered the recent global crisis with its head well above water.

II. Debt problems of developing countries

At the moment of writing few issues exercise the minds of development economists, government officials and politicians as much as the debt problems of developing countries. The manner in which these are resolved will have a profound impact on the future of development and on the entire range of North-South problems.[17] The debt issue generates tremendous controversy: on the one hand is the view that the problem really does not exist or, if it does, is being taken care of; on the other, there is the position which claims that unless the problem is resolved satisfactorily there will be no hope of world economic recovery and of accelerated development for many years to come.

UNCTAD's interest in the debt issue is a long-standing one. From the early days when the external debt of developing countries was still small, UNCTAD has been drawing attention to the burden that it imposes on the development process and calling for its alleviation.[18] This concern has grown with the size of the debt burden; during the seventies the total debt of developing countries more than quintupled.

Total disbursed debt and debt service of developing countries, 1971–1983

	($ billion) 1971	1977	1983 est.
Total debt	90	274	592
Total debt service	11	42	99
(of which interest)	3	13	47

Source: OECD, *Development Cooperation*, 1983 *Review*, Paris, 1983, p. 213

The debt burden of the Third World has come to symbolize the malfunctioning and the inequity of the international economic system, representing as it does the accumulation of the negative effects of insufficient and costly external finance, unsatisfactory trading conditions and the lop-sided institutional structures governing the world financial and monetary systems. The course of economic events in the seventies added to these woes. The total debt of developing countries is now probably the single most frequently cited indicator of the injustice of the international economic system.

The increase in the total external debt has been accompanied by important changes in its composition. The share of commercial debt with market-related interest rates has been rising and with it the cost of servicing the debt. Moreover, short-term debt appears to have become relatively more important, although it is not easy to reach an accurate conclusion on this score. In a very large number of developing countries, the servicing of the external debt, as well as the creditors' perception of such debt, have become decisive factors in those countries' development process.

Yet when they come to negotiate the issue multilaterally with the North, developing countries have shown a certain equivocation, which illustrates the difficulties they face. An increasing debt burden is in fact a logical outcome of their demands for access to private capital markets and for more external development finance in general. Developing countries could therefore be accused of confused thinking if they asked for more resources while simultaneously complaining of a high debt burden. There is a vague notion that a 'debt service ratio' (i.e. debt amortization plus interest as a ratio of total exports) of 20 per cent is the upper limit of financial prudence, but even this is controversial. In addition and even more important, creditworthiness as perceived by creditors is a key determinant of solutions to a country's liquidity problem.[19] It does a developing country little good, in trying to convince prospective lenders of its creditworthiness and sound financial management, if at the same time, in international gatherings, it complains about difficulties in coping with the burden of past debt.

Furthermore, debtor countries, especially the larger ones, tend to feel that they can get a better deal bilaterally, in private negotiations with their own creditors, than through a multilateral process involving other debtors and creditors. This view conforms to the philosophy of the officials of finance ministries and central banks who normally deal with debt problems; these officials are notoriously sceptical about multilateral financial negotiations, shy of attracting international publicity to their particular debt problems, and keen to maintain the impression that these problems are entirely manageable and under control. Thus, key debtor countries like Argentina, Brazil or Mexico shun any talk of multilateral initiatives on debt which go beyond mere generalities. Yet, no meaningful multilateral action on debt is conceivable if the larger debtor countries will not participate in it.

Against this background, four main areas in UNCTAD's work on debt problems can be identified, namely, debt relief measures, guidelines for debt operations, the institutional framework for debt negotiations, and technical assistance to debtor countries.

(a) Debt relief

Calls have been made on several occasions for measures of immediate and generalized relief of the official debt of developing countries, mainly arising from ODA. Such calls are almost always grounded on the difficult balance-of-payments position of the debtor countries at a given moment of time. One of the negotiating successes of UNCTAD, in fact, is a 1978 ministerial decision of the Trade and Development Board under which creditor countries agreed to grant relief to low-income developing countries on their ODA debt. A large number of OECD countries wrote off over $3 billion worth of ODA debt as a result, and softened the terms on an additional $2 billion.[20] Over 40 developing countries benefited from these relief measures.[21]

While subsequent resolutions in the United Nations and UNCTAD have called for the continuation of such debt relief, it may be observed that the particular measures endorsed by the 1978 resolution suffer from serious technical limitations. In effect, creditor countries were asked to soften the terms of ODA debt (interest rates, grace and maturity periods), including where applicable to convert loans to grants, so as to apply retroactively to outstanding ODA loans the benefits of the significant softening of ODA terms which had occurred during the seventies. The logic was that developing countries should not have to continue servicing past ODA debt on hard terms if they were currently recipients of much softer ODA from the same sources. The snag is that the amount of debt relief that can be granted in ths way is constrained by the amount of softening in new ODA that has actually taken place, and is limited to those donor countries that have softened their ODA. Furthermore, it has been argued that this debt relief formula discourages donor countries from further softening of ODA terms on account of the cost of applying the new terms to old debt. Nevertheless, the political appeal of this technique to several donors is undeniable.

However, the United States, which is the largest ODA creditor within the OECD group, declined to give debt relief under the UNCTAD resolution.[22] The objection of the United States Administration is a fundamental one, going deeper than technical criticism and stemming from the belief that debt relief is an improper channel for resource transfers. If additional aid is to be given, it is argued, it should be a readily recognizable new expenditure. Moreover, the United States Congress takes a particularly austere view of bad debtors and requires the Administration to submit to it an annual report identifying recalcitrant debtor countries. The fact that the largest ODA creditor has declined to join other creditors in giving debt relief under this resolution has effectively dissuaded the latter from continuing the relief measures.

The United States has also argued strongly that there is no case at the moment for across-the-board debt relief and that it would contemplate debt relief strictly on a case-by-case basis. Most other industrial countries also remain generally committed to the case-by-case approach.

In its more recent proposals on official debt relief, UNCTAD has extended the argument for relief to cover official export credits as well as ODA debt. It has also proposed a different and less complicated technique of debt relief, namely a straightforward moratorium for two years on the service of certain categories of official debt, with a simultaneous extension of the amortization period for two years. This would be a once-for-all measure to alleviate the current critical situation of developing countries. The proposal was tabled at UNCTAD VI (Belgrade, 1983) but no action could be taken there.

UNCTAD's progress on the now all-important issue of private debt has been much more modest. At UNCTAD IV (Nairobi, 1976) a proposal was made for a refinancing facility for private debt. This proposal was akin to some of the recent suggestions from outside the United Nations for restructuring the existing developing country debt by lengthening its maturity through a refinancing facility. The larger debtor countries, particularly those in Latin America, showed remarkably little enthusiasm for the 1976 proposal in UNCTAD. The reasons for this general reluctance by large debtors to participate in multilateral initiatives on debt have already been alluded to. These constraints on UNCTAD's ability to act on private debt have excluded it from one of the main present-day dramas on the development front, and created a major lacuna in its work.

(b) Guidelines for debt operations

The second main area of UNCTAD's work on debt problems has interesting longer-term implications, namely the formulation of internationally-agreed rules and principles for dealing with debt problems. The argument here is that the manner in which developing country debt problems are addressed is lacking in consistency and faulty in objective. Debt problems are dealt with essentially in the context of balance-of-payments difficulties, and that too only partially and, more often than not, belatedly. The case-by-case approach, eschewing uniformity, leaves the debtor country in a great deal of uncertainty as to how its debt problem is to be treated. Against this, creditor countries would argue that non-uniformity is the essence of sound debt management, since no two debt problems are alike. UNCTAD would counter that there is in fact a great deal of similarity in the external causes of developing countries' debt difficulties, notably in the contributory factors represented by declining terms of trade, protectionism and high interest rates. Furthermore, UNCTAD would argue that the principal objective of creditor countries, as manifested by them through their 'Paris Club', is merely to restore as soon as possible the repayment capacity of the debtor country. The long-term development objectives of the debtor do not enter into the creditors' consideration. The creditors adopt an essentially short-term approach to debt problems, which results in the inadequate terms (short consolidation and grace periods, high interest rates and short maturities) on which debt relief is granted, when it is granted at all.

After several years of deliberation and much haggling a set of agreed guidelines for debt operations was adopted in UNCTAD in 1980. These guidelines set out the following general objectives of international action in the event of debt problems, specifying that such action may vary according to the nature of the problems dealt with: "[it] (a) should be expeditious and timely; (b) should enhance the development prospects of the debtor country, bearing in mind its socio-economic priorities and the internationally-agreed objectives for the development of developing countries; (c) should aim at restoring the debtor country's capacity to service its debt in both the short term and the long term, and should reinforce the developing country's own efforts to strengthen its underlying balance-of-payments situation; [and] (d) should protect the interest of debtors and creditors equitably in the context of international economic co-operation."[23]

This was an important step forward, with much potential for future action. Nevertheless, the impact of the UNCTAD guidelines on the course of debt negotiations is limited by at least two factors. First, an almost inevitable precondition for debt relief at present is the negotiation of an agreed 'adjustment programme' with the International Monetary Fund.[24] The IMF has come to play a pivotal role in the treatment of debt problems of developing countries; in fact, a great deal of what happens at debt negotiations is determined by the debtor country's prior negotiations with the IMF. The UNCTAD guidelines are not aimed at this key stage in the resolution of debt problems and their impact on the actual outcome is consequently diminished. Secondly, the guidelines can only be as effective as the machinery to enforce and monitor them. So far, no machinery exists for this specific purpose. UNCTAD has a general overall mandate in this respect but much would have to be built on it for effectiveness to be achieved.

(c) Institutional framework

This brings us to the third main area of UNCTAD's endeavours, namely the institutional framework for dealing with debt problems. The existing machinery is the result of a highly *ad hoc* approach in the past. The two main institutions are the Paris Club[25] and the *ad hoc* groups set up by commercial banks to negotiate with individual debtor countries.[26] In addition, World Bank aid consortia and consultative groups have in the past dealt with at least some aspects of debt problems of specific countries.

Developing countries and UNCTAD have criticized these institutions as being largely creditor-dominated and insufficiently development-oriented; further, they cannot always be mobilized when needed by the debtor country. One of the main remedies proposed in this connection is the setting up of an 'International Debt Commission', composed of independent experts and chaired by one of them, which would examine all aspects of a debtor country's problems, including its commercial debt. Both the Paris Club and the *ad hoc* bank groups are creditor-chaired and for the moment each mechanism only deals with a part of the debt problem. There have also been proposals to make the chairmanship of the Paris Club more independent.

These proposals have found little favour with the creditor countries, who regard the present *ad hoc* approach as more flexible and more suitable to the needs of a complex situation. They would naturally not want to detract from their dominance of the existing machinery. It has, however, to be said that reform of the debt machinery is another of those rather numerous proposals on financial and monetary matters that developing countries have presented rather half-heartedly, each with an eye on its individual credit-worthiness and on the prospects of bilateral arrangements. Those debtor countries which have had to resort to creditors' meetings have always obtained some measure of relief from them. Indeed, such meetings take place only when there is an informal prior agreement among the creditors to grant relief at all. As a result, debtor countries' criticism of the debt machinery has been muted, to say the least.

UNCTAD has nevertheless achieved a certain recognition of its competence in debt problems, as confirmed by the observer status which it has obtained at the Paris Club. It now participates in Paris Club meetings with the same formal status as the World Bank and the IMF. In general, the UNCTAD contribution to these meetings presents a broad analysis of the debt problem of the debtor country in question, emphasizing in particular the trade-related causes of the problem (e.g. decline in terms of trade or protectionist measures affecting the country's trade). It also sets out various scenarios for the country's economic prospects under different assumptions of the amount and terms of debt relief. Overall, UNCTAD's presence serves to strengthen the longer-term development dimension of the discussion, which otherwise would be less prominent.

UNCTAD's entry into this field is relatively recent and it cannot be expected to have made a major impact on the process through which solutions to debt problems are sought. It may be stated, however, that UNCTAD's pressure has enhanced the prospects for more rational, far-sighted and development-oriented solutions.

(d) Technical assistance

The fourth aspect of UNCTAD's work on debt is the provision of technical advice and assistance to developing debtor countries. Complex and difficult issues are involved in the process of incurring external debt, in recording it and in dealing with debt problems as they arise. Many developing countries are not fully equipped for this; they do not receive technical assistance on this matter directly from the World Bank and the IMF, except in limited areas. Much remains to be done to assist developing countries in setting up debt recording systems, defining policies on incurring external debt, and strengthening their capacity to negotiate with creditors in difficult times. The UNCTAD secretariat has recently started to provide assistance of this nature and, although its work has extended to only a few debtor countries so far, it has already had some beneficial results. The presence of UNCTAD on the scene opens up new possibilities, including the politically very important prospect of exchanging experience among debtor countries.[27] However, further progress is hampered by lack of sufficient resources for the secretariat's technical assistance work.

All in all, limited but significant success can be claimed by UNCTAD in the field of debt. It is a highly sensitive area, with tremendous political implications, and requires deep study. In the space of a relatively few years, UNCTAD has put itself firmly on the map and has created the basis for a growing future impact.

III. Balance-of-payments problems of developing countries

The high susceptibility of developing countries to balance-of-payments (BOP) problems is the result of several basic factors, which it may be useful to list here:

(i) The vast majority of these countries have strong economic ties to the industrial market economies, which are themselves prone to cyclical and other fluctuations. The overwhelming economic power of these industrial economies permits them to shift a significant share of their adjustment burdens onto their weaker developing country partners. This would be so even if the monetary system did not operate in so asymmetrical a manner as it does at the moment.

(ii) The heavy reliance of a large number of developing countries on external finance as an instrument of development increases their vulnerability to external shocks, over and above that engendered by international trade *per se*. As has been noted, the growing 'privatization' of financial flows to developing countries has increased their cost, their volatility and the importance of 'creditworthiness'.

(iii) In the monetary system, the move towards 'managed floating' exchange rates has increased the influence of countries that can 'manage' their exchange rates on those which cannot. It has thus worked to the disadvantage of the developing countries, the vast majority of which cannot influence their exchange rates except within narrow ranges.

As if all this were not enough, the emergence of large surpluses and deficits in the developing countries following the oil price increases in the seventies has compounded the problems for both deficit and surplus countries, though in very different ways. The surplus countries have been faced with the problem of safeguarding the value of their financial and monetary assets. They have not gained influence on international money and finance in proportion to the importance of their surpluses, for these were recycled through public or private institutions dominated by the interests of OECD countries. Indeed the emergence of these surpluses has significantly increased the power of such institutions. And it must be said that several of the surplus developing countries have a view of the world not essentially different from that of the major industrial countries.

A significant consequence of these trends in the seventies, as they affected the specific sector of BOP finance, has been the shrinkage of IMF quotas in relation to world trade and payments imbalances, and the erosion of the Fund's capacity to play the role envisaged in its Articles of Agreement in contributing to global growth and stability. It should be noted that many of the lower income countries continue to rely predominantly on official finance for their balances of payments, primarily from the IMF, since their access to commercial funds is limited.

UNCTAD's position on the BOP problems of developing countries starts with the basic premise that these problems are qualitatively different from those of the industrialized countries.[28] In particular, they are a result of the development effort of the developing countries. They are therefore mostly structural in character and external in origin, being caused, for example, by recession in industrial country markets, terms-of-trade changes, interest rate changes and capital movements. Structural rigidities in developing economies, including typically a large commodity sector, a small and inflexible industrial sector and resource bottlenecks, inhibit their adjustment to shocks. The industrial countries, with their diversified economic structures, their relative flexibility and their creditworthiness can undertake such adjustment with far greater ease. The combination in developing countries of structural rigidities and externally-induced payments shocks makes their adjustment doubly difficult to control. Moreover, the capacity of the many low-income countries to bear high-cost finance is strictly limited.

Therefore, it is argued, developing countries need large and longer-term facilities for BOP finance at reasonable terms, including concessional terms, and under conditions which take due account of developmental and socio-political realities. This implies that the role of official sources in overall BOP finance should be considerably strengthened in relation to private sources.

A significant part of UNCTAD's efforts has been spent in documenting the nature of developing countries' BOP problems and in making a case for a more generous international response, especially in terms of official finance. Its broad goals have been the enlargement of BOP facilities, the creation of new ones, and the improvement of the conditions attached to BOP facilities.

UNCTAD has given consistent support to the efforts of developing countries to enlarge IMF quotas and to make a greater share of these available to developing countries. IMF quotas in relation to world trade have declined from around 10 per cent in the sixties to around 4 per cent now; developing countries hold around 30 per cent of total quotas. These quotas are reviewed periodically in the IMF, but in recent years the process has become increasingly politicized in the United States, which has a key leadership role to play. In general terms, while the United States attaches the highest importance to the IMF as an institution in which it has the last word, it does not at present believe in massive increases in IMF quotas. This is so not only because of difficulties in obtaining Congressional approval but also because the United States authorities prefer to allow a greater role to commercial banks in BOP financing, with the IMF acting more as a catalyst for commercial finance.

Developing countries have pressed, through UNCTAD and in the Fund itself, for new BOP facilities in the IMF and for the improvement of existing ones. The promptings of the United Nations, prior to the formation of UNCTAD, were instrumental in the establishment in 1963 of the Fund's Compensatory Financing Facility for assisting countries to weather temporary shortfalls in export earnings. This facility is greatly valued by developing countries for its suitability to their needs and for the relatively low conditionality attached to drawings under it. Subsequent improvements in this facility can be largely attributed to the efforts made in and through UNCTAD. However, similar pressures to make the Fund's Buffer Stock Financing Facility (set up in 1969) more responsive to developing country needs, e.g. by making its resources available for national stocking, have not been successful. In more recent years, UNCTAD has argued for a BOP facility in the IMF to enable adjustment in developing countries to be spread over a greater period and in the process to bridge the existing gap between BOP finance and long-term development finance. This argument has not led to any significant action; the IMF has countered that its high-conditionality Extended Fund Facility is in effect a medium-term facility. The World Bank has also been lending for 'structural adjustment', but the amounts are limited, and the conditionality has been quite strict. Other BOP questions also persistently raised in UNCTAD concern the need to issue more SDRs, interest subsidy for low-income countries' drawings from the IMF, and the level of access to IMF funds.

The growing share of commercial banks in BOP finance has led to the intertwining of the issues of BOP finance and 'privatization'. UNCTAD's role in relation to commercial bank financing as a whole is a subdued one for reasons which have been mentioned in the section on debt problems.[29] But the commercial banks, especially in the context of current debt difficulties, rely to a considerable extent on implicit and explicit guidance from the IMF in their lending to the Third World. The IMF's catalytic role in dealing with BOP and debt problems has been reinforced significantly as a result. This has encouraged the tendency for observers and critics to focus on the conditions of IMF lending to developing countries in deficit and on the nature of the adjustment programmes which the Fund imposes on these countries. Much attention has been devoted, in UNCTAD as well as outside, to the highly sensitive, emotional and political issue of 'conditionality'.[30]

While accepting that some conditions must always be attached to lending, developing countries and UNCTAD have argued that the conditions chosen by the IMF are not only conceptually defective but also insensitive to the social and political realities in the borrowing countries and generally oblivious of growth and development aims. In general, the IMF's vision of BOP problems is based on short-term monetarist considerations. Typically, the Fund would argue that BOP problems arise because of excess domestic demand, in which large government deficits are automatically financed by expanding the money supply. In addition, unrealistically high wage levels and social benefits are accompanied by low interest rates (which discourage savings) and overvalued exchange rates (which discourage exports while encouraging imports). Finally, excessive government interference in the economy, including an unduly large public sector, creates an unpropitious climate for private enterprise and foreign investment. Market signals are stifled under these conditions, the IMF would argue, leading to misallocation of resources.

The well-known IMF prescriptions habitually follow: lower public spending, curtailment of money supply, higher interest rates, wage curbs, abandonment of food and other subsidies, devaluation and trade liberalization. In many cases, these lead to 'IMF riots', often deadly. Today the fortunes of dozens of developing countries and of literally hundreds of millions of people in the Third World revolve around the negotiations over conditions for borrowing from the IMF.

The objections to such conditionality centre on several themes. First, the IMF's analysis of the causes of payments problems puts disproportionate emphasis on excess demand, to the relative neglect of supply constraints. The IMF's response is therefore based on adjustment through deflation, rather than on adjustment through growth and development. This is a central issue, and it is a cause for astonishment that it has not received more political attention internationally. For the IMF may be doing a disservice to the world economy by promoting a bias in favour of deflation, without stimulating an offsetting pressure for reflation elsewhere in the global system.

Secondly, the IMF diagnosis puts undue stress on the domestic sources of BOP problems as against their external origins. Yet developing countries would assert that they are 'shock-takers' not 'shock-makers'. It is therefore doubly unfair to expect them to adjust when there is no similar pressure on the creators of the external shocks. Insult is added to injury by blaming domestic mismanagement in developing countries as a source of the problem.[31]

Thirdly, it is argued, the IMF's emphasis on market forces, private enterprise and foreign investment in developing economies is quite misplaced. Structural rigidities and market imperfections considerably dilute the accuracy and utility of market signals in those economies. Moreover, in view of the inequalities in wealth and power that exist in a large majority of developing countries, giving free rein to the market is tantamount to strengthening forces which are already strong, and is contrary to distributional considerations in the development process. Very few developing countries deny the role of private enterprise in the development process; indeed, the private sector plays a key role, if not the dominant one, in a large number of developing countries. But developing countries do make a strong case for government intervention in the economy not only on distributional grounds, but also because this is the only way to accelerate the process of national development and to cope with the country's involvement in the complexities of the international economy. Governments of industrial countries, it is pointed out, are constantly and heavily involved in their national economies. Developing countries should not be denied a similar right to intervene inside their own economies, where problems are perhaps more complex and certainly longer-term in nature.

An important new element in the debate is the arbitrary manner in which IMF conditionality is applied. The situation in the most severely indebted countries of the Third World is now of great concern to the Western financial system and to the governments of the industrial countries. These big debtors are in a far superior bargaining position vis-à-vis the IMF and their commercial creditors than smaller, less threatening, debtor countries can be. Such differences in leverage result in a highly uneven application of IMF prescriptions to different developing countries. The situation is compounded by the commercial banks' haphazard considerations of credit-worthiness. Furthermore, the IMF has often been accused of treating the politically more conservative borrowing countries more leniently than others.[32]

There are no objective criteria by which to assess the severity of IMF conditionality with respect to different countries at a given moment of time, or to the same country at different moments of time. Judgement in this area must therefore be highly speculative and subjective. There are times when the IMF is perceived to be relaxing its conditionality, and other times when it appears to be tightening its fist, depending upon the prevailing opinion in the major industrial countries, the political climate and market conditions.

UNCTAD's work in this area suffers from a major handicap, namely the lack of access to confidential information on adjustment programmes. UNCTAD, and developing countries in general, are therefore on somewhat weak grounds in making generalizations on these programmes. Of course, the borrowing countries possess that information; but strict confidentiality has become the norm in negotiations with the IMF, and few borrowing governments have risked jeopardizing their relationship with the Fund by disclosing the content of their negotiations.[33] As in the case of relations with commercial creditors, individual prudence inhibits collective action.

The IMF thus has a clear tactical advantage. There is no machinery outside the IMF to assess systematically the relevance and effectiveness of IMF programmes. With the privileged access to the data and the media that the Fund enjoys, it is not surprising that the 'success' stories get far greater publicity than the others.

UNCTAD's role nonetheless has been instrumental in giving a certain degree of coherence to the views of the developing countries on IMF conditionality and in generating pressures for liberalization, particularly through the Group of 24. A large number of well-documented case studies have emerged from UNCTAD's work with that Group. Overall though, especially with conservative governments now in office in major Western countries, IMF conditionality is widely regarded in powerful circles as the most appropriate answer to BOP problems. There is today no serious challenge to the Fund's monetarist dogmas.

A certain paradox may be noted in passing. At UNCTAD meetings and conferences, political pressure is routinely exercised by the Group of 77 for the enlargement of IMF resources. Such pressure strengthens the legitimacy of the IMF and adds to its influence, without the developing countries getting much in return, for example in terms of a response to their criticism of strict conditionality.

IV. The reform of the international monetary system

Most discussions in UNCTAD on 'money and finance' are concerned with financial issues. The distinction between financial and monetary issues, made at the start of this paper, is fundamental; yet it is surprising that even knowledgeable people either ignore the international monetary issue, or else subsume it under the heading of 'finance' when discussing world economic problems. At the political level it takes courage, not to mention technical competence, even to raise the issue. Many politicians and diplomats who would not hesitate to expound, say, on the virtues and vices of the transnational corporation, or who would readily harangue their listeners on the horrors of IMF conditionality, usually run for cover when the international monetary issue is raised.

Perhaps the reason for this phenomenon lies in the extent to which the nature and control of the monetary system is tied up with political power itself. Control of, or even influence over, the monetary system gives immense political power to whoever exercises it. This is true both domestically and internationally. By the same token, questioning the monetary system is tantamount to challenging one of the pillars of political power.

In the fifties and sixties, the relative stability of exchange rates around the gold-based US dollar, the initial shortage of dollars caused by US trade surpluses, and the enhanced political stature of the United States made the dollar-based system virtually the 'natural' international monetary system. Developing countries did not have the confidence to challenge or even to question it.

At the time of its establishment, UNCTAD's mandate in the monetary sphere was confined largely to issues that touched upon the trade of developing countries. It is therefore a matter of some credit to UNCTAD that, as early as 1965, its Secretary-General convened a group of experts to examine issues relating to the international monetary system. Indeed most of the ideas and proposals of that group, couched in moderate language and made under very different conditions, have since become part of the conventional wisdom on the subject. Its key conclusion was that there was a need to reform the international monetary system so as to make it more responsive to the needs for economic growth of both developed and developing countries.[34]

The system of course contained the seeds of its own metamorphosis, if not of its own destruction. The rest of the world was dependent on a supply of

United States dollars for its liquidity. Such dollars could only be generated through United States deficits i.e. by the United States acquiring real goods from the rest of the world in return for its IOUs. Yet persistent United States deficits of the magnitude required by the international economy were ultimately bound to undermine confidence in the dollar. The eventual delinking of the dollar from gold in 1971 was the inevitable outcome, at a time when the United States had embarked on a number of mutually-inconsistent policies. This delinking and the subsquent establishment of a managed floating system, with negotiated parities between main currencies, has often been referred to as the breakdown of the Bretton Woods system. One of the central characteristics of the system, namely its dollar basis, did not change in any meaningful respect, however, except that a certain discipline on the dollar was removed. Developing countries played a relatively small or no part in those major changes, which goes to demonstrate their limited ability to manoeuvre on this key issue in international economics.

The increases in the price of oil and the consequent emergence of surplus developing countries had an important political impact on monetary discussions, at least for a while. Developing countries were no longer uniquely deficit countries and hence perpetual borrowers. The new political potential acquired by the OPEC countries enabled them to raise important monetary issues (e.g. those concerning the real value of their accumulated reserves). The scale of BOP surpluses and deficits increased overnight, significantly affecting exchange rates in the process. The emergence of a large Eurocurrency market and the movements of vast quantities of liquid funds began to affect exchange rates violently. Industrial countries themselves for the first time began to question key aspects of the system.

UNCTAD and developing countries' complaints against the monetary system now came to be formulated more cogently, and voiced more coherently. These deserve to be summarized.[35]

First, the adjustment process in the present system is regarded as faulty in several senses. Since deficit countries have few choices other than to borrow, they inevitably come under greater pressure to adjust than do surplus countries. Nor is there pressure on reserve currency countries to adjust. Smaller countries are subjected to much greater pressures to adjust than are larger countries. The argument regarding pressure on deficit countries is particularly important. The development objectives of developing countries are likely to entail large deficits for a long time to come. Given the present limitations of BOP finance, there is likely to be almost permanent deflationary pressure upon them to adjust. Such pressure when applied to isolated cases may be tolerable. However, when a multitude of developing countries move into deficit owing to reasons quite outside their control, as happened in the seventies, the accumulation of deflationary pressure damages the global economy.

Secondly, the system of floating exchange rates is also regarded by developing countries as specially onerous, on account of their heavy trade dependence. The instability of this system introduces an element of uncertainty into import costs and export revenues. The ability of developing countries to manage their own exchange rates so as to counter this uncertainty is highly limited, because of the paucity of their resources with which to intervene in the foreign exchange markets and the smallness of their economies. They are inevitably led to peg their currencies to one of the major currencies or to a basket of currencies. Either way, their rate of exchange comes under the influence of pressures quite outside their control. From a global point of view, too, it has been argued that floating exchange rates have introduced inflationary pressures into the world economy, and have made financial flows even more precarious. Exchange rate changes which are unrelated to real considerations also exacerbate trade problems, since countries are perceived to manipulate their own exchange rates to gain competitive advantage. Developing countries do not necessarily call for fixed rates; they do call for greater stability.

Thirdly, these issues are closely tied to the dollar basis of the system, which UNCTAD and the developing countries, as well as some sectors of opinion in the industrial countries, regard as basically unsound. The dollar base subjects the international monetary system to national policy considerations which can run counter to global economic requirements. In addition it confers a particular liberty of action on the reserve currency country. Developing countries have consistently called for a move towards an SDR-based system.

Fourthly, the creation of liquidity under the existing system is regarded as inefficient and inequitable. This key function of the system is now being increasingly abandoned to the private sector i.e. to commercial banks from the industrial countries. This not only reduces the developing countries' ability to influence the system through their voice, frail though it may be, in the IMF; it also makes the system more volatile, more subject to disparate national and commercial considerations, and less responsive to global economic and developmental requirements.[36]

Finally, developing countries consider that decision-making in the present international monetary system is highly biased against them. Not only is the voting structure in the IMF loaded against them, but the real decision-making power lies in the 'Group of Ten' (now actually 11) industrial countries and its inner circles of five or even three countries. Not even at the height of their financial power did any of the OPEC countries succeed in gaining access to these inner recesses of decision-making on international monetary issues.

UNCTAD's effort in the field of international monetary reform has been at three levels: research, technical assistance and inter-governmental deliberation.

UNCTAD has invested a great deal of effort in researching into monetary issues and in giving a certain analytical coherence to the case for reform, especially from the perspective of world development. It has also provided a great deal of technical assistance to the developing countries in their dialogue with the industrial countries on monetary and related issues. UNCTAD has effectively been the substantive secretariat of the Group of 24,[37] through which developing countries' views and pressures on monetary issues are expressed. Similar pressures are also exercised through the regular Group of 77 meetings in Geneva and New York, also with substantive support from UNCTAD.

However, UNCTAD has serious problems in organizing inter-governmental deliberations on monetary reform. The majority of Western countries, above all the United States, see no need for basic reform in the monetary system. Indeed, the United States at present does not accept that there is any need for modifying the system at all. The nearest it has ever come to agreeing to discuss basic aspects of the system is in the Committee of Twenty, within the IMF framework, in the aftermath of the upheaval of the early seventies. The United States Administration did then see a case for change. While the Committee came up with highly detailed and concrete suggestions, its proposals have remained virtually a dead letter.[38]

More recently, some industrial countries have begun openly to voice their disquiet concerning the monetary system. But these are relatively few (notably France and New Zealand) and their concerns are somewhat partial, even though they have called for a thorough re-examination of the system. They have failed to convince the United States and the other major OECD countries to go along with them. The seven industrial countries' summit meeting in Williamsburg in the summer of 1983 nonetheless agreed somewhat timidly to look into the issue. At the time of writing, no concrete decisions had been taken as a result of that agreement and prospects for reform appear dim.

But even the industrial countries more sympathetic to reform have been reluctant to concede UNCTAD a mandate in this area. The last serious attempt by developing countries to force the issue was at UNCTAD V in 1979, when a resolution was adopted by vote to set up an inter-governmental group of experts to look into monetary reform. The group met only once in 1980, and, under United States pressure, was boycotted by the vast majority of the OECD countries.[39] To all intents and purposes, this particular initiative is now dead. But it is conceivable that the OECD countries, other than the United States, if sufficiently pressed by developing countries, could agree to participate in monetary discussions in UNCTAD. Their past deference to pressures against such participation demonstrates the extreme sensitivity of the United States on the subject. The United States has insisted that monetary issues be discussed solely in the IMF, and that the

United Nations is not the correct vehicle through which monetary reform should be brought about, if it should be brought about at all. This stand has also been the main stumbling block obstructing efforts to get 'global negotiations' started under the auspices of the General Assembly of the United Nations.

Yet attempts continue to be made to place monetary reform on the international agenda. Regrettably though, these attempts suffer from a common defect, in that they tie monetary reform too closely to financial and other issues. In 1983, the Non-Aligned Movement called for an international conference on 'money and finance for development'. In the same year, the United Nations Committee on Development Planning, the Brandt Commission and a Commonwealth study group all voiced their support for a process of consultation and negotiation on fundamental reforms in trade, money and finance, what was to be a 'new Bretton Woods'.[40]

However, on the side of the developing countries, there are two important obstacles to progress. First, there has always been a certain ambiguity regarding international monetary reform, particularly on the part of the Latin American countries. This can be attributed partly to pressures emanating from Washington but it also owes something to the perception in these countries that they have done relatively well out of the existing monetary chaos, particularly as regards the distribution of funds from the Eurocurrency markets and other commercial lending. This perception is yet another sign of the overlapping of monetary and financial issues, which weakens the case for monetary reform. Since developing countries routinely inject financial demands into discussions on monetary reform, it is relatively easy for the industrial countries to dismiss Third World proposals on monetary issues as part of the campaign for 'massive resource transfers'. The political aspect is equally worth reflecting upon: whenever developing countries raise financial issues, they are inevitably cast in the role of 'demanders', thereby directly reducing their political power. Yet many of the arguments for monetary reform are grounded on considerations of global economic efficiency, stability and growth, in the interest of all countries. By making it a purely developmental issue, developing countries effectively dilute, if not give away, the central argument for reform of the international monetary system.

Secondly, there is an institutional problem. UNCTAD's main constituency within the developing countries is the Group of 77 in Geneva. The delegations forming that Group (among which, incidentally, the African Group is rather sparsely represented) receive their instructions mainly from the ministries of foreign affairs and of commerce of their governments. These ministries are loth to get involved in monetary and financial issues, traditionally the domain of finance ministries and central banks. In turn, Third World officials in the monetary and financial domain are heavily influenced by IMF ideology, in part owing to the successful programmes of training and technical assistance run by the Fund. They tend to look askance at UNCTAD, not taking it too seriously and not normally attending its meetings. They prefer to operate through the Group of 24 in Washington, and are generally very measured in their criticism of the Fund's policies in its own forums. Indeed, developing country representatives in Washington appear to be chosen for their moderation on financial and monetary issues; a highly apolitical approach to those issues seems to be an important qualification for upward mobility both at home and into jobs in the Fund or the World Bank. These institutional factors dampen the Third World's thrust for monetary reform by channelling it through the IMF's technocracy where the political impetus is lost.

One can conclude that developing countries have been able to give a certain substantive and political coherence to their views on monetary reform. They owe much to UNCTAD on that count. But they have been far less successful in defining steps toward reform. This is important, for it is difficult, and increasingly so, to envisage monetary reform taking place through swift and comprehensive measures agreed by governments. It is much easier to visualize it coming about through progressive, incremental measures over time, but developing countries have not invested much energy in elaborating such measures and a programme for their implementation. Furthermore, the increasing 'privatization' of the monetary system implies that the developing countries will have to reckon with the market in defining any measures for reform. It would be quite possible for the market to out-manoeuvre inter-governmental attempts to change the monetary system, even under the heroic assumption that the latter were based on a hitherto elusive consensus. The task is now many times more complex.

Yet the political aspect of putting pressure on the United States remains the key question. It is a great pity that the developing countries have not been able to win over more allies within the industrial world on monetary reform issues. A case for South-North consensus on this issue can be built on mutual interest. But it is not clear if a serious attempt has been made to do so.

*   *   *

This paper has attempted to outline UNCTAD's involvement in the main external financial problems of developing countries, including the particular problems of debt and balance-of-payments finance, and in issues relating to the international monetary system, particularly as it affects the process of development.

In all these areas, UNCTAD's role has been manifold. It can be said to have contributed significantly to articulating the developing countries' case, on sound analytical lines, for more appropriate responses from the North. In particular, the case has been made for greater volumes of financial flows on generous terms and in a stable framework. Financial flows to developing countries have indeed increased over the past several years, even though the overall composition of these flows has recently taken an unfavourable turn. A case has also been made for a sounder framework for dealing with debt problems and for improving and enlarging balance-of-payments facilities. In fact, several concrete steps forward have been taken. Finally, a relatively coherent case can now be made by the developing countries for a reform of the international monetary system to make it more supportive of stable growth and accelerated development. Negotiations to this end, however, have not progressed at all.

At the moment of writing, financial and monetary issues are uppermost in the minds of many. This is partly because attention has shifted to the short-term, where the financial element is a key ingredient of any solution. The debt issue preoccupies both the many debtor countries and financial circles in the West. It would, however, be a mistake to envisage exclusively financial and monetary solutions to the current problems. In the long run, the main economic effort of developing countries in their struggle for material advance would have to focus on mobilizing their own savings, investing them wisely, ensuring adequate gains from trade and substantially upgrading economic efficiency. The financial and monetary systems can only help or hinder these more basic determinants of development.

---

1. The substantive distinction between finance and money, which is frequently overlooked or blurred, is worth preserving. Financial issues in international economic relations refer predominantly to inter-country transfers of savings and investments. Monetary issues refer more to the system whereby international liquidity is denominated, created, exchanged and stored, and through which financial transfers take place. There is naturally some overlap between these two sets of issues, notably in the areas of debt and balance-of-payments adjustment.

2. Contrast in this respect, the report presented by UNCTAD's first Secretary-General, Raúl Prebisch, to UNCTAD I, "*Towards a new trade policy for development*", United Nations, New York, 1964, and the views expressed in speeches by its present Secretary-General, Gamani Corea, collected in *Need for change: towards the New International Economic Order*, Pergamon, 1980.

3. "UNCTAD's stand" here refers to the positions broadly taken by the developing countries and the UNCTAD secretariat. For their part, the developing countries express their collective views through the Group of 77, the Group of 24 (an offshoot of the Group of 77 dealing specifically with international monetary and financial affairs) and the Non-Aligned Movement. These various positions coincide, but there are important nuances which we shall touch upon later. The latest UNCTAD secretariat report on finance and money is *International financial and monetary issues*, Geneva, January 1983.

4. See *Some aspects of the outlook for global financial flows in the context of the Third United Nations Development Decade*, UNCTAD, Geneva, June 1980.

5. For a summary of Prebisch's theory, see S. Dell's contribution to this volume.

6. A classic exposition of this statement is to be found in J. Pincus, *Trade, aid and*

development, New York, 1967. Also see J. Bhagwati and R.S. Eckaus, *Foreign aid*, Penguin, 1970. For two very different approaches to these issues, see T. Hayter, *Aid as imperialism*, Penguin, 1971 and P.T. Bauer, *Dissent on development*, London, 1976.

7. This definition was established by the OECD. UNCTAD has in the past questioned the definition, but without determination and therefore without success. Even OPEC countries calculate their aid using this definition, which is somewhat arbitrary at best.

8. OECD data and definitions. See OECD Press Release *Financial resources for developing countries 1983 and recent trends*, Paris, 20 June 1984 and *Development Cooperation, 1983 Review*, OECD, Paris, 1983. The latter annual publication is a basic source of data on financial flows.

9. The composition of aid flows counted towards this target has also been challenged in UNCTAD, but again without much perseverance. For example, aid to colonial territories is included in the calculation of ODA. At one time Portugal's transfers to its colonies like Mozambique and Angola were fully recorded as ODA by the OECD. When these countries gained independence, Portugal suddenly disappeared as a donor country. Recently, France agreed not to include transfers to its colonies (DOM-TOM) towards the aid target; the OECD now publishes two separate figures for the French ODA ratio to GNP. Moreover, OECD data include aid to southern European countries and Israel, whereas these flows are not included in UNCTAD data. The exclusion of aid to Israel from the calculation of the ODA: GNP ratio for the United States reduces that ratio significantly. In principle, military aid is excluded from all ODA calculations.

10. For a useful discussion of the issues involved, from the United States perspective, see *US participation in the multilateral development banks in the 1980s*, US Treasury, Washington D.C., 1982. The January 1984 decision by the United States Administration to restrict its contribution to the current replenishment of the International Development Association (IDA), at the same time as it is promoting a number of major bilateral aid programmes, is strongly indicative of this preference for bilateralism.

11. In principle, all multilateral aid is untied.

12. See *Ways and means of accelerating the transfer of real resources to developing countries on a predictable, assured and continuous basis*, United Nations, New York, September 1976.

13. Note for example the influence of UNCTAD's ideas on key North-South initiatives outside the United Nations in recent years: notably the 1969 report of the Pearson Commission, *Partners in Development*, New York, 1969 and the two reports of the Brandt Commission, *North-South: A Programme for Survival*, London, 1980 and *Common Crisis North-South: Co-operation for World Recovery*, London, 1983.

14. For an attempt by the UNCTAD secretariat to build such an image see *Resource transfers, excess capacity, and industrial regeneration in developed market economies: a review of some available evidence*, Geneva, February 1980.

15. See, for example, the powerful statement in favour of aid through IDA in *IDA in retrospect*, World Bank, Washington D.C., 1982.

16. See G.D. Arsenis, "The system of international financial cooperation for development", in A. Sengupta (Ed.), *Commodities, finance and trade*, Westport, Conn., 1980.

17. See, for example, the importance given to the debt issue by C. Alzamora and E. Iglesias in *Basis for a Latin American response to the international economic crisis*, ECLA, Santiago, May 1983. See also *The Buenos Aires Platform*, UNCTAD, Geneva, 1983 for the position on the debt issue of the latest Ministerial Meeting of the Group of 77. For a perspective from creditor countries, see OECD, *External debt of developing countries*, Paris 1983, which contains a wealth of data.

18. For an early exposition of UNCTAD's view see *Debt problems in the context of development*, New York, 1974. For a broad historical perspective see H.J. Bittermann, *The refunding of international debt*, Duke, 1973.

19. It is a matter of no little surprise that neither developing countries nor UNCTAD have challenged creditors' perceptions of developing countries' creditworthiness. Most commercial banks were not, until recently, geared to evaluating country risk. They also have a strong herd instinct. Yet there is no thorough critical study of this problem from a developing country perspective.

20. It can of course be argued that such debt relief does not necessarily imply any increase in aid. Governments could simply reduce projected future allocations of ODA by the amount of

debt relief. Even if this were so, and additionality in aid is always difficult to demonstrate, debt relief is a particularly desirable form of assistance from the balance-of-payments angle. Also, in this particular case, the debt relief was concentrated on low-income countries most in need of ODA.

21. See UNCTAD, *Implementation of section A of Trade and Development Board resolution 165 (S-IX)*, Geneva, 1982.

22. For the United States view on ODA debt relief see C. Michalopoulos, "Institutional aspects of developing countries' debt problems", in D.B.H. Denoon, (ed), *The New International Economic Order*, New York, 1979. For a fascinating inside view of decision-making in Washington on this matter see S. D. Cohen, *Forgiving poverty: an examination of US policy on developing country debt relief, 1977–79*, mimeographed, 1980.

23. See Trade and Development Board resolution 222 (XXI) on *Debt and development problems of developing countries*.

24. For the IMF view of debt problems, and of its role in handling them see *External indebtedness of developing countries*, IMF, Washington D.C., May 1981.

25. For a history of the Paris Club, see A.C. Cizauskas, "International debt renegotiation: Lessons from the past", in *World Development*, Vol. 7, No. 2., 1979. This issue of the journal, entirely devoted to international indebtedness, contains several other valuable articles on the subject.

26. See Group of Thirty, *Commercial banks and the restructuring of cross-border debt*, New York, 1983.

27. Much recent discussion on debt problems has focused on this key aspect of co-operation among debtor countries. It is a matter for some wonder that developing countries have not gone farther in this direction. After all, creditors co-operate among themselves all the time; indeed, they have recently strengthened their co-operation through the Bank for International Settlements and through the Ditchley Institute recently established by commercial banks to gather, among other things, information on their lending to sovereign countries. It can be argued that the debtors, too, should seek to improve their relative bargaining position in similar ways. Yet talk about 'debtor cartels' is regarded as almost sacrilegious. Developing countries are extremely loth to discuss anything resembling cartel-like activity in this area.

28. For the most recent statement from UNCTAD, see *International financial and monetary issues*, Geneva, January 1983. For an exhaustive analysis of BOP problems see S. Dell and R. Lawrence, *The balance of payments adjustment process in developing countries—Report to the Group of 24*, Report of a UNDP-UNCTAD project, United Nations, New York, 1979. Also Commonwealth Secretariat, *Seminar on adjustment policies*, London, 1981.

29. There has been no systematic thinking in UNCTAD on the issue of how UNCTAD, or the United Nations in general, is to influence the central protagonists in current development problems, the commercial banks. There has also been little study of how governments can or should influence them, except within very narrow confines and objectives.

30. See for example G. Bird, *The IMF and the developing countries: evolving relations, use of resources and the debate over conditionality*, ODI, London, 1981; T. Killick, *IMF Stabilization programmes*, ODI, London, 1981; R. Thorpe and L. Whitehead, *Inflation and stabilization policies in Latin America*, London, 1979. See also the 1979 special issue of *World Development*, Vol. 7, no. 2, and *Development Dialogue 1980:2*, Dag Hammarskjöld Foundation, Uppsala, containing the papers of a 'South-North Conference on the International Monetary System and the New International Order'.

31. That this line of attack is coming to the fore is undoubtedly a spillover of Reaganite 'supply side' thinking into powerful development circles. The World Bank has added its voice in its *World Development Report 1983*, Washington D.C., 1983. Even Third World thinkers are succumbing; see for example I.F. Shihata, "The North-South dialogue revisited: some personal reflections" in *Third World Quarterly*, Vol. 5, No. 3, July 1983. No responsible person would deny the fundamental importance of sound domestic policies in developing countries. But this is relevant at all times; the issue was rarely raised in the sixties and the seventies with the vengeance with which it is raised now. Ironically, the issue is being injected into the dialogue on development when developing countries have been hard hit by external factors.

32. A rather special example of the Fund's arbitrariness is its massive loan to South Africa in

1982, reportedly without any conditions concerning the economic rigidities and inefficiencies caused by *apartheid*.

33. Jamaica did so in 1980. See "The IMF and the Third World: the case of Jamaica" in *Development Dialogue 1980:2 (see note 30)*. But this rebellion was short-lived and was soon followed by a change of government in the general elections of that year.

34. See *International monetary issues and the developing countries*, United Nations, New York, 1965. The group was chaired by the present Secretary-General of UNCTAD, Gamani Corea, then at the Ministry of Planning and Economic Affairs in Ceylon. In the UNCTAD secretariat's *International and financial and monetary issues op. cit.*, the need for "fundamental reform" of the system is evoked once again, with a (rather half-hearted) suggestion for an "International Central Bank".

35. The overall position of developing countries is best summarized in the *Outline for a Programme of Action on International Monetary Reform*, prepared by the Group of 24 and adopted by a ministerial meeting of the Group of 77 during the 1979 IMF/IBRD annual meeting in Belgrade. This document has now been revised. Relevant UNCTAD documents have already been cited, as has *Development Dialogue 1980:2*, which contains a critique of the monetary system from the Third World viewpoint. There are numerous books and articles on the overall subject of monetary reform, including in particular J. Williamson, *The failure of international monetary reform*, New York, 1977.

36. It can be argued that the IMF has not been any more just than the commercial banks in its distribution of the liquidity that it has created. Only 27 per cent of SDRs issued so far actually went to developing countries, in accordance with their share in quotas. A properly structured 'link' between SDRs and development finance, another long-standing proposal of the developing countries in UNCTAD and elsewhere, could rectify this anomaly.

37. A large number of studies have been prepared by the UNCTAD secretariat for the Group of 24. A selection of the main topics covered includes: devaluation in the adjustment process, the substitution account, strengthening of SDRs, a medium-term balance of payments facility, the European Monetary System, impact of exchange rate changes, and structural adjustment policies.

38. See *International monetary reform: documents of the Committee of Twenty: Outline of reform*, IMF, Washington D.C., 1974.

39. See *Report of the* Ad Hoc *Intergovernmental High-Level Group of Experts on the evolution of the international monetary system*, UNCTAD, Geneva 1980. The socialist countries of Eastern Europe, most of which are not members of the IMF, attended this meeting in full force. They have fully and consistently supported developing countries' demands for international monetary reform, with two important differences. Socialist countries, somewhat predictably, have taken a highly political view of the matter, utilizing UNCTAD discussions on monetary issues to highlight their views on Western imperialism in the Third World. Secondly, particularly in the case of the Soviet Union, their views on monetary reform can, in the final analysis, be summed up in one single word, namely 'gold'. This approach creates severe difficulties for developing and other countries.

40. See *Towards a new Bretton Woods—Report by a Commonwealth Study Group*, Commonwealth Secretariat, London, 1983.

ECONOMIC CO-OPERATION AMONG DEVELOPING COUNTRIES: A COMPONENT OF INTERNATIONAL DEVELOPMENT STRATEGY

by Moses T. Adebanjo

I. The evolution of economic co-operation among developing countries (ECDC) as a component of international development strategy

The major motive force that brought the Heads of State or Government of the Non-Aligned States together in 1961 was their interest in political co-operation. While economic issues were not considered unimportant at that time, political questions dominated discussions among developing countries in their own fora and in those of the United Nations system. Many African countries which had become independent in the early sixties joined their voices to those of older States in Latin America and Asia, within the framework of the Non-Aligned Movement, to appeal for peace and justice on our planet. This preoccupation of developing countries, and their commitment to non-alignment in relation to both super-powers, explain why the 1961 Belgrade Summit sent an important message to both President Kennedy and General-Secretary Khruschev in which it advocated the cause of peace and warned of the dangers of war.

By the time the third Summit of the Non-Aligned States took place in Lusaka in September 1970, the developing countries had begun to discuss economic issues with greater purpose. The Lusaka Summit's Declaration on Non-Alignment and Economic Progress and its statement concerning the sea-bed were clear manifestations that the non-aligned countries had begun to give prominence to economic as well as political questions. The establishment of UNCTAD in 1964, as well as the consequent birth of the Group of 77 as a powerful mouthpiece of the developing countries on economic matters, had greatly influenced the thinking and orientation accorded to economic and social issues within the Non-Aligned Movement and the United Nations development system. The adoption of a comprehensive 'Action Programme for Economic Co-operation among Non-Aligned Countries' at the 1972 Georgetown meeting of their Foreign Ministers consti-

175

tuted an important step towards the formulation of a comprehensive ECDC strategy.[1]

The fourth Non-Aligned Summit, held in Algiers in September 1973, launched the concept of a New International Economic Order (NIEO), which was enshrined in the Declaration and Programme of Action adopted by the United Nations General Assembly at its sixth special session the following spring. Subsequent summits, in Colombo (1976), Havana (1979) and New Delhi (1983), dealt vigorously with the trade and development problems of the Third World. Thus, although the Non-Aligned Movement started as an alternative to the military alliances of the super-powers and as a political coalition of the Third World, it has become increasingly, perhaps even predominantly, concerned with economic well-being both as an end in itself and as a defence of political autonomy. Out of this concern have grown the concept of Third World collective self-reliance and the patient efforts of both the Non-Aligned Movement and the Group of 77 to realize this concept by elaborating objectives and implementing measures for trade expansion and economic co-operation among developing countries.

To better understand the thrust towards Third World collective self-reliance and mutual co-operation, it is necessary to recognize the centrifugal forces propelling developing countries in that direction. Many of the international negotiating conferences and meetings held in the last two decades within the North-South framework have brought only marginal progress in some areas of crucial importance to developing countries and in some other cases have resulted in no progress and virtual deadlock. The Bretton Woods institutions cannot be relied upon to meet all the major concerns of their developing member countries. The 'adjustment' programmes of the IMF have resulted in economic and financial austerity for a great many of these countries, with all the negative repercussions that this may have on their development and that of their trading partners. Some Third World countries also regard World Bank loans as, at best, export-oriented and import-dependent, aimed at ensuring an increase in Third World supplies of raw materials to users in industrialized countries. In face of these disagreeable economic phenomena, coupled with the erosion of commitments and undertakings entered into at different international fora, including the NIEO and successive Development Decade strategies, the developing countries have become increasingly conscious of the need for greater economic and political co-operation among themselves and have resorted to a greater use of the tool of collective self-reliance as a means of defending their economic interests vis-à-vis the North.

Economic co-operation among what are now known as developing countries is as old as history itself. In recent times, Third World countries have shared a broad variety of experiences in their quest for greater collective self-reliance and mutual economic co-operation. Some experiences have been satisfying, while others have been traumatic and tragic. It is significant that despite such set-backs both the industrialized North and the developing South are agreed that ECDC is particularly important as a vital component of the NIEO and of the International Development Strategy for the Third United Nations Development Decade (DD III).

ECDC has the double objective of accelerating the development of the developing countries and of strengthening their negotiating capability in their relations with the developed countries. While the main responsibility for implementing ECDC measures rests with the developing countries themselves, there are, within the framework of the current International Development Strategy, obligations which the developed countries are also expected to fulfil in this area. In view of the present difficulties and uncertainties in the international economic situation and the stalemate in important negotiations on economic issues, renewed efforts are required to promote and strengthen support from the North which is needed to place ECDC in its proper context. Co-operation between the North and the South within the framework of NIEO and DDIII cannot be completely divorced from co-operation within the framework of ECDC, particularly in those sectors of ECDC where support measures from the North are of critical importance.

The discussion of international economic problems at the sixth and seventh special sessions of the General Assembly, at its thirty-fifth session (which adopted the Strategy for DD III) and at the fourth, fifth and sixth sessions of UNCTAD, all manifested a growing concern in developing countries to develop a coherent inter-regional programme of economic co-operation among themselves. The fact that these meetings devoted attention to ECDC issues reinforces the view that the strategy for attaining the objectives of the ECDC programme cannot be seen in isolation from the overall strategy for global economic development. Indeed the International Development Strategy itself indicates that while ECDC concerns mainly relations among Third World countries, it also has its North-South dimension and should thus be viewed "as a basic component of the efforts towards the establishment of the new international economic order which, as such, is based on co-operation among all States".[2] Although the Strategy did not spell out in detail the perspective, policy measures and parameters of ECDC during the Decade, it nonetheless made reference to the various policy statements in which ECDC objectives and programmes had been elaborated. These, in turn, identify priorities for action and assign to international organizations and to the developed countries responsibilities for the implementation of a far-reaching, comprehensive and far-sighted programme of ECDC. The General Assembly, in section VII of its resolution 3202 (S–VI) on the NIEO, also sets out a range of major principles and measures for the promotion of co-operation among developing countries.

II. The content of the ECDC strategy

A series of meetings by the developing countries (under the auspices of the Group of 77 or of the Non-Aligned Movement) at ministerial and other levels adopted certain common objectives for ECDC. In summary, these objectives are broadly aimed at promoting and expanding trade among developing countries through the use of new, idle or under-utilized productive capacities in these countries; establishing appropriate mechanisms for joint or collective action, especially in the protection of common interests in commodity markets; defending the sovereignty of developing countries over their natural resources; strengthening the negotiating capability of developing countries through the establishment of producers' associations; intensified economic and technical co-operation through exchange of experience; joint import procurement of essential goods; co-ordinating investment policies; increasing production and productivity through the application of new and efficient methods of production; developing new uses for products; increasing developing countries' share in the processing, marketing and distribution of their products, especially those in which they have comparative advantage; promoting joint action for food security; co-operation in energy production and utilization; monetary and financial co-operation; and co-operation in the area of transportation and other services and in the development of new and renewable sources of energy.

These far-reaching objectives encompass virtually all the priority areas in the programmes of action which the developing countries have set for themselves.[3]

Co-operation among developing countries is both a means and an end for the implementation of a new international economic order; it is a key element for strengthening the developing countries' role in that order. The economic issues which were brought to the centre of the South-North dialogue in the sixties and seventies and at the launching of DD III are significant for ECDC and have their distinctive ECDC dimensions. These fall into about seven broad and interrelated categories, namely, food and raw materials, trade in primary commodities and manufactured products, money and finance, technology, energy, sovereignty over natural resources and over economic activity, and technical co-operation among developing countries (TCDC).

(a) Food and raw materials

In the area of food and raw materials there is a need to pursue actively the agreed objectives of the Integrated Programme for Commodities (IPC). In this connexion international commodity agreements should be concluded. The developing countries are also expected, within the context of equitable distribution of activities related to the production of commodities, to increase their share in the processing of raw materials produced by them. The acquisition by developing countries of improved capacity for the exploration and development of their natural resources is also considered to be a key element of the ECDC strategy which the developing countries may wish to pursue in the 1980s and beyond.

The colonial trade pattern in raw materials imposed a strait-jacket on developing countries and the needs of recent times have dictated that efforts towards co-operation among the developing countries should lead away from the bipolar relationship of the colonial era into an era of fruitful trade in raw materials among themselves. Recent trends in the pattern of trade of developing countries have revealed the immense potential for trade amongst developing countries themselves, particularly in the area of food and agricultural raw materials. There is now a tendency towards a more balanced pattern of interdependence, with developing countries trading more among themselves in their traditional food and raw materials exports in which they have been so dependent on markets in the developed countries.[4] The developing countries need, with a view to strengthening their position in the production and marketing of raw materials, to display the necessary political will to facilitate the conclusion of international agreements or producers' arrangements on individual commodities. The Common Fund, which through its operation would greatly benefit developing countries' producers, should be brought into early effect so that it can play its role as a key instrument of the IPC. The increased participation of the developing countries in the processing, transportation, marketing and distribution of their raw materials also calls for a concerted effort on the part of both the developed and the developing countries for the early establishment of an equitable framework of international co-operation as called for in UNCTAD resolution 124 (V). If the necessary support and co-operation are forthcoming from the UNCTAD member states it should be possible to give further impetus to the work programme in this area through the elaboration of proposals which could prove useful in establishing "the elements of the framework for international co-operation".[5]

Contrary to a generally held impression, trade among developing countries in food and raw materials has shown marked improvement in the last few years. ECDC in this area can be used as a strategic instrument for improving developing countries' self-sufficiency in food during the 1980s and beyond. The recent success of the Andean Group in the areas of arable farming and livestock production is a pointer to what developing countries can achieve through co-operation among themselves. The tools for co-operation in trade between developing countries in this area will have to be sharpened. Policy instruments for trade expansion and economic co-operation will have to be adjusted and adapted to encompass co-ordinated and, where possible, common policies for agriculture, sharing of experiences in food production and importation and in agricultural research and development, and programmes for irrigation, soil erosion prevention, pest control, animal husbandry and general improvement of agriculture.

(b) Trade

In the field of trade expansion, the main concern of the developing countries, as manifested in the many programmes of the Group of 77 and the Non-Aligned countries, is with the deterioration in the conditions of their foreign trade including the continuing decline in the terms of trade of a large number of them. They have therefore called for urgent measures by the developed countries to resolve the trade problems of the developing countries by taking steps to put an end to their protectionist policies and to effect the programme of action for structural adjustment called for in UNCTAD resolution 131 (V). New efforts are to be made to implement the Generalized System of Preferences (GSP) in favour of the developing countries and to enlarge and broaden its scope and its duration.

The developing countries, in their various declarations and programmes of action, were not oblivious to activities within the General Agreement on Tariffs and Trade (GATT). They regretted the lack of fulfilment by the developed contracting parties of the commitments they undertook in the Tokyo Declaration, regarding the granting of preferential and differential treatment to developing countries. They also pointed to the way in which even the modest gains for developing countries in the Tokyo Round were being eroded through arbitrary and unilateral action and the intensification of voluntary restraints, as exemplified by the Multifibre Arrangement in relation to trade in textiles. The developing countries also recommended in their Arusha Programme that a Global System of Trade Preferences (GSTP) among themselves should be established, as such a scheme "would constitute a major instrument for the promotion of trade, production and employment among developing countries".[6] The Caracas High-Level Meeting gave broad endorsement to the work in UNCTAD on a GSTP and the thirty-sixth session of the General Assembly, in its resolution 36/145, requested the Secretary-General of UNCTAD to intensify and complete work in the priority areas of ECDC including a global system of trade preferences.[7] It is expected that, in accordance with resolution 139 (VI) of the sixth session of UNCTAD, further impetus will be given to the implementation of the GSTP with a view to having the scheme established at the earliest possible opportunity.

The NIEO and the Strategies for the Second and Third United Nations Development Decades are not lacking in commitments to an open and expanding world trading system and the promotion of structural adjustments in lieu of protectionist measures. The fulfilment of these commitments should lend support to efforts by the developing countries to promote trade among themselves and enhance access to markets in the developed countries for products originating from the Third World. However, the commitments and undertakings by the developed countries, in the majority of cases, have either not been kept or been frustrated by the domestic problems which many countries have had to face as a result of the recent international economic crisis. It is also evident that, as far as access to markets is concerned, the developed countries have not found it possible or desirable to make any great efforts to improve access for semi-manufactured and manufactured products which are of export interest to the developing countries.[8]

The developing countries themselves are aware that their trading positions cannot be improved merely by obtaining easier access to the markets of developed countries. It is equally necessary to develop trade among themselves and to change the composition of their exports so as to encourage significant trade flows in both processed and industrial products. In this connexion, the developing countries should in their programmes for trade expansion and economic co-operation take every possible advantage of the opportunities for economies of scale which are available in vast economic areas. This is why trade expansion has long been a crucial objective of ECDC.

As far back as the 1960s, a number of economic integration groupings were established in developing countries. Many more have been formed in recent years. While some of these groupings have ceased to exist (e.g. the East African Community), the trade within some of them has expanded more than their trade with the rest of the world. Outside the framework of integration groupings, the objective of trade expansion among members is also being pursued through preferential trading arrangements, such as the GATT Protocol Relating to Trade Negotiations among Developing Countries[9] or the Bangkok Agreement.[10] While there is no denying the importance of these different forms of preferential trading arrangements with limited membership, the potential of a global system of trade preferences, open to all developing countries, would seem to make this project the most attractive at this stage.

In the 1970s trade among developing countries grew faster than their trade with the developed countries; the reverse was the case in the 1960s. As shown in the UNCTAD *Handbook of International Trade and Development Statistics, 1983*, between 1970 and 1981 exports among developing countries increased from 19.8 per cent to 27.3 per cent of their total exports. The recession and slower economic growth in the developed countries, the attendant weakening of their import demand and growing protectionism against competitive imports from developing countries have forced developing countries to rely more and more on themselves and to provide a relatively buoyant market for each others' exports.

The current international economic crisis, which has exacerbated economic problems in both developed and developing countries alike, should serve as a clear warning of the serious drawbacks of concentrating the bulk of exports of developing countries in developed country markets. Any trade strategy of the developing countries should aim at making greater headway in trade among themselves and devising policy instruments which would make possible the expansion of mutual trade among these countries at the sub-regional, regional and inter-regional levels.

(e) Money and finance

Monetary and financial co-operation, either through transfer of resources from capital-surplus to capital-deficient developing countries or through general co-operation in the area of monetary and financial policy, could give a great impetus to trade expansion among these countries and also smooth the way to intensified trade expansion and economic co-operation at the sub-regional, regional and inter-regional levels. In the 1960s, co-operation among developing countries in the area of development financing was mainly through the medium of the regional development banks, the Inter-American Development Bank (established in 1959), the African Development Bank (1964) and the Asian Development Bank (1966).[11] More recent forms of monetary and financial co-operation among developing countries include the establishment of regional or sub-regional payments arrangements in the form of clearing houses, payments unions and reserve funds, the establishment of national and multinational financing institutions for external assistance, the establishment of regional monetary funds and the use of joint ventures in promoting agricultural and industrial development in capital-importing developing countries.[12]

While the developing countries consider monetary and financial co-operation among themselves as one of the cornerstones of their ECDC strategy, they generally recognize that there are a few basic constraints to be overcome in this area. Firstly, the fields open for financial co-operation in the different sectors of their economies are varied and sometimes complex and would therefore require sophisticated infrastructure for garnering funds and channelling them into investments. Secondly, resources that could be made available by developing countries themselves for the promotion of their co-operation activities are limited and would need to be supplemented by resources from outside, from the developed countries and their financial institutions. Prevailing international circumstances do not however augur well for any substantial increase in the flow of official development assistance from developed countries to developing countries in the near future.

Of course, the international community, in various declarations, decisions and programmes of action, has agreed to use its best endeavours to alleviate the problems of developing countries in this area. Such agreed measures include undertakings that, in principle, financial assistance to developing countries will be untied and that measures will be taken to reduce the extent and harmful effect of tying; that an increased flow of aid will be provided on a longer-term and continuing basis; that the procedure for granting and disbursing aid would be simplified; and that a "rapid and substantial increase will be made in official development assistance by all developed countries with a view to reaching and, where possible, surpassing the agreed international target of 0.7 per cent of the gross national products of developed countries".[13] However, the track record of many developed countries in this area does not suggest an early realization of these undertakings.

The views of both the developed and the developing countries do not seriously diverge over what actions would need to be taken in the area of monetary and financial co-operation. There are, however, strong differences of views over how and when such actions should be taken. An important and urgent action which the developing countries consider essential for returning order to the international monetary system is the reform of that system in such a manner as to make it more universal, to ensure more effective participation by developing countries in its decision-making process, and to respond to the liquidity and capital needs of the developing countries. The Western developed countries are neither ready nor willing to contemplate such a reform of a structure which they control and which has served their own needs so well.

It would seem relevant in the light of the foregoing, and as a strategic option for the 1980s, for developing countries to strengthen their own financial institutions (national, sub-regional and inter-regional) in which they have a decisive voice and make them more relevant to their own development perspectives. Such institutions could thus open up new vistas of opportunities for the satisfaction of the diverse financial needs of the developing countries in the areas of agriculture, industrialization, access to technology, transport, communications, and services such as insurance and banking. There is also need to stress here a concept which has been emphasized in many UNCTAD documents and which was endorsed by the United Nations Conference on Least Developed Countries (Paris, 1981), the idea that whatever actions might be taken to ease the economic problems of the developing countries in the monetary and financial area, special measures in favour of the least developed countries are of crucial importance if these countries are not to be left by the wayside in the march towards greater economic and technical co-operation among the developing countries.

(d) Technology

Scientific and technological development hold out great promise for the developing countries. The full realization of this promise will inevitably involve a great deal of social change in order to facilitate the introduction of technology, its efficient utilization and the fair distribution of its benefits. The international community, of developing and developed countries as well as international organizations, fully recognizes that access to and mastery of modern technology "are essential for the economic and social progress of developing countries"[14] and that action should be taken to bring about a restructuring of existing technological relations between the developed and the developing countries. The call for such a restructuring of technological relations should be viewed against the background of the realities of the situation in regard to technological transfer, i.e. "95 per cent of modern technology was originally patented in the industrialized countries and the rights of ownership and control rest mainly with large transnational corporations".[15]

The approach of developing countries themselves can be seen not only in the Programme of Action on NIEO but also in the different decisions and recommendations of meetings and conferences of the Non-Aligned countries and the Group of 77. Disappointed with the lack of progress in this area, the developing countries called for the finalization of a universally-applicable Code of Conduct on the Transfer of Technology. Since the question of the transfer of technology is closely related to the activities of transnational corporations, it is not surprising that efforts at finalizing work on the Code have been thwarted by countries with the greatest vested interests in the activities of transnational corporations. Whether or not the Code is agreed soon, the aims and objectives of ECDC would be well served if the developing countries were to begin to implement the terms and conditions of the draft Code nationally, sub-regionally, regionally and internationally in all their transactions among themselves relating to the transfer of technology.

The developing countries could also, in devising their technological strategy for the 1980s and beyond, give positive consideration to strengthening their co-operation in those areas where technology is not commercialized and where they could take initiatives in encouraging mutually beneficial development and transfer of technology. The areas of agriculture and health, where many national governments of developing countries engage in important research and development activities, easily lend themselves to such positive consideration.

(e) Energy

Energy is another important issue not only within the framework of South-

North negotiations but also within the ECDC context. Policy measures agreed upon in this area within the South-North and South-South fora relate essentially to actions required on the part of net oil exporters and in particular the countries belonging to the Organization of Petroleum Exporting Countries (OPEC). The need for secure supplies of oil to industrialized oil-importing countries predominates in the discussion of policy measures in this area. Stability of the income of producing countries and of world market prices for oil has not received the same amount of attention, as action in this area might be interpreted as offending against the classical philosophy of a free market mechanism. Events of the last few years have revealed, however, that on oil policy most net oil-exporting countries tended to follow the OPEC lead, especially in regard to price quotations for crude oil. The United Kingdom and Norway, for example, during the month of February 1982 followed the OPEC lead in cutting prices of oil, thus accentuating the downward spriral in oil prices.

Co-operation among developing countries in the field of energy is of crucial importance to their development. Some of these opportunities for co-operation are listed in the Havana Non-Aligned Countries' Policy Guidelines on the Reinforcement of Collective Self-Reliance among Developing Countries. These policy guidelines, as well as those enunciated in DD III and by the Nairobi Conference on New and Renewable Sources of Energy, contain important measures on which to base whatever energy strategy the developing countries would wish to pursue in the 1980s and beyond. The objectives include the development and expansion of all energy resources of the world with a view to providing long-term solutions to the world's energy problem, facilitation of transition from the present world economy based on hydrocarbons to one that will increasingly rely on new and renewable energy resources, effective implementation of the results of the UN Conference on New and Renewable Sources of Energy and meeting "the needs of energy-deficient developing countries through co-operation, assistance and investment in relation to conventional as well as new and renewable sources of energy".[16]

In implementing an energy strategy among themselves, the developing countries will have to rely on the support, co-operation and understanding of those of them that are substantial net exporters of oil to the world market, i.e, on the support of OPEC countries and other important net exporters within the Third World. Trinidad and Tobago, Mexico and Venezuela, for example, have begun to implement measures to alleviate the financial burden of oil-importing developing countries and to ensure adequate supply of oil to them. These positive steps, coupled, as appropriate, with transfer of energy-related technology to oil-deficient developing countries, will serve the objective of economic co-operation and help to sustain the collective self-reliance of the Third World.

(f) Economic sovereignty

Sovereignty over natural resources and over economic activities is an issue which usually evokes emotive discussions within all the South-North fora which have had to deal with this subject. Both the Charter of Economic Rights and Duties of States and the Declaration and Programme of Action on the Establishment of a NIEO recognize the rights of States to exercise sovereignty over their natural resources. The issue of the right of developing countries to nationalize, expropriate or otherwise dispose of the assets of foreign companies operating in their territories, in accordance with their own national laws, is not unrelated to the wider issue of sovereignty over natural resources. The developed countries, of course, hold the view that just, fair and timely compensation should be paid, in accordance with international law.[17] The adoption of the Charter, albeit against some Northern opposition, represented a big victory for the Third World in its struggle for a new philosophy of development which corresponds to the principles and ideals of the Charter of the United Nations.

Both the Non-Aligned Movement and the Group of 77 feel seriously disadvantaged in negotiations with the developed countries on the issue of sovereignty over natural resources. In a spirit of comradeship, the developing countries tend to fashion out a common negotiating stance on almost all issues hinging on this question. An important refrain which runs through their decisions and declarations on this subject invariably reaffirms the right of developing countries to take necessary steps for exercising sovereignty over their natural and other resources, including the raw materials produced by them. In this connexion, the DD III Strategy calls for "the rational development, management and utilization of natural resources" in order, inter alia, "to prevent early exhaustion of finite resources and overburdening of renewable resources".[18]

Encouraged by the success of OPEC countries in exercising some measures of control over their oil resources, the developing countries decided to pursue as a deliberate policy the strengthening of existing producers' associations and the establishment of new ones in sectors where they do not at present exist. Such a strategy, it is believed, will improve their negotiating leverage. Several producers' associations have been established in recent years by the developing countries.[19] They vary a great deal in their organization, structure and scope of membership. In spite of these diversities, the successes marked up by many of them, particularly in the area of collective bargaining with the developed consuming countries, are likely to give further impetus to the formation of more producers' associations of developing countries in the future.

(g) TCDC

In the implementation of their strategy for economic co-operation and collective self-reliance, developing countries will have to intensify technical co-operation among themselves. For any ECDC strategy to succeed it must be complemented and supported by technical co-operation among developing countries (TCDC), as was made clear in the discussions at the United Nations Conference on TCDC (Buenos Aires, 1978). The NIEO, the DD III Strategy and the developing countries themselves recognize the role of technical co-operation in the development process.

Some of the areas of potential mutual benefit in the context of TCDC include joint ventures in project development, joint efforts in research and development and in the adaptation of technology, and exchange of information, particularly where significant research and development activities are being carried out by the developing countries' governments, as in the fields of agriculture and health. Many TCDC activities are taking place in all regions of the developing countries. The prospects for future TCDC are particularly bright. It has great potential for "facilitating and supporting, *inter alia*, investment, research, training and development".[20] The developing countries should strive to use it as a deliberate policy instrument for achieving self-reliance.

III. Problems, constraints and prospects in ECDC

Although there are a few success spots on the ECDC landscape, progress towards well co-ordinated and harmonized ECDC has been painfully slow. Co-operation arrangements have been bedevilled with problems and conflicts in very many instances. It has to be said that some of these problems are inherent in the juridical, financial or institutional nature of the arrangements for ECDC and constitute impediments to effective work in this area. Their removal is an important task to which developing countries should address themselves.

In the area of trade, the share of trade among developing countries in their total exports rose from 22.3 per cent in 1960 to 24.8 per cent in 1980, although there was a decline to 19.8 per cent in 1970.[21] In 1981, the corresponding percentage was 27.3. This performance is not considered adequate by many developing countries, taking into account the objectives which they have set for themselves in the area of trade. Sharp increases in trade among members of integration groupings with programmes of trade liberalization constitute an important component of the increased share of developing countries in their total trade. Empirical studies carried out by the ECDC Division of UNCTAD indicate that in the Andean Group and LAFTA, for example, tariff concessions were effective at a first stage of development and above a minimum preferential margin. Beyond that stage, further trade increases would appear to require harmonization of economic policies among participating countries.[22] This study underlines the well-known fact that the objectives of trade integration cannot be achieved through tariff reductions alone and that such policy will have to be complemented by exchange rate adjustments and long-term stability of other schemes which constitute an integral part of a co-ordinated and harmonized strategy.

Lack of a commonly accepted instrument for financing South-South trade has hindered the achievement of a spectacular expansion in this area. Trade deficits are settled through convertible currencies or bilateral arrangements. This deficiency in the financing of South-South trade can be overcome through the establishment of a trade financing facility by the developing countries either on its own or within the framework of a commercially viable Bank of the Developing Countries, which some developing countries have advocated should be established.

In the area of development financing, where the different regional institutions can lay claim to a good track record in their pursuit of development objectives, some óf these financing organizations are severely constrained in the modalities and purposes of their lending.[23] The terms and conditions of lending in some of these institutions tend to be too influenced by the philosophy of economic and financial austerity associated with IMF 'adjustment' programmes for borrowers from the Third World. This is due to the banks' proclivity to over-cautiousness and thereby failure to respond positively to the development needs of their clients. It is claimed by some developing countries, for example, that lending policies of the Asian Development Bank and the Inter-American Development Bank are essentially designed to promote the production of exports needed by the developed countries, while lending to meet basic development objectives is apparently lower in the order of priority.

Other obstacles to the achievement of effective economic co-operation among developing countries include resistance to change on the part of some developing countries and their unwillingness to take a plunge into co-operative arrangements, timidity on the part of others in restructuring the bi-polar relationship between themselves and the metropolis, unwholesome competition (political and economic) among developing countries which tends to undermine their cohesiveness, their negotiating leverage and their collective self-reliance, a rather sad lack of trade intelligence in regard to what competitors are up to in the markets of other developing countries and which potentials exist in those markets, a lack of competent and trained personnel to put into operation programmes of economic co-operation among these countries, and a pitifully tenuous linkage or indeed a total lack of linkage between institutions of developing countries in the trade, money, finance and development spheres. Mere identification of these obstacles is not enough, however. What is important is to devise policy measures specifically directed at removing these obstacles and making ECDC truly operational.

Several lessons could be drawn from the experiences of developing countries arising from a practical application of measures of ECDC. Co-operation among developing countries will not just grow, 'like Topsy'. It needs to be carefully nurtured by Third World political commitment at the highest possible level. The concerns of the economically weaker and geographically disadvantaged developing countries should be duly taken care of within the framework of any co-operation arrangements if harmonious relations and cohesiveness within groupings are to be maintained. In this connexion, it would be highly desirable to explore potentially complementary relations between members of groupings in the areas of raw materials, finance, human capital and know-how for co-operation schemes and projects.

Developing countries have had varied experiences with the diverse economic co-operation arrangements which they have so far put into effect.[24] The experiences of the Andean Pact countries, LAFTA, UDEAC and the defunct East African Common Market are particularly relevant in this respect. The benefits and costs of co-operation have in many cases not been shared equitably. Some have been badly shaken by their own ECDC experiences; as in any other human venture, risks cannot be completely discounted in economic co-operation. The developing countries must learn how to co-operate among themselves even when there are great costs to be incurred. The least developed and the economically disadvantaged among the developing countries need to be reminded that, while their concerns and apprehensions should be taken into account in all ECDC endeavours, such co-operation ventures cannot be in all cases without some costs to them, as well as benefits. The urge for ECDC can only be kindled if all developing countries, irrespective of their economic and social philosophies and of their levels of development, carry out their undertakings in this area with utmost seriousness, sincerity and steadfastness. President Julius Nyerere of Tanzania put the ECDC issue in its proper perspective when, in an address to the Group of 77 at Arusha, he stated that "we must ensure that we continue to speak with one voice and that none of us makes a separate bilateral or multilateral deal which weakens the overall Third World bargaining position" and that "the basic question which we should be asking ourselves now, after years of hard talking and little progress, is this. What can we do, among ourselves, to strengthen our position in future negotiations?"[25]

IV. North-South dimensions of ECDC

As already observed, economic co-operation among developing countries is an essential part of a global economic system. It is "an important element of

the New International Economic Order and as such is based on interdependence, common interest and co-operation among all States".[26] In an
interdependent world, neither the developing nor the developed countries
can afford to abandon co-operation at the global level. The developing
countries are already doing a lot to promote economic co-operation among
themselves within the framework of their sub-regional, regional and inter-
regional arrangements. These arrangements, which cover almost all the
whole range of co-operation among developing countries, have their North-
South dimensions. Some of these arrangements would require some resources from the North for their effective implementation, as well as honest
and sincere dialogue on how and when these resources would be made
available.

International monetary and financial institutions, development finance
institutions of the North and Northern aid agencies can be obstructive or
constructive towards ECDC depending on whether their lending policies
have a negative or positive effect on such co-operation. Increased financial
and technical assistance to the poorest and least developed among the
developing countries, especially in the development of their infrastructure
and industries, would increase their capacity and willingness to participate
in ECDC schemes. ECDC could also be positively encouraged through the
channelling of an increasing share of assistance to regional and inter-
regional institutions which are required by their terms of reference to
promote ECDC.

Tying of aid could adversely affect ECDC. Untying of aid should be
encouraged for procurement in developing countries, particularly in areas
where comparable products or services that are the subject of tying could be
supplied by other developing countries. The untying of aid in such circumstances will give further stimulus to ECDC.[27]

Triangular arrangements, by which resources are provided by a capital-
surplus developing country to another developing country for the implementation of development projects needing inputs from the industrialized
North, have been used in the past as a means of promoting ECDC.
Arrangements of this type have been used for the development of communications in Africa and their success has encouraged negotiation of similar
triangular arrangements in other sectors of the economy at the sub-regional
or regional level.

The developing countries have over the years been accumulating information and know-how on what their problems are in certain areas of ECDC,
especially over agriculture, food production and health issues. Many information-gathering units are government establishments or multinational
research institutions of developing countries. The time has come for advantage to be taken, in certain of these cases, of opportunities available in
developed countries, aiming at the exchange of information and know-how

applicable to similar situations in both groups of countries. Such exchange of experiences between developed and developing countries will help to broaden the capacity of the latter countries in such areas and could also help them to adapt modern research techniques to their own co-operation programmes. In the area of adaptive research, the developing countries can also gain a lot from developed countries by exploring the existing information available in those countries and adapting it to their own local conditions.

One of the major constraints on multinational schemes of co-operation and joint ventures among developing countries is that of funding. Resources available within developing countries participating in such ventures may be inadequate and recourse will have to be had to sources of funding from the developed countries or from their capital markets. Such additional or supplementary funding will only be possible if such ventures are 'bankable'. Support for ECDC by developed countries should involve more than mere declarations of good intentions. It should involve a deliberate and voluntary sharing and exchange of technical resources and capabilities. It is inconceivable that a balanced planetary development could be peacefully achieved without such deliberate altruistic acts by the North in support of the South.

The developing countries, within their own integration arrangements recognize that their co-operation efforts must complement and supplement co-operation arrangements among the developed countries. For example, in the Treaty establishing the Latin American Integration Association, its member countries committed themselves to taking the necessary action to establish co-operation links with integration groupings outside Latin America. It is probably for this reason, and because of the growing importance of investment from the European Community in Latin America, that Latin American countries are seen to be taking measures to enhance their relations with the EEC. This change of relationship will be well understood if one recalls that while the USA held 63.8 per cent of total foreign investment in the Latin American region in 1974, the figure declined to 50 per cent in 1980, with the EEC countries' share growing from 17 per cent to 25 per cent during the same period. The advantage of greater co-operation between integration groupings of developing countries and those of developed countries is borne out by the foregoing figures.

In the area of trade, the developing countries could, through intensified co-operation among themselves, offer a vast new frontier for the expansion of North-South trade. If, through their ECDC activities, developing countries are able to improve their productive activity and economic welfare, their more active and prosperous markets would provide new opportunities for exports from the developed countries. Such trade-related activities will offer major and reciprocal advantages for both sides.

Some, though not many, of the co-operation arrangements among developing countries involve the transfer of technology. Such technology transfer is still restricted to the area of non-commercial technology and rudimentary areas of commercial technology, e.g. woodworking, boat-building, machine tools manufacture, food and beverages, batteries, valves, transistors, iron ore concentrates, and processing of agricultural products to mention just a few. For ECDC to be resilient and to benefit from technological changes, developing countries will need to rely on assistance from the North for building up their own research capacities and also expanding and strengthening their technological capabilities. The issue of the revision of the Paris Convention and the negotiations within UNCTAD on a Code of Conduct on the Transfer of Technology are part of the efforts being made at the global level to meet the needs of developing countries.[28]

In the transport and communication sectors of ECDC, massive investments and large technical assistance programmes would be required, with the support of the developed countries and the international community. The bulk of developing countries' trade is carried to and from developed countries and, even in trade among developing countries, some of the critical bottlenecks to trade expansion are the weak transport and communications links between developing countries and in particular between remote island developing countries and their neighbouring developing countries. Improved transport and communications infrastructures among developing countries and between them and the developed countries can reinforce existing commercial links and open up vistas for new ones. There is still great potential to be tapped in the transport and communications area, whether by air, road, rail, inland waterways or telecommunications. There are projects, planned or already operational, which are intended to improve South-South links while also revitalizing North-South trade flows. Such projects include the Pan-African Highway, the Inter-American Telecommunications Network, the Pan-American Highway and the Western Asia Highway. There are also many proposals in the area of shipping which are expected to link developing countries on the same shipping lanes with their export markets in developed countries. These projects in the transport and communications areas require massive investments and massive transfers of technology and know-how from North to South, emphasizing the need for North-South as well as South-South co-operation and collaboration, and the interdependent nature of activities in these areas.

While the responsibility for promoting ECDC lies mainly with the developing countries themselves, their strategy of collective self-reliance is not designed to build a wall of containment around the Third World that would seal it off from the North. Nor should ECDC be regarded as inimical to North-South co-operation. Rather, it should be viewed as a mechanism for making such co-operation more meaningful and equitable. This is recognized by the NIEO and by the many programmes which the developing countries have formulated to further their collective self-reliance. Understanding and co-operation between the developed and the developing countries is therefore absolutely essential if ECDC is to take its place as an inevitable and essential component of the NIEO. Both North and South will have to learn to shed suspicion of each other when major initiatives are taken in the area of ECDC. Joint responsibility and joint action will be required to meet the inescapable needs of ECDC and to solve some of the daunting problems facing the Third World and its ECDC programmes.

V. Observations by way of a conclusion

The many summits and conferences of the developing countries have brought forth many proposals and recommendations for fostering ECDC. These proposals and recommendations cannot all be implemented in one swoop. Priority attention will have to be given to those that are particularly significant and important for the first critical steps towards effective ECDC. The Arusha Programme, while it is comprehensive in nature, attempts to map out such priority areas.[29] The Caracas Programme of Action, through its comprehensiveness and multisectoral approach to ECDC, attempts to take care of some of the shortcomings in the Arusha Plan.[30]

In addition to priority areas in the field of trade expansion, encouragement will have to be given to the transfer of technology which addresses the needs of developing countries in critical areas of water, sanitation, food, housing, energy, health, education, communications and transportation. ECDC will be a mere empty shell if the needs of the Third World's masses are not significantly satisfied in these areas. Attention will also have to be paid to intensified co-operation in money and finance, and to support to activities of economic co-operation and to integration groupings of developing countries.

Since ECDC is perceived to be an important element of the NIEO and of the United Nations Development Strategy for the 1980s, the implementation of agreed measures to promote ECDC should now be given the decisive momentum which they have hitherto lacked. Access to developed countries' markets for exports from the developing countries is not enough. It is just as important for developing countries to change the composition of trade and other economic exchanges among themselves and between them and the developed countries. This will help in ensuring a transformation of the structure of trade and other economic exchanges which will be conducive to meeting the needs of the age.

At the moment many developing countries are, in their trade exchanges, producing what they do not consume and consuming what they do not produce, with the balance heavily tilted in favour of heavy consumption.

Policy prescriptions for now and for future years should encourage changes in the structure of production and consumption with a view to redressing the imbalance in the composition and direction of trade.

It must be admitted that in an international environment plagued by inflation, unemployment and recession, South-North negotiations face an uphill struggle to reach a consensus on what economic policy measures should be adopted at the international level. With the problems confronting South-North negotiations in an uncertain international climate, collective self-reliance through ECDC assumes increasing importance as a strategy for the development of the Third World. Such an uncertain atmosphere should encourage the quest for greater collective self-reliance and mutual co-operation. However, enthusiasm for ECDC should not be fuelled by adverse circumstances at the international level alone. Collective self-reliance and stronger ECDC should also be based on well thought-out policies and practices and the establishment of flexible institutions and mechanisms which will act as catalysts for economic exchanges among developing countries. A sound basis of this kind is required for a lasting ECDC citadel which can withstand the test of time as well as of adverse economic winds at the international level.

To survive, such a citadel will have to be based on solid foundations which include:

= the recognition of the different stages of development of developing countries and the adoption of deliberate policy measures to take care of their varying concerns;

= preferential treatment for the least developed countries within the framework of economic co-operation arrangements at all levels, especially where the least developed countries have demonstrated the capacity to supply the goods or services required within the arrangements;

= harmonization and co-ordination of policies, flexibly enough devised not to drive off those countries that are very hesitant towards ECDC, nor to make 'prima donnas' of those which are enthusiastically committed to Third World collective self-reliance;

= new forms of co-operation between transnational corporations established in developing countries and the multinational enterprises of developing countries, so as to avoid the manipulation of ECDC to promote the cause of the transnationals (the conclusion of the Code of Conduct on Transfer of Technology and the revision of the Paris Convention should provide developing countries with such operational flexibility as may be required for solving problems in this area);

= appropriate mechanisms, facilities and institutions for underpinning collective self-reliance and economic co-operation efforts, based on the experiences of some of the most successful groupings of the developing countries and of the EEC and the Council for Mutual Economic Assistance (Comecon).

It is not intended to present the ECDC situation as if the developing countries have not scored some significant achievements in this area. But, while some progress has been made, particularly towards the establishment of economic groupings, many problems have also been met which are common to these groupings. The cause of ECDC would be greatly helped if some appropriate forum could be identified within which these groupings could discuss their common problems and learn from each other's experiences and ideas. The outcome of such exchange of experiences should help groupings in refining their conceptual approach to problems and assist them in adopting flexible mechanisms for their resolution, particularly if they discover that their policy prescriptions have been inadequate, inappropriate or out of tune with the prevailing economic philosophy of the groupings concerned. The initiative taken by the UNCTAD secretariat in bringing together the secretariats of integration groupings of the developing countries under one umbrella, to exchange experiences of common interest to their groupings, has helped to cement co-operation and to facilitate collaboration among them.[31]

It would be inappropriate and even regrettable if the focus of ECDC were to be the promotion of economic exchanges at the sub-regional and regional levels alone. It is essential to explore the great potentials that exist for inter-regional linkages among existing economic co-operation arrangements. Intensification of co-operation among developing countries at the inter-regional level seems essential for an effective ECDC strategy. On the other hand, efforts by the developing countries to strengthen and expand inter-regional trade and other economic exchanges among themselves should not be thwarted by the developed countries. While the ECDC concept as such is not a contentious issue, the tactics and strategy to achieve its objectives are being seriously questioned in certain quarters of the developed world. The developed countries would be contributing to the development of the Third World and to their own development by accepting the repercussions which flow from intensified economic co-operation among developing countries. A prosperous and economically strong Third World has historically proved to be a strong and expanding market for the North. It can only be hoped that the developed countries will heed the apprehensions and suspicions generally felt in developing countries that, while the North is in principle not opposed to ECDC, it has not, in practice, demonstrated a firm resolve to support and uphold the collective self-reliance of the Third World.

The United Nations development system has a special interest and even a special responsibility for supporting ECDC. UNCTAD has a singularly important role to play.[32] The Arusha Programme for Collective Self-Reliance, the Caracas Programme and the Non-Aligned Action Programmes for Economic Co-operation all give UNCTAD an important role in the implementation of measures for promoting and strengthening ECDC. More frequent exchange of information and ideas among United Nations agencies at the bilateral level and within inter-agency mechanisms would appear to be of paramount importance for enhancing inter-agency co-operation and co-ordination and further refining policy measures, particularly in sectors where feasible and operational arrangements among developing countries at the inter-regional level are not as yet clearly defined, i.e. air transport, communication and environment.

The geographical, economic and political diversities of the developing countries all go to accentuate ECDC problems. After the Mexico City Plan of Action and the Arusha Programme for Collective Self-Reliance, ECDC issues have begun to move from generalities into the technically more complex aspects. The more complex the issues become the greater is the technical capability required for addressing them. Many developing countries have neither this technical capacity nor the managerial experience required to tackle ECDC issues effectively. While the Group of 77 deals with the question of co-ordination on ECDC matters at the international and inter-regional levels, there is also need for appropriate machinery to be established at the national levels for continuous and operational co-ordination of ECDC matters. Such national co-ordination machinery could be in the form of national focal points situated in a ministry designated by the government. National co-ordination is essential for any effective ECDC policy and will ensure that the goals and objectives of ECDC are taken into account at the national level in the areas of trade, development planning, finance, investment, energy, agriculture, industry and technology. A national focal point would also help to ensure that ECDC activities receive the required political support at the national level.

Secretariats of groupings of developing countries and their regional institutions, such as SELA and OAU, as well as the United Nations regional commissions (ECA, ECLA, ECWA and ESCAP) could also assist ECDC by helping to co-ordinate activities at the sub-regional and regional levels and to elaborate sub-regional and regional positions and priorities in key areas for negotiations among the developing countries. Regular contacts among these organizations through meetings, conferences, seminars and symposia on ECDC issues would also facilitate the march to greater self-reliance among the developing countries. The required support for ECDC at the national, sub-regional and regional levels will encourage the Group of 77 in elaborating appropriate ECDC policies at the inter-regional and inter-national levels and in organizing technical and political support for ECDC activities.

The international community also has a long-term economic, political and security interest in supporting ECDC and the collective self-reliance of the Third World. International organizations could be of considerable assistance to ECDC if through their research work and publications they could use their influence to convince governments of the developed countries of the need to support ECDC. The rapid economic development of the developing countries is essentially their own responsibility but ways must be found to ensure that in our interdependent world the necessary support measures fundamental to such development are made readily available. The reality of our times makes it evident that, as regards international co-operation for ECDC, neither the North nor the South can afford to be an island and there can be no doubt that they both need each other.

---

1. Issues covered in the Action Programme include the strengthening of mutual self-reliance, producers' associations, co-operation in procurement policies, trade preferences, support to integration groupings and the establishment of multinational enterprises.

2. See Annex to General Assembly resolution 35/56 (hereinafter referred to as *the DD III Strategy*) section III J.

3. A list of the programmes of economic co-operation adopted by the Non-Aligned Movement and the Group of 77 since 1970 is given in Annex I.

4. See UNCTAD *Trade and Development Report 1983*, part II, chapter 2, section A.

5. See UNCTAD resolution 156 (VI).

6. See *Arusha Programme*, Chapter II: *Programme for Collective Self-Reliance.*

7. See operative paragraph 15 of General Assembly resolution 36/145 which includes in this priority listing work on a trade information system, state trading organizations of developing countries, multinational production and marketing enterprises, a global system of trade preferences among developing countries, and monetary and financial co-operation.

8. For a detailed discussion of this and related issues, see UNCTAD *Trade and Development Report*, 1981 and 1982.

9. See study prepared by Mahmoud A. Hamza on this subject in UNCTAD document TB/B/C.7/49 which gives a review of the GATT Protocol.

10. The members of the Bangkok Agreement are: Bangladesh, India, Lao People's Democratic Republic, the Philippines, the Republic of Korea, Sri Lanka and Thailand.

11. It should be noted, however, that the control and management of some of these development banks are not wholly in the hands of the developing countries and that the developed countries play a dominant role in the lending policies of some of these banks.

12. Note in this connexion the role which the Arab Authority for Agricultural Investment and Development is expected to play in Sudan's agricultural development.

13. See the DD III Strategy, section III D.

14. See the DD III Strategy, section III G.

15. See *Unequal Partners* by Garret Fitzgerald, United Nations, New York, 1979, section II on transnational corporations.

16. See the DD III Strategy, section III H.

17. See in this connexion the Charter of Economic Rights and Duties of States adopted by the General Assembly on 12 December 1974 (resolution 3281 (XXIX)), and also the proceedings of the twenty-ninth session of the General Assembly.

18. See the DD III Strategy, section II.

19. For a list of these producers' associations, see Annex II.

20. See the DD III Strategy, section III F.

21. See UNCTAD *Handbook of International Trade and Development Statistics, 1983*.

22. See UNCTAD document TD/B/C.7/51, Part I.

23. For a list of these financing institutions, see Annex III.

24. For a list of such co-operation arrangements, see Annex IV.

25. See Address by His Excellency Mwalimu Julius Nyerere, President of the Republic of Tanzania, to the Fourth Ministerial Meeting of the Group of 77 at Arusha in February 1979.

26. See UNCTAD document TD/236, *Arusha Programme for Collective Self-Reliance and Framework for Negotiations*, section on Economic Co-operation among Developing Countries, paragraph 4(D).

27. For a detailed discussion of this point, see UNCTAD document TD/B/C.7/57, R.S. Roberts Jr, *Official development assistance and economic co-operation among developing countries*.

28. See the contribution to this volume by Surendra J. Patel.

29. See also UNCTAD resolution 139 (VI) which lists some critical areas to which attention should be paid in the implementation of UNCTAD's ECDC work programme.

30. Note however that the Caracas Programme of Action does not include all critical sectors for an effective ECDC, e.g. health, nor does it address itself fully to the issue of international support measures for ECDC.

31. For details of activities and co-operation arrangements planned by these groupings, see document TD/B/C.7/55, Annex I.

32. In paragraph 8 of its resolution 34/202, the General Assembly requested the Secretary-General of UNCTAD "within the framework of the mandate of the Conference and in the light of its key role in economic co-operation among developing countries within the United Nations system, to intensify further its efforts in support of relevant programmes of economic co-operation among developing countries".

Annex I

*List of the main programmes of economic co-operation adopted by the Non-Aligned Movement and the Group of 77 since 1970**

A. *The Non-Aligned Movement*

1. Programme of Action for Economic Co-operation among Non-Aligned Countries adopted by the Third Summit of Non-Aligned Countries, Lusaka, 8-10 September 1970.

2. Action Programme for Economic Co-operation among Non-Aligned Countries adopted by the Third Conference of Ministers of Foreign Affairs of Non-Aligned Countries, Georgetown, 8-12 August 1972.

3. Action Programme of Economic Co-operation adopted by the Fourth Summit of Non-Aligned Countries, Algiers, 5-9 September 1973.

4. Programme of Action on Economic Co-operation (including the Plan of Action for Food and Agricultural Production) adopted by the Fifth Summit of Non-Aligned Countries, Colombo, 16-19 August 1976.

5. Action Programme for Economic Co-operation adopted by the Sixth Summit of Non-Aligned Countries, Havana, 3-8 September 1979.

6. Action Programme for Economic Co-operation adopted by the Seventh Summit of Non-Aligned Countries, New Delhi, 7-11 March 1983.

B. The Group of 77

1. The Manila Declaration and Programme of Action adopted by the Third Ministerial Meeting of the Group of 77, Manila, 26 January–7 February 1976.

2. The Mexico City Programme of Action (Measures for Economic Co-operation among Developing Countries) adopted at the Mexico City Conference on Economic Co-operation among Developing Countries, Mexico City, 13–22 September 1976.

3. The Arusha Programme for Collective Self-Reliance adopted by the Fourth Ministerial Meeting of the Group of 77, Arusha, 12–16 February 1979.

4. The Caracas Programme of Action adopted by the High-Level Conference on Economic Co-operation among Developing Countries, Caracas, 13–19 May 1981.

* The texts of the programmes adopted up to 1982, together with other related documents, have been assembled in *ECDC Handbook*, prepared for the Seventh Summit of Non-Aligned Countries (New Delhi, March 1983) and now available from the Office of the Chairman of the Group of 77 at United Nations Headquarters in New York.

Annex II

Producers' Associations of Developing Countries

1. African and Malagasy Coffee Organization (OAMCAF)
2. African Groundnut Council (AGC)
3. African Timber Organization
4. Asian and Pacific Coconut Community (APCC)
5. Association of Iron Ore Exporting Countries (APEF)
6. Association of Natural Rubber Producing Countries (ANRPC)
7. Cocoa Producers' Alliance
8. Group of Latin American and Caribbean Sugar Exporting Countries (GEPLACEA)
9. Interafrican Coffee Organization (IACO)
10. Intergovernmental Council of Copper Exporting Countries (CIPEC)
11. International Bauxite Association (IBA)
12. International Tea Committee (ITC)
13. Organization of Arab Petroleum Exporting Countries (OAPEC)
14. Organization of Petroleum Exporting Countries (OPEC)

15. Pepper Community (PC)
16. Primary Tungsten Association (PTA)
17. Union of Banana Exporting Countries (UPEB)

Annex III

Multilateral Financing Institutions of Developing Countries

1. African Development Bank
2. African Development Fund
3. Andean Development Corporation (Corporación Andina de Fomento)
4. Arab African Bank .
5. Arab Authority for Agricultural Investment and Development
6. Arab Bank for Economic Development in Africa (Banque Arabe pour le Développement économique en Afrique—BADEA)
7. Arab Fund for Economic and Social Development
8. Arab Fund for Technical Assistance to Arab and African Countries
9. Arab International Bank
10. Arab Investment Company
11. Arab Petroleum Investment Company
12. ASEAN Finance Corporation
13. Asian Development Bank
14. Banco Latinoamericano de Exportación
15. Banque Centrale des Etats de l'Afrique de l'Ouest (BCEAO)
16. Banque de Développement des Etats de l'Afrique Centrale
17. Banque de Développement des Pays des Grands Lacs
18. Banque des Etats de l'Afrique Centrale
19. Caribbean Development Bank
20. Caribbean Investment Corporation
21. Central American Bank for Economic Integration (Banco Centroamericano de Integración Económica—BCIE)
22. East African Development Bank
23. Fonds de Coopération, de Compensation et de Développement de la CEDEAO
24. Fonds de Développement régional de la CEAO

25. Fonds de Solidarité et d'Intervention pour le Développement de la CEAO
26. Inter-American Development Bank
27. Inter-Arab Investment Guaranty Corporation
28. Islamic Development Bank
29. Mutual Aid and Loan Guarantee Fund of the Council of the Entente States
30. OPEC Fund for International Development
31. Special Arab Fund for Africa
32. Trust Fund for the Development of the River Plate Basin
33. West African Development Bank (BOAD)

Annex IV

Organizations and Arrangements of Developing Countries engaged in Economic Co-operation and Integration ★

1. Action Programme on Economic Co-operation among Non-Aligned and Other Developing Countries
2. African, Caribbean and Pacific group of States (ACP)
3. Arab Common Market
4. Association of South East Asian Nations (ASEAN)
5. Authority for the Integrated Development of the Liptako-Gourma Region (West Africa)
6. Autorité du bassin du fleuve Niger (West Africa)
7. The Bangkok Agreement (South and East Asia)
8. Caribbean Community (CARICOM)
9. Carribean Development Co-operation Committee (CDCC)
10. Comité intergouvernemental de lutte contre la sécheresse dans le Sahel (CILSS) (West Africa)
11. Comité permanent consultatif du Maghreb (CPCM)
12. Communauté économique de l'Afrique de l'Ouest (CEAO)
13. Communauté économique des pays des grands lacs (CEPGL) (Central Africa)
14. Conference of Islamic Countries
15. Conseil de l'Entente (West Africa)

16. Council of Arab Economic Unity (CAEU)
17. Eastern and Southern African Preferential Trading Area
18. Economic Community of West African States (ECOWAS)
19. Grupo Andino
20. Grupo Urupabol (Uruguay, Panama and Bolivia)
21. Gulf Co-operation Council (Arab States)
22. Lake Chad Basin Commission
23. Latin American Economic System (SELA)
24. Latin American Integration Association (LAIA)
25. League of Arab States
26. Mano River Union (MRU) (West Africa)
27. Organisation commúne africaine et mauricienne (OCAM)
28. Organisation pour l'aménagement et le développement du bassin de la rivière Kagera (East Africa)
29. Organisation pour la mise en valeur du fleuve Gambia (OMVG) (West Africa)
30. Organisation pour la mise en valeur du fleuve Senegal (OMVS) (West Africa)
31. Organization of African Unity (OAU)
32. Organization of Arab Petroleum Exporting Countries (OAPEC)
33. Organization of Eastern Caribbean States (OECS)
34. Organization of Petroleum Exporting Countries (OPEC)
35. Protocol relating to Trade Negotiations among Developing Countries (GATT)
36. Regional Co-operation for Development (RCD) (Iran, Pakistan, Turkey)
37. Secretaría permanente del tratado general de integración económica centroamericana (SIECA)
38. Sistema de la Cuenca del Río de la Plata (South America)
39. South Asian Economic Co-operation Scheme
40. Southern African Development Co-ordination Committee (SADCC)
41. Treaty of Amazonian Co-operation (South America)
42. Tripartite Agreement (Egypt, India, Yugoslavia)
43. Union douanière et économique de l'Afrique centrale (UDEAC)

★ For basic information about these see UNCTAD document TD/B/C.7/51 (Parts I–III), 1982–83.

THE UN CODE OF CONDUCT FOR LINER CONFERENCES: A CASE STUDY IN NEGOTIATION, IN THE CONTEXT OF THE SOUTH-NORTH DIALOGUE

by M.J. Shah

I. Introduction

The United Nations Convention on a Code of Conduct for Liner Conferences was adopted in April 1974 by a conference of plenipotentiaries under the auspices of UNCTAD, following several years of preparatory negotiation in that institution.[1] It entered into force in October 1983.* This Code has come to symbolize the aspirations of the developing countries to secure the recognition of international law for the equitable participation of their merchant fleets in the ocean carriage of their trade. In the specific sector of the shipping industry to which it applies, namely the carriage of liner cargoes, the Code has overturned a century of fiercely-defended cartelistic practices by the 'liner conferences': combinations of shipping companies founded by those which dominated the colonial trades under their metropolitan flags.[2] These restrictive practices were maintained even into the post-colonial era, against the claims of the developing countries' shipping companies for easier entry into liner conference membership and of their traders, or 'shippers', for an effective status as negotiators in the fixing of freight rates for the carriage of their cargoes.

The UN Liner Code made a breakthrough in South-North relations. No multilateral instrument before it had ventured so deeply into the regulation of commercial activities with a view to enhancing the participation of developing countries. It was to serve as a source of inspiration for other efforts at codification in different fields. The Code was also the final achievement of Wladek Malinowski's distinguished career as an inter-

---

* Editor's note: The liner conference system discussed in this paper is, of course, that prevailing before the entry into force of the Code, i.e. the system which the Code was designed to reform and regulate.

national negotiator. Indeed, its adoption by such a large number of countries, including several from the North as well as those of the South, owes much to his clear perception of the objectives of the Code, his perseverance in pursuing them and his tactical skill. On both counts, therefore, a study of the negotiation of this Code is a fitting topic for this volume.

A 'case study' usually encapsulates institutional (particularly corporate) problems, issues or processes, perceived in the context of conflicts of personality or interest or both, and envisages the resolution of these conflicts. Historicized data are projected and analyzed to demonstrate how various possible courses of action, or solutions addressed to the situations described, can best be worked out within the framework of stated goals and objectives. In the case of the Liner Code, visualized as a case study, not only were the data and problems facing the international commercial community at the time of the adoption of the Code prodigious, but the varied and often diametrically opposed nostrums that were advanced during the negotiations had to be woven tortuously around the most sensitive neuralgic points of national and private interest. A comprehensive case study of the Code would accordingly present an undertaking of a magnitude and scope to which restraints of space here could not do justice. The present examination must therefore necessarily be more modest, focusing in general terms only on the more important of the key issues and problems affecting the regulation of liner conferences as viewed in the context of the Code.

II. The object of negotiation: the self-regulating liner conference system

In 1974, as now, there were some 350 or so liner conferences serving almost as many separate ocean cargo trades throughout the world. A 'liner conference' is a combination of several individual shipping companies, or 'lines', of different nationalities, organized in the manner of a private club to provide a regular, tariff-based, common international shipping service among a specified range of ports.[3] Under the system, the member lines retain their corporate and national identities but agree to apply uniform freight tariffs and conditions of service on the routes, or 'trades', covered. The individual member lines do not therefore compete with each other but rather present a united front to their customers, i.e. the shippers of goods. The latter are thereby denied the choice they might have had, if competition had not been foreclosed by the system, to seek better terms from individual member lines of the conference, or indeed from non-conference sources (known as 'outsiders').[4] In fact, liner conferences further stifle competition by 'tying' shippers to exclusive use of conference vessels, in return for which commitment the conferences offer the shippers privileged discounted freight rates, in the form either of special nett rates or of rebates on the normal conference tariff (whereby shippers get back a portion, usually 10 per cent of the gross freight paid by them, after 3 to 6 months of proven 'good behaviour' on their part by not using 'outsider' tonnage).[5]

Approximately two-thirds of the conferences are 'self-regulated', i.e. they themselves evolve and apply their own terms and conditions for use of their services and operate without any governmental controls. The remaining third of all conferences are 'USA-type' regulated conferences; in these cases, of which the paradigm is provided by the conferences serving the USA, the economically more powerful State in a particular trade claims national jurisdiction over conferences serving its imports and exports and regulates them by national legislation.[6] Unless otherwise specified, the observations in the present paper relate to the self-regulating conferences, to which the Liner Code applies *prima facie*. Clearly, unless a regulating State becomes a contracting party to the Code or acquiesces in its operation, the Code cannot be expected to function freely within that State's claimed jurisdictional limits.

The logistics of the conference system operate through a network of 'Conference Secretariats', which we find established in most countries engaged in maritime trade throughout the world, administering multinational shipping services between agreed ranges of ports. Every aspect of each of these services is regulated by the member lines of the respective conference, acting as principals and prescribing their own rules of conduct or practice through their own institutional procedures for supervision and control of the particular 'trade'.

The *raison d'être* of a conference is to exclude competition from a liner trade by bringing all potential competitors under its own umbrella and to do business as a single body offering shipping services entailing, *inter alia:*

—restricted membership;

—common freight rates and mechanisms for changing them;

—common or rationalized ranges of ports served, co-ordinated sailings, cargo-sharing arrangements;

—common terms of carriage and conditions of service;

—common loyalty arrangements agreed with tied shippers who, in exchange for privileged price discounts and under pain of penalty, agree not to use non-conference ships;

—internal mechanisms for settlement of disputes.[7]

The distinguishing feature of the impact of these self-regulating conference practices on the economies of affected countries is that the power exercised over the provision of most of the world's international ocean liner services is largely concentrated in the hands of private interests, i.e. the member lines, whose centres of effective control—their headquarters or seats—are almost invariably located in one of a very few developed countries.[8] It was the purpose of the developing countries as initiators of the Code, seeing their nationals (whether shipowners or shippers) as exploited victims of these practices rather than as independent principals, to bring the operations of the individual conferences under public control through an international regulatory instrument in the form of a legally-binding United Nations treaty or convention. Since conferences "make unilateral decisions which affect vitally the interest of the countries whose trades they serve",[9] a principal aim of the Code as envisaged by the developing countries was to balance or modulate in the public interest conference decisions which would be unilaterally imposed and avowedly based on purely private commercial considerations, seen only from the point of view of the member lines in each trade.[10] The activities of liner conferences may be regarded as analogous to certain aspects of the operation of transnational corporations, which have also attracted international concern. The crucial question arising in both cases is this: should the disposition of forces which affect key economic factors in a country's development and balance of payments, such as ocean transport and related elements, be left solely to self-regulating private interests or be made publicly accountable.

This is not, of course, all there is to the controversy over the conference system, nor the only reason why it excites such highly-charged emotion, *pro* and *contra*. Behind it lours the stamp of its nineteenth-century colonial origins in the UK-India liner trade. It was that provenance which gave the conferences their enduring image as groupings of foreign metropolitan lines dominating colonial ocean trades through the exploitation of secret conditions, imposed under pain of penalty upon captive customers bound by loyalty arrangements. Thence also came the image of the member lines operating unchallenged, unhindered by governmental controls of any kind, as a 'ring' or cartel fixing freight and other conditions to suit their own economic purposes (on the notoriously arbitrary criterion of 'what the traffic will bear'), without apparent concern for the needs of their 'host' countries.[11] Through all the vicissitudes of changing times and despite the increasing admission of Third World lines into membership, these are images which the liner conference have not been able to shake off completely, even to this day.[12]

When therefore, at the instance of developing countries, UNCTAD began to investigate liner conference practices in the late 1960s, with a view to injecting greater oppenness, equity and accountability into the conference system, the major points of tension to emerge were:

—those of a psychological nature, emanating from political history: vestiges of the interplay of colonial patterns and attitudes, casting on conferences the seemingly lasting stamp of monopolistic foreign domination over the economy of poorer countries;

—those of an operational nature, emanating from the workings of the conference system itself: either from indigenous shipping lines of newly independent countries, frustrated by their failures to gain ready membership even of conferences carrying their own national trade, or from the frustration of shippers failing to secure ready dispensation to use 'outsider' non-conference shipping without penalty;

—those of a public-interest nature, emanating from larger, national concerns for the development, the export potential and the balance of payments of developing countries: concern for example, about unilateral 'take-it-or-leave-it' conference freighting practices, affording no opportunity to shippers to consult meaningfully over freight rates, or indeed for governments even to monitor freight levels objectively; or about the failure of shippers, and often of governments themselves, to influence the quality, adequacy and pattern of conference services; or, finally, about the lack of an independent adjudicatory body which could hear disputes over the whole range of conference practices.

Permeating these tensions was a further psychological barrier, not always overtly noticeable as such, but patently discernible to those insiders who could see beneath the surface of the discussions at Geneva over the Code. This added complication lay in what might be termed the fear of the unknown felt by many newly independent governments. While pushing publicly for reform, they did not yet dare to act unilaterally at the national level to break the conference 'rings'. It appeared as if their unfamiliarity with the inner working of what they perceived as an alien system aroused a fear of the unknowable consequences of attempting to pierce that system on their own.[13]

The conference lines, in a position of power enhanced by implicit metropolitan governmental support, did little to reduce all these tensions beyond finally instituting, after considerable pressures, a primitive system of consultations with shippers, which still left the conferences with the last word on almost every issue affecting their services. The principal pro-conference arguments, seeking to placate the above-mentioned tensions and defend the *status quo*, ran as follows:

—Conferences stabilized liner services where otherwise chaos and uncertainty would prevail if competing 'outsider' lines were permitted to lift cargo as and when it suited them, charging whatever rates they pleased for each voyage;

—Conference practices were based on a free market system (it was alleged) with competitive efficiency, as judged by the conferences themselves alone, being the sole criterion for their existence and the rates charged being the most economical consonant with the provisions of the particular service (i.e. 'what the traffic could bear').

The canvas laid bare for discussion of the Liner Code within UNCTAD was accordingly worldwide, the principal actors, including governments, being many and diverse, and the arguments for or against public regulation strongly polarized. There were powerful shipping industry lobbies supporting the conferences' campaign for the *status quo*. Moreover, the conference position was backed not only by the main maritime powers of Western Europe (including notably the UK) and Japan, but also enjoyed the support of the USA, Canada and Australia. Initially, the three last-named major trading countries equally opposed the idea of a regulatory international code of conduct, although, as countries whose primary interests in maritime transport were those of shippers rather than carriers, they might ordinarily have been expected to come out on the side of the developing countries.[14] In the event Australia voted for the Code while Canada abstained, the USA never managing to shake off its anti-trust objections both to the Code and to self-regulated conferences.

III. The core question: control and participation in decision-taking

It is not possible here to detail how exactly, step by step, the multifarious issues and problems affecting the Liner Code were presented, discussed and eventually resolved at different stages within the various deliberative bodies, until and including its adoption. Only a broad picture can be given. The original positions of countries on the various issues, as raised at UNCTAD's Working Group on International Shipping Legislation, were sometimes presented straightforwardly as harmonized positions of the respective groups: developing or developed, or socialist countries of Eastern Europe. At other times, there were varying views held even within these groups themselves, with countries from different groups often sharing similar views that were disconsonant with those of their fellow group members. Often, as discussion, negotiation, and lobbying progressed apace, views of particular countries were observed to change. Thus, the positions held by some countries in the chain of discussions which was strung through the Working Group, the Committee on Shipping, UNCTAD III (Santiago, 1972), the subsequent United Nations General Assembly, the two sessions of the Preparatory Committee for the diplomatic conference, and the Conference of Plenipotentiaries itself, were often quite dissimilar at different points in time.[15]

In these circumstances, this paper will first of all attempt to identify the central core of the debate on the Code and list the major constitutive elements which were seen to flow from it. These will then be further broken down into the various individual practical problems they raised, and from them will be singled out those nodal points of hard contention upon whose disposition one way or another swung the direction of negotiations towards the final solutions. It is hoped in this way to expose broadly the anatomy of the major differences that arose during the negotiations, and to demonstrate how these were gradually overcome in the course of the compromises that were embodied in the Code. Finally, an examination of the Code will be made in the context of the South-North dialogue, of which it was one of the earliest battlegrounds. It is thus intended to illuminate several noteworthy facets of the evolutionary process under which, within ten years, the working of one of the most powerful cartel-like institutions in the international economy was brought under public international accountability.

The records show that the central question debated throughout the various meetings on the Code was essentially whether liner conferences should be controlled, as the developing countries wished, through a mandatory international treaty or convention, or be left, as the developed countries demanded, to continue to regulate themselves.

Embedded within this central question were several contentious individual issues:

—the nature of rights of membership in conferences;

—the allocation of shares of trade (cargoes);

—the role of governments in regard to conference operations;

—the scope and effective basis of consultation between conferences and shippers;

—the need for and nature of a machinery to resolve disputes;

—aspects of freight rates: criteria for fixing rates, period between freight rate increases, etc.;

—the scope and nature of shippers' loyalty arrangements, particularly in regard to sanctions, and dispensation to use non-conference tonnage;

—the scope and nature of regulation of conference operations.

Thorny as these issues were, the common thread running through discussions on each of them was soon enough found to be none other than this: that the governments of developed countries could not accept that powers to take final decisions regarding any single matter appertaining to the operation of self-regulating liner conferences be permitted to rest with any party or authority other than the conferences themselves. This negative attitude on the part of these governments to every issue that was addressed, whether in macro or micro terms, entailed their refusal to concede that shippers or governments should ever receive equal status in negotiations with conferences in the decision-taking process.

Now the very nub of the case of the developing countries was the exact opposite, i.e. that, consequent upon political decolonization and changed perceptions of transport questions, their liner operators, shippers and/or governments, should have rights under law or contract to monitor or share effectively in the decision-taking processes of conferences which affected their vital national economic interests. Accordingly, battle was expected to be, and ultimately was, engaged most fiercely on this one central point of contention, at each confrontation on whatever particular problem was being discussed.[16] Further, since behind the approach of the developed countries there was an equally formidable ideological counter-argument, projected as a sacrosanct historical principle of unhindered 'freedom of the seas' and backed by powerful industrial lobbies which the developing countries could not match, the battle could not be other than hard and long. It was fought at the highest level of technical, political and diplomatic expertise, the developed countries with their 'insider' knowledge of liner conference *praxis* holding all the apparent aces.

IV. Negotiating issues and options

(a) The situation up to UNCTAD III

The proceedings within UNCTAD bodies up to the stage of the preliminary discussions at UNCTAD III in 1972 reveal the following major alternative policy options which, out of the dense mass of liner conference *praxis*, became identifiable as broadly forming the heart of the whole dispute between the contending parties, as to what a code of conduct, if its eventuality were accepted, might or might not contain.[17]

—*Principles and objectives*: whether these should reiterate the better known United Nations declarations on economic development strategy and stress the need to recognize the special concerns of developing countries in expanding their merchant fleets, or that there be no preambular declaration at all or, if any, merely a brief, neutral preparatory statement;

—*Conference membership*: whether to have freely securable 'open' membership, or to operate through 'closed' conferences with stated criteria for admission;

—*Shares of cargo*: whether to offer national and third-flag lines specified cargo-share percentages as a right, or not to recognize any quantified cargo formula, or national or other characterization of lines at all;

—*Publication of conference agreements, tariffs and related regulations*: whether to have open publication of the terms and contents of conference agreements, or to keep them confidential;

—*Consultation machinery*: whether to bring consultation between conferences and shippers closer to true negotiations, or to retain consultation *simpliciter*, i.e. to continue to leave the last word to the conferences;

—*Conference representation*: whether to establish local representatives of conferences in each country with full powers to decide on major issues affecting operations, particularly in regard to membership, shares of trade, freight rating, dispensation, etc., or to have representatives acting merely as a means for transmitting and receiving messages to and from conference headquarters.

—*Freight rates, surcharges, etc.*: whether to institute a system which would permit shippers to negotiate in a real sense, pursuant to agreed criteria, on freight rates (whether specific, general or promotional), surcharges, the degree of flexibility to be applied to notice periods for announced freight increases, times of application, etc., or to continue to have decisions on such matters unilaterally imposed by conferences;

—*Averaging of freight rates*: whether or not to encourage the use of averaging as a rating practice;

—*Loyalty arrangements and 'dispensation'*: whether to permit shippers to have less rigidly enforced ties with the conferences, which would both secure them privileged freights and enable them to use non-conference 'outsider' tonnage whenever reasonably justifiable, or to apply loyalty arrangements rigidly, discouraging dispensation and enforcing penal sanctions for their breach;

—*Quality and adequacy of services*: whether to make these subjects matters for meaningful consultation between conferences and shippers, or to let them remain as purely domestic concerns of conferences;

—*The role of governments*: whether to give governments a role in supervising or monitoring conference operations, or to refuse them any role at all;

—*Settlement of disputes*: whether to establish a mandatory dispute-settlement machinery, or to have none or a voluntary one;

—*Nature of governing instrument and implementation*: whether to have a mandatory code or a voluntary one.

(b) The nature of the Code: mandatory or voluntary?

If we examine these various heads of policy with the aim of building up a case study, we would clearly need to concentrate upon those of their characteristic elements which can be readily identified as being crucial to the liner conference image, and whose slightest variation one way or the other would quintessentially alter the basic institutional character of the conferences. While nuances and emphases may legitimately produce a differing hierarchy of characteristics, according to one's point of view, few publicists would seriously disagree, and the developed countries always made this clear in their utterances, that unequivocal, independent self-regulation by the lines over their entire field of operations represented the core of conference power. Developed countries laid great stress on the requirement that nothing mandatory of whatever nature drawn from non-conference sources should in the least affect or influence conference practices and operations, and in particular those affecting revenue. Put another way, they insisted that no extraneous entity be permitted ever to over-reach or adjudicate on the unhindered power of conferences to:

— admit members,

— allocate cargo shares, sailings, etc.,

— plan and operate services

— set freight rates, surcharges, etc.,

— control loyalty arrangements.

Thus the question of whether to have a mandatory international convention or a voluntary instrument was seen very early on to be at the very heart of conference concerns, as was also the question of whether to have a mandatory arbitration system which would place the power of final adjudication beyond the sole reach of conference decisions. Accordingly, it could be expected that countries favouring conference operations untrammelled by any form of public regulation would hold out to the bitter end against the establishment of any system which favoured an international convention or mandatory arbitration. It was not surprising, therefore, that the final negotiating battles between the developed and developing countries ultimately reduced themselves to testing the extent to which the various controls the developing countries sought to introduce into the system could be rendered ineffective, diffused or neutralized. The developed countries exerted their utmost efforts to ensure that whatever new system might emerge would approximate as nearly as possible to the *status quo,* and the developing countries in turn sought a system which would irrefragably secure for them the substance, if not every jot and iota, of the rights they claimed. Negotiations accordingly ranged equally heatedly not only over fundamental issues, such as the nature of the regulatory instrument and the adjudicative provisions, but also over specific practices covering membership, trade participation, freight rates and so on.

Circularity of reasoning became, in fact, a distinctive feature of the discussions over the Code. If one discussed what type of regulatory instrument was required, it would be stated: we must first agree on the subjects to be covered. When one tackled these subjects, it would be inquired; what type of instrument is contemplated? For this reason, the inistence by the developing countries which led the 1972 General Assembly to resolve that the Code should be a binding legal instrument was of the most profound significance.[18] Yet even the august source of this strong mandate did not deter the developed countries from pressing at every subsequent meeting to whittle down its implications. The Code negotiations never became an occasion for the representatives of the various interests involved to sit amicably together to evolve solutions to problems, under the guidance of terms of reference laid down for them by their political bodies. It was more a case of continuous attritional strife, with the developed countries questioning every single concept or idea which ventured to suggest the slightest change in the pattern of conference practice, and the developing countries resolutely defending their innovatory demands. This was not a happy recipe for constructive convention-making, nor was the situation really improved until the final phase of the negotiations.

(c) Progress at UNCTAD III

An analytical look at the results of the discussions on the Liner Code at UNCTAD III reveals how some of the previously-held extreme positions on both sides were either tacitly dropped or muted under the pressure of negotiations and in deference to an understanding of political and commercial reality.

The general position which emerged at the closure of the session was as follows:[19]

— *Principles and objectives*: While disagreement persisted on some of the finer points of controversy, the diversity of views was not expected to be a major hurdle in the final negotiations.

— *Nature of the regulatory instrument*: Almost all countries agreed that a 'universally-acceptable' Code of Conduct be prepared and implemented as a matter of urgency, but the extent of its flexibility or mandatory nature was left open. This convergence of views was a decisive advance over the earlier stand of developed countries which had either wanted no code at all or sought acceptance of the CENSA Code of Practice.[20] They continued to maintain that an international convention would be too rigid and formal, and preferred a resolution or recommendation from UNCTAD. However, the developing countries, in view of their unsatisfactory experience with the implementation of past UNCTAD resolutions on liner conference practices, reiterated their preference for a binding instrument such as a convention. The socialist countries of Eastern Europe did not express a position on this issue as a group.

—*Conference membership:* While several developed countries agreed with most of the developing and socialist countries that conferences should be 'open', there remained considerable disagreement as to the rights of third-flag fleets. Developed countries believed that these should have equal rights of admission with national fleets and that no preference should be shown to national-flag vessels.

—*Shares of cargo:* The developing countries proposed that, where no third-flag carrier participated in a conference trade, the combined share of the shipping lines of each of the two countries served by that conference should be equal; and that, when third-flag lines participated in a conference, their aggregate share of trade should not be more than 20 per cent, although *ad hoc* consultations could establish a higher share. Developed countries could not accept cargo-sharing in the code, particularly if based on a formula and purporting to give preference by flag. Cargo-sharing was not, however, repugnant to the socialist countries.

—*Role of governments in consultations:* While the developing countries continued to seek a major role for governments in consultations between conferences and shippers, they and the socialist countries of Eastern Europe conceded that it need not be mandatory. Most developed countries did not consider government participation in consultations appropriate, although they could visualize a role for governments in the implementation of the Code.

—*Freight rates:* Developed countries felt that, while conferences should provide information to shippers and consult with them, the lines should be left free to fix their rates so as to earn a reasonable return on capital. They could not accept arbitration in case of disputes, nor unreasonably long minimum periods for intervals between freight rate increases. The developing countries felt that it would not be possible to define return on capital precisely; they proposed in agreement with the socialist countries a provision in the Code that freights "shall be fixed at as low a level as commercially feasible", which would not only be objective and practical but also reflect a concept not too far removed from that advanced by the developed countries. There was also a whole range of issues and sub-issues in regard to promotional freight rates, surcharges, currencies, averaging of freight rates and classification of tariffs, on which disagreements of not too serious a nature persisted. The developing countries maintained their position that specific procedures were necessary for advance notices of, and intervals between, freight increases, so as to protect shippers from arbitrary and too frequent increases. Arbitration was also held by them to be essential, so as not to leave final decisions to conferences alone.

—*Settlement of disputes*: The developed countries moved away from earlier positions opposing independent dispute-settlement procedures for the whole range of conference disputes, by conceding a system of mandatory conciliation in the event of a failure in consultations. They could only envisage arbitration in the event of both parties agreeing to accept it. The socialist countries of Eastern Europe also emphasized consultation but, while prepared to accept compulsory arbitration only where 'appriopri-ate', preferred conciliation. The developing countries persisted with their views that consultation as practised was limited in its results and largely unsatisfactory and continued to argue that, if compulsory arbitration were not agreed, countries would increasingly enact legislation to protect national interests.[21]

V. Dénouement: compromise, confrontation and conflict resolution

(a) A package deal

Despite the progress made at UNCTAD III, where a draft code of conduct embodying the views of developing and socialist countries was adopted against the votes of the developed countries,[22] and at the two sessions of the Preparatory Committee which the General Assembly subsequently established, discussion reached deadlock half way through the first part of the Conference of Plenipotentiaries in December 1973. A small 'Contact Group' was then established by the President of the Conference to resolve the impasse.

Given that even at that penultimate stage of negotiations the Code had to be looked at afresh as an integral whole, the Contact Group had to reconsider whether a strictly regulated, comprehensive and mandatory public order was to be created at all at the international level, or whether the *status quo* in the conference system should be preserved, or modified so as to permit voluntary regulation in limited areas of conference operations.

In the event, none of these options prevailed. The tenacious partisan pressures exerted uncomprisingly on each side were such that a viable middle ground of common agreement, consonant with the terms of the General Assembly resolution requiring a binding instrument to be elaborated, had to be found at the very beginning of the negotiations, if the diplomatic Conference was to rise from its deliberations with any credibility. Clearly here the developing countries were under greater pressure than their opponents to ensure a positive outcome. They had initiated the exercise in the first place. Further, from clamant demanders of what they perceived as their legitimate rights, they found themselves, as the negotiations dragged on, being increasingly cast in the role of supplicants. They were expected to be grateful for what they might receive, if they lowered their demands, from the hands of those who held the master-cards through their control of liner conference operations and the deployment of high-powered lobbying. The latter played upon the fears of many developing countries that they would be unable to 'go it alone' in managing liner services without foreign co-operation and assistance. The discussions thus continued to focus as much on the legal nature of the instrument that was to emerge from the negotiations as on its contents. Choice came to be forcibly narrowed into deciding whether to go 'hard' on content and 'soft' on the nature of the instrument, or 'hard' on the nature of the instrument and 'soft' on content.

However, despite mounting a most punishing campaign, equally dazzling in strategy as in tactics, combining historical principles with pragmatic exposés, adroitly designed so as to undermine each bastion which the developing countries held dear, the developed countries failed ultimately to budge their opponents from strict adherence to the wording of the General Assembly resolution which called for a 'multilateral legally-binding instrument'. That was the sticking point, the limit beyond which the developing countries would not surrender the sanction of positive international law for the rights they sought. They could not, in other words, trust and therefore concede to the benignity or goodwill of foreign-dominated conferences to meet their needs.

Once this fact seeped into the consciousness of the representatives of some developed and socialist countries, whose nationals also often found themselves on the periphery, as it were, of conference operations, those countries moved cautiously towards embracing the positions advanced by the developing countries. They began by accepting the concept of a legally-binding international instrument and, as a corollary, recognizing a role for governments. The 'packeteers', as the countries from the three groups came to be called, then sat together to ensure that, from the impact of the truly spectacular lobbying of the 'hard-line' developed countries to water down the contents of the Code, a viable Code could still be salvaged as a package deal, in a form which assenting countries at the diplomatic Conference could adopt without loss of credibility. A crucial decision thus became imminent, in the closing stages of the first part of the Conference, as to whether those countries from the three groups which would be voting for the Code would be receiving sufficient concessions of a substantive nature from each other in exchange for what they were giving in return.

As a beginning, on 7 December 1973, after conducting personal negotiations, the President of the Conference recommended a number of principles which were accepted by the developing and socialist countries and some developed countries. A certain role was conferred on governments in consultations and in conciliation proceedings. It was also recognized that preference had to be given in cargo shares ('participation in trade') to the national lines of exporting and importing countries, but that some rights had to be acknowledged for third-flag countries;

As a result of the close consultations that were held within the President's Contact Group, the following package of proposals was then placed before the delegations at the Conference:

— *Participation in trade*: National lines at each end of a trade should have equal rights in aggregate, with a share of 20 per cent to be allocated to third-flag lines "where they exist" (the well-known 40:40:20 principle). Uncarried portions of allocated national-line cargo shares would revert to a cargo pool, to be shared *pro-rata* (the lines themselves deciding whether or not to carry their allocated shares, and in what quantities). National lines within a region at one end of a trade would have the right to make adjustments among their shares.

— *The role of governments*: Conferences should supply information, on request, to governments. Government representatives should have the right to be present during consultations, participate fully in discussions, make suggestions and promote agreements between the parties, but without a decisive role. Governments were given a similar role in regard to conciliation proceedings.

— *Freight rates*: These are to be fixed, as recommended by the socialist countries of Eastern Europe, at as low a level as commercially feasible; the minimum period between freight rate increases to be twelve months.

— *Settlement of disputes and implementation*: Every effort should be made by the parties concerned to reach settlement of disputes during consultations. Where this was not possible, the dispute would be submitted to mandatory international conciliation; among matters which might be dealt with in this way are "questions relating to freight rates, surcharges, currency adjustment factors, etc." Recommendations would be binding if accepted by both parties. If a party to conciliation rejected the conciliators' recommendations, it would have to state its reasons comprehensively in writing. A Conference to review the Code would be held every five years after its entry into force, "with particular reference to implementation".

From this package, it became clear that the basic trade-off had been the recognition by the participating developed countries of trade participation rights for fleets of exporting, importing and third-flag states, in exchange for the developing countries giving up mandatory arbitration and accepting mandatory conciliation. The recognition of a role for governments was also significant. It was assumed, without its being stated, that the governing instrument would be an international convention, as had in fact earlier been specified by the General Assembly. Problems which were less than central, such as averaging of freight rates or 'way-port' conferences, were just shelved, since in any case they could be dealt with in individual liner conferences or at Review Conferences on the Code.

(b) Adoption of the Code by majority vote

Having thus solved the major problems in areas of dispute, the President's Contact Group turned its attention, at the resumed session of the Conference of Plenipotentiaries in March/April 1974, to dealing in greater detail both with the agreed principles and with other remaining items of controversy, in moves to secure the widest possible consensus among the participating countries. Reconciliation continued to be built around the flexibility shown 'by prominent maritime countries, such as France, the Federal Republic of Germany and the socialist countries, in approaching and embracing the views of the developing countries. The issues discussed in detail at the final session were as follows:

—principles and objectives,

—participation in trade,

—non-conference lines,

—joint inter-governmental liner services,

—the transitional period,

—implementation of a general freight rate increase pending a recommendation by the conciliators,

—alternative recourse measures in regard to disputes on freight rate matters (i.e. other than international mandatory conciliation),

—the question of the need to have a 'paramount clause' in conference agreements, and related arrangements giving effect to the Code of Conduct,

—rules of procedure for conciliation,

—institutional machinery for the implementation of the Code of Conduct,

—entry-into-force requirements of the Convention.

After a long series of votes on many of the specific provisions of the Code, the complete Convention was eventually adopted on 6 April 1974 by 74 votes to seven, with five abstentions.[23] It contains principles and objectives, substantive provisions and final clauses, and is accompanied by two resolutions of which one relates to non-conference operations. An abstract of the Code is given below.

The *principles and objectives* are designed to stimulate development of regular and efficient liner services and to assure a balance of interests between the suppliers and users of liner services, non-discrimination against shipowners, shippers or foreign trade of any country, and emphasis on meaningful consultations between shippers and conferences with (upon request) the participation of appropriate authorities.

The main substantive provisions of the Code are as follows:

Article 1 establishes, subject to stated criteria, rights to membership of conferences by national and third-flag shipping lines.

Article 2 sets out, with the proviso "unless otherwise mutually agreed", the principle of equal shares in any pooling or other similar arrangements for lines in importing and exporting countries, with "a significant share", indicatively given as 20 per cent, for third-flag lines where such exist.

Article 7 notes that loyalty arrangements with shippers are authorized but that they should be based on the contract system or any other system which is also lawful.

Article 9 provides that tariffs and related conditions and/or regulations should be made available at reasonable cost to shippers and other parties concerned.

Article 10 provides for annual reporting by conferences of their activities.

Article 11 establishes that consultations be held between conferences and shippers.

Article 12 sets out criteria for freight rate determination, with a proviso that other criteria might be agreed.

Article 14 provides for notice of freight rate increases and reference to international mandatory conciliation for disputes which may not have been resolved through consultation.

The Code also provides (articles 23 to 46) procedures for the settlement of disputes through mandatory conciliation. The parties can agree on other lawful procedures provided these are not inconsistent with the principles of the Code, but for disputes on freight this freedom is only available if shippers are not debarred by national legislation from exercising it. Conciliators' recommendations only bind parties if they are not rejected by one or more of them.

Finally, provision is made for the Code to enter into force six months after 24 States, whose combined general cargo and container tonnage amounts to at least 25 per cent of world tonnage (based on the 1973 Lloyd's Register statistical tables), become contracting parties to it; and for five-yearly Review Conferences.

(c) Resolution of problems

We can perhaps now more easily run through the main problems outstanding after the end-1973 package deal, to see if and how they were eventually resolved in the Code.

—*Principles and objectives*: Predictably, these were only agreed in the final days, once it was clear what the nature of the Code would be and what it would eventually look like as a whole. The rhetorical language and references to United Nations declarations on development strategy and so forth, on which the developing countries had insisted earlier, were dropped. Key sentences stressing meaningful consultation, the triggering mechanism of the Code, and reference to special concern for the growth of fleets in developing countries were retained. The developing countries here sacrificed reiteration of already declared principles for substantive gains of a concrete nature. Developed countries also did not appear to mind finally conceding the special position of developing countries, so long as their various concessions were not specifically tied to conceptions they held to be abstract.

—*Non-conference lines*: It being found clearly impossible, without much further study, to include definitive provisions in the Code to cover non-conference shipping operations, it was decided to address the situation in an accompanying resolution. The resolution acknowledges the right of non-conference lines to operate on commercial criteria, thus retaining an element of competition in liner trades. It is difficult to imagine what else could have been done on this matter in the circumstances, since clearly the Code, directed as it was primarily to conference operations, could not be expected within the time-frame of its adoption to solve every possible problem in liner shipping, including the treatment of non-conference competition. This too was a victory for pragmatic considerations over abstract concepts.

—*Bilateral inter-governmental agreements*: It did not ultimately prove to be a tenable position for developed countries to insist that the Code recognize a mechanism for assimilating bilateral inter-governmental agreements with conferences, given their completely different structure, range and type of operations. The problem is quintessentially one which only experience and evolution of further practice can unravel, and the Code at the time of its adoption was, perhaps correctly, not felt to be the place for settlement of this issue.

—*Transitional period*: Developing countries were chary of accepting too long a transitional period for switching over to the new system, in case the delay tended to perpuate the *status quo*. A period of six months was finally agreed. The main point here is that, while one could quibble over how long the period might be, what was felt to be more important was that the principle of transition be recognized.

—*Implementation of a freight rate increase pending conciliator's recommendations*: This was one of the many points on which the developing countries had to back down. It has caused a problem for at least one developing country which on signature (not yet ratified) has made a reservation. However, given the negotiating structure round which the Code is built, it is to be hoped that the provision would not cause chronic problems for those countries which feel strongly about this matter.

—*Settlement of disputes*: Having agreed to drop mandatory arbitration, a main pillar of their cause, the developing countries accepted mandatory conciliation. There was considerable pressure from the developed and socialist 'packeteers' to avoid mandatory arbitration, to the extent that the compromise package deal would almost certainly not have gone through if arbitration had been insisted upon by the developing countries.

—*Paramount clauses*: This question was automatically solved under the provision in the Code that each contracting party would take such legislative or other measures as may be necessary to implement the Code, and the further provision that conference agreements, trade participation agreements and loyalty arrangements should conform to the applicable requirements of the Code.

—*Rules of procedure for conciliation*: These were drawn up, annexed to the Code, and require no special comment.

—*Institutional machinery to implement the Code:* No institutional machinery as such was specified. However, taking our cue from consultations, and the explicitly stated need for governments to adopt regulations giving effect to the Code, we may conclude that conferences and shippers are expected to convene together and draw up the necessary measures to operate conference services under the Code.

—*Entry-into-force requirements of the Code:* The extraordinary stringency of these provisions was the final concession which the developed countries voting for the Code exacted from the developing countries. The required number of contracting parties was attained well before the minimum tonnage, the latter requirement acting, as expected, as a brake on the process of entry into force. The combined minima were met on 6 April 1983—nine years to the day after the adoption of the Code, which thus came into force on 6 October 1983.[24]

VI. Assessment and conclusions

How does the Code shape up to the expectations of its progenitors, particularly in terms of the South-North dialogue? As we have seen, the major complaints against conferences concerned the inability of fleets of developing countries to gain ready admission to conferences, the inability of shippers to participate meaningfully in consultations and to secure ready dispensation to use more competitive non-conference carriage, the inadequacy of most conference services and the absence of independent machinery for settling disputes.

To redress these grievances, it was clear that the levers of control over liner operations, hitherto the sole preserve of conferences, had to be shifted so that they were compelled to respond to agreed norms sanctioned by law. Under the Code, unfettered conference power is indeed diffused. Shippers are to play a meaningful role and the benign guidance of governments is consecrated in its provisions. However, from the point of view of a case study in negotiation, the Code no less than other international conventions must be evaluated with the aim of judging the extent to which concessions negotiated in it are found to be viable and lead to a reasonably satisfactory compromise between aims and realities.

The principal concessions made by the developing countries were that they agreed to exchange mandatory arbitration for mandatory conciliation, accepted the punishing entry-into-force conditions of the Code and accepted a substantial element of flexibility in various provisions of the Code which closely affect conference revenue.[25] In exchange, they received acknowledgement of the rights of exporting, importing and third-flag States to cargo-sharing within an agreed framework of what were felt to be equitable principles, acceptance of an international Convention as the designated regulatory legal instrument, institutionalization of meaningful consultation over a comprehensive range of subject matter, including freight, as a principal co-ordinating mechanism for the implementation of the Code, and a mandatory dispute-settlement machinery.

Now, while one could speculate *ad infinitum* as to which side came off better or worse under the Code, we need to look above the purely business aspects of conference operations to arrive at a mature judgement in the matter. It is not enough to assess what was lost and by whom, in narrow economic terms, under the package deal that was put together by the developing and socialist countries and some developed countries. We need to look at the forces which pressed upon and underlay the deliberations and, bearing in mind the overall settlement that was reached, draw our measured conclusions in the wider context of how and to what extent the needs and concerns which strove for mastery behind those forces were accommodated.

It is at this point that the 'South-North' aspects of the Code really come into clearer focus. Liner carriers and shippers are to be found in both North and South; but, while one would have thought that their respective interests and views would be generally identical within each of these occupational categories, such was not to be the case in the debate on the Code. The conference system was approached as if it were an unbending Northern institution, forcibly imposed upon Southern interests. In crude terms, what was primarily seen to be at stake was how the total 'cake' of liner-shipping traffic, of which Northern shipowners appropriated large 'slices' in most conferences, could be shared, if at all, with their Southern counterparts. The North felt that Southern shipping interests should strive for their share of the 'cake' on a commercial basis and they they did not need the backing of international law to do so. Undeniable, however, was the crucial fact that the controlling forces which apportioned rights to carry trade and decided freight levels were either institutionally located in Northern developed countries or were dominated by their shipowners. The South was either incapable, or felt itself incapable, of penetrating or overcoming on its own this perceived core of Northern economic power. Hence, the expressed need of the South for countervailing positive law enshrined in an international convention.[26]

With this background, the 'bottom line' in discussing the Liner Code in the context of the South-North dialogue always leads to this inescapable conclusion: that equitable rights in international trade of goods or services can be secured only through the medium of public law for so long as the North is unwilling to loosen its hold on historical practices which, in the eyes of the South, favour its own dominant private ends. However, this conclusion carries the risk that such rigidities as the law might then institutionally infuse into commercial practices could, if wrongfully applied, subtly subvert any good the law may otherwise confer. It was this fear, then, which the North exploited to the full in its interventions against the Code. This it did, as we saw, by a brilliant amalgam of conceptual and pragmatic arguments.

At the conceptual level, the Northern lobbyists asserted:

— that shipping was a financially unattractive proposition, warranting a low level of priority in economic development planning and strategy, and was therefore an inappropriate area of entrepreneurship for developing countries to enter;

— that freights would rise as a result of the Code's provisions on cargo-sharing and monitoring of freights, and that shipping services would be disrupted as a consequence, to the ultimate detriment of the developing countries themselves;

— that insurmountable juridical problems and conflicts would arise at national and international levels from the imposition upon (allegedly) 'freely competitive' liner shipping of the legal technique of a national convention and of mandatory arbitration.

These attacks on the Code were reinforced at more pragmatic levels by concrete insinuations that:

—cargo would not be lifted by any ships which might happen to be on berth but were not of the 'correct' flag;

—operations generally would come to a standstill or be hopelessly delayed while disputes on freight and other questions were being resolved through the provisions of the Code, since the last word would no longer be with conferences for quick unilateral decision;

—consultations would bog down in the hopeless search for an ideal synthesis, which would always remain beyond the reach of prompt business-like solutions;

—arbitrators would not have sufficient technical expertise to adjudicate shipping disputes; and that

—rights enjoyed by 'cross-trading' maritime nations would be jeopardized.

What had therefore to be sought in the resulting dialogue was to distil from the South's rhetoric, and perhaps too highly pitched national maritime ambitions, pragmatic solutions which could co-exist both with the deep-seated technical nexus of Northern practice and conservative outlooks which dominated international shipping politics, and with the more realistically sustainable demands of the Southern petitioners for change. And behind the dialectics of it all, there lay, as we saw, the ultimate need to ensure that solutions reached were mandatorily enforceable upon the stronger party, i.e. the liner conferences. This final requirement remained the *sine qua non* throughout the entire exercise, having its genesis, as we also saw, in the history of failure of non-binding UNCTAD resolutions to secure any significant change in the disposition of liner conference operations, and in the isolation experienced by Third World interests in attempting to tackle liner conferences on their own, unsupported by public law.

Can we assess whether and how Northern arguments against change were validly resolved by the Code in terms of credible trade-offs? To begin with, their conceptual arguments could not really stand up to close and informed reasoning: the fact that the entire socialist bloc, as well as maritime powers such as Japan, France and the Federal Republic of Germany eventually came round to the point of view of the developing countries, bears this out irrefutably. Clearly, not only is shipping usually profitable when efficiently conducted, but its position is unassailable as a major factor in a country's economy and development, and its enormous value is undeniable. It was unrealistic for the North to assert in one breath that shipping was financially unattractive and in another to fight tooth and nail to preserve its privileges in this domain! As for the arguments about rising liner freights, these unfailingly rise anyhow, Code or no Code, usually annually and often even more frequently, by large percentages. Furthermore, dispute and delay is endemic in the liner conference system, and it was perhaps a species of special pleading to blame the Code proleptically for classes of problems which would arise in any case, whether it existed or not. Moreover, liner shipping has not been run on a genuinely competitive basis for over a hundred years, except during sporadic outbursts of tonnage over-capacity. The South was thus able to maintain without too much difficulty its scepticism about the fears inspired by the North that the Code would impose jurisdictional conflicts and disrupt a proven system. The criticism about the incompetence of arbitrators was too puerile for refutation, while the fear of 'cross-traders' being chased out of lucrative trades could hardly hold water in the face of the specific provision in the Code for third-flag participation.

Rationalized in this way after the event, it might sound as if the battle over the Code should have been easy. This, we saw earlier, was not the case, for there had been the almost convincingly persuasive pressures of the forces marshalled by the North to be dealt with. These pressures were:

—political: i.e. governmental, but initiated by, drawing sustenance from, and reinforced through private industry lobbying;

—industrial: addressed from lobbies in Western maritime countries to their fellow shipping industrialists in developing countries;

—professional, academic and commercial: channeling the views of various disciplines and occupations through organizations such as CENSA, the International Chamber of Shipping, and the International Chamber of Commerce.

As against this formidable line-up, the South mustered as follows:

—politically: formidably strong in voting power at face value, and particularly if one took account of the support of the socialist countries of Eastern Europe;

—industrially: largely muted, since they lacked capacity anyway—the main purpose of the Code being to acquire capacity—and, in the few trades where they had capacity, they were such relative newcomers as not to carry much weight;

—professionally: uninfluential, in that they either had no effective forum though which to project their views, or lacked international influence.

On the basis of voting power, it might appear that the developing and socialist countries could have imposed whatever type of code they wished, regardless of the views of the minority group of countries to the contrary. In practice, though, since most of the tonnage in the conferences serving their external trade was owned by opposing interests, that would have been a pyrrhic victory. This fact of life was certainly a constraining element in the armoury of the South, and its consequences ran thoughout the debates over the Code. As a counter, however, it was equally clear that the unrestrained hold of conferences over liner services affecting developing countries could not long continue in face of prevailing chronic problems and attacks upon the system. If there were no relaxation of the more implacable conference practices, the various services would soon enough be 'broken' one by one, beginning with those where countries were strong enough to impose their will by unilateral action, as is indeed the current experience in some major conference trades.

Thus, South-North confrontation focused finally on a single pivotal issue: how best to satisfy the need for a controlling mechanism over conference operations which would be of a legally compelling nature yet sufficiently flexible not to obstruct liner shipping, while imposing acceptable limits of restraint on the abuse-prone practices of the conference system.

In the search for viable solutions to secure such a balance, the appeasement of the Northern governments and industry lobbies which sought to retain the *status quo* played a major part. The extent to which these Northern governments followed their own independent national policies at national levels or were merely overborne by the private interest lobbies is arguable. Be that as it may, the technical and pragmatic arguments adduced by the lobbies were undoubtedly the toughest nuts which the South had to crack to secure their objective: a viable code of conduct which would stand up credibly both to Northern professional scrutiny and to their own cherished aims. It helped that the requirement that the Code bear limiting parameters had become inescapable. These, to have any practical value, had clearly to be sited beyond rhetoric and pietistic resolutions, and be seen actually to grapple with 'structure', structural change being a prime objective of Southern negotiation with the North. To that extent the *status quo* argument of the lobbies was demolished. The structure of liner shipping, including controlling mechanisms over questions of membership, freight, trade participation, dispute settlement, etc. had therefore to be modified in concrete terms. That much was clear.

But how were the parallel compulsions of pragmatism to be met? First were established the necessary parameters over conference practice, through legal sanctions imposed by the instrumentality of an international convention. These sanctions bore the burden of effecting fundamental structural change in liner operations. They could not be overborne by contractual freedom which conferences of shippers might abuse. This over-riding constraining element met the South's demand for mandatoriness. Conferences could not legally opt out of their obligations under the Code, nor conduct unilaterally their accustomed cartelistic practices. Analogous restraints were placed upon shippers, and the dispute-settlement provisions were a further mandatory safeguard against irresponsible behaviour. However, the North's concern for commercial flexibility had equally to be respected. What was required therefore, as the second step in the unfolding of the solution, was that sufficient manoeuvrability be written into the appropriate article of the Code to enable conferences and shippers not only to press their aims under juridical sanctions but also to accept reasonable restraints on them.

The substance and content of the Code, and the manner in which the various compromises were effected, were earlier described and need not be repeated. It is rather the legal technique that was used to secure the required mix of 'pliable rigidism' and disciplined contractual freedom which is more revelatory here. The accommodation of combined South-North wishes was finally accomplished by establishing in the text of the convention what was basically a set of fundamental norms and not rigid law. Conferences and shippers were directed to consult together and function within those limits, and against them performance under the Code was to be measured. This solution offered the best of both worlds. It had the sanction of law under flexible norms, permitting the parties to negotiate equitable rights of trade and operate agreed practices. It also firmly entrenched limits beyond which stronger parties could not for long operate unchallenged. Seen in this light, the Liner Code could be said to have largely appeased both the South, which wanted rights and obligations established by sanction of law, and the North which, while finally conceding that wish, still pressed for commercial flexibility.

Can this outcome provide a sound model for other areas of the South-North dialogue where similar needs and concerns arise? Can a lesson be drawn from the Liner Code in South-North terms? Yes, put in the simplest terms possible, on these lines: First of all, when dominant interests are disinclined voluntarily to share real control of key areas of commercial activity, legal measures become mandatory. Basically, these would be addressed to modulating equitably the one-sided disposition of resources or operations in areas of vital economic and developmental concern to affected States. Secondly, legal instrumentalities introduced to redress such imbalances should not be drafted in such a way as to stifle commercial practice when, subject to the norms set by a governing legal instrument, measured discretion could safely be left to the concerned parties under agreed consultative or analogous procedures. These concerns, as we saw, were met in the Liner Code, and due credit must be given to those socialist and developed countries which responded to Third World aspirations in liner shipping and together helped to usher in what hopefully will prove to be a new era in ocean enterprise, which seeks to secure equitable rights for carriers and shippers from exporting, importing and third-flag countries.

---

1. The text of the UN Convention on a Code of Conduct for Liner Conferences, 1974, is contained in UN document E.75.II.D.12, New York, 1975. See also document E.75.II.D.11, Reports of the Conference of Plenipotentiaries and other documents.

2. The first liner conference is generally believed to have been the Liverpool-Calcutta Conference established in 1875. Its members shared a 'pool' or 'purse' when dividing revenue.

3. See *The Regulation of Liner Conferences*, a report by the UNCTAD secretariat which describes the different types of regulation under which liner conferences operate, UN document E.72.II.D.13, New York, 1972.

4. For a fuller explanation of liner conferences and for bibliographical references, see "The UN Liner Code of Conduct: Some key issues regarding its implementation" by M.J. Shah, in *European Transport Law*, Antwerp, December 1981.

5. "The general effect of conferences is to eliminate price competition": see para. 410 of the 'Rochdale Report', *Report of the Committee of Inquiry into Shipping* (Chairman, Viscount Rochdale), H.M. Stationery Office, Cmnd. 5447, London, 1970. Also: [The power of conferences to] "maintain rates higher than those that would result from free competition is monopoly power", Vol. 78, *Harvard Law Review* (1964–65), p. 636, in note on "Rate regulation in ocean shipping".

6. At the time of writing, the USA is reviewing its maritime policies with the apparent intention of moving nearer to elements both of the Liner Code and of the self-regulating conference system.

7. Law is usually invoked only when shippers litigate to justify their breaches of loyalty agreements, but their chances of success are scant in most jurisdictions which honour valid contracts.

8. The term 'developed countries' is used in this paper to refer to the market-economy countries which are members of the OECD, unless otherwise indicated.

9. *The Regulation of Liner Conferences, op. cit.*, p. 3, para. 6.

10. In their public pronouncements, most liner conferences do state that in taking their decisions they also have the needs of shippers in mind. This, however, is a point which shippers usually dispute.

11. The 1907 (UK) Royal Commission on Conferences was specifically addressed to 'shipping rings'; see its Report, H.M. Stationery Office, Cmnd. 4668, Vols. I and II, London, 1909.

12. "In form and object, most of the activities of shipping conferences resemble the restrictive practices in other commercial fields which have in recent times been prohibited or subjected to control in many countries", the 'Rochdale Report', *op. cit.*, para. 456.

13. During one of the joint UNCTAD/IMCO/ILO regional technical assistance missions to developing countries, a revealing episode occurred when a local public authority executive remarked to one of the team: "Shipping? Oh yes, isn't that when foreign countries send their ships over to us and take our goods away?". It never occurred to him that shipping might be an undertaking in which his country could participate with benefit to its economic development. Shipping was perceived as quintessentially an activity of foreigners!

14. As we have noted, the USA had its own statutorily-imposed system of conference regulation, which it was able to apply uncontested in its liner trades. Canada was perhaps too remote geographically from the classically self-regulated conferences to worry overmuch about changing the existing system, which in any case did not appear to affect its overall interests significantly.

15. The dates of the meetings on the Liner Code were as follows: Committee on Shipping, May 1970 and April 1971; Working Group on International Shipping Legislation, February 1971 and January 1972; UNCTAD III, April/May 1972; General Assembly (resolution), December 1972; Preparatory Committee, January 1973 and June 1973; Conference of Plenipotentiaries, November/December 1973 and March/April 1974.

16. While national lines of many developing countries had increasingly secured membership of conferences, it was the common understanding during the debates over the Code that the voices of these newcomers in decision-taking were generally ineffective. It was also an open secret that, in many conferences, new members had only been accepted in recent years on giving an understanding that they would not support cargo reservation, freight reduction and other such measures which were unpalatable to the conferences.

17. In the list which follows, the first option shown against each heading expresses the position favoured by the developing countries. The second option indicates the position of their developed adversaries.

18. General Assembly resolution 3035 (XXVII), adopted by 96 votes to none, with 28 abstentions from developed and socialist countries.

19. This assessment is based on a summing-up which was issued at the time by the Chairman of the Committee discussing the Code at Santiago.

20. This voluntary Code, drawn up by the Committee of European National Shipowners' Associations, was criticized by the developing countries for lack of 'teeth' for the protection of their interests against those of the conferences.

21. In fact, the relevant provision in the draft code jointly put forward by the developing and socialist countries, which emerged from UNCTAD III, reserved several major classes of dispute (e.g. over levels of freight rates and general increases) for reference to international arbitration only if national legislation or regulation of the country from which the cargo originated did not provide otherwise.

22. Draft code annexed to Conference resolution 66 (III), adopted by 74 votes to 19, with two abstentions. Alternative proposals for a code by developed countries that were then made are not discussed as such in the present paper for reasons of space, but the views expressed in those proposals are mentioned in the narrative of the unfolding of the discussions.

23. 58 developing countries voted for the Code (plus Turkey which is classified geographically with the developed countries of Europe), and they were joined by the socialist countries of Eastern Europe, by China, and, among the developed countries, by Australia, Belgium, France, the Federal Republic of Germany and Japan. The abstentions came from Canada, Greece, Italy, Netherlands and New Zealand, while Denmark, Finland, Norway, Sweden, Switzerland, UK and USA voted against.

24. At that date, there were 59 contracting parties with 28.68 per cent of world tonnage.

25. These provisions relate principally to membership, trade participation, freight and the conciliation mechanism.

26. It had in fact been argued at the very first session of UNCTAD in 1964 that 'equal treatment' between nations at the commercial level could only be appropriately applied to 'comparable cases', and could not in justice be extended to trade relations between developed and developing countries. See, in this connexion, the discussion of 'duality of norms', 'compensatory inequality' and related concepts of international development law in Paul Berthoud's contribution to this volume.

POSTSCRIPT ON MALINOWSKI AND THE CODE: A PERSONAL COMMENTARY

by K. H. Khaw

Mr. Shah has made a very useful analysis of the issues and developments relating to the Code of Conduct for Liner Conferences and of the significance of the Code ·negotiations in the larger context of the South-North dialogue. It brings back memories of the many aspects of the drama of the negotiations, the battles that were fought, the obstacles that were overcome, the alliances that were forged, the agreements that were made, the compromises that were reached, and the final victory that was achieved.

The story of the Code is one of the most interesting episodes in the history of UNCTAD and perhaps also in the annals of international co-operation for development. It is also the story of one man and his efforts. I would like to make some brief personal reflections on the latter, not only because it is appropriate to do so in the present volume, but also because they concern a number of matters that remain topical today.

Wladyslaw Malinowski conducted the secretariat's work on the Code with the redoubtable courage and fighting spirit that had already earned him wide respect and admiration. When the work began there was some doubt and scepticism about the feasibility of its objective, and this was felt even by some of his senior colleagues. Malinowski viewed the Code as a means of helping to promote an equitable balance of interests between old-timers and newcomers to international shipping on the one hand, and between shipowners and shippers on the other. He felt that the prevailing system was weighted heavily against the formation of merchant marines by developing countries and that, on the grounds of the infant industry argument at least, some effective measure was needed to assist the developing countries which wanted to develop or expand their shipping lines. This measure was to be in the form of a legally-binding and universally-applicable regulatory instrument. As such an instrument was being proposed for an international commercial activity with long-established practices and powerful protagonists and as it involved many complex issues, the objective was indeed formidable. No wonder then that it was at first seen by some to be unrealistic.

Further, the members of the Group of 77 placed different emphases on various aspects of the Code, depending generally on their relative strengths, either as shipowning or as ship-using nations, *vis-à-vis* the liner conferences which served their trade. The task of reconciling the differences among them was not an easy one, particularly in the context of a legal instrument. Early in 1972, the Group of 77 had in fact two preliminary drafts of a code, one prepared by Asian and African countries and the other by Latin American countries. Malinowski was not a man to hide his convictions, and found himself exposed to the charge of dividing the Group, an accusation which did not fail to reach his superiors. But all this did not prevent him from actively helping the Group to arrive at a unified text, which was achieved at UNCTAD III (Santiago, May 1972).

Moreover, for a long time, the Committee of European National Ship-owners' Associations (CENSA)[1] pressed for the alternative approach of self-regulation. Early on during the negotiations CENSA had come up with its own 'code', based on the philosophy of self-regulation, which was viewed favourably by many Western governments. The issue of regulation versus self-regulation was in fact central to the debate at the Santiago Conference on whether the Code should be embodied in an international convention or in a resolution or recommendation of the Conference. The issue was so fundamental that, despite the many intensive efforts made, including those at the highest level towards the end of the Conference, the differences between the Group of 77 (supported by the socialist countries of Eastern Europe and by China) and the OECD countries could not be resolved. Consequently, the resolution calling for a plenipotentiary conference to adopt a convention was carried by a majority vote.

The battle for a legally-binding code was thus fraught with difficulties and encountered fierce opposition. In the face of such a situation, a man of lesser conviction might have settled for self-regulation but Malinowski stood firm on his position that self-regulation was equivalent to non-regulation.

As an international civil servant Malinowski was a remarkable activist. He kept a list of confidants to whom he wrote constantly, keeping them up to date on the developments relating to the Code and constantly reminding them of the issues involved. He worked actively with a close circle of outstanding individuals from the Group of 77, who gave cohesive and purposeful leadership to the Group during the negotiations and who contributed immensely to their successful outcome. He regularly attended the meetings of the Group of 77 on the Code and spoke freely and openly, without fear or hesitation, whenever he felt the need to do so. He was sometimes controversial, but his audience always listened to him. Above all, he was respected for his conviction and commitment not only by members of the Group of 77 but also by delegations outside the Group. Malinowski knew that the support of the latter was essential for a successful outcome and, recognizing the likelihood of a less than unanimous result, made every effort to encourage the widest possible support for the Code. In the process, he demonstrated that among his many talents was that of acting successfully as a broker between groups. When the final vote on the adoption of the Code was taken on 6 April 1974, six OECD countries voted in favour of the Code with the Group of 77, the socialist countries of Eastern Europe and China, seven OECD countries voted against, while five of them abstained. As the OECD countries, except for one abstention, had voted as a bloc against the Santiago Conference resolution referred to earlier, this was no small achievement. The adoption of the Code was in fact a personal triumph for Malinowski. To the many sceptics and doubters, he proved that politics is indeed the art of the possible.

The focus of these observations is very much on the Group of 77. Malinowski's work on the Code showed that the Group of 77 can be an instrument both of confrontation and of constructive dialogue, and that efficient working methods leading to an effective negotiating strategy of the Group can produce positive results. In the Code exercise, the Group of 77, with good leadership and sound preparations, acted effectively and constructively in negotiations involving complex issues; it combined cohesiveness in representation with flexibility in negotiating methods and contributed greatly to the successful outcome.

This short commentary is about an outstanding individual and his remarkable efforts in the pursuit of a difficult cause. These efforts formed an important part of his constant endeavours to seek constructive change in international economic relationships not only for the benefit of the developing countries but also in the wider interest of the international community as a whole. His work on the Liner Code provides lessons, of courage, conviction and commitment, upon which his successors in the international civil service would do well to ponder.

---

1. After 5 February 1974, it became the Council of European and Japanese National Shipowners' Associations.

PART THREE

Perspectives and Prospects

COLLECTIVE SELF-RELIANCE: TURNING A CONCEPT INTO A REALITY

by Manuel Pérez Guerrero

The Caracas High-Level Conference on Economic Co-operation among Developing Countries (May 1981) opened a new phase in bringing Third World collective self-reliance to the operational stage. Its significance now depends on the implementation of the comprehensive programme of action which was adopted on that occasion.

The critical economic situation which the world is going through makes it more urgent—although not necessarily easier—to implement this programme of action. Indeed, international economic co-operation is in the grips of a crisis without precedent, and the projected new round of North-South global negotiations has not yet been launched, in spite of the impulse it received from the Summit Conference held at Cancún, Mexico, in October 1981.

The world is faced with a historic challenge. Two scenarios may be imagined. In the first, we have a fruitful advance towards our common goals through global negotiations, overcoming the difficulties cropping up on the way, and, in parallel, a sound and resourceful programme of economic co-operation among developing countries, aimed at intensifying and extending their financial and trade exchanges. In the second scenario, the difficulties confronted by the global negotiations are not overcome and these negotiations continue to linger hopelessly, while economic co-operation among developing countries progresses along its own path. Many intermediate scenarios could be imagined between these two, but let us spare no effort to ensure the realization of the first. The second scenario would not bring about a sound, balanced development of the world economy and would certainly not respond to the aspirations of all peoples and nations. Yet it cannot be ruled out.

* * *

Collective self-reliance has emerged in the last decade as one of the major aims and means in the search for a more just, equitable and resilient world economic system. The two conferences of the Group of 77 held at Mexico City (1976) and at Arusha (1979) represent important formative stages of

235

this process. The Movement of the Non-Aligned Countries gave it unquestionable impetus and political significance.

The New International Economic Order, launched by the United Nations in 1974, comprises two clearly distinguishable strands: the restructuring of the South-North economic relationship and the emergence of economic co-operation among developing countries (ECDC). The latter is not an alternative to the former. They are mutually supportive and reinforcing. Admittedly, there are clear political and economic differences among countries of the South, as there are among countries of the North. Yet in the present period of human history no other valid approach exists than for these two broadly-based groups to tackle forcefully, realistically and radically the host of interlocking problems that beset humankind, with far-reaching implications for its future.

Our common determination is not to exacerbate the contradictions and opposing interests of developed and developing countries, rich and poor. It is rather to look for converging aspirations and complementary strivings on both sides. ECDC should be implemented in this perspective. It is quite natural that the developing countries, whatever their stage of development, should aim at promoting their self-confidence and enhancing their economic strength, building on the many and diverse affinities, common interests and complementaries that the member countries of the Group of 77 have identified among themselves. In addition, through ECDC, these countries will promote a better balance in the interdependence of all nations on the planet.

The concept of interdependence has acquired greater significance since the New International Economic Order was launched. Interdependence in this framework presupposes that the developing countries will evolve individually and collectively from the situation of economic dependence in which they still find themselves. In order to achieve a greater degree of economic autonomy, thereby reducing their present vulnerability, their collective self-reliance has to be promoted and developed, steadily and with conviction. Though a legitimate goal in itself, national self-reliance, which should not be confused with self-sufficiency or autarky, would hardly stand a chance of surviving in the interplay of international economic transactions without being buttressed by broader schemes of collective self-reliance.

This reality has led the Group of 77 to approach collective self-reliance through comprehensive programmes of economic co-operation among developing countries. It has appeared essential to strengthen the inter-regional framework for such co-operation, in the conviction that efforts already being made at the regional and sub-regional levels would be strengthened by coherent action encompassing the different regions of the Third World.

This was the scope of the High Level Conference convened in Caracas by the Group of 77 in May 1981. The Caracas Programme of Action covered seven inter-related substantive fields of action: trade, technology, food and agriculture, energy, raw materials, finance and industrialization. It also dealt with technical co-operation among developing countries (TCDC), an effective instrument for implementing ECDC, taking account of the follow-up to the United Nations Conference on TCDC (Buenos Aires, 1978). Services, like shipping and insurance, have not been covered specifically by the Caracas Programme, but they are dealt with in several of its sections and work in this field is expected to be undertaken.

The Caracas Programme aims at establishing a comprehensive, balanced and equitable basis for the effective, progressive realization of the potential for mutual co-operation that exists among developing countries. The results of such co-operation should be of benefit to each of them individually, as well as to the group of countries as a whole. No such division as that between donor and recipient countries exists, although it is recognized that some countries have greater possibilities than others. The complementarities of their economies lend themselves to the fruitful and beneficial development of all.

Such co-operation involves, as a primary objective, learning from one another through an exchange of experiences and information that can and must be adapted to the particular circumstances of the interested countries. It also promotes favourable treatment for the trade flows among developing countries, as is the aim of the projected Global System of Trade Preferences (GSTP) at the inter-regional level. It lays emphasis on joint ventures and multinational enterprises that could be brought about through such mechanisms as action committees. It stresses the significance of mutually supporting and reinforcing actions and the need to resort to such institutions as national centres of multinational scope in the field of training and research, which have already proved effective in a number of regions and sub-regions of the Third World. These actions will expand and consolidate the personal contacts among professionals of the developing countries, enhancing their motivations to direct their efforts towards the major problems of the Third World and helping to arrest the brain drain afflicting the Third World. This does not preclude but rather encourages contacts with professionals from other parts of the world, i.e. the industrialized countries, with the aim of adapting their experience in fields of real interest to the developing countries. The emphasis in ECDC is placed on actions with broad potential impact on the living conditions of the people and not on indulging in gadgetry and superfluous items in obsessive imitation of the rich countries.

It is hoped through all these means to stimulate an inter-disciplinary approach to the problems in the various fields which would lead to effective inter-related solutions more resistant to the impact of the obstacles that may arise in the path of their implementation.

Building institutions for ECDC is a task which has to be managed with a great sense of responsibility in order not to slide towards the proliferation of new institutions. Nonetheless, there is room for setting up a limited number of important agencies or restructuring existing ones to meet the intensified and extended requirements of co-operation schemes. This is particularly true in the financial field, in which the Third World countries have been so dependent on institutions from the North. The situation has improved to some extent in the last ten years, but serious gaps remain to be filled in order to support actions in other fields and, eventually, to establish a framework that would evolve progressively and soundly in relation to the corresponding institutions of the industrialized countries, transnational and otherwise, with their wealth of experience. Co-operation between the South and the North should thus become more effective and fruitful. The international responsibilities of the industrialized countries in the field of financial co-operation with the developing countries would not be consequently diminished. However, more efficient direct co-operation by developing countries in such fields as food, agriculture, energy and industrialization would ensure actions more specifically oriented to our own requirements and circumstances.

Similarly, the Caracas Programme should acquire a new and effective overall dimension through a network of technical information on development matters which has been at the launching pad for the last few years. The Development Communication Network (DEVNET), as it is now called, would enable the developing countries of all regions to follow closely the new projects and experiences emerging in any part of the Third World, which may be of interest to them. The Group of 77, at the ministerial level, has given its support to this idea in the expectation that it will be implemented expeditiously, though progressively to ensure technical effectiveness.

The Caracas Programme did not deal with social questions such as education, health or the environment, all of which are essential for the balanced development of the developing countries, but co-operation already exists in some of these fields in the Third World, particularly at the sub-regional level, and this should be developed in the future. There is a continuous interaction between the economic, social and cultural spheres of development, which makes it essential to co-ordinate and evaluate, at the various levels, the overall results that may be obtained.

Together with its comprehensiveness and its emphasis on operational activities arising from the concept of collective self-reliance, the Caracas Programme of Action represents a turning point in economic co-operation among developing countries as it establishes a carefully designed scheme for ensuring its co-ordinated implementation. Indeed, the Programme would have been incomplete, ineffective and fragmented if such a scheme had not been devised. In effect, the last section of the Programme of Action deals with mechanisms for co-ordination, monitoring, follow-up actions and evaluation.

An Intergovernmental Follow-up and Co-ordination Committee (IFCC) stands out as the major policy instrument. Its membership is made up of senior officials responsible for ECDC. It is entrusted with reviewing the progress of the Caracas Programme and agreeing on measures designed to give more impetus and impart greater operational character and coherence to the Programme. It is open to all countries of the Group of 77 and is to meet once a year, preferably in a developing country. At each session, the IFCC reviews the results of technical meetings held the preceding year.[1]

The Programme also envisages sectoral review meetings dealing with matters concerning each of the various sectors of the Programme. These will be held at intervals of approximately two years.

The conclusions of all these meetings will be transmitted to and acted upon by the annual Ministerial Meeting of the Group of 77 which is held at the beginning of the regular session of the General Assembly. Every second year, this meeting will concentrate its main attention on reviewing and appraising ECDC activities under the Caracas Programme, and providing steady guidance with respect to policy issues in operational matters and, in general, to further strengthening these activities.

It was also envisaged to make effective use, in the context of ECDC, of the bi-annual meetings of the chairmen and co-ordinators of the Group of 77 in the various United Nations centres: New York, Geneva, Rome, Vienna and Paris. The Caracas Programme has made the Group of 77 chapters at these centres specifically responsible for programme implementation, taking into consideration the nature of the activities carried out by the international organizations located there. The effective participation of all of them is of critical importance to the Programme. It is also recognized that the expert advice of the United Nations system is a necessary support that one should resort to as far as practical, provided that the management of the Programme remains firmly in the hands of the Group of 77.

Within the United Nations system, UNCTAD is well placed to provide such support. Already in the early years of its existence, its secretariat established a Special Programme on Economic Integration among Developing Countries (which later became the Division for ECDC) and UNCTAD was the first, and remains so far the only organization to set up specific inter-governmental machinery in this area, the UNCTAD Committee on ECDC. It deserves to be noted here that Wladyslaw Malinowski always attached the utmost importance, political and substantive, to ECDC and was influential in promoting UNCTAD's early involvement in supporting the efforts of the developing countries in this area.

Yet whatever the help that may be forthcoming from the United Nations system, the Caracas Programme has made two important provisions to ensure its autonomous operation.

In the first place, it has established a small 'core' of assistants, nominated by Governments, to help the Chairman of the Group of 77 in carrying out his responsibilities in respect of ECDC matters, including the preparation of the meetings of the IFCC and the scheduling of technical meetings. This arrangement has been devised so as to ensure a proper balance between continuity and rotation. It is expected that, besides contacts with the United Nations agencies and regional commissions, the Programme should develop fruitful relationships with other pertinent inter-governmental organizations and non-governmental organizations active within the context of ECDC, for example in research activities concerning economic problems dealt with in the Programme.

In the second place, the Caracas Programme provides for contributions to a Group of 77 account for ECDC, to finance, as required, activities referred to in the Programme such as collection, collation, printing and distribution of documents and information regarding meetings of expert groups.

It is clear that the Caracas Programme of Action is under way. It constitutes a major landmark in economic co-operation among developing countries. All countries of the Group of 77 should benefit from it whether they are endowed with a variety of natural resources and are already well engaged in their development, or whether they are still among the 'least developed'. The solidarity that these countries have to demonstrate, through well planned and balanced action, should bring them ever closer together. Their diversity, on account of geographical, cultural, economic, social and political factors, should encourage and enrich their common development efforts. In the present circumstances, the developing countries cannot but succeed in advancing towards the goals set out in the Caracas Programme of Action. The spirit of unity and purpose that was present at the historic moment of its birth will prevail to make it a living reality. Indeed, seen from a broad perspective, Third World collective self-reliance will become a fact of life and is bound to play a major role in bringing about the New International Economic Order. What has happened in the recent past in our tormented world fortifies the determination of the developing countries to take effective action in pursuit of this aim.

*   *   *

In pursuing their common objectives through their mutual co-operation, the developing countries cannot fail to project themselves into what the future may have in store for them. Innovations are emerging that have a profound bearing on the modes of production and on our very life-styles. The course of our development and our advances towards effective self-reliance are at stake. Forward-looking studies are needed to focus on such questions as the emergence of new patterns of energy, which have been discussed extensively since the oil warning shook the world in 1973, as a result of the irresponsible overconsumption of a non-renewable resource. Yet, in the same context, attention has to be given to another vital question, namely the pervasive potential influence on all human activities of the microprocessor revolution which is already affirming its impact in the field of computer-based information systems. This revolution will affect our public and private lives, individual and collective. It is presently being geared to remodel life in practically all its external aspects, and may well, therefore, transform economic and social interchanges among peoples and nations. These new developments, as we can tentatively forecast, could either usher in a renewed era of domination by the highly industrialized countries, with the help of their transnational corporations, or instead serve as an instrument of progress and well-being for all the peoples of the world.

If we were to let this revolution proceed with an unhampered mercantile motivation, it would breed domineering attempts and further greed-inspired competition and tensions, with dangerous and negative outcomes. Conversely, if these impulses are tamed, channelled and oriented by the joint responsibility and participation of the world community, the micro-revolution could evolve as a common tool for accelerating the solution of our problems in the developing, as in the developed countries. To ensure this positive outcome, the Third World would have indeed to participate actively, in a spirit of partnership, with the industrialized countries, whether market-economy or socialist. We would thus facilitate a smooth and constructive transition, as is our overall determination in the restructuring of international economic relations. South-South co-operation is essential in this connection to ensure a sound harmonization of technical developments with the traditional assets worth preserving from our cultures.

If individual developing countries were to face these issues single-handed, in face of the sophisticated industrialized countries, they would risk being captured in the latter's zone of influence, with all that would entail. However flattering and attractive they may look, we are bound to lose heavily in such deals.

Nor can we let matter gain hold over the spirit: the human values again being overwhelmed and stifled by the materialistic, impersonal and turbulent flood of useful and harmful goods and services. This is of vital concern to all mankind—something that really matters.

And would this new technological wave deprive great numbers of workers of gainful employment? Or would it generate a much greater number of jobs, as the promoters seem to believe? Mistakes have been made in the past which are costly to repair.

A common reflexion on and scrutiny of these issues and their implications, among ourselves and with some of our sensitive partners in the North, should take place in parallel with our joint efforts to extend and intensify our economic co-operation in pursuit of collective self-reliance.

Let us act with a sense of urgency and purpose and, at the same time, assess the new signs along the way and thus advance with assurance towards the achievement of our common objectives. Together, we should be able to step up our progress on the road to a balanced development of all our countries and regions in pursuit of greater social and economic equality among nations and peoples, in freedom and peace.

---

1. The IFCC has held two sessions: in August 1982 in Manila and in September 1983 in Tunis. A third session is scheduled for September 1984 in Cartagena, Colombia.

TRADE AND DEVELOPMENT: A PROSPECTIVE VIEW OF UNCTAD

by Ignacy Sachs

I. The crisis and the debt trap

The prospects for UNCTAD must be evaluated against the background of the severity of the present crisis, the unpreparedness of the international system to cope with it, and the disappointment caused by the Belgrade Conference (UNCTAD VI, June 1983).

The documentation prepared for UNCTAD VI ought to have convinced even the most sanguine optimist of the gravity of the situation and the dismal prospects for the Third World. Since 1980, the world economy has been in the throes of the most pervasive crisis since the Great Depression, in which underlying problems of a structural and systematic nature have been compounded by cyclical factors.[1]

Mass unemployment in OECD countries is likely to persist even in the uncertain event of a recovery fuelled by the current upswing in the United States. A reasonable long-run response to the technologically-induced unemployment in these countries, caused by the spread of automation, must rest on a mix of carefully planned policies for growth, employment and income, protecting those who are being displaced.[2] The urban populations of semi-industrialized Latin American countries, subject to drastic contractionary adjustment policies and lacking adequate social protection, are living through the worst social crisis in their history. All over the Third World, heavy social and economic damage has resulted from the combined disruptive effects of shrinking foreign markets, on account of the recession and rampant protectionism, falling prices of non-oil commodities, declining terms of trade and rising foreign debt aggravated by the unprecedented level of real rates of interest.

Two decades after the creation of UNCTAD, in clear contradiction of the hopes and ideals that were instrumental in shaping that organization, the restructuring of the international environment in line with the needs of the Third World seems as distant as ever. No significant progress has been achieved in instituting the New International Economic Order, since the eventful special session of the General Assembly in 1974, even though considerable work on principles and new approaches to development has been carried out by the various United Nations bodies. As a matter of fact, the actual working of the world economy looks like the NIEO upside down!

To repair the harm already done will call for a carefully balanced and vigorous international strategy, an equitable sharing of the cost of adjustment policies, and a radical overhaul of the existing monetary, banking and trade institutions.

While there is considerable room for improving the strategies and performances of individual Third World countries, even their most rigorous efforts will be undermined so long as the working of their economies and of the world economy is left to the free interplay of market forces. State intervention, based on social and ethical principles, is necessary at both the national and the international levels to overcome the present structural asymmetries.[3] As Raúl Prebisch rightly reminded the Belgrade Conference, Third World countries should not expect too much at this stage from a revived world economy. Yet, in Belgrade, the United States delegation and those of several OECD countries insisted that the present recession was just a cyclical downturn in the process of being overcome. They asserted that the renewed prosperity in sight in the industrialized countries would trigger off an upsurge in the Third World countries, provided that these curbed inflation effectively through policies of monetary restraint and demand-contraction. Instead of seeing in the reactivation of the development processes in Third World countries an important stimulus for the world economy, they maintained that the linkages of interdependence would work the other way round in conformity with the conventional (and rather discredited) 'trickle-down' theory of growth.

The single most explosive issue facing the international community at present is the debt problem. What is at issue is not so much the amount of debt accumulated by the large debtors, which is not exceptional in relation to their real capacity to repay, but the severe payment terms and extremely high interest rates. Under prevailing conditions and in the present international economic environment, the debt simply cannot be repaid. The question is not whether a *de facto* moratorium should be proclaimed, but simply when and how the debt should be renegotiated. Solutions must be sought at the political level: payments must be stretched out and interest rates drastically reduced. The windfall profit of the private banking system ought to be curtailed. The alternative is political turmoil in countries forced by the IMF to accept socially-unbearable austerity packages and a serious threat to what remains of the international financial system (or 'non-system'?). The private banks with excessive exposure in the Third World will have to be bailed out by their central banks.

In the meantime, after a 'lending orgy' made possible by the availability of petro-dollars,[4] net private lending to Third World countries has come to a standstill while ODA is blatantly insufficient. The recession is being used by the industrialized countries as a pretext not to fulfil the modest targets previously agreed upon and to revert to the practice of tied aid. The situation is particularly ominous in the low-income countries which do not enjoy access to private sources of external finance. These countries are being asked to shoulder almost the entire burden of corrective action, even though the major part of their current payments deficits has little to do with their domestic economic policies. "What is very unfortunate about the inequity of the high conditionality now being demanded of the developing countries is that this demand is being spearheaded through the International Monetary Fund, an institution which, all said and done, is still part of the United Nations framework and could be said to subscribe to the broad development perspective of the United Nations Organization".[5]

The inappropriateness and the danger of the IMF package of prescriptions have been lately acknowledged by none other than Henry Kissinger, an author not hitherto suspected of having a pro-Third World bias. The IMF's original purpose was to lend to individual countries that found themselves in temporary balance-of-payments difficulty. It was not designed to deal with a durable crisis affecting many countries at the same time. "The heart of the problem is that the current rescue efforts pretend to 'solve' a debt problem that is in fact insoluble in the immediate future. In the process, it does provide an excuse for banks to continue lending. But our real objective must be to promote a sustained process of growth in the developing world; without it, all the frantic activity of rescheduling is simply delaying the inevitable crisis".[6] The IMF conditions can be quite dangerous when they are fulfilled: "A policy of forcing developing countries to reduce their standard of living drastically over a long period is likely to weaken precisely those moderate governments that are the most likely to accept Western advice".[7]

As a matter of fact, the IMF package is inspired by the 'monoeconomic'[8] theories of neo-classical obedience which are not suited to the socio-economic setting in Third World countries. The problems of a country like Brazil cannot be solved by applying a short-term policy used in developed countries, as if Brazil had the same mechanisms to protect society from the adverse effects of the cure.[9] One may indeed argue that the IMF's priorities are reversed with respect to the real needs of Third World countries: it makes little sense to 'help' a poor country by further depressing its economy and reducing social services in order to cut the public deficit. The same reductions in imports sought by the IMF could be obtained by selective import controls leading to import substitution. This kind of protection would not impede international trade any more than do the IMF's depression-inducing policies.

Solutions to the debt problem are to be found in a reduction of the excessively high interest charges, the more so as the international banks did nothing to earn them. They were, so to say, a gift from the Federal Reserve Board, whose tight-money policies drove up interest rates.[10] In other words, to play a positive role in the present situation, the IMF ought to increase its low-conditionality loans considerably, as well as changing its high-conditionality criteria[11] drastically and, above all, trying to curb the disruptive effects of the dollar-based 'non-system' which gives to the United States the unique privilege of spending, soldiering and investing abroad, generating international liquidity through the creation of dollar liabilities.[12]

The convening of 'Bretton Woods II' can only be a matter of time. In spite of their hostility to the idea, the United States and the international bankers would be forced to change their mind in the eventuality of a collapse of the present *ad hoc* management of the debt crisis.

Given the magnitude of the problem faced by the Third World debtors, the twenty 'structural adjustment loans' voted by the World Bank since 1980, the Bank's 'Special Action Program' amounting to $2 billion to be disbursed over three years, as well as its new co-financing programme limited to $500 million over a two-year testing period, amount only to a small fraction of present financial needs.[13] It is less and less likely that these will be met by the private banking system on conditions that would not be self-defeating from the point of view of Third World countries. A fundamental reform of the international lending institutions is therefore called for to enable less painful structural adjustment policies in the Third World.

To complete this brief review of the inadequacy of the present institutions, we should mention that the GATT has been unable to contain the wave of protectionism in industrialized countries. For a short while it appeared that one of the few positive results of UNCTAD VI was the promise of actions by the North to bring about a standstill in protectionism and a rollback of protectionist measures against Third World exports. But only a few days after the closing of the Belgrade Conference, the United States imposed new tariffs and quotas on imports of speciality steel from 20 countries, in blatant contradiction of President Reagan's pledge, at the preceding Williamsburg economic summit, to begin to dismantle the protectionist barriers to global recovery. Beggar-my-neighbour policies are spreading under the cover of free-trade rhetoric.

II. South-North dialogue: from Cancún to Belgrade

The proposed North-South 'global round' has still not been launched. The expectations attached to the Cancún summit of Octber 1981 did not materialize, and that event was soon forgotten. It is true that President Reagan felt obliged to pay lip service there to the principle of North-South global negotiations within the United Nations. But even this apparent procedural concession was qualified by his Philadelphia speech, delivered shortly before the Cancún meeting. There, President Reagan emphasized the roles of the GATT, the World Bank and the International Monetary Fund, "free associations of independent countries who accept both the freedom and the discipline of a competitive economic system", and went on to praise private capital flows, commercial lending and private investment, now accounting for almost 70 per cent of total financial flows to developing countries. "It is impractical", he said, "not to mention foolish, to attack these flows for ideological reasons". The United States would therefore seek to increase co-financing and other private financing with the multilateral banks,[14] an approach which had already been commended by the incoming President of the World Bank, A. W. Clausen.[15]

The United States position appeared even more clearly in articles reflecting the views of the Administration published on the occasion of Cancún. In a special report, *Newsweek* bluntly dismissed the NIEO as unrealistic on account of the crisis in the industrialized countries: " . . . such slogans ring with more noise than reason when the North itself is struggling with unemployment, inflation and high interest rates".[16] According to that magazine, the United States fears that global negotiations represent a Third World attempt to seize control of the post-war economic system, so comfortably controlled by the USA through the World Bank, the IMF and the GATT. The London *Economist* whose symphathies for Reaganomics are as notorious as its distaste for the United Nations, went a step further by condemning the very notion of global negotiations within the UN in an editorial entitled "the Cancún *cul-de-sac*".[17] We may end this press review of Cancún by a quotation taken from an essay by the well-known ecologist (and misanthrope), Garret Hardin, printed in the *Newsweek* special report already referred to: "Most of the World's wretchedness is caused by the crunch of overpopulation, which will only be made worse by the drug called 'aid' . . . ".

Against this background, UNCTAD VI met in an atmosphere of pessimism. The stakes were high and in many respects UNCTAD was the best possible forum to attempt once more a breakthrough in the South-North stalemate. The Non-Aligned countries and the whole Group of 77 spared no effort to prepare themselves for the Belgrade negotiation. The Buenos Aires Conference of the Group of 77 spelled out in detail the common position of the Third World countries, including draft resolutions for consideration in Belgrade which were conciliatory in their tone, moderate in their demands and inspired by the desire to avoid another sterile confrontation. Most of this effort proved vain because of the intransigence of the United States, the pusillanimity of the other OECD countries and the indifference of the East European bloc. The second report of the Brandt Commission pinned some hopes on the emergence of the informal grouping of 'like-minded' countries in the North, more sympathetic to the development needs of the South.[18] However, in Belgrade, these countries behaved in a subdued manner even though they did not conceal their disagreement with the United States on many substantive issues. The solidarity of the rich nations continues to carry considerable weight, even though the United States ended up politically isolated in the adoption of the final statement of the Conference.

Assessing the Belgrade Conference, the Secretary-General of UNCTAD, Gamani Corea termed it "a missed opportunity".[19] The Belgrade Conference recognized the primordial importance of the development process in the present world economic crisis. But it failed to respond to the need for a rigorous programme of recovery and development. Third World delegations left Belgrade disappointed, as the measures adopted fell far short of the required action. Their frustration was put on record in the final plenary session of the Belgrade Conference by the spokesman of the Group of 77, who made it clear that the 77 accepted the package of resolutions only in order to prevent the total failure of UNCTAD and the inevitable damage which that would do to the already fragile spirit of international co-operation.[20]

The most positive result of Belgrade was that UNCTAD survived as an institution without major paralysis. This may not be much, but leaves at least some hope for the future. Institutional pluralism within the international system is important in a period of turbulence, when the need for a thorough institutional reform is clearly perceived but there are conflicting and still confused ideas about the direction to take. The record of UNCTAD in its twenty years of existence may be quite modest by the yardstick of expectations nurtured when it came into being. But without it the situation of the Third World countries would have been worse.

UNCTAD provides a negotiating forum and a source of information, expertise and ideas *different* from those to be found at the World Bank, the IMF, the GATT, not to speak of the OECD. This *differentia specifica* ought to be cultivated in spite of the political pressures exerted by the United States and the other OECD countries. The North-South global negotiations, if ever they start, will be protracted. Bretton Woods II and other conferences of the kind are not for tomorrow. Meanwhile, UNCTAD is all we have.

III. Self-reliant strategies for coping with the crisis

The prospect for the Third World countries, other than a handful of capital-surplus oil exporters, is dismal. They must cope with a formidable array of mutually-reinforcing negative features on the international scene:

—slow growth or even stagnation of industrialized economies;

—deterioration of terms of trade for primary commodities other than oil and food;

—further increase of real prices of energy and food, of which most Third World countries are net importers;[21]

—rise of protectionism, of beggar-my-neighbour policies and of schizophrenic attitudes in the North towards free trade, recommended in theory and obstructed in practice by restricting the market access of Third World industrial goods;

—further curtailment of the already-reduced share of public funds in financial flows to the South, increasingly dominated by transnational private banks;

—continuation of the armaments race, imposing severe world-wide distortions on economic activities and on R and D efforts, not to speak of the threats to security;[22]

—further intensification of the present trend towards capital-intensive and environmentally-disruptive technologies in the North, fostered under the pretext of ensuring competitiveness in international markets, and which, when transferred mimetically to the South, are likely to prove socially and ecologically disruptive;

—the automation of hitherto labour-intensive industries (e.g. textiles, garments, electronics) in the North, with a consequent fall of Northern demand for the products of these industries in the South.

The first volume of a welcome addition to the series of annual reviews issued by the various international organizations, the *Trade and Development Report, 1981*,[23] prepared by the UNCTAD secretariat, opens significantly with a sentence on the discouraging beginning of the 1980s. The dilemma of our times is summarized by its authors as follows: "Low growth for developing countries is unsustainable from the point of view of their own social dynamics, while high growth for these countries is not feasible in the context of the existing international system". In these circumstances, the Third World countries must find ways and means of loosening the dependence of their rate of growth on that of industrialized countries, rather than accepting the friendly advice that they should wait for the renewed prosperity and expansion of the industrialized economies.

Interdependence is a major structural phenomenon in the world economy as shaped by four centuries of capitalist development. It applies equally to the centre and to the periphery. The crisis in the North would have been worse without the booming exports to the Third World countries, financed through the recycling at ever higher interest rates of petrodollars deposited in Northern banks by Middle-Eastern capital-surplus oil exporters. Many Third World countries have thus been lured into the trap of foreign indebtedness and, as we have seen, are facing severe balance-of-payments problems compounded by the high prices of oil and the exorbitant cost of foreign debt service. But, at the same time, they have been acting as 'engines of growth' for the ailing Northern economies. The present situation certainly gives more reason to Keynesianism (or, if one prefers, to Rosa Luxemburg) than to supply-side Reaganomics. It justifies the concept of a planetary 'New Deal', on condition that massive flows of foreign resources are not used to impose an exogenous development model on Third World countries.

If such a course were to be adopted, interdependence would bring about 'inter-development'.[24] But the chances for it, on a global level, are slim. Even bilateral 'co-development' agreements, announced by the French Socialist Government, have yet to materialize. At the other extreme of the spectrum of possible action, we must dismiss de-linking as unrealistic and very costly in economic and social terms, only possible, if at all, in a handful of exceptionally large countries, like the Soviet Union or China. Even there, the confusion of autarky with self-reliance had harmful results.

In between, the operational question for the Third World countries is how 'to restructure their economies away from excessive dependence on external factors as sources of economic growth and towards new patterns of development in which the external factor is adapted to serve the needs of the domestic economy".[25] UNCTAD addresses itself to this problem in a somewhat different form, enquiring under what conditions the developing countries could accelerate their development in a world economy characterized by slow growth. Two important directions in which solutions must be sought are clearly identified by UNCTAD in its *Trade and Development Report:* increased trade among Third World countries and a higher degree of import substitution. A third one, of a more qualitative nature, should be added: the ability to use available import capacity to serve genuine development priorities. A comment on each of these is in order.

It is highly significant that, for his Nobel lecture, Sir Arthur Lewis singled out the collective self-reliance of the Third World as the only way of offsetting the slowing down of North-South exchanges.[26] His basic assumptions are that the 'Less Developed Countries (LDCs)' need to have their exports grow at 6 per cent per year, while the (industrialized) 'More Developed Countries (MDCs)' will increase their imports from them only at 4 per cent per year, given the unwillingness of the latter to allow LDCs a greater share of their markets. Simple arithmetic shows that, in these circumstances, LDCs' sales to the rest of the world must increase initially at about 11 per cent per annum. This could only happen by sharply accelerating South-South trade, which Lewis considers feasible. "Currently the LDCs' depend on the MDCs for food, fertilizers, cement, steel and machinery. Taken as a group. LDCs could quickly end their dependence for the first four and gradually throw off their dependence for machinery". This new South-South trade would be worldwide and not tied to regional arrangements.

This optimistic long-run view is shared by Celso Furtado, who considers that Brazil and India could become centres of technological innovation geared to the needs of the Third World. To achieve this, however, Brazil must free itself from the trap of short-term problems and radically transform its participation in the international economy. "The dynamics of our present insertion in the international division of labour cause uncontrollable imbalances and tend to impose growing costs in foreign exchange on the development of our economy. It is as if Brazil, while developing, had to pay an external tax increasing more rapidly than output".[27] Furtado rightly points out that Brazil can adopt an outward-looking strategy only at the price of accepting to underpay its labour force turning out exportable goods and of indulging in a predatory exploitation of its natural resources. The country's development prospects are, on the contrary, linked to the expansion of the internal market, in his view.

This brings us to the discussion of the balance between outward and inward orientation in development strategies. Bela Balassa[28] and, more generally, the World Bank are engaged in a systematic promotion of outward-looking strategies as a panacea for all the Third World countries, with little or no regard for their size, natural endowments, degree of economic development and political regime. Practically the same prescription is considered applicable to Hong Kong and to China! More often than not, it goes in the same package as the advice to rely more heavily on private sources of ever-more expensive finance, despite the risk of getting trapped in foreign indebtedness, and to abide by the IMF's draconian policy of austerity at the expense of working people. This is not the place to expose the often fallacious arguments advanced in support of outward-looking strategies, nor to examine in detail the long list of IMF casualties. The present writer does not have a bias in favour of de-linking and against trade acting as an engine of development. In point of fact, the challenge facing UNCTAD is to transform the world economic scene in such a way as to make development through trade possible and advantageous, reducing in this way its social costs. But the opportunities for outward-looking strategies for growth, not to speak of development, are just not available for most countries. Raúl Prebisch has explained this point time and again: "Frequently, voices from the centres have condemned peripheral import substitution. However, this has not been originally a matter of doctrinaire preference. It has been something imposed by facts, and continues to be so. The more the centres are reluctant to follow a liberal policy, the more the periphery is forced to substitute domestic production for imports in so far as it cannot expand exports. This does not condone the frequent abuses of protectionism and the numerous shortcomings and incongruities of import substitution".[29]

The industrialized countries persist in not recognizing that their own enlightened self-interest should push them into a totally different policy from the one they pursue at present; they could only gain by opening their markets wide to LDCs' products and using their present idle capacity to turn out goods in short supply in the Third World. Financing development aid is a reasonable substitute for unemployment allowances, not to speak of the terribly wasteful and dangerous arms race. It is true that such a policy reversal would require far-reaching internal adjustments in the industrialized countries, but how one can expect the present crisis to be overcome without a drastic overhaul of economic and social policies?

The debate about outward-looking versus inward-looking strategies is now, to a great extent, an abstract one. The real problem for those few Third World countries who can count on the expansion of their trade is to see that trade is not only an engine of growth but also a factor of development. In this connection, the experience of the NICs (newly-industrialized countries), heralded as an example for the rest of the Third World by the advocates of outward-looking strategies, deserves a close look. Whose comparative advantage is being taken into consideration: that of the TNCs looking for wage differentials and/or cheap raw materials, or that of the people in the host country? In a well-documented article, Calcagno and Jakobowicz[30] reach the conclusion that the type of development attributed to NICs cannot be generalized: "The open industrialization model based on present comparative advantages tries to promote the low cost of labour and natural resources (often non-renewable), does not contribute to consolidating the national economy or providing the people with goods, and may lead to the veritable cultivation of underdevelopment". Besides, a model based on labour discipline and low wages is very difficult to maintain without an authoritarian regime. In other words, the model applies essentially to countries that do not have any other alternative owing to their lack of natural resources and the reduced size of the internal market.

On the other hand, a look at some oil exporters will make it clear that booming exports do not *per se* bring development. The case of Mexico, a NIC *and* an oil exporter, is very instructive indeed. According to the supporters of the outward-looking model, Mexico's belonging to both these privileged categories should have boosted its economic growth and ensured lasting prosperity. Yet the Mexican economy almost collapsed in 1982. Nor should import substitution be looked at as an intrinsic goal and a sufficient condition for development. Indeed, the shortcomings and incongruities of import substitution, mentioned by Prebisch and often used as an argument *a contrario* for outward-looking strategies, should be attributed to a confusion between means and goals.

In the absence of a development strategy translated into a set of economic and social priorities, the market mechanism is likely to work in favour of import substitution of non-essential consumer goods and durables, for which a strong demand exists on the part of local elites. But these goods are precisely the ones that can be foregone, at least in the initial period of development. Banning their imports is thus a correct measure only on condition that they will not be substituted and that the resources thus released will be used in accordance with the priorities established in the development strategy. The evaluation of foreign trade performance, and for that matter of foreign aid impact, is impossible without taking a global view of the economy.[31] This calls for a planning framework with explicit socio-economic goals and evaluation criteria going beyond the narrow economic cost-benefit concept. For the planner, the problem does not consist in pushing import substitution against export promotion, but in finding the best opportunities in both directions (comparable in terms of net domestic cost of the foreign exchange unit saved or earned) and then making the best possible use of the available capacity to import. In an import-sensitive economy,[32] development performance will ultimately depend on this ability. But far from being a sectoral problem, this is a matter of the right choice of development models, of refusing to imitate the consumption styles and production patterns of the North, and of setting as the paramount goal the mobilization of the national resources to satisfy the essential needs of the whole population. As Keith Griffin put it provocatively, "if each Third World country would embark on a programme to abolish poverty within its borders, the world would soon be changed in the process".[33] Perhaps a new international order would be brought about by this synergic effort of Third World countries more effectively than by discussion in international fora.

This statement should not be taken by the industrialized countries as an excuse for maintaining the present asymmetric and exploitative North-South relations, any more than the impasse in the South-North dialogue should be invoked by Third World elites to justify the continuation of inequitable and often authoritarian regimes. Far-reaching changes are necessary both at the international and national levels, the industrialized countries being no exception. The challenge to the UN system in general, and to UNCTAD in particular, is to help these changes along by making the most, and more than hitherto, of the scant margins of initiative conferred upon the Secretariat by the United Nations Charter.

IV. UNCTAD in the years ahead

Let us then look at UNCTAD's future role in a broader historical perspective. We still live in a world to a great extent shaped by the outcome of the second World War. In spite of its internal inconsistencies and weaknesses, and of the wide spectrum of political regimes represented in Africa, Asia and Latin America, the emergence of the Third World is the most significant structural phenomenon to have occured in the second half of this century. Of course, UNCTAD's coming into existence is related to it. 1973 was another watershed, in so far as for the first time in history a group of developing countries was able to assert sovereignty over such a strategic natural resource as oil and to put the major industrial powers on the defensive.

One should not draw too optimistic a conclusion from these events, however positive they may be. The balance of economic power in the world is still overwhelmingly tilted in favour of the North. International finance and trade continue to be ruled by institutions controlled by the United States and their Atlantic allies. Formidable pressures are exerted to maintain in life the collapsed Bretton Woods system and to prevent the long-overdue reforms aimed at more democratic power-sharing within the IMF and the World Bank. The NIEO proposals do not embody a coherent set of trade rules and, by default, continue to echo the GATT doctrine of open trade based on comparative advantage.

Conservative dynamism demonstrates its vitality in all international fora. Meanwhile the TNCs and the Northern private banks have been consolidating their positions in the world economy and, more particularly so, in many places in the South. Colonialism is dead, but the capitalist system has demonstrated its adaptive powers, inventing new and changing forms of effective exploitation of the Southern economies. The latest show of its ability to turn an initial setback to its advantage is provided by the recycling of petrodollars. Private loans extended by Northern banks to developing countries lured them, one by one, into the trap of foreign indebtedness and made them vulnerable to the point of having to abide by the conservative rules of conduct dictated by the IMF.

Quosque tandem? A day may come when the huge debt accumulated by the developing countries will become their major lever to force the industrial powers to negotiate new arrangements for international trade and finance. But we are not there yet. Meanwhile, the Third World must accept progress by the millimetre on the way to the NIEO, the more so given that in its negotiations with the North it cannot count on the support of the Eastern bloc. The socialist industrialized countries have missed their historical chance to develop meaningful economic and technical co-operation with the South through some kind of planned sectoral division of labour, translated into long-term contracts. Instead the Eastern bloc has chosen to compete with the Third World countries on Western markets as a source of commodities and of industrial goods produced by cheap labour.

Moreover, the asymmetric relations between North and South are inseparable from other highly negative results of the post-war settlement: the acceptance of a biased interpretation of the Yalta agreement as the cornerstone of the world balance of power; the overwhelming military and political roles of the two superpowers, in spite of the emergence of Europe and Japan as major economic powers and of China as a second pole in the socialist bloc of nations. As a tragic corollary, the armaments race not only threatens mankind with a holocaust but also casts its staggering burden on the world economy: over $600 billion are spent each year on weaponry, the equivalent of the GNP of the poorer half of the world's population. World poverty will not be overcome, nor will social progress and international security be achieved, unless a new balance of forces emerges on the world scene, forcing the two superpowers to abandon their present arrogant course. This new balance is vitally important to the Third World, as well as to the European countries, at least to the so-called like-minded ones and, perhaps, even the EEC as a whole. Thus, ways of bringing these two groups nearer to each other should be actively pursued, all the more so in that the present international economic order, highly discriminatory with respect to Third World countries, also poses many problems to European countries, like France today, which aim to bring about social and economic reconstruction at home.

What can UNCTAD do to help bring about the necessary yet still remote restructuring of the international economic system? Its possibilities with respect to this broad objective are fairly limited, but far from insignificant. The world economic scene now is very different from the one, twenty years ago, when UNCTAD came into being. The problem before Raúl Prebisch, Wladek Malinowski and the first core of UNCTAD architects and managers was how to ensure that the Third World countries received a fairer deal and a greater share in rapidly expanding world trade and production. Their generous endeavour was predicated on two assumptions: that the world economy would pursue its steady growth and that the Bretton Woods institutions, as well as the UN system, could be made to work both efficiently and equitably. Accordingly, removing trade barriers, promoting a model of multilateralism with built-in safeguards and concessions for the developing countries, negotiating commodity agreements, stepping up the flow of public aid and granting access to technology on fair terms appeared as both important and feasible components of an international development strategy of direct concern to UNCTAD.

Unfortunately these assumptions did not hold true; the growth of the world economy cannot be taken for granted any more, the monetary system is in a shambles and, in spite of its modest goals, the NIEO has not been accepted by the United States and most industrialized nations. The defensive reactions of governments, unable to deal with the present crisis except by passing the problems across their national frontiers, have created a situation in which the increased interdependence achieved through the massive growth of trade in the last twenty years, is now taking the world economy on a downward spiral.[34]

In the present situation, UNCTAD cannot by itself reverse this trend and set the world economy on an upward course. After the disappointment of Belgrade, UNCTAD's most urgent task is to preserve its integrity and its potential role as an active agent of change in the international system, asserting its right and duty to address itself to the overall world economic situation in all its complexity, including financial and monetary issues. UNCTAD should reaffirm its mandate as the main UN agency for development and trade, entrusted with thinking about development as a whole.

The UNCTAD secretariat ought, therefore, to continue its efforts to monitor the present crisis in its structural as well as conjunctural aspects, outlining a bold agenda for a global reform of the world economic system. The UNCTAD secretariat has an important analytical and conceptual role to play and, if it wishes to live up to the standards of its founders, a moral obligation to state issues frankly, dramatically and in their entirety. It is important at this critical point not to shun controversy by seeking refuge in the verbal compromises so often resorted to at the United Nations. In particular, the onslaught of the marketeers must be vigorously resisted. UNCTAD was born of the conviction that unrestricted free trade and free enterprise could not by themselves solve the development problems of the world; that a fair measure of planning, resource redistribution, international regulation and market organization were necessary even in times of high conjuncture. The argument is valid *a fortiori* in a period of crisis. From the fact that industrialized countries are discriminating against developing countries through protectionism and bilateralism, it does not follow that concessions should be made to a doctrinaire reaffirmation of the pretended virtues of free trade and multilateralism as such.

A permanent task for UNCTAD should be to monitor not only what goes on in world trade, finance and development, but also the realm of intellectual work on these matters, in particular in Third World countries. The South-South option postulated by Third World leaders[35] has also an intellectual dimension, up to now too neglected. Development thinking in all its aspects must be decolonized and the many original contributions of Third World scholars made better known to their counterparts throughout the Third World. UNCTAD has gone farther along this road than any other UN body, but the task ahead is still enormous. UNCTAD can best play its fundamental role of generator of ideas by becoming a clearing house of new thinking about development and trade and the inevitable reform of the international economic, trade and financial systems. It goes without saying that the effort to ensure that contributions from the South are not absent should not be understood as a discrimination against bright new ideas coming from whatever quarter. UNCTAD's orientation must remain oecumenic and pluralistic.

UNCTAD's capacity to act as the spearhead of world economic reforms would be greatly enhanced by the creation of an 'OECD' of Third World countries capable of discharging UNCTAD from the function of supporting the Group of 77, a function at present assumed with a certain degree of ambiguity and difficulty, as proved by the debate on ECDC.[36] But a strong 'OECD' of the Third World will take years to become operational, even once the decision to create it is taken by the Group of 77 or by a substantial number of its members. We are not yet there, in spite of some positive steps taken recently. In the meantime, while monitoring the economic and social impacts of the structural crisis, nourishing the NIEO debate and preparing for global negotiations, UNCTAD should give considerable priority to all ECDC and TCDC activities for three reasons:

—South-South co-operation constitutes, along with their national development strategies, the only margin of freedom for the Third World countries to offset the negative impact of the world crisis on their economies. The greater the obstacles to a meaningful expansion of ECDC, the more necessary is the involvement of UNCTAD, and generally of the whole UN system, in such aspects of this activity which are practical and likely to yield positive results even in the short term.

—Expanding South-South relations in the realm of trade, finance and technology is tantamount to strengthening the overall bargaining position of the Third World countries in the South-North confrontation and in the eventual global negotiations. It may yet prove the most effective lever to overcome the likely deadlocks in the protracted process of negotiation.

—Last but not least, building South-South co-operation is a positive contribution to the NIEO.

UNCTAD's involvement in ECDC will probably require the strengthening of its capability for technical assistance of various kinds to Third World governments. As a breakthrough towards global negotiations is not likely to occur soon, technical assistance in such areas as development planning for import-sensitive economies, or management of foreign trade and finance under conditions of growing strain, may become increasingly important to several Third World countries hit by the crisis and caught in the foreign debt trap, yet unwilling to accept the high-conditionality package and the orthodox policy prescriptions administered by the IMF.

It goes without saying that these ambitious and difficult tasks should not deter UNCTAD from its patient day-to-day pursuit of continuing negotiations and its stop-gap efforts to prevent a further worsening of the plight of Third World countries in commodity trade and other areas of its traditional concern, even though in the absence of more fundamental reforms of the international economic system the efficacy of such measures may appear limited.

---

1. See UNCTAD VI, *Report of the Working Group on the World Economic Situation* (TD/L.260, 2 July 1983) in the report of the Conference (TD/325 and Add. 1).

2. See W. Leontief, "What hope for the Economy?", *New York Review of Books*, 12 August 1982.

3. This point was made forcefully by Raúl Prebisch in the first Raúl Prebisch Lecture at UNCTAD on 6 July 1982.

4. At the peak of this 'orgy', commercial bank lending increased at a rate of 25% per year and accounted for almost two-thirds of the total flow of capital to the Third World (M. Miller, *Coping with the International Liquidity Problem*, paper read at the Annual Conference of the Federation of Financial Analysts, Toronto, 16 May 1982).

5. I. S. Gulati, "International Finance: Asymmetries, Old and New", *Economic and Political Weekly*, vol. XVIII, No. 11, 12 March 1983, p. 395. See also S. Dell, "Stabilization: the Political Economy of Overkill", *World Development*, vol. 10, No. 8, August 1982.

6. H. A. Kissinger, "Saving the World Economy", *Newsweek*, 24 January 1983, p. 19.

7. *Ibid*, p. 18. It is a pity that Kissinger's forceful article did not carry conviction with the US delegation in Belgrade!

8. The term has been proposed by A. O. Hirschmann to denote economic theories claiming to have universal validity. See *Essays in Trespassing*, Cambridge University Press, 1981.

9. Interview with Celso Furtado in *Gazeta Mercantil*, 6 July 1983. Furtado advocates a unilateral moratorium followed by negotiations and the repudiation by Brazil of its agreement with the IMF.

10. W. D. Slawson, "The Fund's Priorities are Reversed", *International Herald Tribune*, 16 July 1983. Compare A. Bressand in *RAMSES 82*, IFRI-Economica, Paris, 1982, p. 154: "Paradoxalement, la force du dollar se nourrit de la faiblesse de la politique économique américaine".

11. A. Bressand, *op. cit.*, p. 178, points to the need to establish conditionality criteria based on development performance.

12. Between 1973 and 1979 the US current account surplus was of only $5.1 billion. However, its additional investments abroad were sixty times higher, adding up to $307 billion (Gulati, *op. cit.*, p. 395).

13. Data taken from Miller, *op. cit.*

14. As reported in *The New York Times*, 16 October 1981.

15. Address to the Board of Governors, 29 September 1981, World Bank, Washington.

16. *Newsweek*, 26 October 1981.

17. The Economist, 31 October 1981.

18. *Common Crisis North–South: Co-operation for World Recovery*, The Brandt Commission 1983, Pan Books, London, p. 149.

19. Statement to the UN Economic and Social Council on 7 July 1983.

20. *The Observer* of 10 July 1983 wrote: "Four weeks of haggling at the United Nations Conference on Trade and Development in Belgrade, culminating in three consecutive all-night sessions, had achieved absolutely nothing. Most of the blame for the failure lies with the rich countries, particularly the United States. For the first time the West recognized in Belgrade that its prosperity depends on progress in the Third World. But the United States, backed by Britain and West Germany, refused to accept any of the developing countries' proposals for action—maintaining, against most of the evidence, that recovery in the rich countries would automatically 'trickle down' to the poor. A change of attitude in these three countries is urgent and overdue".

21. According to some forecasts the cost of food may double by the end of this century, imposing great hardship on the poor all over the world. See *Global 2000 Report to the President,*

"Entering the Twenty-First Century", a report prepared by the Council on Environmental Quality and the Department of State, Volume 1, Washington 1980.

22. Impressive evidence on the disrupting and perverting effects of the armaments race has been assembled in the *Report on the Relationship between Disarmament and Development*, prepared at the UN by a group of experts, Document A/36/356, Annex, 5 October 1981.

23. Document TD/B/863, 31 July 1981, presented to the twenty-third session of the Trade and Development Board, p. 14.

24. The term has been proposed by J. Saint Geours, *L'impératif de coopération nord-sud*, 1981, Dunod, Paris.

25. Analytical Report of the Director-General for Development and International Economic Co-operation, document A/S–11/5 of 7 August 1980, p. 106. See also Sachs, 1965, *Foreign Trade and Economic Development of Underdeveloped Countries*, Asia Publishing House, Bombay.

26. W. A. Lewis, "The Slowing Down of the Engine of Growth", *The American Economic Review*, vol. 70, No. 4, Sept. 1980, pp. 555–564.

27. Celso Furtado, "El Orden Económico Internacional y el Brazil", *El Trimestre Económico*, vol. XLIII (3), No. 191, July-Sept. 1981, pp. 523–537.

28. See, for example, B. Balassa, *The Process of Industrial Development and Alternative Strategies*, World Bank Staff Working Paper No. 438, October 1980 and, by the same author, "Structural Adjustment Policies in Development Economies", *World Development*, Vol. 10, No. 1, January 1982, pp. 23–38.

29. R. Prebisch, *Crisis of Advanced Capitalism*, Third World Lecture 1981, p. 8. In 1973, I published a paper entitled: "Outward-Looking Strategies: A Dangerous Illusion?" in P. Streeten, *Trade Strategies for Development*, London, Macmillan, pp. 51–61. Today, I would suppress the question mark in the title.

30. A. E. Calcagno, and J. M. Jakobowicz, "Some aspects of the international distribution of industrial activity", *CEPAL Review*, No. 13, April 1981, pp. 8–33.

31. See M. Kalecki, and I. Sachs, "Forms of foreign aid: an economic analysis", *Social Science Information*, Paris, Vol. V, No. 1, 1966, pp. 21–44.

32. An import-sensitive economy is characterized by a low ratio of imports to GNP, yet a very high dependence on essential imports which cannot be substituted.

33. K. Griffin, "Economic Development in a Changing World", *World Development*, Vol. 9, No. 3, 1981, p. 226.

34. See the statement by Gamani Corea at the meeting of the Trade and Development Board on 8 March 1982.

35. See *inter alia* The Third World Lecture 1982 by Julius K. Nyerere; Soedjatmoko's Jawaharlal Nehru Memorial Lecture, 13 November 1982; and Raúl Prebisch's "La Crisis Inflacionaria del Capitalismo", *El Trimestre Económico*, Vol. XLIX, No. 193, January–March 1982.

36. See on this subject K. O. Hall, "The Group of 77—Strengthening its Negotiating Capacity", *Third World Forum Occasional Paper*, No. 11, 1979.

GLOBAL MANAGEMENT OF PROCESSES OF CHANGE AND ADJUSTMENT

by Stein Rossen

Post-war economic history has amply demonstrated the need for global management of processes of change and adjustment in the world economy. This need was recognized by most participants in the discussions and negotiations on multilateral rules and mechanisms in the years 1943–1948, but it was far from adequately translated into the IMF/GATT system that was actually created by the developed market-economy countries (DMEs) under the leadership of the United States.[1]

Part One of this paper briefly reviews the IMF/GATT system in the context of post-war economic trends and with particular reference to the issue of global management. Attention is drawn to the fact that the system became subject to increasing strains in the latter part of the period of fast growth in production and especially in trade, which came to an end in 1973. Subsequent years have been characterized, on the one hand, by world economic disturbances and slow growth and, on the other hand, by the absence of global management rather than by its exercise. The conclusion is that there is a need for a comprehensive reform of the system, including, in particular, new multilateral rules and mechanisms designed to ensure development-oriented management of change and adjustment. While the main lines of reform in the monetary and financial areas have been identified at the conceptual level, the problems appear to be much more intractable in the case of trade, mainly in view of the discrepancy between the principles and the practices of the DMEs with respect to trade-related processes of structural change and adjustment.

The problems in the trade field are examined in Part Two of the paper with reference to structural change and adjustment in manufacturing industry. The main subjects discussed are the prospects for far-reaching structural change during the remaining part of this century, the roles of the major actors: the governments and the transnational corporations (TNCs), and proposals put forward with a view to introducing elements of international management in this area. The problems inherent in any move towards international management are fully recognized, but the paper argues that the pace of the industrialization of the developing or Third World countries (DCs) and the preservation of an open trading system may well depend on the readiness of governments to consider constructively new and pragmatic approaches to rules and mechanisms regarding structural change and adjustment.

Part I

The IMF/GATT System, Post-war Economic Trends and the Issue of Global Management – An Overview

The Great Depression of the early 1930s brought about the breakdown of the gold standard and the imposition by governments of restrictions, often of a discriminatory nature, on trade and payments, with the deliberate aim of increasing domestic output and employment. These restrictive policies met with only limited success, since they failed to take their adverse repercussions on other countries into account. Unemployment was high in most countries at the outbreak of the second World War.

In view of the inter-war experience, governments gave serious consideration during the war to a multilateral system of trade and payments. Agreement was reached in 1944 on the IMF and on the IBRD, presently known as the World Bank. It proved more difficult to reach agreement on the international trade regime. This reflected primarily the fact that, while the maintenance of high levels of employment and economic activity was generally recognized as a condition for the introduction and preservation of a liberal system of trade and payments, different opinions were expressed on the priority of full employment policies and their implications for the trading regime.

A multilateral negotiating process was initiated in 1946 and a Charter for an International Trade Organization (ITO) was signed at Havana in 1948 by 53 countries. The commercial policy provisions of the Charter did not meet the particular needs of the DCs, nor did they meet all the preoccupations of those DME goverments which favoured purposive direction of their economies. However, these provisions should be seen in conjunction with those contained in the other substantive parts of the Charter. The ITO was conceived as a very active organization concerned with virtually all issues in the areas of trade, employment and development and, in the final analysis, with the management of the world economy. More specifically, the avoidance of unemployment and under-employment was considered as not being of domestic concern alone, but also as a necessary condition for the achievement of the objectives of the Organization. The ITO was, therefore, empowered to take concerted action against the international spread of a decline in employment, production or demand.

The ITO did not materialize because of the failure of the United States to ratify the Havana Charter.[2] This led to the emergence of the General Agreement on Tariffs and Trade,[3] administered *de facto* by an organization referred to as GATT, as the trade component of the international economic system. The aims and activities of the Contracting Parties to the Agreement were much more limited than those envisaged for the members of the ITO. In fact, the General Agreement corresponded essentially to the commercial policy provisions of the Havana Charter, thus treating commercial policy separately from other fields of economic policy.

Taken together, the components of the post-war international economic system set out principles and rules for trade and payments designed to achieve and preserve trade liberalization and convertibility of currencies for current transactions. The basic principles called for non-discrimination and reciprocity and for reliance on tariffs as the sole instrument of protection, to be reduced over time. Departures from the latter principle were subject to detailed rules intended to protect the value of tariff concessions. The bulk of world trade was expected to be carried out by private enterprise under conditions of fair competition; no provisions were made for the control of restrictive business practices, including abuse of dominant market power.

As far as the DMEs were concerned, it was largely left to the Marshall Plan, the Organization for European Economic Cooperation (OEEC) and the European Payments Union (EPU) to overcome the dislocations caused by the war and to create the conditions necessary for the actual establishment of the system. The latter objective was attained towards the end of the 1950s, although a number of 'hard core' restrictions remained in agriculture and certain traditional industries. From that time onwards, the balance of payments adjustment process as well as trade-related processes of structural change and adjustment were in principle to be left to market forces operating within a framework set by tariffs and macro-economic policies. The Articles of Agreement of the IMF provided for elements of global management, in particular the financing of reversible deficits and a system of fixed and unified exchange rates,[4] which could only be altered after international consultations. The main purpose of the latter was to prevent member countries from using currency devaluation as an instrument of beggar-my-neighbour policies.

According to the General Agreement, the Contracting Parties were to co-operate with the IMF in order to ensure policy co-operation, but in practice the co-operation extended little beyond the acceptance by the former of the latter's judgement on any plea of balance of payments difficulties advanced by a GATT member as justification for invoking the special provisions of the General Agreement.[5] However, the DMEs recognized the need for co-ordination and harmonization of national macro-economic policies. This task was carried out by limited fora of major DMEs and by the OECD, the successor of the OEEC. The OECD endorsed the view that the achievement of economic growth and the expansion of world trade on a multilateral basis required a favourable economic climate, including the maintenance of virtually full employment and a state of reasonable equilibrium in the balance of payments.[6]

The IMF/GATT system did not suit the DCs, which had to rely on active government policies, including selective import controls, in order to transform the structure of their economies. On the monetary side, the DCs were allowed to apply payments restrictions by reference to the provision which sanctioned the use of such practices in the 'post-war transitional period'. By contrast, the General Agreement contained an article on goverment assistance to economic development, which from 1955 onwards also incorporated special provisions for DCs regarding balance of payments safeguards. Further consideration within GATT of the particular problems of the DCs resulted in 1964 in the addition to the General Agreement of a new Part IV on Trade and Development, which *inter alia* introduced the concept of non-reciprocity,[7] stressed the role of exports in economic development and called upon the DMEs to accord high priority to measures designed to improve the terms of access to their markets of products of particular interest to the DCs. These innovations were not unrelated to the Prebisch doctrine[8] and the developments leading to the establishment of UNCTAD, also in 1964.

Notwithstanding Part IV, the Kennedy Round of trade negotiations (1964–1967) confirmed the interest of the DMEs in reducing tariffs on advanced products and their reluctance to introduce a significant degree of free trade in the products of traditional industries. In 1970 agreement was nevertheless reached within UNCTAD on generalized tariff preferences in favour of DCs (the GSP), for which GATT granted a waiver. However, the importance of this achievement was reduced by the *de facto* establishment, in connexion with the enlargement of the EEC, of a free trade area in manufactures covering virtually the whole of Western Europe and, in general, by the failure of DMEs to give full effect to the GSP scheme as originally conceived. UNCTAD also succeeded in obtaining recognition of the trade gap[9] associated with development and the related target for official development assistance, which in principle were to be observed by the DMEs in deciding on measures of balance of payments adjustment.

From the early postwar years up to 1973, the DMEs experienced economic growth, high levels of employment and an expansion of trade largely exceeding that of output. This period also witnessed substantial changes in the geographical patterns and commodity composition of world production and trade. The DCs benefited from the expansion, but their share in world trade declined sharply and the gap between their *per capita* income and that of the DMEs widened.

The liberalization of trade and payments undoubtedly contributed to economic expansion, but other factors were also at work, in particular the supply of funds and technology from the US. Moreover, in assessing the role of the economic system, account should be taken of the fact that it became subject to increasing strain in the course of the 1960s, as shown by the recurrent monetary crises and the trend towards erosion of the trading regime.

The monetary crises in the 1960s reflected such factors as the reliance on US deficits as the principal source of international liquidity, the fixed price of monetary gold in terms of US dollars, the rigidity of the foreign exchange regime, the reluctance of surplus countries to participate in the balance of payments adjustment process and the decline in the relative economic strength of the US.[10] The US deficits had made it possible for Japan and most Western European countries to pursue policies of economic growth and liberalization of trade and payments, while rebuilding their foreign reserves. But this process could not go on forever. By the end of the 1960s, the US was no longer prepared to face a decline in its market shares at home and abroad, while other countries were reluctant to finance US deficits by adding to their dollar holdings. Attempts were made to solve the resulting conflicts between the trade and payments objectives of the major countries, but these failed largely on account of the weaknesses inherent in the monetary system. In 1971, the US placed the issue of monetary reform before the international community by suspending unilaterally the convertibility of the dollar in terms of gold and other reserve assets. The IMF responded in 1972 by establishing an *ad hoc* committee, known as the Committee of Twenty, for the purpose of elaborating proposals for reform.

The erosion of the trading system reflected the extensive use made by most DME goverments of selective policy instruments other than tariffs,[11] the emergence of the concept of market disruption,[12] the growing share of preferential trade in world trade, the trend towards internationalization of production and trade under the auspices of TNCs and the related expansion of intra-firm trade. As far as manufacturing industry was concerned, governments both promoted and reacted to structural change by means of selective policies, which tended to be oriented to growth and efficiency in advanced industries and protectionist or defensive in traditional industries. According to the Rey Report, published in 1972, "The situation . . . is characterized by an absence of international discipline, making countries relatively free to introduce a wide variety of safeguard measures" which, as noted by the Report, were often discriminatory in nature.[13] Addressing itself to the trading regime in general, the Report drew attention to the emergence of the EEC and Japan as great trading powers, the persistent difficulties of the

DCs and the increasing interdependence of national economies, and called "for a fresh examination of the concepts and mechanisms on which world trade is based".[14] The three main trading powers, the US, the EEC and Japan, were also concerned about the trading system, as shown by their 1972 declarations which led to the Tokyo Round of Multilateral Trade Negotiations (MTNs).

In 1974–75 the DMEs experienced a substantial decrease in industrial output and steep increases in the rates of inflation and unemployment. The recession was triggered off by a variety of forces, including the commodity price boom and the long overdue increase in the price of oil. However, the recession had roots both in the shortcomings of the international economic system and in the economic, social and institutional changes which had taken place in the national economies during the period of expansion. Some of these changes, in particular the increased rigidity in price and wage formation, added substantially to the problems of bringing inflation under control.

The DMEs agreed to finance the trade deficits caused by the increase in the price of oil, since any other course of action would have aggravated the situation. However, as a group, the DMEs achieved a recession-induced surplus in 1975, small deficits in 1976 and 1977, and a substantial surplus in 1978, thus shifting a considerable part of the burden of adjustment to the oil-importing DCs. On the other hand, they failed by relatively large margins to reduce the rates of inflation and unemployment to pre-recession levels. Faced by a second round of oil price increases in 1979, the DMEs attached top priority to the fight against inflation by means of restrictive monetary policies, thus bringing about another recession in 1980–82 accompanied by a steep increase in interest rates and a collapse of non-oil commodity prices.

The years of recession or stagnation in the world economy have been associated with a failure to provide for and exercise global management which, as shown below, has had particularly serious economic consequences for the DCs. The objective of a comprehensive monetary reform was given up in 1974, though it was agreed that an evolutionary process of reform should be initiated. Some measures were in fact adopted, including the acceptance of floating exchange rates, but no substantial progress has been made in the direction of improving the balance of payments adjustment process and bringing the creation of international liquidity under multilateral control. Erratic changes in exchange rates have continued to hamper trade and investment, while a substantial measure of control over international liquidity has been shifted into private hands. The latter shift has been associated with the growing importance in world monetary and financial affairs of international banks, which have been entrusted with the task of recycling payments surpluses.[15] By contrast, the Special Drawing Rights, created by the IMF in 1968, have served mainly as a unit of account, in spite of the objective of making them the principal reserve asset of the monetary system.

On the trade side, the Tokyo Round of MTNs was concluded in 1979. Its results included a declaration confirming the liberal macro-economic approach to the balance of payments adjustment process, but the Contracting Parties failed to agree on its micro-economic corollary: a multilateral safeguard system governing the imposition of restrictions on particular products. An important discriminatory policy instrument, the 'voluntary export restraint' or 'orderly marketing arrangement', remains, therefore, outside multilateral discipline.[16] The trend towards officially-managed trade appears also from some of the results of the MTNs, such as the code on subsidies and countervailing duties, which reflect a 'managed' approach to world trade rather than the original GATT 'free trade' approach designed to minimize government interference.

The MTNs did not arrest the erosion of the trading system, which not only continued to affect the DCs adversely, but also led to conflicts between major trading nations. Only two years after the end of the MTNs, the Contracting Parties decided to convene their annual session in 1982 at the ministerial level with a view to improving the functioning of the system. However, this objective was not attained; if anything, the Ministerial Session has left the trading system in greater disarray than before.[17]

Notwithstanding the policies of the DMEs and the vulnerability of DCs to the serious shortcomings of international monetary and financial arrangements and the trading regime, the non-oil DCs as a group adjusted much better in the mid-1970s to the disturbances in the world economy than did the DMEs.[18] However, the adjustment performance varied greatly within the group. Some countries with relatively diversified economies managed to re-order their import priorities, maintain growth and high levels of savings and investments, and expand exports of manufactures in spite of the growing wave of protectionism. Their performance was associated with substantial capital inflows from private markets, reflecting their credit-worthiness as perceived by international banks. By contrast, most of the countries with limited industrial activity experienced declining growth rates in view of their inability either to expand exports or to attract growing amounts of external finance on terms and conditions appropriate to their economic circumstances. The role of the IMF as a source of finance was very modest, mainly because of the demand-management type of conditionality attached to its lending.

The adjustment efforts of the non-oil DCs were associated with a rapid accumulation of debts, especially by the major exporters of manufactures. This process could only continue in circumstances allowing for swift growth of exports. However, as we have seen, the external environment deteriorated sharply in 1980–82. The non-oil DCs became reluctant to increase their borrowings on the onerous terms prevailing in private markets, while at the same time the attitude of the banks changed from an urge to lend towards refusal to accept further exposure, thus revealing the risk inherent in reliance on private finance. Consequently, growth rates and import volumes faltered; the latter contributed to a deepening of the recession in the DMEs. On their side, the oil-exporting DCs experienced a steep decrease in export volumes followed by a substantial deceleration of import growth. World output and trade stagnated or declined in 1982 and acute debt crises, threatening to bring about a global financial disaster, occurred in several countries.

The economic developments in the latter part of the post-war period have amply demonstrated the need for translating the awareness of inter-dependence into new rules and mechanisms for global management in three inter-related fields, namely, the balance of payments adjustment process, structural change and adjustment in particular sectors producing tradeables, and the maintenance of high levels of economic activity and employment. The objectives of global management should be development-oriented. The new rules and mechanisms should therefore be framed with a view to enabling DCs to pursue their efforts to transform their economies in the face of disturbances beyond their control. It should also be recognized, in practice as well as in principle, that servicing debts contracted for develop-ment purposes depends not only on the efforts of the debtors, but also on the terms of access of their exports to world markets, and that the industrialization of the DCs must be accompanied by adjustment in the developed world.

The major DMEs have a particular responsibility for the co-ordination and harmonization of policies with a view to maintaining high levels of employment, but activities to that effect should be carried out in representa-tive, multilateral fora. There is, in general, a need for more equitable and democratic processes of taking decisions reflecting development objectives as well as the increasing weight of DCs in the world economy.

New rules and mechanisms should be integral parts of the long-overdue reform of the international economic system. On the monetary and financial side, the main lines of reform are relatively well known. The Outline of Reform prepared by the Committee of Twenty called *inter alia* for the introduction of SDRs as the principal reserve asset, a system of stable but adjustable exchange rates, an effective and symmetrical adjustment process, and the establishment within the IMF of a Council with the necessary decision-making powers to supervise the management and adaptation of the monetary system.[19] Account should also be taken of the proposals for monetary reform made in 1979 by the Group of 24 DCs and endorsed by the Group of 77.[20] The main differences between these proposals and the Outline lie in the importance attached by the DCs to growth and employment objectives and in their insistence, on the one hand, on a link between SDR allocations and additional development assistance and, on the other, on the need for a medium-term facility designed to finance adjustment by DCs on terms and conditions related to the causes of their payments deficits.

On the trade side, attention has been increasingly focused on the rules and mechanisms which might be designed to govern trade-related processes of structural change and adjustment in particular sectors of economic activity. The UNCTAD secretariat has identified two main options: a return to the tariff-based GATT system or the elaboration of a new set of rules and principles for ensuring management of trade in an equitable and development-oriented fashion.[21] The first option cannot but appear unrealistic in view of the failure of past efforts, even during the period of expansion, to enforce multilateral rules regarding selective measures firmly embedded in the national policies of the DMEs, and also on account of the growing importance of trade managed by governments or TNCs.[22]

The second option, broadly interpreted, is examined in Part Two of this paper with reference to structural change and adjustment in manufacturing industry. However, it should be noted here that in the case of the highly diversified DMEs, the ideas of management of micro-economic processes may be rejected as being inconsistent with the traditional macro-economic approach adopted by these countries to the balance of payments adjustment process. The rules and mechanisms governing the management of the two kinds of process should of course be consistent but, in view of the considerations set out above, consistency should be achieved by adopting a less doctrinaire approach to the balance of payments adjustment process as well, and by attaching high priority to development objectives and to the maintenance of high levels of economic activity and import demand.

Part II

Towards Global Management of Structural Change and Adjustment in Manufacturing Industry.[23]

I. Aspects of past and prospective developments

The unprecedented expansion of the world economy from 1950 to 1973 was associated with far-reaching changes in the patterns of world production and trade. The volume of world exports rose substantially faster than that of output, with manufactures, spear-headed by engineering goods, being the most dynamic components of both production and trade. The DMEs expanded their output at a lower rate than the socialist countries of

Eastern Europe (SCEEs) and the DCs, but they consolidated their position as the leading traders. They were also the source of most of the new technologies which found their way into world production and trade.

The US emerged from the war as by far the strongest economic power, but its weight within the group of DMEs was gradually reduced in the course of the period of expansion. While the US recorded productivity increases in line with historical trends, most West European countries and Japan experienced exceptionally fast productivity growth, reflecting the continuing process of catching up with US standards in consumption as well as in production.

The SCEEs, pursuing central policies of planned development, recorded a substantial increase of their share in world output, especially of manufactures. This development was associated with profound changes in economic and social structures, but not with a commensurate rise in the share of the SCEEs in world trade. The production and trade structures in Eastern and Western Europe became increasingly similar during the period considered, but this was not reflected in the composition of East-West European trade. In particular, technology-intensive products accounted for a much larger share in the East-bound flow than in the flow from East to West.

In the course of the 1960s, the combined share of manufactures, public utilities and construction in total value-added of the DCs as a group overtook that of agriculture which, however, continued to employ the bulk of the labour force. Within the manufacturing sector, heavy industry expanded faster than light industry. In terms of their foreign economic relations, the DCs remained dependent on the DMEs, which in the early 1970s absorbed close to three-quarters of their exports. An important aspect of this dependency was the persistence of a vertical division of labour between the two groups of countries. The share of the DCs in world exports declined sharply from 1955 to 1973.

From the end of 1973 onwards, the process of structural change in manufacturing industry slowed down substantially in the three major groups of countries.[24] Among the factors which contributed to change in the DMEs during this period were the increase in the cost of energy, technical advance, changes in the pattern of final demand, increased competition among these countries in their own as well as in third markets, and increasing imports from the DCs.

The rise in the cost of energy has been accompanied by an increase in the overall efficiency in energy use by the DMEs, as measured by the ratio of total energy requirements to total output. In the case of manufacturing industry, this development has resulted from progress in reducing energy requirements in particular sectors and from the decrease, partly on account of cyclical factors, in the share of energy-intensive sectors such as basic metals in total industrial output. It appears that there is scope for further energy saving by sectors, but this would require costly investments.[25]

Technical advance has mainly taken the form of improvements in existing products and processes, serving such purposes as economies in the use of labour and energy and compliance with regulations dictated by environmental considerations. These changes have as a rule taken place within existing plants, reflecting not only low rates of growth of GDP and investment, but also the increasing importance of replacement demand in total demand in certain areas characterized by fast growth in the past. The electronics industry seems to be a major exception in these as well as in other respects; technological development within that industry are expected to result in a 'micro-electronics revolution' bringing about profound changes in virtually all human activity.[26]

The increased competition among the DMEs has been associated with slow growth and large import bills for oil. The export drive has given rise to conflicts, but so far major trade wars have been avoided. However, the sharp increase in Japanese exports to other DMEs of such products as cars, colour television sets, video tape-recorders and machine tools, has led to the adoption of restrictive measures, including the conclusion of 'voluntary' restraint agreements, and to the establishment of Japanese subsidiaries or joint ventures in importing DMEs.

As a group, the DCs increased the volume of their exports of manufactures at about 13 per cent per annum during the period 1963–65 to 1971–73. This rate was then maintained until 1977–79 in spite of the deceleration in output growth as compared to the earlier period.[27] It appears that the export expansion slowed down in 1980 and 1981, but the DCs retained their position as the most dynamic exporters of manufactures also in these years. Their share in world exports of manufacture rose from 5 per cent in 1970 to 9 per cent in 1980. The DMEs remained by far their most important market, absorbing around 60 per cent of the exports of the DCs in the 1970s. The corresponding share of the DCs themselves was about 36 per cent, but it reached somewhat higher levels in the recession years 1975 and 1980.[28]

The DMEs reacted to the changes in competitiveness in favour of DCs by raising their barriers to imports from these countries. Nevertheless, the share of the DCs in the total imports of manufactures by the DMEs doubled from 1970 to 1980, reaching almost 8 per cent in the latter year.[29] The protective measures taken by DMEs affected mainly the 'sensitive' products which were also subject to restrictions in earlier years. Import penetration was particularly high in these products, levelling off in the case of clothing at about 35 per cent of total imports in 1979 and 1980. But the restrictive measures also reflected the fact that they were supported by both employers and workers in traditional industries. The steep increase in the imports of certain engineering products since the late 1960s encountered much less resistance. According to GATT statistics covering the imports into industrial areas from non-oil DCs of seven major categories of manufactures, engineering products had exceeded clothing in value as early as the beginning of the 1970s and accounted for 37 per cent of the total increment in these imports from 1973 to 1981. The corresponding figure for clothing in that period was 21.5 per cent.[30] The difference in attitudes and actual practices cannot be explained by reference to import penetration only. It should also be seen in conjunction with the internationalization of production, which plays a much larger role in the TNC-dominated engineering industry than in the clothing industry.

So far, the exports of manufactures from DCs have been heavily concentrated in a few major exporting countries. Moreover, notwithstanding the gains achieved since the mid-1960s, such exports accounted in 1978 for only 1.9 per cent of apparent consumption in the EEC, Japan and North America combined.[31] It would appear, therefore, that both the DMEs and the DCs are concerned not only and perhaps not even mainly about the present, but also—for different reasons—about what might happen in the course of time if other DCs were to join the group of fast-growing exporters of manufactured goods.

Scenarios and industrial studies indicate that in the course of the next two decades, there may be an extensive redistribution of world industry, among countries as well as among sectors. As regards the former aspect, the UNIDO high-growth scenario results in an increase in the share of DCs in world manufacturing output from 8.5 per cent in 1975 to close to 24 per cent in the year 2000 (China is excluded from both the numerator and the denominator).[32] According to scenario B.2 prepared by the research team in charge of the OECD Interfutures Project, the DCs will increase their share in world output of manufactures from 7.1 per cent in 1970 to 16.7 per cent in the year 2000, and in world exports of manufactures from 10.3 to 20.9 per cent in the same period. The scenario also foresees major shifts in the shares of output and trade of principal developed countries and areas (China is included in the OECD aggregates, but treated as a separate group).[33]

The growth rates for GDP as well as for manufacturing output are lower for both developed and developing countries in the OECD scenario than in that of UNIDO, but both scenarios foresee that the latter countries will grow substantially faster then the former. The increase in the DC share of world manufacturing output derived by the OECD team is less spectacular than that envisaged by the UNIDO secretariat, but nevertheless represents a tremendous change, taking into account the fact that the share in question rose by only two percentage points from 1960 to 1978.[34] The result obtained in scenario B.2 in respect of the trade share of DCs also points in the direction of accelerated structural change in world manufacturing industry.

The UNIDO scenario assumes implicitly that many basic policy changes, considered as essential by the authors, will in fact be realized. Thus, there will be an abatement in the wave of new protectionism, an increase in the flow of resources to DCs and improvements in the extent and quality of international industrial co-operation. As regards the implications for the structure of industry, the UNIDO secretariat foresees, for example, that heavy industry will continue to grow faster than light industry in the Third World, that processing of raw material by DCs will increase and that the participation of these countries in world trade, particularly in intra-industry trade, will grow. The volume of their exports is expected to grow faster than that of their output. Growth of intra-DC trade at a higher rate than total exports is considered to be a pre-condition for achieving the scenario results, though the developed countries are expected to remain the major markets for DC exports of manufactures.

The industrial studies undertaken in connexion with the Interfutures Project indicate, as is to be expected, that traditional industries will grow much faster in developing countries than in developed countries. The latter will, however, remain competitive in many lines of production. Shipbuilding, which is considered a traditional industry, will face a substantial slow-down in world demand, related to trends in maritime transport. The location of this industry will change in favour of countries of the Third World as far as the construction of conventional vessels is concerned. Chemicals and motor vehicles are cited as examples of industries that have been among the driving forces in the past industrial growth of the OECD countries and which now face large-scale changes. Both these industries, which are dominated by TNCs, will face a slow-down of demand in the developed countries. In the case of chemicals, the factors pointing in the direction of a relocation of industry will be offset to some extent by the development of new technologies. As regards passenger cars, replacement demand may account by 1990 for 85 per cent of total demand in North America, Japan and Central and Northern Europe. Production will be gradually transferred to regions where demand will be growing faster, in particular Latin America, Southern Europe and some Asian countries. Given the present importance of the car industry in the industrialized countries, the problems likely to be encountered by this industry in the last decade of the century "might well be of another order of magnitude than those now faced by textiles (including clothing) or steel."[35]

Electronics and capital goods, on which the 'micro-electronics revolution' is expected to have its largest impact, will be the most dynamic industrial sectors of the OECD countries. The competition between the larger countries will be especially keen in these sectors, which also involve issues related to the control of the new international division of labour as well as of the productive systems of the countries concerned.[36] The fragmentation of production processes and the transfer of labour-intensive activities to DCs will continue, with the TNCs maintaining their mastery of production as a whole and of the trade networks. The DCs will make further progress in the production of machinery and equipment, but will remain dependent on the industrialized countries.

The scenarios referred to above cannot but appear as over optimistic in the light of developments since 1979. However, they remain valuable as indicators of what could happen if the international community were to tackle constructively the task of promoting development-oriented growth involving, in particular, far-reaching structural change and adjustment in world industry. Governments, acting individually and collectively, should assume responsibility for world economic development but, in so doing, they should take duly into account the activities of the TNCs. The next section examines briefly the roles of these major actors, the governments and the TNCs, in determining the patterns of production and trade in manufactures.

II. The roles of governments and transnational corporations—the case for global management

(a) The role of governments

—in developed market-economy countries. Throughout the post-war period, most governments of DMEs have been engaged not only in demand management, but also in the management of supply. The latter has been closely related to policies of structural change in pursuance of general as well as specific economic, social and security objectives. Market mechanisms have played an important role, but it has been generally recognized that the play of market forces should be guided by incentives and disincentives and, when required, supplemented or even replaced by more direct forms of intervention. Supply management has been widespread, not only in such sectors as agriculture, mining and housing, but also in manufacturing industry.

In the course of the post-war period, governments have become increasingly concerned with two sets of problems, related to the growing competition from low-cost producers and the steep increase in trade ratios, i.e. the shares of imports in consumption and of exports in production. Some aspects of these problems are discussed below; the activities and policies of the TNCs, which are relevant to both problem areas, as well as the interplay between governments and TNCs, will be considered later.

According to conventional international trade theory, the emergence of low-cost producers should have as its counterpart the transfer of production factors from labour-intensive industries to industries which make intensive use of capital and/or skills and to tradeable services, such as consultancy and managerial services. Governments of DMEs have in fact promoted advanced industries, especially those with a considerable growth potential. Such forward-looking, positive policies also serve the purpose of maintaining and strengthening the position of their countries as industrial leaders in the world economy. In France, the Federal Republic of Germany, Japan, the United Kingdom and the United States, the electrical/electronics industry accounted in 1975 for between one-fifth and close to one-third of total R and D expenditure in manufacturing industry. More than half of this expenditure was financed by governments.[37]

The emphasis on advanced industries has, however, not been associated with a move of production factors out of traditional industries along the lines envisaged by conventional theory. Admittedly, output has declined in some of these industries in many DMEs, but this trend has been slowed down not only by protection at the frontier and by support to domestic producers, but also as a result of defensive policies, i.e. private and public efforts to restore the competitiveness of traditional industries through technical advance and rationalization, involving for example mergers, various forms of co-operation among firms, abandonment of certain lines of production and improvements in management. Thus, in the years 1973 to 1977, productivity rose substantially faster in textiles, leather and clothing in the Federal Republic of Germany and Italy than in their manufacturing industry as a whole. In several other countries it advanced at the average pace of total industry.[38]

From the point of view of the DMEs, technical advance in, and rationalization of, traditional industry mean exploitation of their comparative advantages. They also mean loss of jobs, in fact a much greater loss than that caused so far by increased imports from DCs. However, the alternative policy of increased emphasis on capital-intensive advanced industries is also associated with adverse effects on employment. It may be argued, therefore, that DMEs should attach increasing importance to their service sectors. In fact, since 1973 virtually all mature DMEs have experienced a strengthening of the trend towards increasing employment in services and declining employment in industry. Nevertheless, it appears that these countries continue to consider manufacturing industry as the major engine of technical advance and structural change in production and consumption.

In view of the high trading ratios, no credible or realistic strategy can be formulated for industrial sectors without a rational assessment of the prospects of trading partners regarded both as markets and as competitors. The absence of an adequate basis for such assessments has not prevented governments from pursuing defensive as well as positive industrial policies. It appears, however, that governments have supplemented such policies through more active participation in trade. In this connexion, attention has been drawn to the trend towards a certain 'bilateralism' in trade relations between DMEs and other countries, reflecting such factors as the keen competition among the former, especially in respect of capital goods exports and technology transfers, as well as the importance of DCs and SCEEs as markets and the role played by the governments of the latter countries.[39] However, this trend appears also to be present in DME intra-trade, for example, in trade related to oil activities in the OECD area and trade in armaments. According to *Technical Change and Economic Policy*,[40] the play of market forces tends to be partly replaced by inter-governmental negotiations, especially in high technology sectors.

—in developing countries. Virtually all governments of DCs pursue active industrialization policies, which may be classified into three groups, namely import substitution related to the structure of existing domestic demand, export promotion related to the structure of world demand, and self-reliant or endogenous policies related to the structure of the basic needs of the domestic economy. In practice, a DC may combine elements of different strategies; it may also change its strategy over time.

It is generally recognized that import-substitution policies are suitable at the initial stages of industrialization, but that continued emphasis on such policies may hamper both industrial and overall development. Past experience indicates that import-substitution policies, especially when associated with the maintenance of large domestic income differentials, tend to neglect the development of intermediate and capital goods industries. They thus produce, or threaten to produce, a fast-growing trade deficit in manufactures, which cannot be offset, even under favourable external circumstances, by a trade surplus in primary commodities. However, the increasing emphasis on export-promotion policies by a number of DCs since the mid-1960s reflected not only the need for industry to earn foreign exchange, but also the dynamism of the DMEs, which seemed to open the door to export-led growth. These policies were successful but, in assessing their applicability to DCs in general, account should be taken both of the particular economic and other features of the major exporters of manufactures and of the risk, demonstrated by recent experience, associated with increased dependence on the DMEs and their enterprises.

Endogenous policies form an integral part of self-reliant long-term development policies based on the fullest possible use of local human and natural resources. Such policies involve the achievement and maintenance of a fairly egalitarian distribution of income, a relatively large element of rural industrialization, the development of national technological capabilities and, in general, far-reaching government intervention in the economy. Self-reliant policies do not mean 'de-linking', but regard exports as a means of paying for essential imports, rather than as a major source of growth. GDP may initially grow less fast than in economies pursuing outward-looking policies, but the emphasis on the building-up of a diversified economic structure may pay substantial dividends in the longer run. However, given the small economic size of most DCs, self-reliant policies at the national level need to be supported by co-operation at the regional or sub-regional level, especially for the purpose of establishing intermediate and capital-goods industries.

Increasing attention has in fact been given to industrial co-operation within the framework of ECDC for political as well as for economic reasons, including the prospects for continued slow growth in the industrialized countries and, consequently, the need for export policies designed to meet the demand of DCs rather than that of developed countries. ECDC is seen by the Third World as an undertaking involving all DCs, irrespective of whether or not they pursue self-reliant policies at the national level.[41] However, the DCs have adopted a 'managed' approach to trade expansion among themselves, combining planning elements with measures designed to facilitate the play of market forces. This implies a 'managed' approach also to issues of structural change and adjustment arising in economic relations within the Third World.

—in socialist countries of Eastern Europe. The gradual evolution of the planning methods of the governments of SCEEs in the course of the post-war period has been associated with reduced possibilities for extensive growth, a larger role for enterprises in the conduct of foreign trade, and increasing emphasis on the importance of trade for economic development. Different systems of planning are applied within the CMEA area, but in all countries the overall conduct of foreign trade has remained the prerogative of the central authorities, which cannot be expected to be guided exclusively by the potential benefits to be derived from exchanges with other countries. Account must also be taken of the risks involved. This may explain the fact that, in contrast to the experience of DMEs and DCs, the SCEEs as a group have recorded a faster growth of output than of trade in manufactures.[42]

The SCEEs have joined the DCs in their complaints about protectionism in DMEs. The latter have responded by drawing attention to the small share of DCs in the total imports of manufactures into the SCEEs, which in their view reflects protectionism in the CMEA area. This argument over-looks the difference in system: the concept of protectionism, defined, as is usually the case, by reference to discrepancies in the terms of competition between domestic and foreign producers in domestic markets, does not apply to planned economies. On the other hand, the governments of such economies are able to exercise a much larger degree of control over trade-related structural change than those of DMEs. However, given the impor-tance attached by planners to stability in major trade flows, the acceptance of such change depends in no small measure on the extent to which exports and imports can be planned by the trading partners concerned. Trade conducted under long-term co-operation and specialization agreements has been growing rapidly in the CMEA area,[43] but elements of planned division of labour have also been introduced in trade with third countries and their enterprises, in particular TNCs.

(b) *The role of transnational corporations.*

The role of TNCs in world investment, production and trade is well known in general terms, but the statistical data available on TNC activities are still as a rule inadequate. This applies also to TNC intra-trade, which is particularly important in the present context because it reflects the internationalization of production and trade managed by central decision-making bodies.[44] However, available evidence indicates that TNC intra-trade accounts for a very substantial proportion of world trade.

According to the UN Centre on Transnational Corporations, intra-firm trade accounted for approximately 46 per cent of US imports in 1974, while roughly 50 per cent of US exports were within the transnational system in 1970. The Centre also reports that 29 per cent of Swedish exports in 1975, 30 per cent of UK exports in 1973 and 59 per cent of Canadian exports in 1971 were on an intra-trade basis.[45] More recently, the share of TNC intra-trade in world trade has been estimated at about two-fifths;[46] it is most probably well above that level in the case of trade in engineering goods.

The bulk of TNC intra-trade takes place between the DMEs, but the SCEEs and the DCs are also involved. In the case of the latter countries, · transnational networks may well have accounted for an increasing part of their exports of manufactures, raising questions regarding the functions allocated to TNC-controlled firms in DCs. Some aspects of these questions may be illustrated by reference to one simple and one complex case.[47]

In the simple case, the labour-intensive processes of the production of finished products are transferred by a TNC to an affiliate in a low-cost country. The TNC provides the technology, whatever material inputs are required and often also management and supervision. The total output of the affiliate is exported to units of the same TNC located in other countries. The affiliate is totally dependent on the parent company; in economic terms it forms an enclave in the host country, irrespective of whether or not it is located in a free zone.

In the complex case, on the other hand, the unit or units in a host country participate in TNC intra-trade in both finished products and processed inputs. A finished product, incorporating foreign as well as domestic inputs, produced in the host country is sold also in that country, while other brands or models of the same product are imported from units of the same TNC located abroad. The imported finished products may incorporate inputs produced in the host country in question. Complex networks of this type are found in the automobile industry.

The simple case applies mainly, if not exclusively, to DCs, while complex arrangements involving two-way flows similar to or approaching those described in the second case are typical of DMEs. However, a few DCs with diversified industry, technological capacity and relatively large and growing domestic markets may also participate in complex networks. An example is the participation of Brazil in the production and trade of automotive products. Other DCs, wishing to make use of TNCs in their industrialization efforts, would consider participation in most aspects of the complex TNC networks as an objective to be achieved over time. Arrangements of the simple type reflect essentially huge discrepancies in levels of development; they will at best make an indirect and limited contribution to industrialization and development in the host country.

Relations between TNCs involve co-operation as well as competition. One important aspect of competition is precisely the location of labour-intensive processes in low-wage countries. The economies realized by means of such arrangements may be substantial, since wage differentials are as a rule far from offset by differences in productivity. Co-operation among TNCs includes, for example, sub-contracting arrangements and joint R and D; new or improved products resulting from the latter activities, e.g. car engines, may be produced by a joint venture. Common interests of TNCs are also reflected in their participation in international agreements regarding prices and market shares.

(c) *The interplay betwen governments and transnational corporations.*

Relations between governments and TNCs are characterized by co-operation as well as by actual or potential conflicts. The TNCs contribute in many ways to the economic strength of their home countries, while their foreign investments are associated to varying degrees with the introduction of new technologies, import substitution and export promotion in host countries. However, the objectives and the geographical scope of the two actors differ. The TNCs are basically profit-oriented and their area of operation is world-wide. The economic and social policies of governments, on the other hand, are dictated by objectives related to the development and security of their national territories.

Governments of DCs are increasingly engaged in negotiations with TNCs already operating, or contemplating investing, in their countries, with a view to ensuring and, as far as possible, enhancing the contribution of the foreign companies to national development. In particular, efforts are made to induce TNCs to accept performance criteria defined in terms of domestic value added and/or exports. Increasing attention is also given to the possibility of achieving a greater degree of national control over TNC activity through joint ventures or non-equity contractual arrangements,

"take into account possible impacts on other countries and involve a fair sharing of the costs of adjustment".[57]

The research team in charge of the OECD Interfutures Project also favours market mechanisms and free trade but it fully recognizes the role of governments and, in contrast to the Orientations, also that of TNCs. The importance of these two actors is not considered as a temporary phenomenon. According to the team, the development of international trade in the period ahead may be governed by two trends, viz., a growth of trade within TNCs and increasing government intervention. Co-ordination of government policies and concerted action would be required to promote structural change while avoiding excessive disturbances, e.g. the emergence of substantial surplus capacity, which might provoke governmental reactions jeopardizing the open trading system. Decision-making by governments, as well as by enterprises, should be facilitated by the establishment of an industrial information system and by the examination of industrial adjustment problems at the world level. The latter should be undertaken on the basis of sectoral studies carried out with the co-operation of major sectoral enterprises, a recommendation reminiscent of indicative planning practices at the national level. Finally, the Interfutures team concludes that the improvement of the functioning of international markets would also require "new rules of the game and codes of conduct both for enterprises and for governments".[58] The contents of the new rules and codes of conduct are not spelled out, but the conclusion implies that the team does not consider existing OECD instruments as adequate for the purpose of managing structural change.

The policy recommendations of the OECD team are addressed to members of that organization. Miriam Camps, on the other hand, deals with structural change and adjustment in connexion with her proposals for a New Global Trade Organization,[59] which all countries may join subject to the acceptance of a few common principles. According to Camps "the two biggest institutional requisites in the general area of trade policy are the need to incorporate developing countries more fully into the global trading system and the need for more international concern with problems related to the process of structural change."[60] The first requisite is reflected *inter alia* in the proposals made for associate and ultimately full membership of advanced DCs in one of the main semi-autonomous bodies of the envisaged Organization, namely the Tariff and Trade Code, which would be the successor body to GATT.[61] As regards the second requisite, Camps takes the view that in the light of the experience of GATT, a number of policy measures cannot be outlawed, because they are too embedded in national policies. Camps also argues that, while most structural issues are related to trade, they extend well beyond the areas at present covered by GATT. International concern with structural change should not focus on national policies only; consideration should also be given to international action "to identify areas in which change is desirable and to assist the process of adaptation to new patterns of production".[62]

The envisaged Global Trade Organization would have a representative Advisory Council on the structure of the global economy with responsibility for the constant study of, and dissemination of information about, the changing patterns of production and trade. The Council, which would be assisted by a highly qualified research team, would develop the main lines of a global industrial policy and the implications of such a policy for the adjustment of national policies. The operational function of the Council would be indirect, i.e. that of advising the Trade Policy Review Board, the principal trade policy body of the new Organization, representative of the entire membership, on all matters related to structural change and adjustment. In this context, the Board would be concerned with linking exceptional trade restrictions to specific time-tables for adjustment, negotiation and surveillance of special sectoral arrange-ments, consideration of policies not ready for or susceptible to codification, and review and settlement of complaints.[63]

Camps also deals with issues related to TNC activities. In her opinion, only part of the problem lies in removing restrictions and outlawing practices which restrict or distort markets. The other part of the problem is the need for "some positive judgement about the kind of action that should be encouraged if production patterns are to reflect changes in comparative advantage and to meet the needs of an evolving global economy".[64]

(b) *Development-oriented approaches.*

The three development-oriented approaches to industrial restructuring dis-cussed here originate in UNIDO (1975), UNCTAD (1979) and in the proposal of a group of Dutch economists/politicians for a New World Employment Plan (1980).

Development-oriented approaches to structural change and adjustment constitute an integral part of the broad suggestions put forward by the UNCTAD secretariat in a report to UNCTAD V[65] and of the proposal made by J. Tinbergen, J.M. den Uyl, J.P. Pronk and W. Kok for a New World Employment Plan.[66]

The UNCTAD report draws attention to the persistence of structural and institutional rigidities in the DMEs and to the inconsistency between the market-oriented rules of the game and the reduced role of market prices in determining the allocation of resources within the national economies. The report further notes that the reconciliation of conflicting national objectives is difficult, if not impossible, in the context of slow growth and structural disequilibria and suggests that planned structural changes would be needed in order to break away from the vicious circle of instability, recession, inflation and payments imbalances. Such changes would involve large investments on a worldwide scale, requiring collective action focused on the development of the Third World by the international community as a whole. The operational conclusions of the report call for the establishment of a high-level advisory group assisted by small working or study groups, as appropriate, for the purposes of examining the problems related to the management of the world economy, especially policies in the fields of trade, payments and finance and their relationship to development; assessing the consistency of those policies with longer term development objectives; and recommending, for consideration at the inter-governmental level, concerted measures that would promote structural changes in the world economy and thus provide a favourable environment for sustained development at the global level. The Conference took no action on these suggestions, the relevance of which have increased with the passage of time.

The aim of the proposal by Tinbergen and associates is "to launch a large-scale international operation to stimulate the economies of, and to raise employment in, both the industrialized countries and the Third World countries". The emphasis on employment reflects not only the right to participate in economic activity, but also the fact that many pressing human needs remain unsatisfied. The proposal combines two policies: promotion of anticipatory structural adjustment of industries in developed countries and large-scale international income transfer to DCs. Both policies would be designed to maximize employment instead of economic growth. A central thesis of the proposal is that attempts should be made to approach an optimal international division of labour based on comparative advantages viewed in a dynamic way. It is argued that the DMEs "should turn to knowledge-intensive and up to a point capital-intensive activities", but attention is also drawn to the need for new activities in sectors producing non-tradeables, which are complementary to activities in sectors producing tradeables, or which would meet social needs in industrialized countries. In order to promote employment in DCs, the increased international income transfers should be invested mainly in infrastructure, which is too costly to be financed by individual countries, in integrated rural development schemes and in small-scale industries.

The proposal emphasizes that the envisaged structural adjustment cannot be brought about through market forces alone. Planning elements would therefore have to be introduced. Investment decisions should be based on social considerations pertaining to the direction of production and the distribution of employment. This in turn may require "inter-governmental control of the long-term investment policies of transnational companies". World demand should be steered, for example, by means of price policies and income transfers, in accordance with social objectives. The employment plan would also include international trade measures "based on (indicative) long-term planning of the world's industrial development". Government support for weak and infant industries, in richer as well as in poorer countries, may be accepted on a temporary basis, provided that "such support enables inter-governmental planning of the sectors concerned".

Attempts to stimulate global inter-governmental action on structural change, adjustment and protectionism have been made in UNIDO and UNCTAD.

The Lima Plan of Action on Industrial Development adopted by the Second UNIDO Conference in 1975 set a target of 25 per cent for the share of the DCs in world industrial production, to be reached by the year 2000. It outlined various policies and institutional arrangements required to achieve that target, including a System of Consultations. By the spring of 1980, consultations had been conducted on an experimental basis in eight industrial sectors. Information of value to public and private policy-makers was derived from the examination of the changing pattern in a sector, the main trends governing its future and the particular problems faced by DCs in the sector. However, the consultations did not have any significant impact on government policies, since the developed countries regarded the consultations as a forum in which information and views could be exchanged without entering into any commitments.

In 1980, the UNIDO Board decided by consensus to establish the System of Consultations on a permanent basis and to enhance its operational significance.[67] However, it appears that—notwithstanding some progress made since that time—the objective of policy-oriented consultations has not been attained.[68]

While UNIDO concentrated on industrial restructuring, efforts were made within UNCTAD to tackle the related issues of protectionism and structural adjustment. A resolution adopted at UNCTAD V in 1979 seemed to open the door for action-oriented examination of these issues by the Trade and Development Board. However, it proved difficult to reach an agreement on how to proceed. Substantial progress was achieved in 1981 and 1982, but governments have yet to demonstrate their readiness to take concrete action, bearing in mind their agreement to the effect that "the interests of the developing countries are an essential dimension of the whole exercise."[69] As noted in Part One of this paper, the UNCTAD secretariat has in the meantime drawn attention to the option of elaborating new trading rules and principles with a view to ensuring management of trade in an equitable and development-oriented fashion.*

---

* *Editor's note:* Since this paper was completed early in 1983, it should be noted, in this connection, that UNCTAD resolution 159 (VI) of June 1983 has called upon the Trade and Development Board to study developments in the international trading system and make proposals to strengthen and improve the system to make it more universal, dynamic and responsive to development needs.

(c) *Elements of appraisal.*

The market-oriented approaches reflect the very real interdependence among the DMEs, in particular the West European countries. The internationalization of production and the high trade ratios have reduced the ability of governments to manage their economies in accordance with national objectives, and it would be difficult, if not impossible, to turn back the clock. Hence the emphasis on exchange of information, industrial studies and the acceptance of some common principles or guidelines which, it is hoped, would facilitate decisions by governments and enterprises and help to avoid conflicts among nations. However, attention has also been drawn to the need for co-ordination of government policies.

Efforts are being made within the OECD along the lines just indicated, but the DMEs have so far not been prepared to participate meaningfully in policy-oriented discussions in global fora such as UNCTAD and UNIDO. On the other hand, a few more-industrialized DCs have been invited to participate in the deliberations of OECD bodies dealing with structural change and adjustment, but these countries have refused to become involved.[70] A move away from defensive policies, in accordance with the OECD Orientations, would improve the access of DCs to OECD markets in traditional products, while the increased reliance on market forces and the emphasis on positive adjustment policies would protect and perhaps even strengthen the predominant role of the DMEs and their enterprises in the world economy. In the light of recent experience it seems likely, however, that the OECD countries will continue to apply defensive as well as positive policies in pursuing their national objectives.

Camps' proposals have been classified as market-oriented because she takes a Western-type trading system for granted, as shown by her concern about the progressive integration of DCs into such a system, and because she tends to neglect such primary objectives of economic policy as the maintenance of high levels of employment and the development of productive resources. However, she provides for participation by all countries in the New Global Trade Organization and she takes a broad and pragmatic approach to issues of structural change and adjustment. Camps' proposals deserve serious consideration by all those who are preoccupied with the future of the trading system.

The development-oriented approaches regard trade as an instrument rather than as an end in itself. There is a striking difference between the top priority attached by Tinbergen and associates to the creation of employment and the satisfaction of human needs, and the emphasis put by the OECD Orientations on GDP growth and efficiency.

The DCs have so far concentrated their attention on their own industrialization and the related need for 'planned' adjustment by developed countries in sectors where comparative advantages have changed or are about to change in favour of DCs. They have given relatively little attention to international management of global structural change and adjustment. However, issues arising, for example, in DME intra-trade are also of concern to other countries; they should not be left for consideration within OECD only.

The common feature of development-oriented approaches is the perceived need for at least some planning or concerted action at the global level. The UNIDO secretariat has emphasized the need for some control over change for constructive purposes. Taking a broader approach, the UNCTAD secretariat has called for concerted action to bring about desirable structural change and to relaunch the world economy. On their side, Tinbergen and associates have outlined an ambitious plan of action which, however, does not address itself to such issues as the trading rules and mechanisms that would be required to attain the stated objectives.

(d) *Features, objectives and problems of global management.*

No attempt will be made here to propose a blueprint for global economic management, but some comments are made below on certain desirable features and objectives of international management and on some of the complex problems arising in that connexion.

All countries should be given the opportunity of participating in the search for new rules and mechanisms designed to govern processes of structural change and adjustment. This is indeed an issue of concern and interest to every one of them. Given the differences among countries, in their economic and social systems and their levels of development, the objective of universality points in the direction of the elaboration of a few common principles and a fairly heavy reliance on consultation procedures.

Global management should promote development in accordance with internationally-agreed objectives and facilitate the achievement and maintenance of high levels of employment by all countries. One important consequence of the priority attached to development is a strong presumption against any action to the detriment of new producers in DCs. The cost of adjustment and the time required for carrying it out should be recognized, and account should also be taken of the fact that the ability to adjust depends on the level of development.

The approach taken to structural change and adjustment should be broad, covering industry as a whole, as well as all features of substantial relevance to industrial activity as an integral part of economic and social development. Thus, account should be taken of factor incomes and working conditions, technological developments, prices, rates of consumption and availability of non-renewable raw materials, pollution and other environmental factors. The broad approach should, of course, not prevent the international community from giving special attention to specific problem sectors, but the problems and prospects of such sectors should be examined in the light of the main lines of a global industrial policy designed to promote desirable patterns of change.

Many of the problems encountered in the search for arrangements for international management centre on the functions and authority of the institution which would administer such arrangements. It is neither feasible nor, in principle, desirable to prevent governments from pursuing national objectives, but they should be expected to take duly into account internationally-agreed objectives and to refrain from any action likely to cause serious injury to other countries. The 'managing institution' would be responsible, for example, for elaborating the main lines of a global industrial policy which would cover issues related to all major trade flows, for providing a forum for consideration of the implications of such a policy for national policies, and for strict surveillance of such sectoral arrangements as might be negotiated under its auspices. As argued by Camps, no attempt would be made to outlaw policy measures which are firmly embedded in national policies, but the institution would keep patterns of investment, production and trade under continuous review and administer procedures for the settlement, through consultation and conciliation, of disputes generated by actual developments.

A stronger institution would be concerned with such matters as the establishment of development-oriented trade targets with varying degrees of operational significance and the application, as required, of various kinds of pressures to a country designated as the offending party in a dispute but reluctant to take any remedial action. A major weakness of GATT has been that the final sanction of an offending party is retaliatory action by the affected party, a procedure which fails to take into account the big differences among countries in economic size and retaliatory power.[71] It may also be noted, however, that in actual negotiations, questions regarding the decision-making power of the institution would most probably be linked to the issue of weighted voting.

Notwithstanding their weight in the world economy, the TNCs are at present not accountable to the international community and accountable for only part of their activities to individual governments. The institution would need to be adequately informed about relevant TNC activities and also about the interplay between these private entities and governments. This information should be duly taken into account in considering the global industrial policy and its implications. The exercise of control over the TNC activities would be left to governments or groups of governments, which may act within the framework of international rules elaborated for this purpose.

Arrangements for international management would legitimate various forms of selective intervention by DMEs in their economies. They are, therefore, likely to be resisted, at least by some of these countries, on doctrinal grounds. It may be noted in this connexion that the lack of substantial progress towards a common EEC industrial policy reflects differences in economic-political philosophy among member countries. However, such differences have not prevented the EEC from managing parts of its imports from developing and certain other countries.

For more than twenty years, the DCs have pursued their efforts to improve the terms of access of their products to the markets of the developed countries. However, notwithstanding the GSP, the trade regimes of the DMEs remain biased against imports of traditional products and processed goods from the Third World, while the SCEEs continue to absorb only a small fraction of the DCs exports of manufactures. It would seem, therefore, that new approaches to structural change and adjustment would be in the interest of DCs. There is, however, a danger that given the present distribution of power and the asymmetry of interdependence among nations, international management of structural change and adjustment would tend to reflect the interests of developed countries, focusing on ways and means of preventing the emergence of substantial excess capacity in the world economy, to the detriment of new producers. A move towards international management should therefore be accompanied by a further strengthening of ECDC, a development which, as already noted, is also required for other reasons.

Finally, there are the problems concerning the criteria to be applied in the search for an international division of labour conducive to development. Within the limits of its validity, the concept of comparative advantage can undoubtedly provide general guidance for the division of labour among countries which are at very different levels of development in most relevant respects. It remains true, however, that in the case of many industrial activities, comparative advantages as revealed in the market are subject to frequent changes not only as a result of movements in factor costs, but also in response to learning effects, economies of scale, product differentiation and related publicity, restrictive business practices and shifts in economic power. References to comparative advantages viewed in a dynamic context are not likely to be of much help to policy-makers faced with decisions regarding the industrial future of their countries.[72] High priority should be given to research on criteria for the international division of labour, taking into account market distortions, learning effects and industrialization strategies, as well as the important objective of DCs to reduce over time their dependence on imports of technology and advanced capital goods from the developed countries.

(e) *Concluding remarks.*

Any attempt to introduce elements of international management in the process of trade-related structural change and adjustment in world manufacturing industry is bound to be problematic. But this should not be used as an argument for inaction. Notwithstanding the important differences in objectives and emphasis between market-oriented approaches and development-oriented approaches, even the former recognize the need for mechanisms of international management including efforts to co-ordinate government policies. As Diebold states in concluding his analysis of industrial policy as an international issue, "there will be a deterioration of international economic relations if things go on as they have".[73] The preservation of an open trading system and the pace of industrialization of the DCs may well depend on the readiness of governments to consider constructively new, pragmatic approaches to the issues in this area.

As stated in Part One of this paper, new rules and mechanisms for global management of structural change and adjustment should be an integral part of a comprehensive reform of the international economic system, also incorporating global managerial elements in respect of the balance of payments adjustment process and the maintenance of high levels of economic activity and employment. On the trade side, the process of reform might involve the establishment of an inter-governmental group of experts, selected to represent the international community as a whole, for the purpose of exploring ways and means of dealing at the global level with structural change and adjustment not only in manufacturing industry but also in agriculture and other relevant sectors. The experts, who might be assisted by study groups, would be expected to examine new arrangements as well as the relationship between possible courses of action and existing rules and mechanisms in the area of trade in the wide sense. This in turn should lead to renewed consideration of the establishment of a comprehensive trade organization (CTO) to fill the gap resulting from the failure to give effect to the Havana Charter. This important issue remains on the agenda of UNCTAD by virtue of its terms of reference.

A CTO would administer the world trading system, including rules and mechanisms in such fields as transfer of technology and restrictive business practices, and, in particular, be responsible for the management of trade-related structural change and adjustment within the framework of a broad approach to trade and development issues. Close and constructive working relationships would have to be established between a CTO and the IMF in order to ensure complementary and development-oriented management of macro-economic and micro-economic processes of change and adjustment in the world economy.

---

1. It should be understood that the IMF/GATT system, also referred to in this paper as the international economic system, has never been either universal, i.e. accepted by all trading nations, or comprehensive, in the sense of covering all important aspects of international economic transactions.

2. With one exception, the other signatories made their ratification conditional upon that of the US.

3. Henceforth referred to as 'the General Agreement' or 'the Agreement'.

4. The exchange rate regime was based on a commitment by the US to buy and sell monetary gold at $35 an ounce, combined with the obligation assumed by most other countries to maintain currency parities in terms of US dollars.

5. *Economic Bulletin for Europe*, United Nations Economic Commission for Europe, Vol. 16, No. 2, 1964.

6. *The OECD at work*, OECD, Paris, 1969.

7. It was agreed that, in the course of trade negotiations, the DCs should not be expected to make contributions which were inconsistent with their individual development, financial and trade needs.

8. For an outline of the Prebisch doctrine, see Sidney Dell's contribution to this volume.

9. See Dell, *op. cit.*

10. See *The International Monetary Situation*, UNCTAD document TD/180/Rev.1, 1972, for a brief analysis of the relationships between these factors.

11. The importance of the tariff as a policy instrument had been reduced over time, not only as a result of reductions in, and binding of, tariffs in successive negotiations, but also owing to the practical difficulties inherent in any attempt to raise tariff levels through renegotiations of concessions under the relevant provisions of the General Agreement, as shown in UNCTAD document TD/B/913, July 1982.

12. This concept, which was not, and is not, embodied in the General Agreement, has been used as a justification for restrictive measures against imports from particular sources, especially 'low cost' producers, taken unilaterally or by reference to sectoral agreements, starting with the cotton textile sector in 1962.

13. *Policy Perspectives for International Trade and Economic Relations*, Report by a High Level Group, OECD, Paris 1972, p. 82.

14. *Ibid.* p. 21.

15. See the UNCTAD *Trade and Development Report, 1981*, UN, New York, 1981 for a discussion of the 'privatization' of the international monetary system.

16. Except that, in the case of textiles and clothing, such restrictions are imposed by reference to the Multifibre Agreement. The latter, however, bears no relation to the principles and rules of the General Agreement.

17. See the contribution by R. Krishnamurti to this volume for an evaluation of the 1982 GATT Ministerial Session.

18. See the World Bank's *World Development Report 1982* and the UNCTAD *Trade and Development Report, 1982*, UN, New York, 1982.

19. *International Monetary Reform*, IMF, Washington D.C., 1974.

20. The proposals are reproduced in UNCTAD document TD/B/AC.32/L.2.

21. TD/B/913, *op. cit.*

22. See *Protectionism, Threat to International Order*, Report by a group of experts, Commonwealth Secretariat, London, 1982.

23. This Part is a modified and slightly updated version of parts of a study entitled *Notes on Rules and Mechanisms governing International Economic Relations*, published by the Chr. Michelsen Institute, Bergen, Norway, in October 1981.

24. See the indices of structural change presented in the UNCTAD *Trade and Development Report, 1982*, UN, New York, 1982, tables A.33 and A.23.

25. *Ibid.*

26. *Technical Change and Economic Policy*, Report of an OECD Expert Group, Paris 1980, p. 55.

27. *Trade and Development Report, 1982, op. cit.*, tables A.13 and 26.

28. Based on data (for SITC 5 to 8 less 68) supplied by the UNCTAD secretariat.

29. *Ibid.*

30. *International Trade 1981–82*, Geneva 1982.

31. *UNCTAD Handbook for International Trade and Development Statistics, 1981 Supplement.* The average of 1.9 per cent conceals important differences among the major categories of manufactures. By far the highest share, almost 12 per cent, was recorded by clothing.

32. *World Industry since 1960,* UN, New York 1979. The scenario assumes that (i) the GDP of individual developed countries will grow at rates one percentage point below those realized from 1960 to 1975, (ii) developing countries with exceptionally fast growth in the past will maintain their pace in the future and (iii) each of the other developing countries will realize growth rates two percentage points higher than in 1960–1975. The increase in value added in manufacturing industry is estimated for each country as a function of *per capita* income; as growth in *per capita* income continues, growth in manufacturing industry will proceed, but at a declining rate.

33. *Facing the Future,* OECD, Paris 1979. The B.2 scenario, which is one of six, is characterized as one of moderate growth. It assumes, *inter alia,* convergence in the relative levels of productivity in the OECD countries and increased participation by developing countries in world economic exchanges. According to the limited information provided on the numerical aspects of the scenarios, GDP growth rates for OECD countries were calculated on the basis of assumptions some of which can be expressed in quantitative terms, e.g. rates of change in the labour force, participation rates and productivity. These rates, and presumably also those selected for other countries, were used as inputs for a model constructed on the assumption that many aspects of the world economy can be described in neo-classical terms.

34. *World Industry in 1980,* UN, New York, 1981.

35. *Facing the Future, op. cit.,* p. 356.

36. *Ibid.* p. 335.

37. *Technical Change and Economic Policy, op. cit.,* p. 31. See also *Facing the Future, op. cit.,* pp. 336–346.

38. *Technical Change and Economic Policy, op. cit.,* p. 70.

39. William Diebold, Jr., *Industrial Policy as an International Issue,* McGraw-Hill, 1980, pp. 159–160 and 231–232.

40. *Op. cit.,* p. 21.

41. It should be noted, however, that the Lagos Plan of Action for the Economic Development of Africa, adopted by the Heads of State of the OAU countries in 1980, calls for self-reliant policies at national, sub-regional and regional levels.

42. UNCTAD document TD/B/805, tables I and VI.

43. According to document ECE/EC.AD.15 published by the United Nations Economic Commission for Europe in 1977, trade in machinery and equipment conducted under long-term specialization agreements may have accounted for one-quarter of total CMEA intra-trade in such products in 1970 and for one-third in 1975.

44. The internationalization of production involves also various forms of sub-contracting, the common characteristic of which is that the principal does not have any substantial ownership share in the firm of the sub-contractor. TNCs play an important role in these forms of sub-contracting which, however, may not be counted as TNC intra-trade.

45. *Transnational Corporations in World Development,* UN, New York, 1978, p. 43.

46. *Trade and Development Report, 1981, op. cit.,* p. 137.

47. The simple and the complex cases correspond broadly to cases D and B described in C.A. Michelat's study published in *International Sub-Contracting,* OECD Development Centre, Paris, 1980. The complex case may involve sub-contracting arrangements between TNC subsidiaries and local firms.

48. *Transnational Corporations in World Development, op. cit.,* p. 11 (on regional co-operation) and pp. 133 and 134 (on adverse effects on other DCs).

49. Japan has become a major industrial power without experiencing a similar period of large scale penetration by US TNCs.

50. *Ibid.* p. 25. By contrast, DCs are predominantly host countries, although enterprises located in more industrialized DCs have in recent years invested in joint ventures or subsidiaries in less industrialized DCs.

51. Bergsten, Horst and Moran, *American Multinationals and American Interests,* The Brookings Institution, 1978. The authors consider that domestic value added requirements have the same trade-restricting effects as import quotas. However, a typical objective of such requirements is to substitute local production for 'tied' inputs imported from another entity of the same TNC, i.e. imports not subject to competition.

52. *The Case for Positive Adjustment Policies,* OECD, Paris, 1979, p. 94.

53. *North–South Technology Transfer; the Adjustments Ahead,* OECD, Paris, 1981, pp. 90 and 91.

54. *Technical Change and Economic Policy, op. cit.,* p. 103.

55. According to the UNCTAD study *Fibres and Textiles,* UN, New York, 1981, the clothing industry is experiencing far-reaching innovations, which will reduce labour input and hence tend to erode the major advantage of DCs in this sector.

56. *The Case for Positive Adjustment Policies, op. cit.,* p. 3–8.

57. *Ibid.* p. 8.

58. *Facing the Future, op. cit.,* p. 414. It appears from other parts of the report (see for example p. 268), that the team has new rules in mind for TNCs.

59. See Miriam Camps, with Catherine Gwin, *Collective Management: the Reform of Global Economic Organizations,* New York, McGraw Hill, 1981. The references below are to Camps' original presentation of her proposal in *The case for a New Global Trade Organization,* Council on Foreign Relations Inc., New York, 1980.

60. *The case for a New Global Trade Organization, op. cit.,* p. 18.

61. This code is expected to be accepted mainly by DMEs. It would cover tariffs, quotas and those rules regarding other non-tariff barriers which can be enforced in trade among OECD countries. The members of the code would continue to observe commitments undertaken under the auspices of GATT, such as tariff reductions made in past negotiations. However, there would be no automatic extension without reciprocity to non-members (apparently with the exception of the least developed countries) of further trade liberalization measures made among the full members of the code. Questions regarding trade among DCs would be assigned to another semi-autonomous body, in which only DCs would be represented.

62. *Ibid.* p. 18.

63. This function should be seen in conjunction with the acceptance by all members of "the general principle that national actions in the fields covered by the organization may have damaging external consequences and that another member state which considers itself adversely affected has a right to have the situation reviewed according to agreed procedures" (*Ibid.* p. 31).

64. *Ibid.* p. 22.

65. UNCTAD document TD/225, *Policy Issues in the Fields of Trade, Finance and Money and their Relationship to Structural Change at the Global Level.*

66. In *IFDA Dossier 21,* January/February 1981, International Foundation for Development Alternatives, Nyon, Switzerland. For the sake of brevity, reference will be made in the text to the proposal by "Tinbergen and associates".

67. UNIDO document ID/B/248.

68. The UNIDO secretariat has expressed the view that industrial restructuring is increasingly dependent on broad policy decisions taken at the national level and has drawn attention to the need for consultations to clarify the global consequences of such decisions and to co-ordinate development (see *World Industry since 1960, op. cit.*).

69. Report of the Board on the first part of its 24th session, March 1982 (TD/B/900).

70. Camps, *op. cit.,* p. 17.

71. The understanding reached in the MTNs regarding dispute settlement etc., contains a provision envisaging the possiblity of joint action by the Contracting Parties to protect the rights of a DC. It remains to be seen, however, whether such action will in fact be taken.

72. G.K. Helleiner (Chairman), *The Refsnes Seminar,* Norwegian Institute of International Affairs, NUPI Rapport no. 49, 1980.

73. William Diebold, Jr., *op. cit.,* p. 280.

UNCTAD: THE CHANGING SCENE

by Gamani Corea

The several essays in this volume have reviewed UNCTAD's work and its contributions in various fields. Three aspects stand out in this review—UNCTAD's role as a forum for the international debate on development issues, its general influence on thinking and policy-making, even outside of UNCTAD itself, and the specific decisions and agreements that have been negotiated in UNCTAD, extending in some cases to the creation of instruments of a legally-binding character. What is unique about UNCTAD is that the ideas that have been disseminated and the agreements reached have mostly been initiated by the developing countries, subsequently receiving the endorsement of the international community. This has hardly been the case in other international organizations concerned with economic issues, such as the Bretton Woods institutions and the GATT. This is not a criticism of these other institutions, for decisions taken or agreements reached on the basis of consensus must be seen as serving the interests of all, no matter where the initiative came from. But the fact that the main thrust of proposals agreed upon in UNCTAD came from the developing countries has put some balance into the total array of decisions on international economic issues.

The contribution of the UNCTAD secretariat, through its studies and analyses, has also been distinctive. These have had a particular focus on the international environment for development, highlighting the factors and policies that accelerate development and those that retard it. They have also, because of UNCTAD's broad mandate, been able to take account of the interrelationship between such issues as trade, money, finance and development, and also to pay attention to such subjects as technology transfer, shipping, insurance, trade with socialist countries and co-operation amongst developing countries.

UNCTAD's task over the last twenty years has been difficult. The thrust of the developing countries' efforts was to make changes in the *status quo* in a way that was beneficial to them, whilst the developed countries invariably saw themselves as being pressed to make concessions. Many people have pointed to the analogy with the process of collective bargaining in labour relations but that analogy cannot be pushed too far. The developing countries did not have the leverage of trade unions in collective bargaining—the capacity or the willingness to act in concert to cause financial loss or inconvenience. In the 1960s and 1970s they had a certain political power that was inherent in the emergence of many of these countries as newly independent nation states and their coming together in such coalitions as the Non-Aligned Movement and the Group of 77. There had to be some response to their pressures and aspirations, but this reponse was influenced also by the perceptions of the industrialized countries of their own interest in political and economic stability in the Third World. The Point 4 programme of the United States and the launching of bilateral aid programmes by virtually all developed countries, as well as the establishment of international financial institutions for development, had their origins long before the creation of the Group of 77 and UNCTAD. UNCTAD's effectiveness and achievements would not have been possible in the absence of these wider perceptions and the acceptance by the developed countries of the need for, and value of, a forum in which developing country aspirations could be voiced as a basis not only for debate but also for adopting specific proposals.

None of UNCTAD's negotiating successes was easily achieved. For example, the Generalized System of Preferences and the Integrated Programme for Commodities won acceptance as a result of negotiations that were long, difficult, and often dramatic. Once adopted and put into operation they were seen to be beneficial by all groups of countries at least in terms of their broad objectives. To put it another way, there was a broad acceptance of the legitimacy of the UNCTAD thrust, with its analogy to collective bargaining, even though the specifics of every action proposed were the subject of hard-fought battles.

UNCTAD's effort since its creation can be seen as a step-by-step process to improve the international economic environment for development. It has not succeeded in bringing about a total overhaul of international economic relations. Prebisch's vision of a new trade policy for development has still to be realized. But every UNCTAD decision, every agreement, has been a step in favour of the developing countries, a step taken with the eventual acquiescence of the industrialized countries. The step-by-step process was never a smooth progression; there have been periods of movement and periods of lull. The phase following UNCTAD IV, for example, was one of intensive negotiating activities in UNCTAD centering around such subjects as the Common Fund, individual commodity arrangements, the codes on technology, multimodal transport and restrictive business practices and debt rescheduling.

In the recent period, however, the loss of momentum has been particularly marked. There has been a setback in the climate for negotiations that goes beyond the hesitations and inertia of the past. While this setback is related to the mounting tensions on the international political scene, it has much to do with the emergence of economic problems in the developed countries since the early seventies. Rapid inflation was followed by the deep recession of the last two or three years, itself brought about by the policy response to the problem of inflation. Cuts in government spending naturally affected aid budgets, despite some creditable efforts to protect and even enlarge them. It was not only aid that suffered; the thrust towards improving market access for developing country exports and stabilizing commodity prices was also weakened in the changed environment.

These difficulties were not merely of a short-term character. Longer-term forces were pointing to a slowing down of the trend of growth in output and productivity in the developed countries, with subsequent strains in their economic, political and social situations. At the same time, changes have also taken place in the developing countries. Some of them have acquired impressive new capacities to produce industrial goods for export, as well as to mobilize financial resources from private capital markets. Oil-exporting countries brought about changes in price relationships with profound long-term effects for the entire world economy. They generated the financial surpluses which were a source of funds to world capital markets. New regional groups of some economic strength have also been emerging amongst the developing countries.

All these changes inevitably affected the character of North-South relations and the way in which the industrialized countries perceived their responses to Third World needs. In the context of the constraints facing them, both short-term and long-term, these countries have become less willing to promote a step-by-step progression along directions that had earlier been accepted, for example, the expansion of concessional aid and other financial flows, as well as of market access. At the same time, again in the new context, there is a greater resistance to the political pressures exerted through the universal institutions of the United Nations system where the dominant voice is that of the majority of member countries—a majority greatly influenced by the accretion of member states from the Third World.

The present situation is, therefore, one of impasse in the negotiating process on North-South issues. This impasse has been apparent in UNCTAD as witnessed at UNCTAD VI (Belgrade, 1983) and even earlier, though less evidently, at UNCTAD V (Manila, 1979). The stalemate, however, has not been specific to UNCTAD. It is a generalized stalemate reflected, in one way or another, in every forum: the 1982 Ministerial Meeting of the GATT, the negotiations in the World Bank and the IMF on the question of greater resources for these institutions, the blockage of consensus on global negotiations in the United Nations General Assembly. The Cancún Summit itself did not achieve a breakthrough. It is not only developed country attitudes that underlie this situation. The collective negotiating leverage of the developing countries has also been weakened by their own vulnerability, brought about by the recession and their desperate search for financial accommodations through bilateral rather than multilateral arrangements or actions.

However, the present phase is unlikely to persist. In the first place, the extent of the impasse should not be exaggerated. There are still innumerable instances in UNCTAD and in other bodies where dialogue and negotiations are in progress. Though the tempo of advance is slow, these processes have not been terminated. At UNCTAD VI, for example, a number of solid mandates were adopted, virtually in all cases on a unanimous basis, for continuing efforts by UNCTAD in a number of critical fields. These included the Integrated Programme for Commodities and the Common Fund, protectionism and structural adjustment, trade in services, the evolution of the trading system, as well as several issues in the area of money and finance. In the second place, to the extent that the limited responses of the developed countries were due to the recession, some amelioration might be expected to follow from the process of recovery. This is still weak and fragile but it is under way in a number of industrialized countries. A strong recovery could strengthen commodity prices, discourage protectionist pressures, facilitate the adoption of larger aid budgets by the industrialized countries, and generally improve the climate for international dialogue and negotiation.

Perhaps most decisive is the fact that the present critical situation in the developing countries is too dangerous to be allowed to continue. If it does and the devastating experience of recent years is not reversed, there could be serious political and social destabilization with global repercussions. That this danger is already perceived is evident from the fact that there is a case-by-case response to particular situations, for example, situations of indebtedness. But to the extent that such a response proves insufficient—and there is much to suggest that it may—it would need to give way to more imaginative and extensive efforts of a more global kind. The disquieting question is whether these efforts would be brought about by the march of events or by a timely anticipation of the dangers involved.

It would seem, therefore, that the present situation will sooner or later give way to a new phase in which there will be a greater readiness to respond to critical problems and therefore a better climate for the resumption of negotiations between South and North. In this new phase, UNCTAD will have a new responsibility and a new opportunity. The new phase cannot, however, be a return to the past. Account would have to be taken of the longer-term changes in the world economy and approaches and negotiating styles fashioned accordingly. The central factors in the new phase, in so far as it concerns North–South issues, would be the changing position of the developing countries in the world economic scene, together with the medium to long-term prospects in the developed countries themselves.

UNCTAD was established in a setting of rapid, indeed unprecedented, growth in the developed countries and a parallel expansion in world trade. The developing countries sought to share in that process and thus reduce the growing gap between themselves and the developed countries through a number of mechanisms such as increased aid and preferential access to markets. These mechanisms would have enhanced the 'trickle down' of growth from the North to the South. The present context is significantly different. On the one hand, the prospects of the developed countries, at least in the medium term, are for relatively slow growth in comparison to the 1950s and 1960s, even on the assumption of a recovery from the present recession. The prospect of 'trickle down' and the environment for supplementary measures of development co-operation of a traditional kind are therefore considerably less promising than in the earlier period. On the other hand, there has been a change in the relative position of the developing countries themselves in the world economy. The concept of the centre and the periphery is still by and large valid, but it has been modified by recent changes. The economic experience of the developing countries is now a factor of some importance in the smooth working of the international economy. Their setbacks could trigger off setbacks for the industrialized countries. A continued and vast contraction of the imports of developing countries, a failure to service their debts, a disruption in supplies and prices of oil and other essential materials could all engender far-reaching effects on the world economy and thus on the economies of the industrialized countries. Conversely, the acceleration of growth in the developing countries could stimulate global recovery and expansion. What is new is not the fact of interdependence but the changed character of this interdependence in which economic impulses, whether positive or negative, are now flowing increasingly in both directions.

This changed perception of interdependence must underlie the new phase in the dialogue and provide fresh stimulus for positive responses. It has implications for immediate actions to deal with the current recession and even more significantly for the longer-term thrust of the negotiating process in both the North-South context and the wider context of the evolution of international economic relations. The new interdependence was indeed the underlying theme of the Belgrade Conference, widely shared by all groups of countries, even though the time had not come for translating it into specific actions.

The motivating factors now are not only the political need to respond to the problems of newly-emerging nations or the humanitarian compulsion to alleviate poverty and reduce the widening gap between the rich and poor countries. There is now also the need for a framework of international economic relations which provides for the maximum utilization of mutually reinforcing and interacting forces for growth and prosperity throughout the world economy, a framework which would embrace all groups of countries —the developed market-economy countries, the socialist countries of Eastern Europe and the developing countries. The articulation and identification of these interactions as a basis for policy is one of the crucial tasks for the future, a task which if well accomplished could create a climate that would change the existing character of negotiations on development as well as on international economic issues.

The changing character of interdependence would be of relevance to UNCTAD's future work in each of the critical areas with which it is concerned. It is of relevance to UNCTAD's approach to commodity issues, where greater price stability and the strength and good functioning of commodity markets should be seen not just as objectives that are specific to particular products or particular groups of countries, but as essential requirements for strength and stability in the global economy and for the macro-economic policies of the developed countries themselves. It is of central importance to the question of trade policy, since the future of an open and non-discriminatory trading system cannot be sustained by rules alone but requires a new dynamic of interacting growth and expansion throughout the world economy. It is of vital concern in the area of money and finance, where the question of resource flows to developing countries has to be seen in the context not only of the fight against poverty but also of the dynamism of the world economy. In one way or another, it would also provide a new rationale for UNCTAD's work in other specific areas such as the transfer of technology, shipping, and trade among countries having different economic and social systems.

If the dynamics of future world economic growth require a vigorous growth process in the developing countries as an essential component, two objectives are of crucial importance and UNCTAD has to contribute to each of these. First is the objective of economic co-operation among developing countries. This is essential because the growing production surpluses of developing countries cannot be absorbed by the developed countries alone. They have to be exchanged in increasing proportions among themselves. Economic co-operation among developing countries is not a second-best or fall-back answer to a lack of response from the industrialized countries to the demands of development co-operation. It is an imperative for the good functioning of the future world economy and is therefore an objective in which the developed countries themselves have an obvious and important stake.

The second objective relates to systemic change in the international institutional framework. Rapid growth in developing countries would require—save in the case of a dramatic change in export prices and earnings, as happened in the case of oil—a level of imports in excess of their exports. It is in the global interest that this trade deficit be made possible through adequate and sound financing. At UNCTAD I the theme was enunciated of a trade gap to be bridged by a combination of greater exports and aid. In the present and future context, there are constraints to each of these. In the case of aid, there is little prospect that the bulk of the prospective trade deficits of the developing countries would be filled by flows of concessional aid. Nor can direct private capital, however strongly it is encouraged, in practice satisfy the whole of the residual need, whether in terms of quantity or in terms of distribution. The commercial banks for their part, as recent experience has demonstrated, cannot be relied upon to resume the role they played in the 1970s as major lenders. The international financial and monetary system as a whole must play its part in finding an answer. The post-war system designed at Bretton Woods was heavily focused on short-term capital flows as an instrument of sound economic management. Long-term flows were not ignored—the World Bank was set up for this—but they were not clearly integrated as an essential element of the dynamics of the world economy. This is a gap that needs to be filled. As recent experience has shown, a large and growing number of developing countries can reach high rates of growth if they have recourse to external financing. The task for the future is to ensure the flow of such financing on terms and maturities that are appropriate.

Similarly, so many changes have eroded the world trading system that it can hardly be restored to its earlier character simply by insisting on the observation of rules. The system itself and its rules have to be adapted to take account of the several changes that have taken place, including the growth of common markets and other integration arrangements, of trans-national intra-firm trade and of state trading. They have to reflect the need for structural adjustment in an open trading system, and to provide for the dynamic accommodation of the trade of developing countries in the context of their progressive growth and transformation.

The evolution and adaptation of the international economic systems must engage the attention of several fora. This is an area in which UNCTAD can make a vital contribution because it is particularly well suited to consider the interdependence among issues and their development dimension. Raising the question of systemic change should not be seen as a grab for power on the part of the developing countries or as a threat to institutions that have functioned well. Such suspicions have resulted in needlessly defensive attitudes which have impaired a serious consideration of the subject. UNCTAD should seek to elaborate and propose improvements in the functioning of the international economic systems; its responsibilities and experience enable it to make this contribution. The underlying theme for systems adaptation must be the incorporation of a 'development consensus' comparable to the 'full employment consensus' which was written into the post-war systems. This is not, by any means, a sectional interest of the developing countries. It is an imperative for the world economy and hence for the developed countries as well.

The new scene will have its implications for negotiating styles and modalities. The group system has been criticized as being unconducive to efficient negotiations. Negotiations in large fora have been faulted. So, too, has the tendency to deal with large and sweeping issues instead of concentrating on smaller, more specific and therefore more manageable ones. Where there is some substance to these views and criticisms, and where organizational and procedural changes are needed and possible, they should most certainly be undertaken. But it would be seriously wrong to conclude that the lack of positive results in international negotiations, particularly in the North-South context, has been primarily due to organizational and procedural deficiencies, and that action to remedy such deficiencies should therefore be the central issue. North–South negotiations have failed to make progress even when taken up in smaller fora and outside of the traditional group system; the Paris Conference on International Economic Co-operation and the Cancún Summit are examples. The central issue has been and will be political: the perception of national interests and the capacity to reconcile these interests in new actions brought about through the negotiating processes.

In recent times, the developed countries have given voice to new concepts that are a departure from the thrust of the earlier consensus. The graduation and differential treatment of developing countries in trade and the narrowing of the list of recipients for concessional aid are amongst these suggestions, some of which have already been reflected in bilateral actions. There can be no gainsaying of the need to review and, if necessary, modify earlier principles in a context of change. However, if this process is to be a movement forward in North–South negotiations and not a step back, it has to be brought within the ambit of a new and agreed framework of overall policy which remains predicated on the need to support the development process in the developing countries in the interest of the workings of the global economy. In such a framework, the dialogue between North and South could make fresh headway and transform the current climate of confrontation and stalemate. UNCTAD, for its part, could assume a new vitality and a new relevance as an instrument and a forum for international economic co-operation.

As UNCTAD evolves and adapts to the changing scene, it should preserve and nurture the spirit which was instilled in it by its founding fathers, among whom Wladek Malinowski played a crucial role in shaping the organization and influencing its character. Those original impulses are of the essence of UNCTAD and remain a source of inspiration and guidance for the forward thrust of its work.

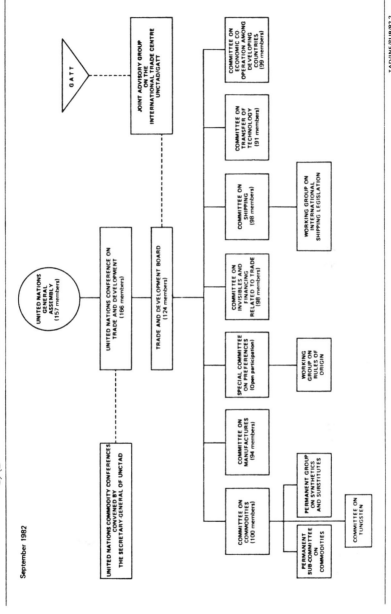

UNCTAD : its structure

September 1982

UNCTAD Information Unit
United Nations Office at Geneva

TAD/INF/PUB/82.2
Printed at U.N. Geneva
GE.82-57088 –September 1982 – 5,000

ABOUT THE AUTHORS

Note: Most of the contributors to this volume are or have been members of the United Nations Secretariat, of which the UNCTAD secretariat forms part. Their countries of origin are indicated only to convey the diversity of the national experiences which they brought to the United Nations. The views which they express in their contributions to this book are their own and should not be held to represent the official positions of the United Nations or its Secretariat. For reasons of space, bibliographical references have not been included in these brief biographical notes.

Moses Taiwo Adebanjo (Nigeria) has been Director of UNCTAD's Division for Economic Co-operation among Developing Countries since 1981. The early part of his career was spent in the service of the Federal Government of Nigeria; he was a delegate to UNCTAD I and II and, from 1966, the Head of the Commercial Division of the Nigerian Permanent Mission to the UN Office at Geneva. He joined the UNCTAD secretariat in 1969 as Deputy Secretary of the Trade and Development Board and later was Secretary of the Board and Chief of the Conference Affairs Service (1974–79) and Chief of the New York Office (1979–80).

Paul Berthoud (Switzerland), a lawyer by training, served the United Nations Secretariat from 1951 to his retirement in 1983, after having started his professional career in the Swiss Federal Public Service. He contributed to the work of the United Nations in the social, economic, developmental and legal areas from a variety of staff and field positions. His posts in UNCTAD included those of Secretary, Trade and Development Board, Director of Technical Co-operation, and Director of Programme Support Services. He was also Secretary of UNCTAD IV and UNCTAD V.

Zenon Carnapas (Cyprus) joined UNCTAD's Division for Invisibles in 1967. He contributed to a number of major activities in UNCTAD's work programme on maritime transport and was particularly active in work to promote economic co-operation among developing countries in that area. In 1976, he was transferred from the Shipping Division to the New York Office of UNCTAD, which he now heads.

Gamani Corea (Sri Lanka) has been the Secretary-General of UNCTAD since 1974. Before that he had contributed to UNCTAD's work in a number of capacities, including as chairman of the Working Party on Shipping at UNCTAD I, of the 1972 UN Cocoa Conference and of two expert groups on international monetary issues. His other international assignments have included the chairmanship of the UN Committee on Development Planning from 1972 to 1974. In the service of the Government of Ceylon/Sri Lanka from 1952 to 1973, he held a number of senior positions in the areas of planning and finance, among them those of Permanent Secretary of the Ministry of Planning and Economic Affairs and Senior Deputy Governor of the Central Bank. His last governmental assignment was as Ambassador of Sri Lanka to the EEC and the Benelux countries.

Sidney Dell (United Kingdom) is at present the Executive Director of the UN Centre on Transnational Corporations (CTC). After spending a short period as an economist at the Board of Trade in London, he joined the United Nations Secretariat in 1947 and has served it since then, specializing in problems of world trade and payments. He was an Executive Assistant to Dr Prebisch before and during UNCTAD I and from 1965 to 1973 was Director of the New York Office of UNCTAD and of its Division for Financing related to Trade (then also located at UN Headquarters). He subsequently served as Assistant Administrator (Programme) of the United Nations Development Programme and as Special Adviser to the UNCTC.

Iqbal Haji (Tanzania) has been a member of the United Nations Secretariat since 1967. He worked for several years in UNCTAD, with spells in its Divisions for Invisibles and for Money, Finance and Development, as well as in the Office of the Secretary-General and the New York Office. He is presently attached to the Office of the Director-General for Development and International Economic Co-operation at UN Headquarters.

K. H. Khaw (Malaysia) has been Special Assistant to the Secretary-General of UNCTAD since 1979. He joined the UNCTAD secretariat in 1970 in its Division for Invisibles, where he served as Special Assistant to W. R. Malinowski from 1972 to 1974, the period of the negotiation of the Code of Conduct for Liner of Conferences. Subsequently, he worked in the Office of the Secretary-General with responsibility for liaison with the Group of 77, and in that capacity was the Secretary of the third and fourth Ministerial Meetings of that Group.

R. Krishnamurti (India) served the United Nations Secretariat from 1947 to his retirement in 1979. After working in the Economic Commission for Asia and the Far East, where he came to head the International Trade Division, he joined the UNCTAD I team as an Executive Assistant to Dr Prebisch. On the establishment of the UNCTAD secretariat, he was successively Special Assistant to the Secretary-General, Director of the Manufactures Division (1967–77) and Director of the New York Office of UNCTAD (1977–79). He is now an independent writer and consultant.

Alfred Maizels (United Kingdom) is a Fellow of the Institute of Development Studies at the University of Sussex, England, and an Honorary Research Fellow at University College, London. His positions in the UNCTAD secretariat, where he served from 1966 to 1980, included those of Deputy Director of the Commodities Division and Director of the Economic Policy Evaluation and Co-ordination Unit. Prior to joining UNCTAD, he worked at the National Institute of Economic and Social Research, London.

Surendra J. Patel (India) headed the UNCTAD secretariat unit responsible for work on technology from 1969, initially within the Division for Invisibles, and held the post of Director of the Technology Division from 1978 until his retirement in 1984. His career in the United Nations Secretariat started in 1950 at Headquarters. Pursuing his interest in problems of economic growth and development planning, he went on to work for three of the regional economic commissions—those for Europe (1956–62), for Africa (1963–64) and for Asia and the Far East (1965)—before joining the UNCTAD secretariat in 1966.

Manuel Pérez Guerrero (Venezuela) was the Secretary-General of UNCTAD from 1969 to 1974. His international career, in the service of international organizations or of his country's Government, now spans five decades and covers the institution-building conferences of the mid-forties as well as the development dialogue which started in the mid-sixties. He has been Permanent Representative of Venezuela to the United Nations (1967–69), Co-Chairman of the Paris Conference on International Economic Co-operation (1975–77) and Chairman of the Group of 77 in New York (1980–81) at the time of the Caracas Conference on ECDC. In the Government of Venezuela, he has held the Ministries of Finance, Planning, Petroleum and Mines, and International Economic Affairs, the latter of which he now occupies once more.

Raúl Prebisch (Argentina) was the first Secretary-General of UNCTAD (1963–69). In 1949, well-known as a central banker and an academic economist, he was appointed Executive Secretary of the UN Economic Commission for Latin America (CEPAL). He was also Director-General of the Latin American Institute for Economic and Social Planning (ILPES). His work in those years had a profound effect on trade and development theory and provided the intellectual foundation for the establishment of UNCTAD. Since resigning his UNCTAD post, he has continued to reflect and write on development issues. He directs the *CEPAL Review* and has undertaken special assignments for the Secretary-General of the United Nations. In 1980, Dr Prebisch became the first recipient of the Third World Prize, awarded by the Third World Foundation, London, for outstanding service "to the general good of the peoples of the Third World".

Stein Rossen (Norway) is a Senior Research Fellow of the Christian Michelsen Institute, Bergen, Norway. Most of his professional life has been spent in the service of the United Nations, from the early post-war years onward. He directed the Research Divisions of the UN Economic Commissions for Africa (1959–63) and for Europe (1963–70), before being appointed Deputy Secretary-General of UNCTAD. He was the first ever incumbent of that post, which he held until his retirement in 1979.

Ignacy Sachs (France) is a Professor at the Ecole des Hautes Etudes en Sciences Sociales and the Director of the International Research Centre on Environment and Development (CIRED), both in Paris. He has held these positions since 1968, before which time he was the Director of the Centre for Research on Underdeveloped Economies in Warsaw. He is currently also a programme director for the United Nations University and has been a member of the Executive Committee of the International Foundation for Development Alternatives, Nyon, Switzerland, since its establishment.

M. J. Shah (Pakistan), Barrister-at-Law of Gray's Inn, London, joined the UNCTAD secretariat in 1969, with a legal, diplomatic and commercial background, to take charge of the work programme on maritime legislation of the Division for Invisibles, later the Shipping Division. He retired from the service of the United Nations in 1983 as Deputy Director of the Shipping Division. He is an Honorary Fellow of the Canadian Marine Transportation Centre, University of Dalhousie, Halifax, Nova Scotia.

Michael Zammit Cutajar (Malta), who edited this volume, started his United Nations career as Special Assistant to W. R. Malinowski in UNCTAD's Division for Invisibles (1967–71). He next worked for the incipient United Nations Environment Programme, returning to UNCTAD in 1974 as Deputy Secretary of the Trade and Development Board and later Special Assistant to the Secretary-General (1975–78). After an assignment to the International Foundation for Development Alternatives, Nyon, Switzerland, he resigned from the United Nations Secretariat in 1980 and now works as a consultant.

Index